The Accomplished Senator

The Accomplished Senator

by

WAWRZYNIEC GRZYMALA GOSLISKI

new introduction by
PROF. KENNETH THOMPSON,
UNIVERSITY OF VIRGINIA

*The American Institute
of Polish Culture*
MIAMI

1992

Copyright © 1992 by The American Institute of Polish Culture
All rights reserved
The American Institute of Polish Culture
Miami, Florida 33141

Typesetting by Jeffrey Young & Associates
in Adobe Caslon.
This edition is a line-for-line, page-for-page
reproduction of the 1733 edition.

Printed in the United States of America.

Library of Congress Number: JC145. G6

Library of Congress Cataloging-in-Publication Data

Goslicki, Wawrzyniec, 1530-1607.
The accomplished senator.
1. Political science.   2. Political ethics.
1. Title.
JC145. 62313   1992   320´.01   92-53234
ISBN: 188128405-0

PREFACE

In 1568 a Polish statesman named Wawrzyniec Grzymala Goslicki (Laurence Grimald Gozliski) planted the seed of political philosophy which would bear fruit in the American Declaration of Independence and the U.S. Constitution. Goslicki (1530-1607) whose latinized name is *Laurentius Grimaldus Goslicius*, published that year in Venice a remarkably modern treatise on statecraft entitled *De Optimo Senatore* (The "Perfect" or "Accomplished" Senator). A second printing came out of Basel in 1593 and English translations appeared no less than three times, in 1598, 1607, and 1733.

The importance of *The Accomplished Senator* cannot be overstated. A renaissance work by a true "Renaissance Man," it was studied and debated by such leading political writers and philosophers as John Locke, Helvetius, Montesquieu, Rousseau and others, who adopted in their own writings many of the principles enunciated by Goslicki.

The Accomplished Senator is the product of Goslicki's broad and rigorous education at the Jagiellonian University of Cracow and the Universities of Padua and Bologna. He demonstrates a detailed and comprehensive knowledge of ancient cultures, laws, leaders, and writers of classical Greece and Rome. The book is also the product of his astute analysis of the contemporary political conditions in Poland and elsewhere in Europe. As a Minister of State and Secretary to King Sigismund II of Poland (and a Roman Catholic Bishop) he was uniquely situated to observe and evaluate diverse political systems, laws, and public servants.

Thomas Jefferson (through his reading of Locke, if not directly from Goslicki's treatise) incorporated in the Declaration of Independence these same justifications for severing American ties to England and for forming a new government. The Constitution of the United States is similarly indebted to Goslicki for defining ideas of a modern, democratic form of government, accepted now four hundred years later by most of the world's civilized nations.

Goslicki's treatise was brought clearly into focus during the conference "Constitutionalism and Human Rights in America, Poland and France" held in April of 1989 at the White Burkett Miller Center for Public Affairs of the University of Virginia in Charlottesville, Virginia. Prof. Kenneth Thompson, Director of the Center, to whom I will always feel indebted for organizing this conference as well as the American, Polish and French scholars of constitutional law, who participated in this conference, inspired me to publish this enlightening work, a copy of which, fortunately, was located at the Library of Congress in Washington, D.C.

The Accomplished Senator cannot be dismissed as merely yet another work of great historical significance. Public officials and the electorate would do well to study his portrait of the ideal public servant. There is still much to be learned from this remarkable Polish statesman.

Blanka A. Rosenstiel
Founder and President
The American Institute of Polish Culture

INTRODUCTION

The Accomplished Senator is a remarkable work of political philosophy and statecraft that is timeless. Goslicki is a European thinker even more than a Polish nationalist. The universality of his thought is demonstrated in the response in England to his writings in the period from the 16th through the 18th century. While his concern is for the government and the political life of Poland, his writings are addressed to those concerned with governance everywhere. He rests his political theory on Aristotle; the traditions of state he emphasizes are rooted in Greek and Roman political institutions.

The Accomplished Senator is a classic work because it deals with all the fundamental questions: freedom and order, liberty and justice, aristocracy and democracy, law and politics, the electors and the people and authority and the limits on power. From Aristotle, Goslicki draws on the analogy comparing the state and the body, the necessity of the state for both moral and political life, restraint and regulation as a hedge against excess, the relation between the law and the sovereign and the law as limited by expediency and necessity. *The Accomplished Senator* is a counsel to the ruler on war and peace, justice and equality. The Senator is the epitome of the practical philosopher. Not all philosophers can be statesmen; Goslicki in particular excludes theorists who shun the discipline of hard choices within institutions and philosophers who are recluses and solitary figures immersed in speculation. Schools and universities should be training grounds of virtue and wisdom, not of a "sleepy, dreaming and speculative sort of knowledge."

Goslicki warns against moral decay and the three dangers he sees inherent in democracy, which he praises but finds historically sometimes inferior to aristocracy and monarchy. However he also defends democracy. Nonetheless he discovers in democracy a tendency toward personal gain at the expense of honest and right action, unrestrained passions that may degenerate into absolute government and the tyranny of the majority which can override justice. The masses are changeable and given to excess and extravagance. Tyranny by the majority is even more dangerous than that of the individual ruler. Nonetheless, Goslicki calls for limitations on the executive, equality of all citizens and equal rights before the law. There can be no democracy without freedom but freedom presupposes responsibility and the moral life.

Any statesman must view politics from a certain historical perspective because history is the only way of looking at politics from the standpoint of action. Only history enables men to understand change. Man depends on his understanding of principles derived from the past. He cannot act without being aware of the past. The school for the statesman has three stages: philosophy, history and practice. They form a unity, a Crocean "circle of the spirit." Thought must not be separated from action. Philosophy for its own sake has no value. Knowledge is the basis for practice as practice is the fulfillment of knowledge. Goslicki warns that not all questions are appropriate for politics and deliberation. Some lie beyond the reach of the state. So firm was his sense of religious toleration that later monarchs banned his work. Goslicki was a religious liberal but a progressive conservative in politics. He eschewed reckless innovation and taught respect for traditions, institutions and values.

Because of the universality of the message, *The Accomplished Senator* speaks to our times as well as the sixteenth and seventeenth centuries. Because of his love of freedom which has lived on through Poland's many adversities, his message finds resonance in the differing experiences of democracy, especially in England and the United States. Not least the concern for practical morality and prudential judgments in politics strikes a sympathetic chord in the midst of present problems. In a striking way the problems that are addressed in *The Accomplished Senator* are our problems as much as they are Poland's. As peoples and political leaders struggle to preserve and practice democracy, the writings from another century strike to the heart of our own age. Senators and congressmen, teachers and philosophers can profit from reflecting on the lessons of *The Accomplished Senator.*

Professor Kenneth W. Thompson
Director of the White Burkett Miller
Center for Public Affairs, University of Virginia

March 23, 1992

THE Accomplished Senator.
In TWO BOOKS.

Written Originally in LATIN,

By LAURENCE GRIMALD GOZLISKI, *Senator* and *Chancellor* of *POLAND*, and *Bishop* of Posna or Pozen.

Done into ENGLISH, From the Edition Printed at *VENICE*, in the Year 1568.

By Mr. OLDISWORTH,

Omnis in Hoc Uno variis Discordia cessit Ordinimibus.—— Claudian.

LONDON:
Printed for the AUTHOR, in the Year 1733.

T O

The Most Noble Henry *Duke of* Beaufort;
The Most Noble John *Duke of* Argyll;
The Right Honourable Edward *Earl of* Oxford;
The Right Reverend John *Lord Bishop of* Oxford;
The Right Reverend Peter *Lord Bishop of* Corke;
The Right Hon. and Noble Sir Robert Walpole;
The Right Hon. Sir William Wyndham, *Bart.*
The Honourable Sir James Campbell, *Bart.*
The Right Honourable William Conolly, *Esq;*
Watkin Williams Wynne, *Esq;*
John How, *Esq;*
William Shippen, *Esq;*
Humphrey Parsons, *Esq;*

Most Noble, *Right* Honourable, *Right* Reverend, *and* Honourable!

AT a Time, when the *Party-Names* and Distinctions, which split and divide us, and for almost *Two Centuries* together, weakened and enervated a Great and Powerful Nation, are happily laid aside and abolished

DEDICATION.

abolished; when the Heats and Animosities, which kept us so long in a Feverish and Disordered State, are well Composed and Allayed; and the only Remaining Contention now is, who shall approve himself the most Faithful and Sincere Lover of True *Patriotism;* I cannot think a Work in which *Patriotism* is fully described and set in so Fair a Light, can be an Unacceptable or Disagreeable Present to the Great and Illustrious *Names*, to which in all Humility I have Presumed to Inscribe it.

In my own Name, so very Mean and Inconsiderable, I durst not have ventured upon a Subject of such Importance, had I really all the Abilities, of which the *Great Author*, whose *Works* I have attempted in *English*, was an Undoubted Master: Though I cannot but think it the Just Right and Privilege of every Free-born Subject, to Enquire into the Nature of the Constitution under which he Lives, and to assert the Liberties of which himself is a Legal Partaker. But when I Inscribe This Work to so many *Names* of the

First

DEDICATION.

First Distinction and Lustre, I implore Your Patronage, not so much for Myself, as for *Gozliski*, one of the ablest *Ministers* that ever any *Northern Nation* was blessed with, and therefore every way worthy of Your Protection and Favour.

Any One Such *Name* as is affixed to this *Dedication,* were no doubt sufficient to Adorn and Recommend a much more Valuable Work than I can Presume to be engaged in; But since the *Character* of an *Accomplished Senator* extends to *Both Houses* of *Both* the *Great Councils*, in whose Hands all the Publick Interests of *Two Islands* are Entrusted, I thought it reasonable enough, that a Work of such General Use, should not appear in Publick, without submiting it to the Judgment and Approbation of a *Senatorial Committee* of the *Parliaments* of *Two Kingdoms.*

When the Differences between a *British* and a *Polish* Government (of which I have elsewhere given a short Detail) are removed and set aside, or amicably compremised and adjusted,

DEDICATION.

adjusted, what *Gozliski* hath advanced in Defence of *Loyalty* and *Liberty*, and to make these Two Principles compatible, will, I hope, deserve the Attention of such *Patriots*, as are alike Zealous for the *Prerogatives* of the *Crown*, and the *Interests* of the *People*.

Gozliski wrote at a Time, when the World was Unacquainted with the *Parties*, which have since Harassed and Perplexed Other States and Nations besides our own. Nothing therefore that he has said can possibly be suspected of the least Deviation and Tendency towards what himself hath Condemned in general, with so much Zeal and Rigour. When these *Parties* are no more, now is the Time for him to be Heard, not only Patiently, but with Regard and Deference. If any Fresh Seeds of Discord are just now Sown, or any New Fires ready to be Kindled; and if *Party*, our old Inveterate Enemy, is once more preparing to Visit us under a New Name, and in another Shape, *Gozliski's* Precepts and Institutions are an Admirable Prescription, for Preventing the

DEDICATION.

the Rise and Growth of such a Publick Malady; and by fixing our Minds upon the One Great Fundamental Principle, the *Common Good*, or *Love of our Country*, will Divert us from all Disputes and Debates, unless upon This *One Thing Necessary*, and which alone can Justify us in our Dissensions and Disagreement with our Fellow-Subjects.

THERE have been many *Authors* who have written freely of the Office and Duty of a *King;* and they have met with a Favourable Reception, whilst they kept their *Pens* within the Bounds of That Deference and Submission, which is due to the Superior Grandeur and Dignity of the *Scepter. Gozliski* has with great Delicacy touched upon This Subject, and has settled the *Divine Right* of *Monarchy* in such a Manner, that though he was subject to an *Elective Monarch*, we can by no means think him an Enemy to a Crown, not absoluely, but conditionally *Entailed*, and made *Hereditary:* And he Tasted so plentifully of the *Royal Favour*, both in his *Sacred* and *Secular Capacity*, that it can never be

DEDICATION.

be imagined his Memory should suffer, on account of any the least Suspicion of his being, in the worst Sense of that Appellation, a *Professed Republican.*

From the Regal to the *Senatorial* Character, the Passage is Easy and Orderly. If in treating this Subject, he has used the same Freedom, with which I can imagine he always spoke in a *Polish Dyet*, and for which he is in Fact applauded by the Writers of that Age and Nation in which he Lived, so much the more Consistent is his Behaviour and Conduct, and the greater Regard is due to his Judgment. This however is clearly Demonstrable from his *Writings*, That there never was a more Zealous Advocate for *Publick Liberty* and the *Love of his Country*; and his Sentiments ought to have a more than Common Weight with us, who are Natives of a Kingdom, on many Accounts, so justly Preferable to *Poland*, and which has consequently so much a stronger Title to our Best Affections.

GOZLISKI

DEDICATION.

GOZLISKI has been strictly and remarkably Careful, to avoid all the Common Weaknesses and Errors, which the other *Political Writers*, and too many even of the First Note and Rank, have Indulged themselves in. He has Censured no One Name of Eminence, extant in his Time. His Panegyrick extends rather to Great *Families* than Great *Persons;* to the *Dead* more than to the *Living*: And I know of but One Name, That of the *Great* STANISLAUS, to which he has affixed a Compliment of an Extraordinary Nature; and indeed a Finer was never affixed to any *Name* whatsoever. But considering upon how Clear a Matter of Fact, which subsisted long before *Gozliski's* Time, this High Strain of Eulogy is grounded, the *Good Bishop* must, on this Occasion, stand acquitted of all Appearance and Imputation of Flattery. In Borrowing from the Sentiments and Opinions of Others, by Quotation or Reference, he has made no Use of the Works of his *Contemporaries,* or taken
Part

DEDICATION.

Part in any of their Controversies and Disputes; but has Resorted only to the Old approved *Masters of Divinity, Law, Policy,* and *Philosophy*: And he has no where touched upon any one Prevailing or Contending Interest, any Favourite *Project* or *Scheme of the Day,* or any the Ordinary and *Short-lived Topicks,* which are the Burthen and Substance of Vast Numbers of *Modern Pamphlets* and *Essays,* designed and calculated, like some Creatures of the *Reptile* and *Volatile Species,* only for a *Monthly,* a *Quarterly,* or at most for an *Annual* or *Biennial* Duration: But his Reasoning proceeds altogether upon such Principles, and terminates in such Conclusions, as are of Eternal Veracity, and of Perpetual Use to all States and Societies of Men.

As Zealous as This *Author* is for the Particular Form of Government, the Laws and Institutions of his own Country, he very candidly allows of many Differences in the *Polity* of other Nations, which he would

DEDICATION.

would have them Keep and Retain, so far as they are Consistent with the Fundamentals of Good Government: And since he is of That *Northern Hive,* in which the Curious Frame and Contexture of the *Three Legislative Powers* or *Estates,* was first Woven and Brought to Perfection, and of That Particular Nation, in which the *Regal* and *Popular Rights* have so long and so amicably subsisted together; He may, on all these Accounts, hope for a Kind and Hospitable Reception at the Hands of such *British Patriots,* to whom the Interests of Their *Royal* MASTER, and of Their *Dutiful Fellow-Subjects,* are alike Dear and Inseparable.

WHAT *Gozliski* says against *Tyrants,* falls short of what is really due to That Name, and carries no Reflection along with it upon a *Limited Monarchy.* In a Nation, where *The King can do no Wrong,* the very Name and Suspicion of Tyranny must always be Strangers. There was indeed a Time, when

the

DEDICATION.

the Advocates for *Arbitrary Power* were Permitted, or Encouraged, to Write with more Freedom, than by their own Principles they had a Just Title to. And when These *Mercenaries* were Retained and Kept up, among other Excursions, they often fell upon the *Polish* Nation, which they always treated with a good deal of Obloquy and Contempt; by Representing the Troubles and Disorders, which in some Junctures had Annoyed That Kingdom, in very Hideous and Frightful Forms. Great Mistakes, and some notoriously Wilful and Unjustifiable, were made on this Occasion; and Those Particular Broils, which sometimes attended their *Regal Elections*, we who are under Another Form, are happily Unacquainted with. But neither These, nor any other Disturbances whatsoever, had ever happened, if the Principles laid down by *Gozliski*, had been duly attended to. *Power* and *Liberty* will sometimes be at Variance: But amidst all the Struggles and Contentions of this Sort, POLAND hath preserved its Constitution for

a very

DEDICATION.

a very Long Series of Years, and hath felt none of those Fatal Shocks and Convulsions, which many *Popular States* and *Absolute Monarchies*, its Contemporaries, could not get over, without an Alteration or Overthrow of their Political Establishment. And as its People have all along been noted for their Great Learning and Knowledge, the Inseparable Companions and Sure Supporters of *Liberty*, so they have, in the midst of a Disadvantageous Soil and Clime, always maintained a Character of Dignity and Grandeur; have often Distinguished themselves by their Wisdom, Bravery, and Conduct; and at one Time particularly, in so Glorious a Manner, that they seemed to have a Good Claim to the Title of *The Deliverers of* Europe *from Infidelity and Slavery:* On which account, there is perhaps a good deal of Deference due to them; and they may well be admitted as Advocates for *That Liberty*, which by their Arms they so bravely Defended: At least, they may expect to be Heard with Patience, upon so Agreeable a Subject, by Us, their Constant

DEDICATION.

stant and Firm Allies, of whom, for our Love of *Liberty*, they have had so Good an Opinion, that Remote as we are from Them, they have more than once attempted to set an *Englishman* upon the Throne of *Poland*.

The Labours of *This Excellent Author*, upon so very Nice and Important a Subject, are Carried on and Finished, in so exact a Manner; and he hath Traced his *Accomplished Senator*, from the Cradle to the Grave, and hath Furnished him with all the Proper Ornaments, Vertues, and Perfections, both of Private and Publick Life, with so much Judgment and Accuracy, that to *Persons* who are the *Originals* of that *Picture* which he has Drawn, I can never Think the *Copy* of it will be an Unacceptable Present, from,

Most Noble, *Right* Honourable,
Right Reverend, *and* Honourable!
*Your Ever Devoted, and Most Obedient
Humble Servant,*

W. Oldisworth

THE PREFACE.

*H*istorian*s and* Chronologer*s are generally agreed, that the Kingdom of* Poland *was Founded about the Middle of the Fifth Century, by their First King,* Leschus; *from whom the Race and Descent of their Several Kings are regularly traced down and continued: Though some Antiquarians have carry'd their Original much higher, and mingled it with the* Cimbrian, *and the* Teutonick, *the* Tigurine, Scythian, *and* Sarmatian *Dynasties.*

King Leschus, *or* Lechus, *was at first possessed only of the Upper and Lower* Poland, *with all* Silesia; *to which Provinces, by his Bravery and Conduct, he afterwards added the Great* Duchy *of* Pomerania. *In the Reign of* Boleslaus, Bohemia, Moravia, *and Part of* Russia *and* Prussia, *became tributary to* Poland. *In the Year* 1183, *all* Prussia *was subdued by King* Casimir *the Second, and all* Russia *by* Casimir *the Great, Anno* 1338. *After this, new Conquests were made, by the Reduction of* Walachia, Moldavia, *and* Lithuania. *In the Year* 1500, *all* Livonia *was Conquered; and after this, other Acquisitions were made by King* Ulidislaus, *who annexed the* Duchies *of* Smolensko, Severia, *and* Czernicovia, *with several Provinces in* Muscovy, *to the* Polish *Crown; and in a little time all* Tartary *upon the* Ukraine, *and quite to the Shores of the* Black Sea, *fell under the same Jurisdiction.*

From

PREFACE.

From the Thirteenth *to the Close of the* Sixteenth Century, *this Kingdom was continually making new Conquests, and grew up to such as amazing and formidable Bulk, as could not fail to draw down upon them the Envy, Dread, and Jealousy of all their Neighbours. Their vast Acquisitions, and the Glory of their Arms, were in a good Measure owing to the Unanimity of their* Regal Elections, *and to their Choice of such Kings, as had distinguishd themselves by their Bravery and Conduct. But when some of their Elections were suspended for too long a time, or were attended with Intestine Broils and Contention, and sometimes with Bloodshed; or when they had made a weak or an ill-judged Choice; Advantages were taken of these Errors in Policy, by their Vigilant and Jealous Neighbours, who were closely Confederated against them: And at different Times, the* German, *the* Turk, Tartar, *and* Muscovite, *the* Swede, *the* Dane, *the* Hungarian, Bohemian, *and* Prussian, *exerted themselves in recovering what they had lost, and in reducing* Poland *to the Bounds and Limits, within which it is at present confined: Though after all its Losses, this Kingdom is still equal in Extent to the Kingdom of* France, *but far inferior to it, in the Goodness of its Clime, the Fertility of its Soil, and the Number of its People.*

The Poles *have been ever famous for Arts and Arms; for their Bravery, Good Conduct, and Literature. The* Latin Tongue *is kept up among them, and is familiarly used even by the Meanest of their People, though with a very Particular and Unclassical Pronunciation. The* Three *Great Governing* Orders of Poland, *are the* King, *whose Crown is* Elective, *the* Senate, *and the* Nobility or Gentry ; *under whom the People are kept in a State of entire Submission and Vassalage, especially since the Great Revolt, when they rose against their Masters, slew some of them, drove the rest out of their Country, and for a Time kept all the Power entirely in their own Hands.*

The Senators, *with the* Nobility or Gentry, *make about a* Tenth Part *of the Natives or Inhabitants; and out of these Orders the* State-Governors *are chosen; some of which are nominated and commissioned*

by

PREFACE. iii

by the King, *and the rest are their Hereditary Nobles, who hold their Places in Virtue of their Tenures. Their* Archbishops *and* Bishops, *in Number Sixteen, are always* Senators *by their Order. They preside in the* Estates ; *and during the* Inter-regnum, *the* Primate *is the First Officer of* Poland ; *whilst the* Priests *have a Share in the Jurisdiction of their Lesser Courts. Though the* Poles *set a high Value upon Birth and Nobility, yet no one Subject is born a* Palatine, Senator, *or* Lord; *but these Dignities are annexed to certain Great Offices, and are bestowed by the Crown. The* Lay-Senators *are in Number* 128, *including* 32 Palatines, *the* 10 Great Officers *of the* Crown, 85 Castellans, *and one* Starosta. *The* Palatines *are the same as* Lords Lieutenants of Counties ; *the* Castellans *command Part of a Province, with a Castle, in War-time; and the* 10 Officers *of the* Crown *are the* Marshals, Chancellors, *and* Treasurers.

The Starostas, *or Military Officers, are either with or without Jurisdictions : Those who have Jurisdiction, are the Governors of Cities or Castles, where they try small Causes; and Those who have no Jurisdiction, are only* Tenants in Capite.

The Nobility *or* Gentry *of* Poland *have their own Personal and Body* Guards, *both of Horse and Foot; and some of them have appeared with no less than a* Thousand armed Men *at a* General Dyet. *Where both Parents are* Noble, *the Son has the Highest and Strongest Title to* Nobility ; *though for the sake of Wealth, even Those of the First Rank have of late often marry'd into* Plebeian *Families. The Power of conferring* Nobility, *was formerly in the* Crown, *but is now altogether in the* General Dyet ; *and as this Dignity may be obtained by serving the Office of First Magistrate in some Great and Privileged* City, *so it may be lost and forfeited, by giving away the* Family Arms *to the Vulgar or Ignoble, or by following Trade and Merchandize, or by serving as a Magistrate in any of the Lesser or* Unprivileged Cities.

All

PREFACE.

All the Nobility *or* Gentry *are obliged to have an Estate in* Land. *They who are possessed of only three* Acres, *are entitled to a Vote in the Lesser or* Provincial Dyet, *where the* Nuncio's *or* Deputies *are chosen, and sent up with Instructions (which they are never to alter or diminish) to the* General Dyet *or* Senate, *wherever it is held; and then they make a Distinct* House, *chuse a* Marshal *or Speaker of their own; and during the* Session *(which never lasts above six Weeks) no one* Nuncio *can be chosen a* Senator, *or removed into the Upper House.*

When the Dyet *is opened, and the* Chancellor, *in the* King's *Name, proposes the several Points that are to be debated on, the* King *leaves the House, and is never present at any of these Debates. The Two Houses of the* Senators *and* Nuncio's *have frequent Meetings and Conferences. No Law can pass or be in force, unless it is first proposed in the* Nuncio's *House, who have a Power to* Impeach, *and spend some Time in drawing up their* Bills, *whilst the* Senator's *House is employed in trying Criminal Causes. Towards the Close of the* Session, *when the* Nuncio's *Bills are ready, they come up to the* Senator's *House, and with them make one General and United Body, of which the* Great Marshal *is then Sole Speaker. Both* King *and* Senate *must concurr unanimously in the Passing of every Law or Decree; and in these* General Dyets *they treat of the* Election *of their* King, *of his* Marriage *and* Revenues, *of* War *and* Peace, *of* Taxes, Embassies, *and* Alliances, *and ultimately Hear and Determine all* Appeals *from Inferior Judicatories.*

When Christianity *was first settled in* Poland, *one of the* Jagelonian *Race was at that time upon the Throne: A Family of so much Reputation and Renown, that it produced many* Kings, *and hath given a Name to one particular Æra in the* Polish *Chronicles, which is called* Dynastia Jagellonidarum. *In the Year 1506, one of this Family was chosen* King, *by the Title of* Sigismund *the First,*

PREFACE.

First, Surnamed the Great; *which high Appellation he very well deserved, by a Series of many Wise and Glorious Actions, during a long Reign of no less than 42 years. Under him,* Gozliski, *a Nobleman of very Ancient House, began to exert himself in the State; and before this Monarch died, was admitted into the Senatorial Order. In the Year* 1548, *when* Sigismund the Great *died, his Son* Sigismund *the Second, Surnamed* Augustus, *was chosen King in his room: A very strong and uncommon Proof of the Great Confidence the* Poles *had in the Merits and Vertues of this Illustrious Family! Though some Authors have indiscreetly said, that This Prince succeeded his Father. Thus far indeed he might be said to succeed him, because he copied his Fathers many Excellent Vertues: And so well were the* Poles *affected towards him, that they were prevailed with to acknowledge his Wife for their Queen, which was a very unusual Precedent in* Poland. *He reigned 23 Years in much Peace and Tranquillity, was the last of his Family, and died* Anno 1571, *about the* 13th *Year of the Reign of our Queen* Elizabeth, *having never been charged with any one Vice or Fault, unless what a Good-natured Observer might call by the Softer Name of* Cunctation ; *though some more Rigid Historians have been pleased to give it the Harsher Name of* Procrastination.

When King Sigismund *the Second began his Reign,* Charles *the Fifth was the Emperor of* Germany, *and King of* Spain, Edward *the Sixth King of* England, Mary *Queen of* Scotland, Francis *King of* France, Christian *of* Denmark, Gustavus *of* Sweden, Ferdinand *of* Hungary *and* Bohemia, *and* Solyman *Emperor of the* Turks. *This I thought proper to take Notice of, because of the Observations made by* Gozliski *upon the Monarchs and States Cotemporary with his own. For in this Reign* Gozliski *was advanced to be a* Minister *of the First Note, was made* Chancellor *of* Poland, *and* Bishop *of* Posna; *and when at last he died, full of Years, Experience, and Reputation, was buried in great Pomp at*

the

the Publick Expence, with many High Encomiums upon his Name and Memory, by the Wits *and* Eulogists *who survived him.*

Gozliski *did not live to see the Troubles and Calamities, which followed in* Poland *upon the Death of his Royal Master King* Sigismund *the Second: After whom,* Henry *of* France *was Elected, who Reigned only Two Years, and after him* Stephen Bartoli, *an* Hungarian, *who Reigned only Eleven Years, and who was followed by* Sigismund the Third, *Son to the* King *of* Sweden. *This Monarch, upon the Death of his Father, accepted of the* Swedish *Crown, and held it in Conjunction with That of* Poland : *By which Unnatural Union he added to the Confusion and Publick Disorders, which were begun in the Two Former Short Reigns, and which ended in the Destruction of that Unfortunate Monarch; all which might have been happily prevented, if the Principles advanced by* Gozliski, *and particularly one Great Rule laid down by him in the Conducting of all* Regal Elections, *had happily prevailed and been in force after his Death.*

These Historical *Facts and Accounts I thought fit to communicate to the Publick, in order to give the Reader some Idea of the* Polish *Nation and Government, whereby he may be able to state the Differences between their Constitution and our own, and some General Notions of the* Polish *History, both Natural and Political, and especially of so much of it, as relates to the Reigns and Times in which* Gozliski *flourished, and was a Minister of State. Whoever has a Mind to be more particularly acquainted with the State and Affairs of* Poland, *may at their Leisure peruse the Works of* Martinus Cromerus, Alexander Guagninus, Johannes Leo, David Braunius, Jachomus Pastorius D'Hirtemberg, Bartholomæus Henckelius, Solomon Nangehour, Bernardus Vascovius, Andreas Maximilianus Fredro, Stephanus Forcatulus, Johannes Demetrius Subicovius, Leonardus Gorscius, Snorro Sterlonides, *cum Notis* Peringskioldi, *and* Starvolscius : *From all which Authors, he may receive*

the

PREFACE.　　vii

the utmost Satisfaction upon this Subject, that the Writers of That Age and Nation are capable of giving him.

The Polish *Nation had a Full and Free* Senate, *long before our* Parliaments *were possessed of all Those Rights and Privileges, in which their Liberty and Authority are at present happily Established. Thus much we learn from all their Best and most Approved Historians. And on this Account it fell much sooner in their Way than in ours, to make themselves acquainted with the Nature, Dignity, and Extent of the* Senatorial Office. *Of this They set us a very Early Precedent. But many Years had not passed, before* Gozliski's *Book, in which* Loyalty *and* Liberty *are so well Tempered and Reconciled, and the* Whole Duty *of the* Senator *is so fully and so clearly explained, was happily brought over and imported into* England, *where we never yet had any Particular Tract or Essay written upon this Important Subject, by any of our own Countrymen: For the* Methodus tenendi Parliamentum, *and some few Books to the same Purpose, do by no means enter into the* Senatorial Character, *in the Manner* Gozliski *hath done; who seems entirely to have exhausted this Important Subject. In the* Reign of Queen Elizabeth, *when the Prerogative ran high; and soon after the Decease of* Cromwell, *when the Pretensions to Liberty ran altogether as high, and were flying out into Anarchy and Confusion, some few* Extracts *of This* Work *were Printed in the* English Language, *but so miserably Maimed and Incorrect, that they Died away insensibly, and were soon Lost, as containing only some few Popular Scraps and Fragments, altogether in Favour of the* Republican Scheme ; *whilst all that was said of the* Legal Powers *and* Prerogatives *of the* Crown *was wilfully Concealed and Suppressed.*

In the Year 1612, there was a Book published at Paris, *entitled,* Ciceronis Consul, Senator, Senatusque, *Authore* Georgio Bellendino. *I have not seen it, but imagine, as the Title imports, that it relates only to so much of the* Senatorial Character, *as we find it described by* Cicero, *who is very sparing upon This Subject ; or so much*

of

of it as is agreeable to the Constitution of the Old Roman *Commonwealth. If so, it can be of little Use, unless by explaining some of the* Roman *Customs and Antiquities. Certain it is, that their Boasted Liberties lay but in a very few hands; their Constitution was not made for any long Duration, and was almost in a continual Ferment and Fluctuation. They governd their People, as they did the World, by Brutal Force, rather than with That mutual Tenderness which is due to our Fellow Creatures. Glory was more their Aim, than the Peace and Happiness of Mankind. Except this Work, I never heard of any Other extant upon This Subject: And it might seem strange, that a Work so New, of such great Importance, not only to the Present, but to all Succeeding Generations, so full of the Justest Reasoning, of the most Curious and Useful Learning, and written in a Style of much Purity and Elegance, almost equal to that of the* Augustan *Age, should lie concealed so long, and be secreted in so extraordinary a Manner; that after many and diligent Enquiries, I have not been able, either by searching the Publick or Private* Libraries *and Repositories of the Curious, or by any Acquaintance and Correspondence, to find above* Three Copies *of this Work;* Two *of the* Basil, *and One of the* Venetian Edition; *to which last, as the most Correct and Authentick, I have entirely confined myself in This Translation. But when we consider, that, upon the Death of* Sigismund *the Second, and his Great Minister* Gozliski, *new Measures were taken, and Attempts made upon the Liberties of* Poland, *during the Three following Reigns, and especially in the Reign of* Sigismund *the Third, when* Poland *was in the utmost Confusion and Distress, (of which we have some Account given us in the* Commentary *of* Johannes Demetrius Subicovius) *it is not to be wonder'd at, that Care should be taken to suppress a* Book, *in which Those Measures and Attempts were so justly Censured and Condemned.* Gozliski's *native Country did Justice to his Memory, by a most splendid Funeral, and by a Collection of*

Encomiums,

PREFACE.

Encomiums, *still extant in* Starvolscius; *but his Best Remains, his Works, were not suffered to pass through any of the* Polish *or* Lithuanian *Presses; or if they did pass through them, no* Copies *of any one such* Edition, *so far as I was able to discover, have been suffered to come down to our Hands.*

Before the Dawning of the Sixteenth Century, *which* Gozliski *did not live to see opened,* Learning *and* Liberty *had not entirely recovered themselves, from the Waste and Desolation brought upon them, by* Barbarism *and* Monkery. *Absolute Dominion was at That Time the Great and Favourite Project of most of the Crowned Heads in* Europe ; *and some Schemes were then laid for* Universal Monarchy. *The Freedom of the Press, even in the Infancy of Printing, was a Formidable Objection to every Attempt of this Kind, and therefore fit to be removed.* Gozliski's *Book would, for this very Reason, be particularly enquired after, and all imaginable Care taken to Secrete and Suppress it, even without the Benefit of an* Index Expurgatorius. England *was not at That Time without some Attempts upon its Liberties, which it happily escaped; and how this Work was brought into our Country, though in a very Maimed and Mangled Condition, we have already seen. There was also a* Translation *of it in* Italian, *which I have not been able to come at; but I imagine it to be the Produce of some of those* Free States *or* Cities *of* Italy, *in which there then was, and still is, just as much* Temporal Liberty, *as is able to maintain and support itself, in an Unnatural Conjunction with* Spiritual Tyranny *and* Slavery. *At the Time when* Gozliski *wrote, the* Dutch, *and some other* Republicks, *had not as yet a Being.* Switzerland *and* Venice *were the only Countries, in which the Liberties of the People were allowed and recognized, or made a Part of the Constitution of the Government. And accordingly, when we resort to those two Countries, we find them to be the only Two Places and Sanctuaries, in which the Works of* Gozliski, *upon their being exported or driven out of* Poland, *could find a safe Retirement and Protection. The* Venetian *and* Basil Editions

bear

PREFACE.

bear Date *in Queen* Elizabeth's *Reign: Though it is very certain, that* Gozliski *wrote long before, even so early as in the Reign of our King* Edward *the Sixth. For in the Account given us of the* English *Government by this* Author, *Mention is made of a* King *; whereas it is well known, that King* Sigismund, *to whom this* Work *is* Dedicated, *was advanced to the Throne in* Edward's *Time, after whose short Reign, we had* Two *successive Queens,* Mary *and* Elizabeth; *and before the Middle of Queen* Elizabeth's *Reign,* Sigismund *and* Gozliski *were Both Dead, the Two* Editions *of This* Work, *at* Venice *and* Basil, *bearing* Date *but a few Years before their Decease.*

In These Editions, *so published in Those Two Cities, I do not wonder to find the* Book *declared in the* Title-page, *to be* Opus Aureum, *as well on the account of its Rarity, as of its Weight, Purity, and Value: For wherever Liberty prevails, Learning never fails to grow up and flourish by its Side. And if a Work of this Nature, which establishes* Monarchical Power, *as well as the* Rights *and* Liberties *of the* Subject, *could be so well received and so highly extolled in a Country in which Liberty prevails, as separate from, and exclusive of* Monarchy, *there is all the Reason in the World to depend upon its being well received in a Country, where* Monarchy *and* Liberty *are happily United.*

After what I have said of the Author and his Work, it may not be improper to give some Account of Myself, that whatever Faults the Translator *or the* Translation *has, the* Great Original *may not suffer, or be wounded through my Sides; and that, out of Prejudice to me or my Name, his Fine Sentiments and Excellent Precepts may not lose their Proper Weight and Effect upon the Minds of all his Readers.*

I freely own, that till I had read Gozliski, *I had not so Full and Clear a Notion of the Two Great and Fundamental Principles of* Loyalty *and* Liberty, *in all the Extended Parts and Branches, in which they really or seemingly Differ, and Interfere with each other,*

and

PREFACE. xi

and of the True and Exact Method of Reconciling and making them Consistent. But I was ever a sincere Lover of Both these Principles in Conjunction, long before I engaged in Political Controversy, into which I was in Fact Called and Invited, and did not Press into the Service but of any over-weening Opinion of my own Abilities, or any Fondness for Debate and Contention.

When I engaged on the Side of the Prerogative and Ministry, I never offered at the Least Violence to Those Laws and Claims of Right, upon which the Liberties of my Countrymen were Founded. I had a Sett of Writers, *some of them of the First Name and Character, either Constantly or Occasionally engaged against me. I never Complained of the Common Liberty they made use of, but only of their Abuses of it; and when one of my Antagonists in particular, who was afterwards admitted into the* Senatorial Order, *was threatened with a very severe Prosecution, I used my Best Endeavours, and not without Success, to prevent any Attack of That Kind, which he hath often since acknowledged, and with a good deal of Gratitude.*

The Minister, *under whom I had the Honour to serve, and in whose Good Opinion of me I shall always Glory, was by many Undoubted Proofs a sincere Lover of Liberty in general, and of the* British Liberties *in particular. I have lived to see the World reconciled to his Character. The Cleanness of his Hands, and the Greatness of his Heart, are now generally allowed of: And certainly the Strength and Clearness of his Head were never called in question at any time. Some Severities were perhaps necessary, in order to make a Thorough Difference and Discrimination between Those who were True Lovers of the Liberties of their Country, and Those who were suspected of a Design to Undermine and Subvert them. They who bravely stood all* Tryals, *have not only been honourably acquitted by the General Voice of their Fellow-Subjects; but many of them have been admitted to new Honours and Preferments : And when we are told on Both Sides, that the Personal Heats and Animosities, which once prevailed amongst us, ought to be*

laid

laid aside, there is no Reason why so Mean a Person as Myself should be Excluded the Benefit of this Voluntary and General Amnesty or Act of Oblivion.

Of all the Calumnies which have been poured upon me, in a very lavish and profuse Manner, none ever more sensibly affected me, or was more remote from the Truth, than the Imputation of my being a Mercenary Hireling. What is so easily Advanced, it may be very difficult to Disprove. But it is some Pleasure to me in my Present Circumstances, that they are an Evident Confutation of this Calumny and Falshood. I thank Heaven and my Fellow-Creatures, that I was never yet acquainted with a Man, who in all the Time of my being marked out and noted by the Publick, as a Political Writer, ever offered me what had the Least Appearance of Bribery or Hire: And what was never offered me, I cannot assume to myself the Merit of Refusing. I never solicited even for Empty Promises, nor Complained of being neglected. When I have been Urged and Pushed on, to ask Something, or when an Honourable Offer hath been made me, I readily Declined every thing of this Sort, or which had the Least Shadow of Self-Interest: And had I really some Merit, I had rather Reject what might be called by my Few Friends the Reward of it, than accept of what Others might be tempted to call by a much worse Name, at Least a Retainer, *if not the* Wages of Servitude.

When the Rage of Parties was at the Height, I was often Threatened, but never Persecuted; unless by Those Tormentors of the Press, *who were resolved to make me an* Author, *even when I was gone into an Easy and Quiet Retirement, and had no Mind to be reputed a Constant Retainer to the Press, or a* Trading Writer *and* Author *by Profession. Above* Sixteen *several Pieces, some in* Verse, *and some in* Prose, *some on* Critical, *and others on* Political *Subjects, many of which I had never seen, or heard of, till a good while after they were in Print; some I had only Recommended to the Press, and others*

I had

PREFACE. xiii

I had but slightly Touched upon and Corrected, were Published *in my Name, or under such Personal Marks and Characters, as would not easily fit any other Author. All this ill Usage I patiently submitted to, and was so little fond of a Name on this Account, that I never affixed it to above One Work, or permitted others to affix it for me. I have been called to Account and censured for a Part in a Controversy, in which I was never Concerned. I have been killed by one* News-writer, *and brought to Life again by another, on purpose to be made an Author of; and like some of the* Primitive Christians, *or the* Hunter *in the* Fable, *I have been dressed out by my Persecutors, in the Skins of Beasts, and in all manner of hideous and frightful Forms, on purpose to provoke the whole Kennel of Staunch Hounds, and even the Terriers and Mungrels of the* Press, *to fall on, and worry me.*

I congratulate my Countrymen upon the Extinction of Those Fires, at which none but an Enemy could warm himself, and rejoice at the near Prospect of Dancing at last in our Ashes. It is happy for us that the Storm of Parties *should so soon blow over:*

———Quod optanti Divum promittere nemo
Auderet, volvenda dies en attulit ultro.

But we know who commands the Winds and the Waves, and who restraineth the Madness of the People. It is still happier, that after such a Tempest so Sweet a Calm should follow, and that Patriotism *and the Love of our Country should spring out afresh, and with so Fair and Fragrant a Bloom, that even Strangers are attracted with the Beauty of it; and from being unable to keep Peace at Home, that we are now once more said to be the Common* Arbiters *of the* Peace *of* Europe. *As I have heretofore Publickly, and often since, Privately Lamented our Intestine Differences and Distractions; so I think it*

every

PREFACE.

every one's Duty, to contribute all he can, to the perpetuating of That General Peace at Home, which is now so happily Established: And what is there that can be more effectual to the Securing of this Great and Valuable Blessing to us and our Posterity, than our Best Endeavours to forward the Growth of Patriotism, *just now Reviving and taking Root in our Soil ? Upon which Subject, there never was a Writer yet Extant, who has so fully Explained, so clearly Illustrated, and so strongly Enforced this Noble Principle, as* Gozliski *hath done. Whose* Book *therefore will at this, and all future Times, be no Unacceptable Present to the Publick, as a Means to promote Unity and Concord, to prevent Popular Discontents, and the Rise of any new Parties or Factions, and to preserve and perpetuate the Wellfare and Happiness of all Free States and Governments; by tracing up their Schemes of Policy to the Only Pure and Genuine Fountains, the* Natural *and* Revealed Laws *and* Providential Administration *of the* Great *and* Only Legislator *and* Governor *of the Universe, who* maketh Peace in all the World, *and who* teacheth *our* Senators Wisdom.

I am aware of the ill Use that may possibly be made of many Passages of This Book, *by the Modern Dealers in* Partial Quotations, Applications, *and* Parallels. *To an assuming Arbitrary and Corrupt* Ministry *there never was a more Inveterate Enemy than* Gozliski : *But then on the other hand, he is altogether as Severe, in condemning Those* State-Medlers *and* Demagogues, *who raise or promote Groundless Clamours, Reports, Jealousies, and Suspicions, and attack their Superiors, in an Illegal and Extrajudicial Way. The Freedom of* Satire *is an Admirable Check upon Vice and Folly; but a Downright Personal Accusation and Criminal Charge ought to be supported by plain Matters of Fact, or by Authentick and Unquestionable Evidence. A Full and General Account of any one* Great Office *in the* State, *and of the several Rights, Powers, Duties, and Functions*

PREFACE. xv

Functions belonging to it, is no more a Satire *upon the Person who shall at any Time possess it, than the* Whole Duty of Man *is a* Satire *upon the* Generality of Christians.

Similitude of Constitutions *is as conducive to the making of Alliances between Nations, as Similitude of* Tempers *is to the making of a Friendship between Private Persons. Hence we may in some measure account for That Long and Constant Friendship, which hath for so many Centuries subsisted between our Own and the* Polish *Nation, without any considerable Interruption; though we have often been at Variance with many other Countries, at a much greater Distance from us. We and the* Poles *have indeed, for many Years, been the Only Two Kingdoms, in which* Monarchical Power *and* Popular Liberty *have all along been happily United, and the Union between them, except some few Transient Shocks and Commotions, always preserved with the Utmost Rigor and Exactness. On this Account it is, that whatever Lights or Improvements in Policy, Either Nation can communicate to the Other, in Defence or Support of the Common Liberties of Both, ought to be very well received by so Dear, so Faithful, and so Ancient an Ally and Confederate. Accordingly we find, in how kind and respectful a Manner Gozliski speaks of the* English *Nation with an Entire Approbation of its Scheme of Government. Some Deference is really due to him on this Occasion: And so great is his Moderation, that he not only extols the* French *Nation, because their Monarch governed in such a manner, as to make his Example and Administration the same to his People, as a Body of the Wisest and most Wholsome Laws; but he allows even of those Forms of Government, most strictly* Absolute *and* Despotick, *in which the People, by their Natural Disposition and Manner of Life, are not qualified to Receive and Enjoy the Inestimable Blessing of Liberty. In general, he does not presume to Prescribe to his Neighbours, but (saving Fundamentals) leaves every Nation to its own*

Laws,

Laws, and advises the strict Observation and Execution of them, how much soever they differ from those of his own Country. When therefore the Differences between Our Own and the Polish *Constitution, are duly settled and adjusted, we may then plainly see, how much of* Gozliski's *Scheme we ought to Reject, and how much of it we may safely Retain.*

The Crown *of* Poland *being* Elective, *in defence of this Right,* Gozliski *hath said all, that such a Cause will bear. If indeed the* Polish *Nation had always chosen their* Kings *in such a manner as* Gozliski *advises, and out of such Persons as he Describes, many of those Mischiefs might have been prevented, which in fact have fallen heavy upon* Poland, *in Consequence of their* Regal Elections, *and are an Unanswerable Objection to this Way of Electing. It were easy to shew, that the* Hereditary Form *is preferable to the* Elective, *and that all the Objections advanced against it, are effectually answered, by* Limiting *the Inheritance of the Crown, and by making it Conditional. In this State, it comes as near as it ought to do to the* Elective Form; *and all those Evils are cured, under which* Poland *hath so often and so severely smarted. As* Gozliski, *by his own Principles, must have Opposed or Censured many* Elections *which have been made in* Poland *since his Time; so if he had lived to be acquainted with This Scheme of a* Limited Monarchy, *he must certainly have declared it to be in a good measure reconcilable with the* Elective Form.

When Gozliski *excludes* Foreigners *from being Candidates for the Crown of* Poland, *he advances a Principle, which his own Country hath often thought fit to break in upon, especially since the Times in which he Wrote and Lived. For this they have suffered more than once. But then in* Hereditary Monarchies *it ought to be considered, that the Generality of the Subjects, and especially the Populace, are very often and very egregiously mistaken in the Meaning of the Word* Foreigner. *The* Royal Blood *is not Lost, by Streaming out into many, and some very Wide and Remote Channels. Before, and since the*

PREFACE. xvii

the Conquest, *many of our* Kings *and* Princes *were the Natives of* Foreign Countries. *The same was the Case of many of our Old, as well as Modern* Nobility. *And though in the* Settlement *of the* Crown, *some Years ago, an* Act *or* Clause *of* Naturalization *was thought to be of Use, in order to remove all Popular Doubts and Scruples, yet it was by no means absolutely Necessary; any more than a* Naturalization *was necessary, to make* Augustus *a* Polander, *the* Prince *of* Hesse *a* Swede, *the* Palsgrave *a* Bohemian, Philip *of* Anjou *a* Spaniard, *King* Stephen, John *of* Gaunt, *King* James *the First, and King* Charles *the First,* Englishmen.

The Executive Power *is by* Gozliski *allowed to be entirely in the* Crown, *as it is with us; but when he speaks of the King's* Reverencing *the* Senate, *of his* Submitting *to their Authority and Decrees, and of his being* Accountable *to them; whilst he no where makes any mention of a* Negative Voice; *these Expressions are by no means agreeable to the Just Sentiments which we* Britons *are taught to entertain of the* Royal Prerogative. *He does, however, in many Places and Passages of his* Book *invest* Monarchy *with a* Divine Right, *which he hath admirably well explained in the Fullest and Clearest Manner: And in one Particular we are entirely agreed with him, That the Laws made by the joint Concurrence both of* King *and* Senate, *are the Measure of His Power, as well as of Our Obedience.*

Gozliski *makes no Mention of* Two Armies *or* Bodies *of* Standing Forces *in* Poland, *One the* Army *of the* Crown, *and the Other of the Commonwealth; but he seems to devolve the whole Power of the* Sword *upon the* King, *which is perfectly agreeable to the Laws and Usages of our own Constitution. His Aversion to* Tyrants *can never grate upon the Ears of Those, who have tasted of the Sweets of Liberty; and what he has said upon this Subject can never Interfere with the Duty we owe to a* Good King, *limited in his Power, who makes the Law his Will, and is so far like his Maker, that he can do no Wrong. There is as great a Difference between such a* Monarch *and a* Tyrant,

as

as between a Man and a Monster: And the Destruction or Execution of a Tyrant or Usurper, is (in Gozliski's Sense and Opinion) no more Regicide, *than the Execution of a Parent, who has murdered his Children, is the Detestable and Unnatural Crime of* Parricide.

When Gozliski gives the King *a Power to chuse all his Senators, he may possibly seem to put the Whole of the* Polish *Government into the Hands of the* Crown: *And this single Instance is sufficient to acquit him from any Suspicion of the worst Sort of* Republican *Principles. But when he confines the* Election *to a Particular Order of Men, and describes their several Qualifications in so minute and exact a Manner, he thereby prevents, in some measure, the ill Consequences of so large a Grant, and such an extended Prerogative. With us the Method of* Electing *is quite Different; and unless it were settled in the Manner it is, I cannot well see how our People could be said to have any* Representatives. *Though it is much to be wished, that our* Electors *would confine their Liberty of Chusing to such Men only, who are nearest in Resemblance to the Character of a Good Candidate, as it is Limited and Described by This Author.*

All the Northern Nations *have, for many Ages, paid a more than Common Deference to their* Nobility, *and look upon Blood and Descent, Ancientry and Ancestry, with a good deal of Particular Esteem and Veneration. Such of them as lie upon the* Continent, *and out of the Way of* Navigation, *are very apt to entertain a Low and Mean Opinion of* Traders *and* Mechanicks, *and to treat them at least with an Overbearing Awfulness, if not with Contempt. Upon this Subject* Gozliski *seems to behave with much Candour and Complaisance. He carries his Notion of* Nobility *high enough; but then by the* Nobility *he does not mean a Particular Order of* Peers *and* Palatines, *but admitts the* Old Gentry *into the same Rank and Class; and he makes every the meanest Subject capable of attaining to the Degree of a Nobleman, by the Best Title and Recommendation, his Vertues and Services. With us the several Orders of Nobility are fixed and certain, but the*

Crown

PREFACE. xix

Crown *can at any time increase their Number; and the Merits of every new* Peer *are recited in the* Patent *by which he is Created. Merchants and Traders are indeed admitted into the* Senatorial *Order; and for this there is a very good Reason, considering the Places and Persons they* Represent. Our Situation, *as an* Island, *and as a Trading Nation, is a just Occasion for this Difference: And Allowances must be made for all such Differences between Nations and Provinces different in their Soil and Region. Where the People depend altogether upon Agriculture, and the Produce of their Lands, where there are few or no* Traders, *unless of the Retailing or Mechanick Sort, and where the* Farmer, *the* Planter, *and the* Woodman, *are their Undoubted Superiors; the highest Regard will always be paid to these Orders of the Populace. Thus, for Instance, in Old* Egypt, *a Country naturally formed for Corn, Commerce, and Navigation,* Shepherds *were a contemptible Order of Men; whilst in the Old Inland* Provinces *of Asia, no Order of Men was more Honourable, and the Nobles of those Countries held all Traders in the utmost Contempt: But this could be no Precedent for Those of* Tyre, *of which City even an* Inspired Author *gives this Character,* That Her Merchants were Princes.

The Romish *Religion having been for* Centuries *established in* Poland, *and the Reformation but just then Dawning, when* Gozliski *wrote, it is not surprising that he should insist on so Punctual and Indispensable a Conformity to the National Church, as a Means to preserve Peace and Tranquillity. What he says of the* Christian Priesthood *in general, we may very readily come into; and I observe, that though in all Doctrinal Matters he refers the* Polish Church *to the Judgment and Decisions of the* Latin Church, *yet when he speaks of the* Spiritual Magistracy, *he vests it entirely in the* Bishops *and* Priests, *to whom he annexes a competent Share of Temporal Jurisdiction (which they all along enjoyed in* Poland) *without making any the Least Mention of the* Pope. *The Truth is, the* Church *of* Rome *always had a much better Interest in* Poland, *than the* Court *of* Rome. *The State took*

took Care to maintain its Rights in a much better Manner, than was done in many other Popish *Countries; and such has been the Spirit of Liberty in* Poland, *that the Protestant Religion hath met with much better Treatment There, than in any Nation whatsoever which hath all along been in Communion with the* See of Rome. *It is true, that* Gozliski *has openly declared for the Extirpation of* Heresy: *But then by* Heresy *he means an avowed Revolt from the* Established Church, *whereby the Publick Peace may be Threatened and Invaded: As to* Dissension, *he does not so much as mention it; and we are at Liberty to imagine, that He, who allows of Differences in Lesser Matters relating to Policy, was of the same Opinion in Matters of Religion. That this is no wild Conjecture of my own Invention, the following Historical Fact is a very Material Evidence. During the Reign of* Sigismund *the Second, when* Gozliski *was in Full Trust and Power, the* Nobles *and* Gentry *of* Poland *were permitted to send their Children to the* Protestant Schools *and* Universities *of* Germany; *by which means they brought the* Reformation *into their own Country, where it spread itself far and near, and might possibly have prevailed in a more Extraordinary manner, had not* Arianism, *and its Twin-Monster* Socinianism, *taken Advantage of this Indulgent Grant, and under Colour and Covert thereof, made their Way into the* North, *threatning Ruin and Desolation to the Common Faith of* Christianity. *The* Poloni Fratres *have dressed out These Two Heresies with all the artificial Gloss that Good Language and a Fallacious Way of Reasoning could possibly set upon them; whilst they carefully concealed the Monstrous Errors, Absurdities, and Blasphemies of their* Fellow-Sectaries, *who had written upon the same Subject, and of which there is a very Full and Authentick Collection to be met with in the Works of* Brockman, *a very Learned Professor of the* University of Copenhagen. *Upon the breaking out of these Heresies, some Restraints were thought to be Wholsome and Seasonable, if not absolutely Necessary; and the* Papists *made their Advantage of this Critical Juncture. They*

PREFACE. xxi

They spared no pains for the Extirpation of Heresy, and were too successful in instigating the Poles, *to lay the Whole* Protestant Body *under the same Common Restrictions; which Restrictions no Good* Protestant *could have justly found Fault with, had they extended only to the Suppressing of the* Arian Heresy, *so fatal to the Peace of all* Christian *States and Societies, that even* Cromwell, *amidst the General Indulgence granted to all Sects whatsoever, though some of them were perfectly Wild and Enthusiastick, did not scruple to give out Particular* Commissions *for the Suppressing of This, the very Bane and Pest of all* Christian Governments, *and the sure Fore-runner of their Final Overthrow; of which the once Flourishing Churches and States of* European Greece, *and of* Asia *and* Africk, *are, at this very Day, a most Glaring and most Deplorable Instance. But however these Things be, to avoid all Colour and Occasion of Offence, instead of the* Latin *or* Romish Church, *where it is mentioned by* Gozliski, *I have taken upon me to insert the* Primitive Church, *as the Good Old Standard, to which all* Christian Churches *whatsoever, are more or less fond of making their Approaches.*

These are the most Material Differences between Our own *and the* Polish Constitution, *as they are set out and mentioned by* Gozliski: *And such is his Impartiality, that he differs in some Things from the Customs and Usages of his own Country, and particularly mentions it as one of the Advantages and Benefits of Travel, that we are thereby enabled to Import into our own Country, whatever may Reform or Improve a State, by the Example and Imitation of its Neighbours.*

In all the most Material and Important Instances, extant in Gozliski, *which are of a singular Nature, and Peculiar to the* Polish Government, *I have taken Care to insert some few Words, by which they are Restrained to That Particular State they most properly belong to; that no Offence or Dislike might be taken at these Passages, which do not exactly tally with our Notions and Principles of Government and Subjection, or with the Customs and Usages of our Country.* Gozliski
himself,

himself, who advises all his Neighbors to Retain their Good Old Laws and Customs, however different from those of other States, would, I am sure, have Excused me This Freedom: And my Design all all along was, to present my Countrymen with a Good and Useful Book, *rather than with an Exact and Accurate* Translation.

There are some Minutenesses and Points of lesser Consequence, in This Author's Description of the Accomplished Senator; *as, for Instance, when he mentions his Dress, Diet, and Exercises, and the particular Marks of Esteem and Deference, which his Fellow-Subjects ought to pay him, whenever he appears in Publick: But every thing of this sort the* English Reader *may pass over, or Peruse it rather in the way of Amusement than of Approbation. When he says, that the Opinions or* Votes *of a* Senate *ought to be* Weighed *and not* Numbered, *I do not think he thereby intended to set aside the Right of* Majorities, *which so far prevails in* Poland, *that in many Cases there must be an* Unanimity, *exclusive of any One* Negative; *but meant it only as a Caution to the Wiser and more Experienced Part of such a Body, that by their Assiduity and Constant Attendance, they should take care to prevent their being over-powered or out-voted by their less Able and Experienced* Assessors.

But after all, when these Under-parts and Circumstantials are set aside, the Bulk and Substance of Gozliski's *Book, will, I am persuaded, contribute much to the Improvement of our Minds, and set us right in our Opinion of the True Measures both of Government and Submission, and particularly in our Notions of the* Original *of* Government; *the Account of which, as* Gozliski *gives it us, is much more Clear and Rational, than what is to be met with in the Old* Patriarchal, *or in any Later Schemes. From him we learn, what was the True and Genuine Rise of the* Senatorial Order, *which some have looked upon as Prior to* Monarchy, *and others have derived from the* Northern Nations, (*and particularly from* Poland) *the Earliest Imitators of the* Greek *and* Roman *Institutions: But* Gozliski,

very

PREFACE. xxiii

very wisely waving such a Narrow and Partial Way of Thinking, even in favour of his own Clime and Nation, derives it much higher, from Human Necessity, and the Natural Principles of Good Policy; and makes it Coævous with, and an Inseparable Coadjutor to Monarchy. *Had the Late Earl* Stanhope *read* Gozliski, *the Question put by him to the Learned Abbé* Vertot *might have been spared. I omitt many other Curious Discoveries: But what is the Greatest Value of This Work, it will, in all Probability, be Effectual to the Promoting of Peace and Unity, to the Suppressing of Parties, Factions, and Divisions, and to the Curing of all Publick Animosities, Disaffection, Discontent, and Murmuring. A Wise People will be ready to Learn and take Instruction, even from an Enemy, much more from a Faithful Friend and Ally: And let us only imagine a Sett of* British *Senators, already* Accomplished, *even beyond the Description given us by* Gozliski, *yet still This Author may be of Great Use and Service, by reconciling all their Fellow-Subjects to their Character and Conduct; when they see how great a Likeness there is between the Picture and the Original; and by Leading our Noble and Generous Youth into the same sure and shining Track, that the* Senatorial Succession *may be always preserved, in Wisdom, in Justice, and in Righteousness:*

——Uno avulso, non deficit alter
Aureus.——

I have already observed how far Gozliski *goes into perhaps an Undue Extreme, in those Parts of his Work, where he treats of the Order of* Merchants *and* Traders. *It is much to be wished, that we may never Fly out into the opposite Extreme, which may be equally Dangerous and Fatal to us.* Trade *is no doubt one of the First and Principal Branches; but not (as some Late* Writers *seem to make it) the Sum and Whole of the Publick Interest of This Kingdom. It is for the Glory of This* Parliament, *that they have done so much*

for

for the Landed Interest, *and for* Inland Navigation, *and Agriculture, the Great Points in Policy, which* Gozliski *hath so much Laboured, and so well Recommended. Our Wisest* Monarchs *and* Senates *have always had this Interest at heart. The Great King* Henry *the Seventh took particular Care of it; for which he is justly extolled by one of the Ablest Masters of Learning and Policy this Nation ever bred, the Famous Lord* Bacon, *who Recommends Agriculture in as strong Terms as* Gozliski *hath done, and particularly on account of its serving as a Nursery to our* Fleets *and* Armies; *the Seamen and Soldiers, who have been brought up in this Way, being well Prepared for Fatiguing (now of so much Use in War, since the Late Improvements in Fortification) and having their Full Share of the Well-known Courage and Bravery, which are allowed to be the Undoubted Properties of all their* Countrymen.

What hath been said in general, concerning the Expediency of Certain Set Consultations, *preliminary to the Meeting of every* Dyet, *is not fully and particularly Explained by This Author. With us, there is a Provision made, on the Side of the* Crown, *by the frequent Meeting of the* Cabinet *and* Privy Councils: *And it is much better to leave the* Two Houses *to treat in general,* super magnis & arduis Regni Negotiis *(as we find it worded in the* Summons *to* Parliament*) than to have our* Representatives *tied down by their* Electors, *to Certain Articles and Instructions, which they can never recede from; it being found by Fatal Experience in* Poland, *that this Practice hath often involved the State in many Great and Dangerous Calamities.*

When Gozliski *advises the* Polish *Government not to conferr any* Two Offices *upon* One *and the same Person, he certainly means this of such Offices, as are of the Highest Trust and Greatest Profit, or which are held in one and the same Capacity. But however That be, such a Rule can never obtain in this Kingdom, where the Number of Offices is vastly Superior to those in* Poland, *many of which are Hereditary; and They who are of the* Senatorial Order, *made capable of accepting them,*

PREFACE.

them, are vastly Inferior in Number to the Polish *Nobility and Gentry, of whom, according to* Gozliski, *the very Meanest may set up, as no Improper Candidate, for the Highest and most Profitable Place in the Kingdom.*

The System *of* Morality, *which makes so Considerable a Part of This* Work, *may possibly be looked upon as extending its Obligations to the Meanest of the People, as well as Those of the* Senatorial Order. *But when we observe, what a Happy Turn This Author has given to every One of the Great and Lesser* Vertues, *how well he has fitted them for the Use and Ornament of the* Noble *and* Powerful, *and in how close and particular a manner he hath united the* Moral *with the* Political *Character; all that he has said upon this Subject, will appear to be alike Useful and Entertaining. And when he Founds* Morality *in the* Divine Image *(which was never wholly Defaced in Man) and in our Natural Notions of the* Eternal Rectitude, *and other Attributes of the* Divine Being, *he gives this* System *a much Better and more Genuine Original, than is to be met with in the Works of some Later Writers.*

Consider Gozliski *as a* Divine, *a* Moralist, *a* Lawyer, *a* Philosopher, *an* Historian, Philologer, Orator, *and* Politician, *and he cannot fail of appearing to a very Great Advantage in all these several Capacities; and by his Example, as well as Precepts, may be a Means of Provoking our* Noble *and* Generous Youth *to Excel and Emulate each other in these High and Valuable Attainments, and to make an early Acquaintance with* Divinity, Ethicks, *and* Law, *with* Philosophy, History, Philology, *and* Rhetorick; *this being the Readiest Method of Accomplishing themselves, in their Last and Highest Character, as Good* Politicians. *In the midst of these more solid and weighty Studies,* Gozliski *hath taken Care not to omitt the Politer Arts and Accomplishments, such as* Classical Learning, Musick, Dancing, *and the* Exercises at Arms, *with whatever may Form the truly* Fine Gentleman; *nor yet* Hunting, Racing, Fowling, *and* Husbandry,

bandry, *with whatever may tend to the* Country Gentleman's *Happiness and Improvement. He hath traced his* Senator *from the* Cradle *to the* School, *and thence to the* University, *the* Camp, *the* Bar, *and the* Bench *of* Justice: *He hath followed him in all his* Travels, *and through every Stage and Period of Private and Publick Life, to his Last and Highest Attainment as a* Minister of State. *So that his Book is not only of Use to all our* Nobility *and* Gentry, *but to the Whole Body of our* Electors, *by Directing them how to make a Right Choice, and to take a Due Estimate of the Character and Dignity of their* Representatives.

I have nothing more to add, but a Hearty and Sincere Wish, That the Works of This Excellent Author *may be* Read *with the same Impartiality and Freedom of Judgment, with which* He *Wrote.*

TO THE

Most Serene and Most Potent *Prince*,

Sigismund-Augustus,

King of POLAND,

Great *Duke* of *Lithuania, Russia, Prussia, Masovia, Samogitia, Livonia,* &c.

Our Ever-Honoured, Good and Clement Lord and Master.

Great SIR ! Renowned for Wisdom and Conduct !

EVERY Man may easily know, that Those States and Commonwealths are most truly Happy, in which the Citizen, or Subject, passes his Life in the greatest Ease and Tranquillity: And on the Other hand, that Those States and Commonwealths are truly Wretched and Miserable, in which the Subject has no Solid Foundation or Security for his Ease and Happiness in Life. No Government can be Happy or Miserable, without involving its People in the same State and Condition. But now by what Means a Nation and People are made Happy, is really a Matter of Great Dispute, and much Controverted

verted among the Learned. Some attribute all Publick Happiness to Good and Wholsome *Laws,* and others to the Institution and Observation of *Civil Discipline:* Some Impute it to the Influence and Predominancy of the *Stars* and *Planets,* and to the *Soil* and *Climate,* in which we live, as a Means to Prompt and Encourage us to be Vertuous: And Others to the Example of Great and Excellent *Kings,* by which their Subjects are Provoked to imitate Their Vertues, and to conform to Their Likeness and Similitude. This Last Opinion I readily give into; for many very Good Reasons, but for none more Powerful, than the Consideration of YOUR MAJESTY's Personal Character, and the Right Use You make of Power and Authority.

The Great Quiet and Happiness which the *Polish* Nation hath for some Time Enjoy'd, are entirely owing to YOUR MAJESTY; the Splendor of whose Wisdom and Vertue is so very Great, that it attracts the Eyes of all your Subjects, and directs them how to Form their Lives and Manners, by Copying so Fair and so Bright an Original. To You they all Look up, watch Your Nod, and diligently attend to all the Steps and Movements of Your Administration; in which they see Equity and Clemency so well tempered with Justice, that it is as much their Choice to Love and Admire, as it is their Duty to Obey You. For so Great is Your Authority, that You are not only our Moderator, Governor, and Law-Giver, but are allowed as the General Judge and Censor of the Manners, Vertues, Dignity, and Merits of all Your Subjects; and such is the Justice of Your Reign, that nothing Superior to it can possibly be found in any other Nation under Heaven.

It is enough for Your Glory, that You obtained the High Station in which You at present Shine, not by any Claim of Blood or Hereditary Right, not by Force or Usurpation, but by the Unanimous Consent and Concurrence of the *Polish* Nation,

founded

founded in the Opinion they ever entertained of Your own Merit and Vertues, as well as of Those of Your Illustrious Forefathers. For it is a Notorious Truth, that the *Jagelonian Family* hath really been a Seminary and Nursery of Kings; so very Fruitful, that Foreign Nations, intent upon making themselves Great and Flourishing, have filled their Thrones with the Descendants of This Family: And if it had Remained longer than it did upon the Thrones of *Hungary* and *Bohemia,* and had headed the Armies of those *Christian* Nations, the Infidel *Turks* had not, in all Probability, made such a Progress in *Europe,* as they have lately done.

These, SIR ! are Great Advantages and Accessions to Your Glory; but You are doubly Happy in this, that You have a *Senate* to assist You, in a Wise and Prudent Administration, chosen according to Your own Wishes, and by Your own Direction, and as remarkable for their Prudence and Justice, as for their Illustrious Birth and Nobility; by whose Moderation and Wisdom, our Country enjoys Peace and Quiet, and the Fulness of Reputation and Renown. I make no Mention of the several Inferior Orders of the *Polish* Magistracy, who not only Grace and Adorn their Country, but Add to, and Improve the Common Felicity. So that *Poland* may be justly called the First of all Compleat and Well-established Governments, and the Capital Seat and Mansion of *Liberty*.

Who is there, SIR ! of all your Subjects, that does not look up to You as the Principal Author of all our Publick Blessings? These Things I have often Considered and Admired, even in the Days of my Youth and Nonage. As I grew up, Improved in Judgment as well as in Years, and plainly saw, that the Measures You took, were agreeable not only to the Sentiments of the Wisest Philosophers, but to the Laws and Institutions of the most Renowned Nations and Commonwealths; I readily imagined with
myself,

myself, that I should neither Lose nor Misemploy my Time and Labour, if I collected together all that my own Studies, or the Writings of Other Men, could supply me with, upon the General Subject of Policy and Good Government, and Transmitted it to Posterity, for the Common Good and Benefit of Mankind. To which Undertaking, I always Resolved to Prefix YOUR MAJESTY's Name, for whose Sake I was chiefly Induced to Enter upon it.

So Great is Your Wisdom, that it is above Instruction and Improvement; and I am therefore far from presuming to Direct or Inform YOUR MAJESTY; but it will be some Pleasure to You, to behold the Draught and Resemblance of Your own Vertues: And it must be a Satisfaction to You, to Preside in a Government, not only Good and Well-established in its own Constitution, but agreeable to the Best Plans and Systems of Policy, laid down by the Ancients.

In this Treatise of the *Accomplished Senator*, I have certainly Undertaken a very Arduous and Difficult Task: In the Prosecution of which, I have very little Dependance upon my own mean Skill and Abilities. But the Love of Praise (which is Natural to every Honest Man) and the Desire of doing Good to Mankind, are sufficient to Excuse my engaging in this Work. This I am Confident of, that YOUR MAJESTY will Graciously Accept of my Honest Endeavours: And my Confidence is entirely Founded in That Great and Well-known Clemency, which is so Essential to Your Royal Character, and Derived to You from so many Illustrious Ancestors.

AUTHORS

AUTHORS *and* EXAMPLES
Cited or Referred to in This Work.

LEGISLATORS, EMPERORS, KINGS, PRINCES.

*M*OSES.
Solon.
Lycurgus.
Parmenides.
Hippodamus.
Minos.
Demosthenes.
Cecrops.
Theseus.
Romulus.
Numa.
Draco.
Clisthenes.
Aristides.
Pericles.
Justinian.
Alexander the Great.
Hector.
Julius Cæsar.
Oct. Augustus.
Pyrrhus.
Trajan.
Ariobarsanes.
Hermodorus.
Constantine the Great.
Theopompus.
Agathocles.
Tullus Hostilius.
Tarquinius Priscus.
Tarquinius Superbus.
Agamemnon.
Osiris Ægyptius.
Midas.
Cyrus.
Thrasibulus.
Periander.
Alphonsus, King of Arragon.
Seleuchus.
Dionysius.
Agesilaus.
Scilurus.
Mycipsa.
Taxilis.
Nicocreon.
Ulidislaus, King of Poland.
DIVUS Stanislaus.
Sardanapalus.
Philip of Macedon.
Barsilidas.
Honorius,
Adrian, } Emperors.
Mithridates.

SENATORS, GENERALS, COMMANDERS.

*D*Emetrius, Son of *Antigonus.*
Epaminondas.
Dion Syracusius.
Cato.
Ulysses.
Minutius.
Fabius.
Hannibal.
Hanno.
Cicero.
Cymon.
Aristides.
Themistocles.
Damon.
Camillus.
Scipio.
Cleon.
Philopæmen.
Pompey.
Alcibiades.
Metellus.
M. Coriolanus.
M. Brutus.
Nestor.
Ulysses.

Ulysses.
Ajax.
Sylla.
Cinna.
Carbo.
Marius.
Cataline.
Fabius.
Gracchus.
Clodius.
Clisthenes.
Q. Cepio.
Heraclitus Ephesius.
P. Rufinus.
Æmil. Lepidus.
Sophocles Senator.
Paulus Æmilius.
Curtius.
Scævola.
Marcellus.
C. Crastinus.
M. Anthony.
Regulus.
Pompey the Younger.
L. Q. Flaminius.
Manilius.
M. Curius, Sen.
Hortensius, Sen.
Cassius, Sen.
Q. Tubero, Sen.
Demetrius.
L. C. Cincinna.
Servilius Isauricus.

PHILOSOPHERS, POETS, ORATORS, LAWYERS, HISTORIANS.

HOmer.
Ovid.
Diogenes.
Diogenes Lærtius.
Socrates.
Cicero.
Stilpo.
Plato.
Lysis.
Aristotle.
Anexagoras.
Pythagoras.
Athenodorus.
Charitus.
Artemius.
Plutarch.
Thales.
Livy.
Epicurus.
Crantor.
Demosthenes.
Thucydides.
Polybius.
Xenophon.
Aulus Gellius.
Caius.
Horace.

Juvenal.
Zeno.
Epictetus.
Chilo.
Theophrastus.
Heraclides Ponticus.
Dicoearchus.
Antonius Juriscons.
Cyneas.
Silenus Poeta.
Lucan.
Terence.
Bion Boristhenius.
Crates.
Chrysippus.
Carneades.
Democritus.
Metrocles.
Aristippus.
Tiresias.
Mopsus.
Amphiarus.
Calchas.
Plautus.
Timon.
Ennius.
Salust.
Lælius Juriscons.
Anexarchus.
Isaias Propheta.
Varro.
Euripedes.
Johannes Samoscius.

THE

THE
Accomplish'd Senator,
In TWO BOOKS.
BOOK I. CHAP. I.

The CONTENTS.

The Excellency of Political *Knowledge. The Dignity of the* Senatorial *Character. It differs according to the Differences in the several* Forms *of Government. Which* Form *the Most Perfect.* Man *the Governor of this Lower World. How nearly related to his* Maker. *How deputed by* Him *in the Government of the Earth.* God *the Author of all* Political *Wisdom. How we must Apply to him for it. Our Reason a Part of the* Divine Image. *When our* Reason *is in its best State.* Philosophy *the highest Improvement of* Reason. *The Praise and Excellency of* Philosophy. Philosophy *a sure Introduction to the* Art of Government. *Of the several Kinds of* Government.

OF all the Lovers of Truth, and Enquirers after useful Knowledge, They who employ their Time and Pains in the Pursuit of such Studies, as alike contribute both to the Publick Advantage, and to the Pleasure and Satisfaction of Private Life, are (as I conceive) in a fair Way of attaining that

True

True and Perfect Wisdom, which best deserves the Approbation and Applauses of Mankind; for every wise Man will take care, that his Wisdom may be useful and serviceable to his Fellow-Creatures. But now of all the Arts and Sciences, and all the several Branches of Learning, which serve to the Satisfaction, or to the Improvement of Life, I cannot think there is any one so Pleasant and Profitable, so Excellent in itself, and so Useful to Mankind, as the Study of *Civil Discipline* and *Policy,* or, of the *Art of Government;* by which Men are directed to the utmost Happiness their Nature is at present capable of; and by which both in their Private, and Publick Characters, as Members of a Community or Society, their Conduct ought always to be regulated, and restrain'd. I could produce many Examples for Proof, and in Confirmation of this Truth; and my own Experience, and long Conversation in Publick Business, are enough to convince me, that the most excellent Sort of Wisdom and Knowledge is That, which is conversant in the Direction and Management of States and Publick Bodies; the Government of which ought to depend altogether upon clear Reason and sound Judgment, and not upon false and fallacious Opinion, and the uncertain Caprices of Chance and Fortune. Hence it was, that I came to a Resolution of tracing this Subject through all its Parts and particular Members, and of communicating to the World, what I had to say of the Office, Vertues, Qualifications, and Dignity, of *the Accomplish'd Senator;* that the Publick might reap the Benefit of my Labours and Diligence, and those Men be in some Measure satisfy'd, who are particularly pleas'd and delighted with this sort of *Philosophy.*

In tracing this Subject up to the Source and Fountain of all *Civil Wisdom* or *Prudence,* I thought myself obliged, with the utmost Pains and Diligence, to collect the choicest Secrets from the Archives and Repositories of the greatest *Philosophers,* and to produce Nothing to the Publick, which was not agreeable to
the

the best Sentiments of the wisest *Legislators,* and most prudent *Senators* of former Ages. The Name and Person of *a Good Senator,* are sufficient to sustain the highest Character, because his ripe and mature Age fits him for the Practice of all those Vertues, which render a Man truly Great; and his Dignity and Station are such, that the People, his Fellow-Citizens or Subjects, look up to him, and expect at his Hands, their Common-Safety, Peace, and Quiet, and such wholsome Counsels and Advice, as plainly tend to the Establishment and Happiness of the Constitution. I am not forming to myself an imaginary *Idea* of a *Good Senator,* no where really Extant, but in the Mind; and whose shining Original is only to be found in Heaven; without casting the least Shadow or Resemblance of it upon Earth: *Plato's Commonwealth,* and *Cicero's Orator,* are Airy Topicks, which I shall not presume to meddle with: For my Enquiries are all entirely confined to common Life, agreeable to the Customs of Mankind, and altogether intended for Publick Use and Benefit. Whatever occurs in the wide Extent of *Academical* Learning, in the *Constitutions* of the several Republicks, in the Enquiries after *Civil Wisdom* and *Prudence,* and in the Treasuries of *History* and *Experience,* that may relate to, or make up the *Senatorial Character,* in all its Features, shall be drawn together, and comprized in this *Essay*; and what *Plato* enjoins as a Rule in the Formation of a *good City,* I shall observe in drawing the Portraiture of a *good Senator*; and shall borrow from the several Nations, Cities, and Commonwealths of the World, all the Vertues, Endowments, Precepts, and Duties, which may make up the several Parts and Beauties of the *Good Senator,* and render his Image and Description perfect.

But since there is a great variety in the *Forms* and *Constitutions* of the many *Republicks,* which are, or have been, upon Earth; whence it follows, that there must be also a Difference in the *Senatorial*

torial Character, and in the Vertues and Offices annex'd to it; I shall, for this Reason, endeavour to describe such a *Form of a Commonwealth*, as is most just and perfect, and most prevailing among Men, in which the *Regal Authority* and *Power* of the *People* are happily temper'd, and moderated, by the Prudence and Wisdom of a *Senate*: But preliminary to this, it was necessary for me to say something of the several Republican Models in general, their different Kinds, and Schemes of Happiness; of the good Estate and Condition of the Subject, or Citizen, and of the Education and Discipline necessary to qualify the *Senator* for the due Discharge of his Duty; in such manner, as that he may be well acquainted with the Nature of that Government, in which he is to preside, and be fully instructed in all those Vertues, which adorn Life with Honesty and Goodness, and which may best serve to raise him to the Height, and honourable Station and Dignity of an *Accomplish'd Senator*. These Vertues and Duties are so described, as that the Study and Knowledge of them may be alike useful to the *Senators* of every Commonwealth in the World, as well as to those of my own Country: And since we learn from *Plato*, that a Republick is then most Happy, when either it is govern'd by *Philosophers*, or when they who govern it do make *Philosophy*, or *True Wisdom*, their chief Study and Delight; it will be necessary to enquire, what *True Wisdom* is, and in particular that sort of *Wisdom*, which is conversant in the Affairs of Civil Government; before we can fix and complete the Character of the *Good Senator*.

Of all the living Creatures that are encompass'd within the wide Circuit and Pale of this Earth, upon which we move, the Creature, *Man*, in the Order and Condition of his Birth, has evidently the Superiority and Pre-eminence. He only, of all other Animals, various in their Kinds, and different in their Makes and Nature, was appointed not only an Inhabitant and Citizen of this

this Lower World, but the Lord and Master of it. This high and extensive Dignity he obtain'd immediately from *The Divine Being*, the one Supreme Governor both of Heaven and Earth: Who took him to be, as it were, his Partner in the Government of this World, made for the common Residence of Human Beings, and capable of a Communication with those of a Celestial Nature. Accordingly he breathed into him a Divine Mind and Understanding, the better to enable him, by his Reason and Counsel, to govern the World in a Godlike Manner, with Prudence, Sanctity, and Justice. There is a Social Intercourse and Communication of the Human Nature with the Divine, which is founded in the Reason and Understanding of Mankind; and where these are Perfect, they raise Men to a near Resemblance of their Maker, and produce an Order of mix'd Beings, which may not improperly be call'd, *Mortal Gods*: For herein is founded that Relation which we are supposed to bear towards our Maker, as his Children and Offspring. 'Tis the Divine Presence that animates and sanctifies our Reason. There is a heavenly Seed sown in our Nature, which, if well receiv'd and improv'd by the good Husbandman, will bring forth Fruit agreeable to its true Nature and Original; but if neglected, or depraved, it perishes in a barren Soil; or instead of Fruit, produces nothing but Thorns and Briars. That Man therefore, who has a true Knowledge of himself, will consider his own Endowments, as so many Rays of the Divinity; and his Reason and Understanding, as the Holy and lively Image of his *Maker*: And will accordingly endeavour always to think and do such Things, as are most worthy of, and conformable to, the Divine Privileges and Endowments, of which he stands possess'd. Since therefore, we are in effect associated with our *Maker*, and are so nearly ally'd and related to him, we ought to look upon this World as our great City, or Society, the right Ordering and Government of which is committed to us, by,

and

and in common with our great *Creator*. And since he is the Author of all Things, and the Architect of the Universe, from whom, as the one great common Parent, all other Beings derive their Original; for this Reason, we ought to resort to him, for whatever Counsels, Laws, and Edicts, are necessary to the good Government of the World, his Creature; that the World may know, it is not managed and directed by the Will of Man, but at the Command, and by the Wisdom of its Eternal *Maker*, and according to his good Will and Pleasure. For as Herds are not govern'd by any of their own Cattle, nor a Flock by any of its Sheep, but only by the Shepherd; so neither can Men govern Men, without the Superior Direction, and over-ruling Power of their *Maker*. When it so happens, that presumptuous Mortals set *God* aside, and undertake to bear Rule, without regard to the Divine Will, Wisdom, and Conduct, a State necessarily goes to Ruin; and Calamities and Misery are the unavoidable Portion of the Subject. For unless *God* keeps and preserves the Publick, the Temporal Governor, or *Watchman*, watcheth but in vain. Hence we may learn, that all Human Vertue and Wisdom, are derived to us from our Maker; and for this Reason it was, that our Forefathers erected Publick Temples, and dedicated them to *Vertue, Fidelity, Concord, Wisdom*, and *Peace*.

But in what Manner now must we apply to our *Maker*, for Counsel and Direction, in the right Ordering and Administration of Worldly Government? Must all our Applications for Redress, in every the least, as well as greatest Cause of Complaint, be referr'd to him, and immediately be brought before a Divine Audience? Thus far, indeed, we may comply with this Method, if we address ourselves to him by Prayer; and are particularly careful, that all our Petitions are agreeable to Reason and Justice. The Foolish, the Irrational, and Wicked, are in vain employ'd in lifting up their Hands, and throwing out their Clamours, towards Heaven.

The

The Ears of the Almighty are deaf to their strong Cries, and no Intreaties can be effectual to the drawing down upon such Wretches, that Heavenly Wisdom and Conduct, which are necessary Qualifications for the great Art of Government: Whilst God is always a sure Guide to the Wise and the Good, is ever present with them, and in them; according to that fine Observation of Ovid.

> *There is a* God *in Men, whose Light inspires*
> *The Mind, and warms it with Celestial Fires.*

The Mind of such Men is continually beset and enlighten'd by the Divine Wisdom, which attends so closely upon the Birth of Mankind, as they do upon their Maker, and in some sense may be said to make Gods of Men. It is impossible to be good and wise, provident, artful, and sagacious without the Divine Being. 'Tis Vertue only, that brings us near in Resemblance to the Deity, and Vertue is the genuine Offspring and Effect of Right Reason. It is therefore just and equitable, not (as some have imagined) that because we are Men, we should therefore conform to what is merely Human; but that (as much as in us lies) we should endeavour to shake off the Dregs of Humanity, and conform and live up to that nobler Part, which is ingrafted upon our Nature. What is there in Mankind, which we can call Good? Nothing certainly but Right Reason: In the strength of which, we are enabled to acknowledge our *Maker*, to put all the Vertues in Practice, and to chuse the Good, and reject the Evil. By these Marks we may easily know, when a Man is truly Wise, Magnanimous, Just, Brave, and Perfect in every Vertue. It is therefore evident, that without the Divine Mind and Reason, Man cannot govern the World: And for this Reason he ought, in the Administration of all Affairs, to follow this Guide, and to take all his

Counsels,

Counsels, Laws, Decrees, and Designs, from the Supreme Being; or, in other Words, from that Divine Reason which is implanted in our Nature, and is in effect our only Oracle. By these means we may be well instructed to govern wisely, justly, and in a Manner truly Godlike: For as the Reason of *God* is the Supreme Law, and in effect *God* himself; so in a wise Man the very same Faculty, when rais'd to Perfection, is a Law and a *God* to him. Hence the *Laconians* were used to give those Men the Title of *Divine*, who were remarkably excellent for their Wisdom and Justice; and accordingly *Hector* is thus described by *Homer*:

He seem'd not of a mortal Offspring bred,
But sprung from Heav'n, and of Celestial Seed.

Whoever therefore is in perfect Subjection to Right Reason, and makes That the sole Guide of all his Words and Actions, may be justly esteem'd as a *God* upon Earth; and only such a Man deserves to be recognized as a *King, Prince*, and Governor of the Universe, who well understands, on every Occasion, what Conduct, what Counsels, and what Sentiments to enter upon; and looks upon nothing as truly good, but what proceeds from, or is agreeable to, the Divine Counsel and Wisdom.

Since now it is the common Condition of every such Prince, or Governor, as I have hitherto described, to have his Residence and Part in the Society and Communion of his Fellow-Creatures, and this Society is either general, and inclusive of the whole Earth, or particular, as being subdivided into Kingdoms, Provinces, and Cities: It is an evident and necessary Truth, that the Divine Light, Reason, and Counsel, which ought to be in every Governor, are by him to be wholly laid out and employ'd, for the Security and Benefit of this Society, and Communion among Men. There are then two Sorts of Republicks, or Cities, and both

both subject to Government, the one Greater City or Republick, is that of the whole Earth, not confined within the Bounds of *Africk*, *Asia*, or *Europe*; but measur'd out by the daily Course of the Sun: The other Lesser Republick, is that particular one, to which we are confined by our Birth or Residence, as the Republick or Kingdom of the *Greeks, Latins, Germans, Gauls, Spaniards, Polanders, Lithuanians, Rutinians*, or any other such like particular and subdivided Nation. The Government of the former World is not to be comprehended, but only by the Mind, whose piercing Eye takes in a general Survey of all Things, and by the Strength of its Reason, grasps and collects together the whole Order and Nature of the Universe, by the *Greeks* call'd, the *Macrocosm*, or *Greater World*; and not only the Universe, but of that particular World, in and by which we Live, Breathe, and Understand; I mean the World within us, by the *Greeks* call'd, the *Microcosm*, or *Lesser World*. When the Mind shakes off the Bodily Dregs, and Load of Flesh, with which it is encumbered, and is in the full Exercise of its natural Freedom and proper Offices, when it is well-edg'd, and, by a keen Discernment, separates the Good from the Evil; when it is made acquainted and in Love with Vertue, and has a just Abhorrence of Pleasure and Vice; when it triumphs over, and keeps down the rebellious Appetites, and maintains an absolute Dominion over itself; what is there beyond or above this Mental Power and Dominion, which we can imagine or describe to be more truly Heroick and Divine? In like manner, when the same Mind takes Wing and flies Abroad, coursing over Heaven, and Earth, and Seas, and surveying the true Nature of all Things; when it examines and understands whence they were made and generated, of what Principles, by what Cause, and to what End; when it can find out what is Mortal and Perishing in every one of them, and what Durable and Eternal; what is the Nature of the Stars, where and in what manner

ner the Sun Rises and Sets; what are the Motions of the Moon; how all Things decay and perish; and what is the true Nature and Energy of the several Elements, Animals, and Vegetables; when the Mind is thus employed, and takes in all this mighty Mass of Knowledge, and at every step plainly traces the Almighty Author of all Things, and sees him governing and directing whatever is without himself: How does Man, by these Searches into Nature, and by this collected Wisdom, raise himself to be not only a Citizen and Inhabitant of one City, or a single Province, but to be a Prince of the whole World; which is hereby made Subject to him, as if it really were a particular Society, over which he presided? *Socrates*, being asked, *What Country or Nation he belonged to?* readily answered, *To the Universe:* Thereby intimating, that he looked upon himself, to be a Citizen, or Inhabitant, and in some degree a Prince and Governor of the World. And was not *Diogenes* (as we are informed by *Laertius*) called, the *Cosmopolite*, or Citizen of the Universe? This first Great City, or Society, knows no Servitude, nor is in any Subjection to Tyrants; it is not governed by Laws of Man's Invention, nor has any Occasion for Walls and Bulwarks; it is surrounded by universal *Space*, it is governed by the certain, perpetual, and immutable Laws of *Motion* and *Order*; and the *Elements* are its Fortifications, that guard and compass it on every Side. Its Citizens are called by the Divine Name of *Philosophers*, who have a perfect and reciprocal Power and Government over each other, and carry a Soul within them, which no adverse Blast of Fortune can ruffle or overthrow: From the Dominion and Principality they stand possessed of, no hostile Force can possibly remove them, no warlike Attempts can drive them from it: Neither Fire nor Tempest can break in, and interrupt their quiet Enjoyment of it; and they remain always Unconquered, ever Brave, Happy, and Free, without Danger, and without Fear. When *Demetrius*, the

Son

Chap. I.   SENATOR   11

Son of *Antigonus*, had taken the City *Megæra*, of which *Stilpo*, the Philosopher, was at that Time and Inhabitant, and had given Orders to have him brought into his Presence, he very courteously demanded of him; *Whether in the Sack and Plunder of the City, any Thing had been taken from him*; and readily promised him, it should be immediately restored: But the Philosopher answered, *That he never yet saw the Man, who had it in his Power, to do any Violence to Philosophy, or could possibly take any Thing away from it: That in the Possession of this Treasure, he was truly Rich;* and that *he was entirely regardless of all other external Goods, which were alike common to the Besiegers and himself.*

But now since all *Philosophy*, in the fullest Extent of it, consists partly in Practice, and partly in Theory and Contemplation; hence naturally arises a Division of *Policy*, or the *Art of Government*, into two Parts: The first comprehends all those, who confine their Studies to mere Speculative Knowledge, without proceeding any further; who set up their Rest in unactive Contemplation, and hold the Reins of Government, with only an imaginary Hand: These have an Aversion to Civil Commerce and ordinary Society, and often retire into Solitude, and the Monastick Way of Life, being, as *Homer* describes them, *without Privilege, without House, and without Tribe*. I can only intreat such Men, or (in Imitation of *Plato*) earnestly conjure them, that they would come abroad again, into the free and full Enjoyment of Civil Society, and a Life of Humanity, which is altogether conversant in Usefulness and Practice. For mere Speculative Knowledge, and the Theory of Nature, are of no manner of Use, unless they are to put into Action, and produce such Measures, as serve in the Defence or for promoting the Advantage, of the Publick. Is there a Man so entirely given up to the Study of *Nature*, who, in the midst of his *Philosophical* Contemplations, if a Messenger should bring him the News,
that

that his Fellow-Citizens, his Friends, Relations, Parents, and Country, were in the utmost Danger, unless he came to their Rescue, would not immediately rouze at the Call, and lay aside all Enquiries about the Stars, Elements, and System of the Universe, for the Sake of his beloved Country? We do, therefore, seriously invite the *Contemplative Philosopher* into Action and Business, and give up the *Commonwealth* and Reins of Government into his Hands; not That one Great and General Dominion, which is bounded only by the Sun and Elements; but that Lesser Republick, formed and knit together by an Assembly, or Society of Men, which the Subject claims as his own Country, by Custom, Law, and Birth-right: Because by such a Governor as this, well-versed in all Divine Wisdom, we have good Reason to expect, that Human Affairs should be happily conducted, with so much the more Prudence and Justice. For the Mind of such a Man being well disciplined and instructed, seasoned with the Nurture, and full fraught with the Knowledge of *God's* Wisdom, Reason, and Laws, he will most probably approve himself to be (as it were) a *God* to his Country. With a Mind and a Soul thus happily turned to Wisdom, *Solon* took upon himself the Administration of the *Athenian*, *Lycurgus* of the *Spartan*, and *Parthenides* of the *Eleatick* Commonwealth. In the Laws and Institutes of this Divine Wisdom, was *Epæminondas* of *Thebes*, trained and brought up by *Lycis* the *Pythagorean*; *Dion* of *Syracuse*, by *Plato*; *Alexander the Great*, by *Aristotle*; *Pericles*, by *Anexagoras*; the *Princes* of *Italy*, by *Pythagoras*; *Octavius Augustus*, by *Agrippa*; and many other Governors and Monarchs, by their Tutors and Masters in *Philosophy*. Hence the Ancients always esteemed those Republicks to be truly Happy, which were governed by Philosophers; or in which the Governors admitted Philosophers into their Councils and Friendship. It was for the sake of Improvement in Philosophy and Wisdom, that *Cato*, a

most

most excellent *Senator*, was so fond of *Athenodorus*; *Ulysses* (as we are told by *Homer*) of *Charitus* the Philosopher; *Pyrrhus* of *Artemius*; *Trajan* of *Plutarch*, and *Scipio* of *Panatius*, a Man (as *Plutarch* assures us) of the nicest Discernment between Right and Wrong, and a Perfect Master of Justice and Equity. *Philosophy*, when it has taken up its Abode with a Private retired Man, who gives himself up to Ease and Solitude, and to a listless State of Inactivity, who confines himself to his little Cott or *Villa*, as to a Magick Circle, and leaning on his Staff, and collecting himself within his own narrow Girdle, basks in the Sun-shine, despises every Thing about him, has the Publick in Contempt, and rejects all its Services; such *Philosophy* can be of little Service to Mankind, when it is thus grafted upon a dry rotten Stump, and withers away, and perishes with it. But where the Seeds of this Wisdom fall upon quite other Ground, and where *Philosophy* is professed by a Man or a Governor, formed for Magistracy, born for the Good of others; and fitted for a life of Business and Activity; it never fails to bestow on all such, Wisdom, Greatness of Soul, and a Sort of *Divinity*.

In the mean time, a Question may arise, What sort of *Republick* is proper to be put under the Care and Direction of this Great, Wise, and *Divine Philosopher*, whom we have been hitherto describing? For there are several Kinds of Republicks, and the Ways of Government are as various, as are the Manners, Employments, and Conditions of the several Subjects, who live under it: Though all of them are directed to this one great End, the Publick Good, or Happiness of Mankind; which Happiness we all naturally seek and endeavour after, and yet often differ in the Way and Means of obtaining it; and the Laws and Customs are Various, by which we attempt to fix and secure it. For whoever will carefully examine the Laws of *Hippodamus*, made for the *Milesians*, those of *Minos*, for the *Cretans*, and those of *Lycurgus*

curgus and *Solon*, which obtained in the *Lacedæmonian* and *Athenian* Commonwealths, will find great Differences therein, and much Variety in the several Offices of their Magistrates, and in the Forms and Constitutions of their Government. The *Seven* famous *Wise Men* (commonly so called) *Thales* only excepted, who withdrew himself from all affairs in the State, introduced a great Variety of Institutes, Laws, and Orders, among the People, over whom they presided, either at their own Discretion, or in regard to the several Humours and Dispositions of their Subjects; and differed very much in the Manner and Method of their Administration. Whence have arisen great Contentions, and Various Controversies, not only among the *Academicks*, but those of other *Schools*, who often make it a Question, how many Sorts of *Commonwealths* there are, and which is the most Excellent, and best deserves the Preference. *Plato* and *Aristotle* seem to me to have distinguished themselves, above all other Authors, upon this Subject, who by searching more narrowly into Human Nature, and carefully examining the Temper and Disposition of the several Climates and Regions of the World, have by their Learning and Diligence at last discovered, what Kinds of Administration, what Offices, Orders, and Laws, are in themselves most Excellent, and to what Nations or People they are best adapted. To their Opinion I readily subscribe, and chuse to be numbered with their Followers. Accordingly I reckon *Three* Kinds of Government; the first of which is *Monarchy*, the second *Aristocracy*, and the third *Democracy*; or as the *Latins* describe them, a Government by one *single Prince*, by *many Nobles*, or by the *whole Body of the People*. In the Formation of Man, God was pleased to make him a Perfect Emblem, or Image of the Body Politick. For as the Animal Power is divided into *Three* Parts, and has *Three* principal Seats in the Body Natural, so it is in the Political. Reason, like a *King*, assumes the Uppermost Region, and is seated in the Head,

as

as in a Throne or Tower, and there keeps Guard, holds its Council, and governs all beneath it. Next to the Head, and in close Conjunction with it, are the Bosom and the Heart, the Seat (as *Plato* calls it) of the Passions and Affections, and this is the *Second* Place of the Animal Life's Residence; where it acts in Concert with the Head, and readily and vigorously executes whatever Counsels and Designs the Superior Reason dictates and contrives. The *Third* and Lowest Part, as distinct from the two former, lies below the Heart, in the Belly and Bowels, and resembles the mixed Multitude, who are sometimes Idle, Drowzy, and Slothful, and at other Times Petulant, Noisy, and Turbulent; Slaves to their own Appetites, and liable to be hurried away into any Excess or Extravagance. In this *Threefold* Division of the Animal Life, we have a clear View and Representation of the *Three* Social States, or Kinds of Government. The *First*, or *Regal* State, seems to have a Natural Right to Dominion: The *Second*, though placed in a Lower Degree, is yet equally Useful, if Care be taken to keep it in Subserviency, and Subordination to the First. For as Reason, without the Affections, is as a Monarch without his Guards and Forces, unfit for Action or Defence, and altogether weak and languishing; so the *Senatorial* Power, without its *Monarch* Reason, as a Conductor and Defender to provide against, and to be its Support in every dangerous Action and Adventure, is entirely disabled, and loses all its Strength and Manhood. Hence *Aristotle* well observed, That there were two Parts in Reason, one Perfect, Self-consistent, and Absolute in its Authority; the other Secondary, and Subservient to the former, as a Son is to his Father. *Minutius*, as we are told by *Livy*, seems to have explained this Matter very fully, in the Defence he made for *Fabius*, when he was accused of having engaged too rashly with *Hannibal. I have* (says he) *often heard the best Soldiers argue, That He was the First and Greatest Man, who, upon any Emergence,*
could

could of himself form the wisest Schemes and Counsels; and that the next Best and Greatest was He, who could readily take and follow the good Advice that was given him: Whilst the Wretch, who can neither give nor take Advice, is to be looked upon as sunk and lost in Folly and Contempt. It is the Office and Duty of *Senators*, to follow Reason, as their Monarch, their strong Leader, and sure Guide, in all Undertakings whatsoever; and to exert the Affections, as Spurs amd Incitements to Bravery and Boldness. To which Purpose, *Ovid*, speaking of a Hero, makes this same Observation:

He Rages; but 'tis Heav'n inspires his Rage.

The *Third* and *Last* Part of the Animal Life is the true Image and Representation of Popular Government, when the mixt Multitude set up for a Power to do whatever pleases them, and will not be controuled by any Laws, but those of their own making. Hence it comes to pass, that they often fall into Disorder and Confusion; because they are naturally inclined to follow their own Brutish Inclinations, are governed by their unruly Lusts and Appetites, and have a Low and Vulgar Opinion, and Contempt of that Kind of Life, which is in exact Conformity to the Rules of Right Reason and Vertue.

Besides this, there is another Kind of Analogy or Resemblance, made Use of by *Aristotle*, in his Account of Government; and that is borrowed from the Nature and Constitution of Private *Families*. Monarchy, or Kingly Government, is very aptly represented by the Power and Authority, which a *Father* has over his Children, whose Office it is to be careful of, and watchful over them; to provide for their Sustenance and Welfare, and whenever they are Disobedient and Wicked, to Reform, rather than to Punish them. In the very same Manner, all good Kings ought to

behave

behave towards their Subjects; and hence it is, that *Jupiter*, King over all, is by *Homer* called, *the* Father *both of Gods and Men*. The Authority which the *Husband* has over his Wife, is an exact Resemblance of the Power of a *Few Select Nobles*, in a State of *Oligarchy*. This Authority of the *Husband* ought always to be exercised in the mildest Manner, and with a perfect Regard to the Rules of strict Justice; no Commands are to be laid upon the Wife, but such as are entirely agreeable to Goodness and Vertue. *Democracy*, or the Popular State, is best described by a *Fraternal Society*, or the Agreement among Brethren; between whom there is no Difference, but in the Priority of Birth. Now as a Father, when he becomes eminently Wicked, and is remarkably Cruel and Inhuman towards his Children, does thereby lose the very Name of a Father, and is no better than an Unnatural Tyrant: So when a King is under no Restraint, but of his own Will and Lusts, when he tramples all Law under Foot, is by his Life a Scandal, and in his Government a Plague to his People, he immediately forfeits the Name of King, and cannot justly be called by any other Title, but that of Tyrant. In like manner, when a *Wife* is at open Enmity with her *Husband*, when instead of taking due Care of her Children amd Houshold, she neglects both, or gives them up to Confusion and Ruin, she thereby loses all that Power and Authority, which is the Undoubted Right and Property of every good Parent: And just so it is, when *Brethren* turn Brutes to one another, and fly out into all the Excesses of Unnatural Hatred; when they disturb a Family by Broils and Contentions, or attempt its Ruin by Sloth or Luxury: By which Means they effectually forfeit the Name of Brethren, and lose all the Right and Power which the Priority of Birth gave them over each other.

From this Corrupt State, and these Abuses of Authority, by which the Art of Good Government is debased and vitiated, there

arises

arises another *Threefold* Division of Power, different from, and contrary to that *Threefold* Division, which we have already mentioned. These are, *Tyranny*, in opposition to *Monarchy*, or Kingly Government; *Oligarchy* or *Dinasty*, in Opposition to *Aristocracy*; and *Oclocracy*, or the Wild Outrages and Insolence of the *Mob* and *Rabble*, in Opposition to *Democracy*, or the Government of the People. *Policy*, which in *Plato* and *Aristotle*'s Sense of the Word, does sometimes signify only a Popular State, is but a General Term, importing the Constitution at large, or the Administration of Publick Affairs, without Regard to This or That Particular Form. To these *Six* Parts or Branches of Power and Government, *Plato* hath added a *Seventh*, when he subdivides Kingly Government, and says there are Two Sorts of *Kings*, one *Limited* and bound down to the Observation of Known Laws and Statutes, and the other Free, *Absolute*, and under no Legal Check or Restraint. *The Government* (says he) *of a* Single Prince, *well informed in the Knowledge of Wholsome Laws, and duly restrained to the Observation of them, is of all the other Six Political Forms, the Best* and most Eligible: But where there are no fixt Certain Laws to restrain such a Governor, the Subject can never be truly Easy or Happy under him. And yet it is much better to live under such a State as this, than under any of the other States, (the *Seventh* only excepted) if they too are without Known Laws, as well as the *Monarchical*: Though still the *Monarch governing by Law*, is of all other Powers the Best and most Eligible, and comes nearest in Resemblance to the *Divine Authority*.

It is very easy to trace that apparent Variety, which is to be found in the several Forms and Constitutions of Human Government, and to account for it by the Variety of Manners, Dispositions, Tempers, and Ways of Life and Education, which is commonly observed in Mankind, without resorting to a Divine Decree or Fatality, as the true Cause of it; or leaving it at Random, and in the

the Hands of uncertain Chance and Fortune. The Difference plainly to be seen in the several Climates and Situations, of the several Regions and Provinces of the World, will naturally occasion a good deal of Difference in the several Humours and Dispositions of their Inhabitants, and must consequently produce a like Difference in the several Forms and Constitutions of their Government. Add to this, the many Rebellions, Seditions, Wars, and Tumults, which often shake and overturn the Greatest, Strongest, and Best settled States and Kingdoms, and change the Old Constitution into a quite New and different Form: For such is the State and Condition of all Human Affairs, and Vice is so close a Neighbour, and makes such near Approaches towards Vertue, and Good and Evil are so twisted and interwoven with each other, that it is very common for a Man, or a whole Body of Men, to fall at once from the highest Pitch of Integrity, into the lowest and most groveling Corruptions. Sometimes a *Commonwealth*, though in itself well ordered and constituted, is by the Mismanagement and Mal-administration of those who preside over it, suddenly overturned, and passes from one Political Form into another. Thus it often happens, that *Tyrants* are made out of *Kings*; that the Government of a *Few Select Nobles* dwindles into a *Faction*; and that a *Popular State* is subverted, to make Way for *Mob-Usurpations*, and the *Tyranny* of the *Rabble*. The several other Political Forms are alike Subject to the same Turns, and Revolutions; all which Changes were by *Plato* ascribed to a certain *Fatality*, and to the Motions and Influence of the Heavens, Stars, and Planets. But besides this, there is a Difference in the several Forms of Government, which arises from the Difference there is between Man and Man, in the Order, Condition, and Circumstances of Life. For in some Countries and Nations, the Rich have the Majority, and in others, the Poor. In some the Nobles, the Soldiery, and the Husbandmen make the Majority; and in others, the Merchants, Mechanicks,

Mechanicks, and Traders are the Bulk of the People. Now where there is a Prevailing Superiority of Traders, Artificers, and Husbandmen, the *Popular State* is best adapted to such a Country and Consitution: The *Aristocratical Form* ought always to prevail in those Nations, where there is a superior Abundance of Men Rich and Opulent: And those Countries are fittest to receive a *Princely* or *Monarchical Model*, wherein is the greatest Number of Men, Good and Wise, and excelling in every Heroick Vertue. There are *Three* Things, which are particularly Useful and Serviceable in the Government of a *Commonwealth*; and these, in *Aristotle*'s Opinion, are Liberty, Wealth, and Vertue. Which of these is most Useful, cannot easily be determined: And as to Nobility or Superiority of Birth, which is sometimes reckoned to make a *Fourth Part* in this Division, we can look upon it no otherwise, than as an Attendant upon Two of the abovementioned Qualifications, Wealth and Vertue. Hence it is, that a *Popular State* is said to consist of an even Mixture of the Rich and Poor; whilst a *Faction* of the Rich and Wealthy ends in an *Oligarchy*; and a just Mixture of all Three, that is, of the Rich, the Wise, and the Free, most commonly produces that Form which is usually called *Aristocratical.* The nearest in Resemblance to this Form, was the Old *Carthaginian Commonwealth*, wherein the greatest Regard was always had to Wealth, Honesty, Genius, and Education. All the several Kinds of Commonwealths, which have been established in the World, either by Use and Custom, or which have been set up and founded, by the Wisdom and Industry of Philosophers and Legislators, being thus fully enumerated and described by us; the Discerning and Judicious may very easily discover, which of these Kinds or Forms of Government is the Best and most Eligible. All Orders of Men whatsoever are naturally disposed to extol and magnify their own Country, to prefer that particular Establishment, under which they were Born

and

and Educated, to all others whatsoever, and to chuse it before any Foreign Scheme, or Constitution of the Neighbouring or Remote Nations. Some there are, who are most Fond of a *Regal State,* as being in their own Nature Generous and Heroick, and therefore readily disposed to give up the Supreme Power into the Hands of a Single Person, eminent for his Vertue, and distinguished by his Actions and Exploits. The *Cappadocians*, who have lived under *Kingly Government* for many Ages together, would by no means accept of the *Democratical Form*, when it was offered them by the *Romans:* And therefore *Ariobarsanes* was sent to be their King, and was voted the Friend and Ally of *Rome*. On the other hand, the *Athenians*, who had been used to a *Democratical* or Free State, could never be brought to submit to a Government of a Few Nobles, or of a Single Person. There are other Nations capable of submitting to Tyranny, as particularly the *Sicilians*, whose Government was of this Sort, or very near it: And with these are to be reckoned most of the *Asiatick Nations*, whose servile Nature and Disposition have all along kept, and still keep them in Subjection to Arbitrary and Tyrranick Dominion. In general, That sort of People (says *Aristotle*) are best qualified for Civil Empire or Policy, who out of a Sense of their own Great Actions and Exploits, their Glory and Renown in War, and mindful of their own Honour and Dignity, are readily disposed to take their Turns, either of Dominion or Obedience. But let us now pursue the Subject that is before us, and enquire in a more particular Manner, which of *the several Political Forms and Systems is the Best and most Eligible.*

CHAP. II.

The CONTENTS.

The Peripatetick Philosophy *recommended. Wherein Human* Happiness *consists. Of* communicating *our* Happiness *to others. Of* Civil *and* Philosophical Life. *A* mix'd Life, *most truly* Divine. Plato's *Account of the* Formation of Mankind. *Of the* Monarchical *State. How* Kings *may be said to be* Gods. *Of the* Aristocratical Form. *How it differs from the* Democratical, *or* Popular *Form. The Preference due to* Monarchy *and* Aristocracy. *How these Two* Forms *are to be Mixed or United. The Glory and Advantages of this* Union. *What we are to understand by the Word* People. *Of the* Good Things *belonging to a* Nation. *The several* Orders *of Subjects. Of Counsellors and Soldiers. The Dignity of the Priesthood.*

THE several Writers and Observers upon the Nature of Government, when they come to enquire after That particular Form or System, which has the Preference to all others, and is most Beneficial to Mankind, do in the first place endeavour to know and find out, what Kind of Life among Men is to be esteemed the Best. For unless this Preliminary Question be well and fully resolved, all Enquiries after Good Government and Policy are Vain and Fruitless, and amount to no more than a Wild Wandering and Roving in the Dark, without being able to find a Sure and Right Way to walk in. What it is, that makes Human Life truly Good, and how this Blessing is to be attained, the Philosophers are divided in their Opinions. On this Subject the *Stoicks, Peripateticks,* and *Epicureans,*

are

are at great Variance with each other, and have split Mankind into *Sects* and *Parties*, and occasioned great Differences, both in Matters of Opinion, and in the Choice and Manner of Life. We readily chuse to follow the *Peripatetick Order*, out of whose *School* have arisen Men, most Perfect in the Knowledge of what is really Good, and who to the Full Possession of True Vertue have added the Possession of all other External Goods, as alike necessary to Human Happiness, and not only to make Life Perfect, but to grace and adorn it. Hence it is, that the Discipline and Institutions of the *Peripateticks* have been always found by Experience to be of excellent Use, in securing the Happiness of Mankind, and the Common Good of Societies. We do not however entirely disagree with the *Stoicks*, who fond of an Abstemious and Austere Way of Life, place all Happiness in Vertue only: And we agree with them, in what themselves readily allow, that for the Sake of Vertue, External Goods are in themselves desirable; that they are Provisions made by Nature and Fortune, for the Use, and to serve the necessary Occasions of Mankind; and that the Possession of them is an Advantage in Life, and adds to its Happiness and Perfection. For since Happiness is to be numbered among the Perfections, and Nothing can be Perfect, where there is any Defect; whoever would be truly Happy, must endeavour to be so in the highest and most perfect Degree. Such a Man ought therefore to be Wise, Just, Temperate, Brave, Rich, and Honourable; Handsome, and well made in his Person; and of a Sound, Healthy, and Robust Constitution. Since now Man's Life is made Perfect by Happiness, and since Man consists of a Soul and a Body, it is necessary, that his Happiness should extend to both these: For if there be any Thing wanting, or any Defect in either Part, the Whole Man cannot possibly be said to be perfectly and entirely Happy. Besides, if Happiness consists in the Attainment of Good Things, the Happy
Man

Man ought to abound in these External Goods; and when he is possessed of them, he ought to consider, that he was not Born for his own Sake only, and that it is his Duty, out of the Abundance of his own Happiness, to spread Abroad the Overplus of it among his Fellow-Creatures, and (as *Cicero* advises) to bestow some upon his *Country*, some upon his *Friends*, and *Parents*; and some upon his Relations and Acquaintance. Among all these, he ought to deal out a Share and Portion, not only of Justice and Prudence, and the other Treasures and Vertues of his Mind; but if he would really acquit himself as a Happy Man, of those other Good Things also, which Nature produced and intended for the Use and Benefit of Human Life. A Liberal Man must have Wealth, in order to give Proofs of his Vertue, by Acts of Liberality and Munificence. So must the Just Man, that he may have it in his Power to reward as well as punish: And the Temperate Man ought to be entirely Free, and invested with Authority: For without Power and Freedom, it can never be known, whether he is really a Master of that Vertue, which is ascribed to him.

In the Opinion of the Best Philosophers, there are *Three* Kinds or Conditions of Life. The *First* is employed altogether in Action; the *Second* in Contemplation; and the *Third* in the Pursuit of Pleasure. This last Sort, which is wholly taken up with the Gratification of our Lusts and Unruly Appetites, is indeed the Life of mere Brutes, or of the Scum and Dregs of Mankind, who are little better than Brutes. The *First* Kind of Life, which is Conversant in Action, unless it be duly regulated by Wisdom and Vertue, is the Life of Fools, and often exposed to the greatest Excesses of Vice and Wickedness: And in like manner, the *Second* Sort of Life, which is wholly spent in mere Speculation, is altogether Useless and Unprofitable, unless it produce Fruits worthy of its Knowledge, and its Searches after Truth are

are followed by a suitable Regularity in its Conduct and Action: For as he, who with a Constant, Fix'd, and Steady Eye, gazes upon the Sun, in its full Splendor, will by its Excess of Light soon be made Blind; so the Mind of Man, wholly intent upon itself, and upon those great and dazzling Secrets, which are lodged in, or formed by it, will by degrees lose all its Acuteness and Vigour, and be at last buried in a State of Darkness and Stupefaction. Whoever, therefore, resolves to make Vertue the only Guide of his Actions, and to preserve Happiness as the great End and Attainment of Life, must give himself up entirely to both, as well the *Philosophical Life*, or Life of Contemplation, as the *Civil Life*, or Life of Action. For a mix'd Life, made up and compounded of these Two, is truly calculated for Bliss and Happiness, and nearest resembles the Life of the *Deity*. He, who employs himself in Divine Speculations, and furnishes his Mind with the Best and Noblest Knowledge, cannot but be very Dear to his *Maker*. For whoever follows the Genuine Dictates of his own Mind and Understanding, is most like the *Deity*, and must therefore be beloved by him. Because every Being naturally Loves and Cleaves to his own Likeness.

They, who add Practice and Action to a Life of Theory and Speculation, and are Just and Honest in all their Conduct, do readily give into a Way of Existence, perfectly Happy and *Divine*: For without doubt, the Meanest of Mankind cannot but know, that of all the Benefits and Blessings bestowed upon them by their *Maker*, the Greatest and most Excellent is the Faculty and Exercise of their *Reason*; in the Strength of which we are enabled to bring both Heaven and Earth within the Compass of our own Knowledge, and to make an Acquaintance with the *Deity*, and with the Way and Manner of Serving and Worshipping him aright. They therefore, who in Conformity with the Dignity of their Nature, and by a Right Use of the Benefits conferred on

them

them, take care to improve the *Divine Principle* which is in them, and as well by the Contemplation both of Human and Heavenly Things, as also by a suitable Conduct and Behaviour, endeavour to approach as near as possible to the Likeness and Resemblance of their *Maker*, and to excel in all those Vertues, which are common both to *Divine* and Human beings; These Men seem to be Born of *God*, and ought to be esteemed as *Gods*, among Men. On the contrary, if they lose their Humanity, and forget the Dignity of their Nature; if they follow only their own Sensual Appetites, and Stifle or Resist their Nobler Power, and that Active and Vigorous Principle, which is in them; they are no longer Men, but only in Name and Shape, they become debased and degenerate, and are quite fallen from the proper Station and Dignity of their Nature.

There being a plain Difference and Disagreement in the Various Tempers and Dispositions of Mankind; so that some, by a Right Use and Exercise of their Reason and Vertue, are entirely Free, Noble, Ingenuous, and fitted for Empire and Command; whilst others are of an Abject, Rude, and Rustical Disposition, and seemed destin'd to Obedience and Servitude: Hence it is, that Every *Commonwealth* and Society of Men readily give up into the Hands of the Wise and Prudent, all their Publick Offices, Honours, Dignities, and Power; and always behave towards them with Submission and Respect. ' Tis a Fine Observation of *Plato's*, *That in the Formation of Mankind, their Creator did not mix and temper them all alike; but made them of very different Ingredients and Materials, in their Composition.* Gold, was the Chief Ingredient that was made Use of, in the Formation of Men fit for Power, and designed for Empire and Command: Whilst the Men best qualified to Execute their Commands, and to Succour and Defend a State, were made of *Silver*: And the Husbandmen and Mechanicks were chiefly formed of *Brass* and *Iron*. This

Allegory

Allegory of *Plato* is by *Aristotle* applied to the several Tempers, Dispositions, and Vertues of Mankind. Now, though every Parent is desirous, that his own Offspring should be like himself, because this Likeness serves to improve that Love, which is between Relations; yet it often so happens, that a *Golden* Offspring degenerates into *Silver*, and the *Silver* into *Brass* and *Iron*. Whence our *Maker* has particularly enjoined all Parents, Princes, and Governors, that they should, above all other Things, make themselves acquainted with the True Nature, Disposition, and Inclinations of their Children, and take care, in their Education, to purge out the Drossy Iron Particles, and pour in the Purest Gold; or if they find them Untractable, and Incapable of any such Improvement, that they should never suffer them to be entrusted with Power and Dominion; but give them up entirely into a Private Life. *Crantor, Xenocrates*'s Scholar, directs Men to dedicate the *First* Part of their Lives, to the Exercise of Vertue; the *Second*, to the Improvement of their Healths; the *Third*, to the Enjoyment of Lawful Pleasures; and the *Fourth*, to the Acquisition of Wealth and Riches. Without Vertue, Life is a State of Infamy; and without Health, it is a State of mere Weakness and Childhood. For the Soul, in a Sick or Infirm Body, droops and languishes, and is unable to perform its proper Offices aright. Whence it is, that the wisest *Legislators* have always taken care to provide for the Health of all their Subjects in private Life, by Salutary Laws and Edicts, enforcing Temperance, and forbidding Luxury. For in the Private Happiness of the Subjects, consists the General and Publick Happiness of the *Commonwealth*.

We are now to enquire, with which of the Three abovementioned Forms of Government, this Best, Happiest, and most Heavenly Condition of Life, is most agreeable; and after this Enquery is once finished, it may be easily known, which is the Best

and

and most Eligible Form of Government; and we shall be able to trace it by its own Native Beauties and Excellence.

In *Monarchical* States, where the Government is in the Hands of a Single Person, superior Vertue, and the Glory and Renown of good and great Actions, are the ordinary Inducements, by which Men are directed to look up to one single Person, more Excellent than the rest, to make him their King, and cloathe him (as it were) with Divine Power and Authority; having an Eye to the well-known Proverb, *Do well, and Thou shalt be a King*. Such a Governor, who is superior to his Subjects in Vertue, as well as Power, will exercise his Dominion over the People with Justice and Equity; and treat all under him, not as a Lord does his Slaves and Vassals, but as a Father does his Children. The *Athenians* (as we are told by *Demosthenes*, in his Oration against *Neara*) when their State was first modelled and founded by *Theseus*, had a right of chusing their own King, by holding up their Hands, and always made Choice of the most worthy and excellent Person. Among all the Nations of the World, the Election of a *King* was heretofore accounted a Sacred or Religious Solemnity, wherein the People resorted to Divine *Auspices* and *Omens*, for the Direction and Approbation of their Choice. *Romulus* was elected by the People upon the sudden and extraordinary Appearance of twelve Vulturs, as we are told by *Livy*; or as *Dionysius* assures us, at the Hearing of a great Clap of Thunder, was elected and solemnly inaugurated *King* of the *Romans*. Which People had a Law among them, That no Man should be admitted to the highest or any other great Office in the State, without consulting the *Gods*; and it was a Maxim all along maintained by the *Romans*, that the *Augurial* Solemnity, or Right of *Auspicy*, was of Sacred and Divine Authority. *Homer* and *Isocrates* both agree in the Maintenance of this Truth; That the Sovereignty or Supreme Power in every Kingdom is of Divine Authority

thority and Institution; and that every Monarch does in some measure resemble the Divine Majesty. The *Persians* look'd upon their *Kings* to be as so many *Gods*; and were persuaded that *Monarchical Majesty* was the Tutelar Deity of the Commonwealth. And accordingly the *Old Latins* call'd their *Kings* by the Name and Title of *Indigetes*, and look'd upon them as a *Lower Order* of *Gods* made out of *Men* or *Heroes*. Such, for Instance, were *Æneas* and *Romulus*, whose Bodies, the Remains of their Mortality, were no where to be found. The Right of electing Kings was vested in, and belong'd only to such of the People, who were eminent for their Goodness and Love of Liberty. Such only who stood possess'd of this high Character, were look'd upon as the properest Persons to call those *Kings* to an Account, who were declared Enemies to Vertue; and to execute Vengeance upon *Tyrants*. The *Old Law* of the *God* we worship, directs what *Manner of King* should be chosen, and qualifies such Men only for the Throne, who are eminently Good and Righteous, and Obedient in all things to the Will and Law of their Maker. Those Nations, which are govern'd by *Kings*, in an unalterable and uninterrupted Succession, are (in the Judgment of us *Polanders*) either such, whose People were heretofore of a barbarous and savage Disposition, or much addicted to Tumults and Seditions: And of these we now see many still labouring under the heavy Yoke of absolute Dominion and *Tyranny*. *Aristocracy*, or the Government of a few Nobles and Worthies, consists entirely of Men eminently Vertuous, Popular, and Renowned for those excellent Qualities, in which they shine and abound; and by which they rule and govern, so as to deserve the Character of good and wise Men; still making the Precepts of Vertue, and the Laws of their own Country, the Sole Rule and Measure of their Administration. But now in *Popular States*, Things are quite otherwise: For since Liberty is the only great End and Design of this sort of Government,

in

in which all Things are managed and directed at the Will and Pleasure of the Multitude, and subject to their violent and uncertain Humours; for these Reasons, there is in such a State very little Regard had to Vertue and Right Reason. For in every Government of this Kind, those Men only are reckoned Good Subjects, who serve to aggrandize the Publick; though in Matters of Private Life, they are neither Truly Honest, nor have any Regard to Vertue in their Actions and Conduct: And it is not mere Honesty, but Gain and Profit, and the Maintenance of Publick Liberty, which are in their Opinion the Full Measure and Standard of Political Vertue. It is the common Right of every such State, that all Dignity is to be obtained by *Numbers*, and a Prevailing *Majority*. They never reckon Justice by the Truth and Reality of Good Actions, but by Popular *Vote* and Opinion; and they look upon every Thing to be Honest, which is in Vogue, and extolled by the Multitude. So that if the Precepts and Offices of Vertue are sometimes perverted and set aside in every other Kind of Government, yet this is oftner, and much more commonly the Case in *Democracies*, or Popular States. Among the People under this Form of Government, when there is here and there a good Man found, who has an honourable Contempt of Low and Vulgar Life, and may now and then take upon him to Admonish, Censure, and Reprove his Fellow-Citizens, when they go astray, and are in the wrong; and shall attempt to reform, and bring them back into the Right Paths of Honesty; such a one will be soon looked upon as an Enemy to Publick Liberty, and may perhaps expose himself to Reproaches, Ignominy, and *Ostracism*, and be at last punished with Death. In many of the *Greek* Republicks, such heretofore was the Fate of many of their Best and Greatest Men, as of *Cymon, Aristides, Thucydides, Socrates, Themistocles, Damon;* and among the *Romans,* of *Camillus, Scipio,* and many others. The Case of *Aristides* is

very

very Remarkable, and worthy the Notice of Posterity. This Great, this Wise, and Vertuous Man, by the Integrity of his Life, and by his Perfect and Unsullied Honesty, had very deservedly obtained the Glorious *Surname*, or Title, of *Just*. Upon a Day, when the *Athenians* had appointed a Publick Assembly, for the enforcing and executing the Law of *Ostracism*, a common Boor or Rustick, entirely Ignorant of Letters, came up to him in the *Forum*, and in great Haste, and with much Earnestness, intreated him to write down *Aristides*'s Name in a *Shell*, which he then offered him, being of the same Sort with those, on which the Sentences of *Ostracism* were usually inscribed. *Aristides* was astonished, and asked the Fellow, what harm *Aristides* had done him, or his Country? *None*, (replied the Boor) *neither do I so much as know the Man; but it is intolerable, he should take upon him the Name of* Just, *or be Thought a better Man than the rest of his Neighbours*. Of much the same Mind were the People of *Ephesus*, when, as we are told by *Cicero*, they banished *Hermodorous*, one of their Princes, and drove him out of their City, with this Sentence in their Mouths, *Let no Man amongst us pretend to more Excellence than his Brethren: Whoever does so, let him be gone to another City, and another People*. A worthy Principle this, and well becoming a Popular, or *Mob-Government*! So true is the abovementioned Saying of *Plato*, who declares every State to be Short-lived, the Constitution of which is chiefly made up of *Brass* and *Iron*, or in which Fools and abject Wretches, designed by Nature for Servitude, rather than for Empire, have the Sole Power and Authority. A People of this Temper and Disposition, when their Spirits are set on Float, and they are flushed and elated by any unexpected Success in War, do very easily give themselves up to be flattered and allured by those, whom they have made their Leaders and Conductors in any Warlike and Successful Expedition; who loudly harangue them, upon the Glory of their

Arms,

Arms, and the Greatness of their Vertue; extol them to the Stars, and taking them in the Humour, and in the Critical Season, when, perhaps, from a Low and Inconsiderable Estate, they are Risen on a Sudden, and as it were Glutted and made Drunk with Renown, do by degrees allure and prevail upon them, to depose their former Governors, Men perhaps of the Best Characters, for Wisdom and Conduct; and then thrust themselves forward into their Places, and when they are Masters of Power, exercise it in the most Arbitrary Manner, and know no other Law, but their own Will and Pleasure. Hence it is, that every Government of this Sort is very seldom of any long Duration. A People divided in their Opinions and Sentiments, and void of Wisdom and good Counsel, are easily split and crumbled into Parties and Factions; and after long Broils and Contentions, are as easily delivered up into the hands of a Few, or of a Single Lord and Master. Thus the People of *Athens*, when they had obtained a Great and Signal Victory at Sea over the *Medes*, were so transported and infatuated with their Success, that they soon flung their State, by Tumults and Seditions, into the utmost Disorder and Confusion, in spite of all the Endeavours of their Best and Wisest Citizens to the contrary. Such Tumults and Seditions are very often the Rise and Origin of Popular Governments: Thus it fared with the *Romans*, in their several Struggles and Contentions, both with their *Kings* and *Senates*. Sometimes Popular Governments owe their Rise to the Ambition and Cunning of a Few; when taking Advantage of the vain-glorious and high-spirited Temper of a People, they push themselves into Power, and at last seize upon the Liberties of a Nation. This (as we have already observed) was in Fact the Case of the *Carthaginians*, at the Time of their vanquishing the *Medes*; and of the *Romans*, soon after their Conquest of *Carthage*. Sometimes a People, justly provoked and irritated by the Tyranny and Usurpations of their *Kings*,

take

take upon themselves the undoubted Right of vindicating their own Liberties; and by a well-formed Conspiracy, or by open Arms, shake off the Yoke, drive out their Lords and Masters, and take the Government entirely into their own Hands: And this was very lately, and within our own Memory, the Case of the *Helvetick Cantons*. A Popular Government, when it is well fortified and secured by Good Laws, and these Laws are duly Executed, may be reckoned consistent enough with the Strict Rules of Justice and Good Policy: But *Mob-Governments*, which have no Regard either to Law or Judgment, do by no means deserve the Name of Regular and Well-settled *Commonwealths*. Of *Oligarchies* and *Tyrannick Empires*, I have little to say; because these Sorts of Governments are founded in Injustice, and in direct Opposition to the Rules and Institutes of Publick Vertue, of Civil Life, and Common Honesty.

In all our Enquiries after the Best Constituted and most Perfect Form of Government, and what is the most Excellent of all other National Settlements, there are Three Things to be considered, and chiefly attended to; and these are, Authority, Law, and Liberty. For those Governments well deserve the Preference, in which there is all imaginable Regard had to Justice and Liberty: And the greater still is their Glory, the longer and the more firmly and constantly they remain Fix'd and Immovable, and Well-confirmed in the continual Practice and Exercise of these Vertues, which alone are sufficient to give a People the Character and Reputation of Nobility and Antiquity. It was the particular Glory of the *Lacedæmonians*, that they remained without any Alteration, in their Manners and Customs, in their Laws and Constitutions, or in the Form of their Government, for Seventy Years together: And a much greater share of the same Glory justly belongs to the *Commonwealth* of *Venice*; which State has, for these *Ten Centuries*

ries last past, remained unaltered and unshaken, and without any visible or material Change in its Constitution.

The Design of our having been so very particular in tracing and describing the several Forms of Government, and the Nature of the People, who are in Subjection to each of them, was no other than This; That we might be thereby convinced of the Superior Excellency of the *Monarchical* and *Aristocratical Forms*, as being justly Preferable to all other Forms whatsoever. The *Latter* of which is truly Excellent, because the Best and Wisest Men in it are entrusted with the highest Offices, and have the Administration of Publick Affairs put entirely into their Hands. And the *Former* is so too, because it sets up Reason as a Queen over all, and unites the Hearts and Minds of its Subjects in one common Principle, the Good of the Publick; with a View to which the Best and most Excellent of Subjects is singled out and honoured above all the rest, and the Supreme Power committed entirely to his Care. Under these Two Forms of Government, Human Life appears to the best Advantage, and shines out with the greatest Lustre and Dignity: Such a Life, as truly denominates not only Private Persons, but Publick Societies happy. Some have been of Opinion, that the Best-settled Constitutions consist of *Three* Orders or Degrees of Men in Power; and accordingly, that the *Lacedæmonian* State was well formed and constituted, because all Power therein was divided between a Single Person or *King*, a *Senate* or Body of Nobles, and the *People* represented by their *Ephori*, who were Elected by and out of their own Body. *Polybius* extols the *Roman Government* above all others whatsoever, because it consisted of *King*, *Senate*, and *People*: Three Powers, so well tempered and mingled together, that the *King* could not fly out into Tyrannick Insolence, for fear of the *People*; nor the *People* despise or insult their *King*, for fear of the *Senate*: Which Sort of Government hath been ever reputed, and with very good Reason, to be the best Constituted and

and most Excellent. For as it is in Musick, either Vocal or Instrumental, where a Multitude and Variety of distinct and different Notes are put together, in order to make Just and True Concord: So from an Agreement between the *Upper, Middle*, and *Lower* Orders of Mankind, arises (as *Cicero* speaks) That True *Political Concord*, which answers to *Harmony in Sounds*, and which is cemented and held together, by what it naturally produces, the common Good and Welfare of the Society.

This Form then, and Constitution of a Republick, we do readily preferr to all others, which naturally produces the Best and most Vertuous Subjects; and wherein the *Three Orders* of *King, Senate*, and *People*, have all the Power committed entirely to their Care. Above all Things it is to be wished, that the *King*, by his Actions and Conduct, would set an Example of Vertue and Goodness to all his Subjects, would be directed by the Counsels and Advice of his *Senate*, and conform to the Laws of his Country in every Thing. For the Law is the Publick Reason and Sense of the Community, and whoever obeys the Law, does at the same Time obey his Creator too: For *God* is Reason itself, and the First Great Intelligence of the Universe. By the Example of their *King*, the *Senators* ought also, in like Manner, to be strictly Good and Vertuous; because they are to stand between *King* and *People*, and by their Deliberations and Advice, to take care from time to time, that the Safety and Welfare of the *Commonwealth* may be always duly provided for, and firmly established. Counsel and Judgment, and Authority, are the Sum of that Power, which is lodged in their Hands. Every Good *King* will consider them as his Bosom and Faithful Counsellors, always in readiness to direct him with their Advice, and to assist him with their Strength. Whence every such *King* is said to have many Hands, Eyes, and Feet, continually about him, and ever ready to be employed in his Service, upon any

great

great or sudden Emergence. There is almost a *Divine*, or at least something more than a mere Human Capacity, required in That Man, who singly or alone, or in the Conceit and Opinion of his own Abilities, rashly ventures upon the Administration of all the Publick Affairs, and Interests of a Nation. But where there are many Counsellors and Advisers, upon every Publick Emergence and Undertaking; and what they dictate and advise, is left to the *King*, or to a Single Person, to transact and put in Execution; there is the greatest and surest Prospect of Success. Whoever depends on his own Private Opinion, and affects to be Singular in his Judgment, is rather Proud and Rash, than truly Wise. The Counsels and Decrees of many are of Great Service to the Publick, when they are put into the Hands of a *King*, or Single Person, to Execute them; but if many Hands are entrusted with the Execution of them, all such Undertakings are commonly Vain and Unsuccessful. When a Master gives out an Order or Command to many Servants at once, he only puts them in a Hurry and Confusion, and will have Nothing done, or Nothing done as it should be: But his Business shall be well and soon dispatched, when once he pitches upon a Single Person, fit to undertake it. Just so it is in the Affairs of Government; where, when many are empowered to execute, what many have advised, they only lie upon the Watch, and stand at Gaze on each other; no one will undertake, what is the Business of All; and thus the Publick Offices come to be neglected, and the Business of a State to go backward, or to lie Unfinished, and in Confusion. A Multitude of Rulers is (according to the Proverb) a Publick Grievance. Let there be only *One King*, and with him, let all the *Executive Power* be Entrusted.

In the Constitution of Human Bodies, the Separation of the Head and Heart, is sure and immediate Death: And in the Body Politick, a Separation between *King* and *Senate*, is proportionably Dangerous;

Dangerous; is always followed with Civil Discord, Dissension, and Confusion, and easily brings on the Ruin and Overthrow of a Government. Of the two Powers, the *Senatorial* may possibly be reckoned the most Beneficial to the Publick; because it constantly supplies both *King* and *People*, with good and wholsome Counsel and Advice. In the Animal Life, the Heart is of the greatest Use, because it gives Strength and Vigour to the Head, which is the Seat of the Rational or Intelligent Faculty: And the Heart is the Resemblance of the *Senatorial Order*. But then the *King* is alike Useful, because, by taking the Advice of his *Senate*, he makes their Wisdom his own, and in the Strength of it, governs the whole Body, just as Reason governs the whole Man; though not without the Proper Informations and Assistance borrowed from the Senses, on which account it is more Noble than them All. A *King* therefore, who will be under the Direction of his *Senate*, and collect together within himself the united Wisdom of a Great and Wise Body, and govern by the Rules and Dictates of it, must be truly Perfect in Reason, in Counsel, and in Discipline, and far Superior to the mix'd Multitude and Mass of People, over whom he presides. Such a Monarch cannot but govern wisely, and with the most Consummate Prudence: Because he never relies on his own Private Opinion, which may often vary, and lead him into Errors; but on the Common Reason, and United Counsel of his Senate, by which his own Private Reason is made Perfect: And, whatever Governors are under this Direction, ought really to be considered and esteemed as *Gods upon Earth*. As the Hand, the Emblem of Strength, is divided into Fingers, and by this Partition is made stronger and fitter for any Manual or Mechanick Operation; so, in the Administration of Publick Affairs, a Single Ruler or Governor receives double Strength and Assistance, from a Select Number of Faithful *Senators* and Counsellors. Every Man has his own particular Talents, and no one Man is equal to all the

Affairs

Affairs and Offices of Publick Life. The *Macedonian Alexander* could with a small Force subdue great Armies: *Pyrrhus* was an excellent Camp-Master: *Hannibal* often Victorious, but never able to make a Right Use of his Victories: *Philopæmen* was esteemed a Good Commander at Sea, and *Cleon* at Land: *Cicero* excelled as an Orator, *Pompey* as a General, and *Cato* as a Senator: *Scipio* was truly Great in Both these Characters; and many others have had their Proper and Peculiar Excellence: For according to the Proverb, Every Man is a *Roscius* upon his own Stage, or a Master of his own Art. We heartily wish, that in our *Commonwealth*, the Order or Body of the People, who have a Share or Part in the Government, did really consist of Men, Well-born and Bred, and throughly Conversant in the Knowledge and Practice of every Vertue: And that the Bulk of them were fit to take the Second Place, and come next in Order to the *Aristocratical* or *Senatorial* Dignity. For then in Fact, the Body of the People would make a Seminary, or Nursery of Men, well qualified to appear in the *Senate*, and to Execute all the *Magisterial* Offices in the State: There being no other Difference between the Magistrates and the People, but this; That the Former, on account of their Experience and Vertue, are advanced to a Higher Station and more Honours; whilst the Latter, that is the People under them, are alike employed in the several Offices of Civil and Private Life, and in Acts of Obedience towards their Superiors.

By the Word *People*, I do not mean a Mix'd Multitude of Rusticks, Boors, and Mechanicks, the Mob and Rabble, the Scum and Lees of a Country; but a Regular Body of Citizens and Subjects, generous by Birth, civilized by Education, and every way duly qualified to fill the Publick Offices of a State, whenever they shall be legally Invited and Advanced thereto. For since we have all along undertaken to treat only of such a Form of Government, as was the Best and most Excellent in its Kind;

since

since That Government is certainly the Best, in which the People are most Happy; and since Vertue is the Cause and Foundation of all Happiness; it must necessarily follow, that every good Government ought to be well-furnished with a Set of Men, by their Nature and Disposition well-turned and qualified for the Practice of Vertue and Honesty, and for the Enjoyment of True Happiness. For this Reason it is, that we *Polanders* exclude all Mechanick, Mercantile, and Servile People, from any Share in the Government of the *Commonwealth*, as being an Order of Men perfectly Degenerate, and sunk in the Dregs of Low Life, and utterly unacquainted with the Knowledge and Practice of true Solid Vertue. But still, as unqualified as they may really seem to be, for any Publick Trust or Office, because they are wholly taken up with Employments altogether unfit for, and unworthy of a Generous and Free Temper and Disposition of Mind, they are Useful to the Publick, as they are the Strength and force of the Society; and on account of their Hardiness and Numbers, are very fit to be employed in the Defence of it. *Constantine* the *Emperor* took care, by a particular Law, or Public Edict, to keep out all Mercantile Subjects, and those of the Lower Order of the Populace, from any Place or Office in the Government. For Cities were Originally founded, and Societies instituted, not so much for the Sake of those Men, who by their Employments are barely necessary to support Human Life, as for the Sake of Those, who by their Wisdom, Vertue, and Integrity, Bless and Adorn it. And yet it is by no means Just and Right, that those of this Lowest Order of Men should be looked upon with Contempt, or exposed to Disgrace or Misery, by Oppression or Maltreatment: Neither is it for the Peace or Welfare of the Publick, to make them Desperate, and leave them without any Hopes, or Prospect of Rising to Wealth or Honour. For their Merit is, that the Heaviest Toils and Publick Burdens lie wholly upon them, and

without

without them no Government can be of any long Continuance. There are certain Offices and Honours in the State, fit to be bestowed upon them, and to be made the Incitements to their Vertue, and the Rewards of it. So that among them too, as well as among the Noble and Generous, there should be always an Encouragement to Excel, and a proper Price set before them, either of Profit or Honour, to spur them on to Vertue, and to requite their Labours, and Services done to the Publick.

Aristotle, and his Master *Plato*, do both agree in reckoning up the several good Things, by the Abundance of which a City or State is preserved, and without which it must inevitably come to Ruin. These good Things may be reduced to *Six* several Heads. Under the *First* are ranged, all Provisions or Consumables, necessary to the Support of Human Life; and these are furnished by the Husbandman and the Shepherd. Under the *Second*, are contained all Arts and Mechanick Employments, in Use among Mankind, for the supplying them with Proper Conveniencies, as the Cloathing of their Bodies, and the Providing of such other Necessaries, as serve to the Maintenance and Well-being of our own Species: And these are dealt out to us, by the several Handicrafts and Mechanicks of a Nation. Under the *Third* Head are comprized Arms, Ammunition, and all Kinds of Military Stores. For in case of any Foreign Attempt and Invasion, or in order to suppress any Intestine Commotions and Insurrections, it is absolutely necessary, that every State should have a Well-disciplined Force always in Readiness, to keep Peace and Quiet at home, and to Protect and Defend the Liberties of a Country, against the Hostile Incursions of its Neighbours. Under the *Fourth* Head, may be reckoned Money and Treasure, necessary for the Support both of the Civil and Military Establishment. Under the *Fifth*, the Care of Religion, and the Administration of Publick Worship. And under the *Sixth* Head are to be reckoned, Counsel and Justice, both

for

for the Well-ordering and good Government of the Publick, and for preventing and suppressing all Manner of Wrong, Violence, and Iniquity; and the restraining of the Disorderly and Wicked by proper Penalties and Punishments, from living by Rapine, and in Contempt of the Laws, and from Acts of Violence, Injustice, and Oppression. Hence it is plain, that every State, or Body Politick, may be very commodiously divided into Six Sorts or Orders of Men; Husbandmen, Mechanicks, Traders, Soldiers, Priests, and Judges, or Counsellors. Of these Six, the Three *First* are by no means duly qualified to take upon them, or to be admitted to, any High Trust, or Office of Power in the State. They are neither Born to, nor Designed for, Government; but are a mix'd Multitude, intended for Labour, and to supply the Lower and Servile Functions and Offices of Life. To make a Nation truly Happy, it must be furnished with a Sett of Men, Generous by Birth, of a Free and Liberal Education, and at leisure to Study and Improve themselves in Useful Knowledge. For such only are fit to Preside in the State, and to make a Country Happy: Whilst the Mob and Populace have no Opportunity of attaining these necessary Accomplishments, and are altogether of a Sordid and Servile Nature. The Two Orders of Men, who have the best Pretensions to Power and Authority in a Government, are Soldiers and Counsellors. For since there are Two Seasons, which have their due and alternate Influence upon every Country, a Time of Peace, and a Time of War; it is certainly Right and Just, that these Men, who are alike Serviceable to the State, as well by Defending it in Times of War, as by Administring to the Good Government of it in Times of Peace, should be esteemed as the Best and most Useful Subjects, and be promoted to the Highest Trusts and Offices therein. Every Nation, in a State of War, is best preserved by Valour; and in a State of Peace, by Counsel; And therefore Counsellors and Soldiers are the fittest Persons to be entrusted

with

with Power; because they are chiefly concerned and employed both in the Defence and Good Government of the Society. To that Order of the People, properly so called, belongs the Right of chusing their Magistrates, and all other Privileges necessary for the Preservation of Publick Liberty, and the Promotion of the Common Happiness; not to the whole Order in general, but to a Select Number of Men, of distinguished Vertues and Abilities. The Youth of a Nation are fittest to be employed in its Armies and Forces, on account of their Health and Vigour, the Srength of their Bodies, and the Bravery of their Minds. Whilst their Elders are best qualified for Magistracy, and the Publick Offices; because the greatest Wisdom and good Conduct is to be expected from their Mature Age and Experience. It is a necessary Consequence, arising from this ordinary Distribution of the Publick Offices and Places of Trust in any Government, that the Common Good is no where so well provided for, nor the Magistracy so well executed, as when the Elders and most Prudent among the People are advanced to the Highest Posts of Honour and Authority, without doing any Injury to those Beneath them; who, by reason of their Youth and Inexperience, are not as yet arrived at the same Merit and Dignity.

Of all the Orders of Men, which we have hitherto recounted and described, the most Excellent is the *Priesthood*, or That Order of Men, whose Business and Duty it is, to attend upon, and to administer in things Sacred and Divine. The *Priesthood* was ever held in the Highest Esteem and Veneration, on the account of the Dignity and Excellence of this Holy Office. Among the Old *Egyptians*, their King was not permitted to enter upon the Exercise of his Power, without the Consent of the *Priesthood*. It was a Principal Part of their Office, to make Oblations, and offer up Sacrifices to the *Gods*, for the Safety and Prosperity of the People: And to implore the Blessing of Heaven, and draw down from the

Divine

Divine Bounty all the Good Things necessary to the Happiness of the *Commonwealth* in general, and of every Private Subject and Member thereof. Hence it was, that when *Alcibiades* was publickly condemned by the *Athenians*, and Part of his Sentence was, That He should be openly cursed by those of both Sexes, then in the *Priesthood*; one of the *Priestesses* very bravely refused to join in the Office, alledging, That the *Priesthood* was instituted only to Bless, and to offer up Holy and Righteous Prayers, and not to pour out Wicked and Unjust Execrations. *Plato*, in his *Commonwealth*, makes it a Standing Law, That the Election of every Priest was to be left entirely to *God*, and this Election to be decided by casting of *Lots*: That before a Candidate was admitted to the Decisive Tryal, he should be first strictly examined, whether he were perfect and well formed in his Person, without Defect, and without Blemish, a Freeman, Well born and Educated, and of a Generous or Noble Descent, taken out of a worthy Family, and the Issue of Good and Honest Parents; and whether he were pure from all Imputation of Blood, and not polluted by any of those Vices, which never fail to obstruct the Due Performance and Efficacy of all Divine Offices. *Plato* further ordained, That no Priest should continue any longer in the Performance of Divine Worship, than for one Year only: And that no one should be admitted to this Holy Office, till he was Sixty Years of Age. These, and many other Rules and Precepts of this Great and Wise Philosopher, relating to the *Priesthood*, seem to have been dictated to him by *Divine Revelation*: And we may easily believe that he borrowed them not from the School of *Socrates*, but from the Institutions and Discipline of *Moses*. For he had much of his Education from the Priests of *Egypt*, and their Opinions and Sentiments are often mingled and interspersed with his Works. So that his Sayings are looked upon, as more than Human, and himself is often called the *Divine*. *Aristotle* sets up a Sort of Holy and Sacred Magistracy,

distinct

distinct from the Secular and Political Administration, and commits it entirely to the Care of such Men, who are grown old, and have behaved well in the Service of their Country. For since the Worshipping of our *Maker* is the great indispensable Duty of every Citizen and Subject, and since we have made it plainly appear, that every Society consists chiefly of Two several Orders of Men, which are Soldiers and Counsellors, and that no Servile Mechanick, or Trading Subject, nor any of the Vulgar and Sordid Multitude, ought to be admitted into the Order of the *Priesthood*; it remains, that only the Military and Civil Officer are duly qualified to receive this High Honour, and even they too are not to be invested with it, till by the Maturity of their Age, and after an Entire Conquest over their Fleshly Lusts and Passions, they are fitted for the Service of the Altar, and qualified to intermeddle in Affairs, which are altogether of a Pure and Heavenly Nature. It is but just, that They, who are in the Flower of their Youth, have expended their Strength and Vigour in the Service of the State, and are fixed and worne out with the Load and Hurry of Wordly Business, should Retire, and be at Ease in the Sacerdotal Office, and make the Altar their Resting-Place, and the Sanctuary of their Old Age. With such Men therefore as these are, the Care of Holy Things, and the Offices of Religion ought most certainly to be entrusted. I pass by the *Atheistical* Opinion of some *Philosophers*, concerning a merely *Political Priesthood*, and the Wild Notions of Others, not altogether so wicked as the Former, but yet widely differing from us, who have the True *God*, and his Worship, Religion, and Priesthood, happily made known to us. What I have borrowed upon these Subjects from the *Schools* of the *Philosophers*, was intended for no other purpose, but to bring us acquainted with the Ancient State of Religion; and to shew us, how Sincere and Diligent even the *Pagans* were, in the Worship of their *Maker*. I have no Design to enquire, by whom and in what manner, all Elections

tions to the *Priesthood* are to be managed and decided, in the Church and Nation to which we belong: But I shall speak freely of the Pretensions of the *Priesthood*, to intermeddle in Secular Affairs, and to be preferred and advanced in the State. It is enough evident, that their Order was originally instituted by our Blessed Saviour J E S U S   C H R I S T, the Sole Author of all Good to us, and our Great and Only Lawgiver, who, from the First and Earliest Times, was himself a *Priest* after the Rules, and of the Order of *Melchisedech*, whereby he became the Head and Founder of an Everlasting *Priesthood*: Than which Order therefore, no other whatsoever, either in Heaven or on Earth, can be more truly Noble, Sacred, Excellent, and Divine. For to them he has committed the Promulgation of his Laws, the Dispensation of his Holy Rites and Mysteries, and the Denunciation of his Decrees and Judgments; making them as it were his *Vicars* upon Earth, and Partakers of his own Divine Authority. Hence it is, that the Governors of every Well-constituted *Commonwealth* have always thought it Just and Necessary, as well as Beneficial to the Publick, to take in the *Priesthood* as their Companions in Power, and Partners in the Administration of Government. And for this there is very good Reason: For what can be more for the Dignity and Advantage of a State, or conduce more effectually to the due Management of all its Affairs, with Justice and Piety, with Advantage and Success, than to have those Men entrusted with Power and Authority, who borrow their Wisdom, not from the *Delphick Oracle*, but from the *Eternal Mind* and *Reason* of all Things; and are by him instructed to preserve and direct a Nation, in the Ways of Righteousness, Holiness, and Justice. None, but the Sons of Violence, a Rude, Ignorant, and Barbarous People, Strangers to the Name of a *Commonwealth*, truly *Christian*, Vicious, Wicked, and the professed Enemies of all Religion, would ever agree to keep out such Men from all Share of Power and Authority over them. For since every
Government

Government is preserved by Religion, in the Knowledge and Practice of which the *Priesthood* is presumed to excel all other Orders; Those Governors certainly may be supposed to act in the Best and Wisest Manner, who make Priests their Partners in Power; by which means a State may come to be under the Direction of the most Worthy and Religious Men in it; may have the Law of *God* fully made known, and faithfully interpreted; and the Whole Body of their People thereby preserved from every Vicious and Hurtful Infection, and in a State of Health, Safety, and Prosperity. This in Fact was the Case of the *Roman*, the *Egyptian*, and *Jewish*, and of many other Nations. And since to this Order of Men, *God* has committed the Care of the Eternal Happiness and Salvation of his People, it is certainly impossible for us to be so very Weak, Foolish, and Mad, as to imagine, that it is either Unreasonable or Unnecessary for us, to entrust them with the Care and Oversight of our Families, Fortunes, Liberties, and Properties.

CHAP. III.

The CONTENTS.

Instances of some particular Forms *of Government. The Old* Athenian *State. Of the* Lacedæmonian *and* Roman. *Of the* German, French, Spanish, Polish, English, *and* Venetian Constitutions. *What Things contribute to the Publick Happiness. Law is the Great and only Rule of Government. The General* Qualifications *of all* Candidates, *for any Publick Office. Of the* Three Powers *in every* Monarchical State. *The Original and Necessity of the* Senatorial Order. *Instances of its Rise among the Romans and Spartans. What a* Senate *is, and what is meant by the Word* Senator. *More Proofs of the* Dignity of this *Character. The General Qualifications for this Office. Every* Senator *ought to be a Native of that Country in which he is* chosen, *or advanced to any* Place *of* Trust.

Hitherto we have endeavoured to shew, in the clearest and most convincing Manner, what is the Best Form of Government; what Kind of Civil Life is the most Eligible; and what Ranks and Orders of Citizens, are the most Useful and Beneficial to the Publick. We have described a State or Society; in which, if the several Offices of Vertue are duly Executed, and if it abounds in all the Provisions of Fortune and Good Things of this Life, and has a Due Sense, and can make a Right Use of its own Happiness, nothing under Heaven can be found or imagined, more Lovely, Blissful, and truly Divine, than such a Constitution. In this Description we have not copied from *Plato* and his *Ideal,* or imaginary, Way of Writing. The *Common-*

wealth, of which we have drawn the Picture, is not, like his, without an Original, or such as never was, nor is, nor (in all probability) ever will be, extant among Men. We think it necessary to produce some Instances or Examples of that Kind of Government, which we have been hitherto recommending. And though we agree to the General Reasoning and Wisdom of the Ancient Philosophers, yet as their Way sometimes is, whenever they follow Fancy only, and indulge their own Airy Conceits, without accommodating their Notions to Publick Use, and the general Good of Mankind, we take our Leave of them, and reject whatever is to be found in their Sayings or Writings, which is no ways Applicable to the Present Times, and to the Uses and Advantages of Civil Life. In vain do we look for the Republick of *Plato*, among the *Venetians*, *Helvetians*, and *Ligurians*; or expect to find it in any other Nation or Community. The *Cyrus* of *Xenophon* is perhaps an inimitable Original, and was never yet copied by any Monarch, in any Court whatsoever. I pass by many other Writers of the same Sort, and upon the like Subject. For us, and our Undertaking, the Method and Manner of Writing, we propose to follow, are entirely adapted to common Use, and fitted to the Necessities and Customs of Mankind; and therefore, we have all along taken care to mingle *History* with *Philosophy*, and to let them both go on Hand in Hand together. It is very easy to find the True Copy and Perfect Resemblance of that most Excellent Form of Government, which I have endeavoured to describe, in the Old *Athenian Monarchy*. For the Inhabitants of that Part of *Greece*, being in a Wild and Dispersed State, and wandring up and down the Fields, like Sheep without a Shepherd, were first by *Cecrops*, and afterwards by *Theseus*, reduced to a more Civilized Way of Life, and drawn together within the Compass of one City. The former of these Two Leaders was the Founder of this City, which he called by his own Name, *Cecropia*, and which afterwards

wards called *Athens*. He too first instituted a Government among them, which was afterwards handed down to Posterity. After so long a Tract of Time, and for want of Proper Lights from *History*, it is not easy to know, in what Relation the then *Senate* stood towards their *Kings*, or with what Powers they were invested. We may however very easily conjecture, that they had a Select Number or Order of Wise and Prudent Men among them, whose Advice upon all Occasions they made use of, in the Well-ordering and Government of the *Commonwealth*. For according to the Testimony of *Thucydides*, their *Kings* very often resorted to the People for Advice, and were determined by their Suffrages or Votes, in all Cases of Doubt and Difficulty, or whenever they were at a Loss what Resolution they ought to take, or by what Opinion they were obliged to abide. But now the First State and Condition of this Republick did not last long. The *Commonwealth* was soon changed; and in the Various Courses and Ebb of Time, the Great Author of all Human Turns and Revolutions, it declined and dwindled, and sunk at last into the Hands of an Abject and Sordid Set of Men; who by Force and Violence seized all the Power into their own Hands, and executed it entirely at their own Will and Pleasure. The *Commonwealth* of the *Lacedæmonians*, (as I have already noted) consisted of *Three* several Orders of Governors, the *King*, the *Nobles*, and the *People*. And what shall I say of the *Romans?* For among them, the *Regal State* was always called, the *Golden Age*. *Romulus*, their *First King*, elected (as we are told by *Livy*) and placed in the Throne, by the Common Consent and Suffrages of the People, not without the Concurrent Assent and Approbation of the *Gods*, laid down the Original Scheme and First Rudiments of their Government; which at the Beginning were very Narrow and Imperfect. He would not take upon himself the whole Power and Administration of Publick Affairs; but appointed a *Senate*, or Assembly of an *Hundred Men*, whom he made his Partners in the

the Government: And these, on account of their Superior Age and Character, as being Eminent for their Wisdom and Vertue, were called *Fathers*. At the same time, lest the People should imagine they were excluded from having any Share in the Publick Honours and Offices, and should thereupon be provoked to Enmity, both against *King* and *Senate*, he admitted them into the Lesser Trusts and Places of Authority; gave them a Judicial and Decisive Power, particularly in the great Important Article of making Peace or War, and invested them with many other Privileges. Happy had it been for the People of *Rome*, if this State of their Constitution had never been altered, or if their Government had never gone off from its First Foundation. Many Toils, and much Blood might then have been spared, which was so lavishly expended in the Defence of their Liberties, and for the Enlargement of their Empire. The General Tranquillity would not then have been so often interrupted, by Civil Seditions and Tumults; which were so very frequent among them, that they seldom had much Time to breathe in, or had any long and lasting Enjoyment of True Happiness.

From this Excursion among the Ancients, let us draw homeward, and come nearer down to our own Times. In *Germany*, the Government consists of an *Emperor*, of an Assembly of *Electors*, *Princes*, and *Nobles*, and of the *States*, or Deputies of the People. But this great Body of the *Empire* is divided into so many Principalities and Jurisdictions, different in Name and Power, that it would really take up too much of our Time to run through and describe them all. In *France*, the Government is strictly Monarchical. The *King* is not Restrained by any Law, or Accountable to the People for his Administration, Ruling Absolutely, and according to his own Will and Pleasure: But yet, such is his Wisdom and Conduct, that he never breaks in upon the Well-known Rules and Precepts of Righteousness and Equity, and by all his
Actions

Actions endeavours to set the World an Example of a Good and Wise Governor. The *Palatines*, or *Nobles* of *France*, are in their Language called, *Peers:* The People are divided into *Three Orders*, the Quality, the Priesthood, and the Commons: Out of these, the *King* elects a certain Number, and calls them together in one Assembly or Council, in which, upon every Emergence, all the Great and Arduous Affairs of State are brought into Debate, and finally determined. This Great Council is called, the *Assembly* of the *Three Estates*, and resembles the *Panætorian*, or *Pylaick* Council, among the *Ætolians*, often mentioned by *Livy;* and the General Council of *Ionia*, which was called *Panionium*. In *Spain*, the *King* has the Supreme Power in his own Hands; but yet he often calls a *Council Royal*, in which the Nobles have a Seat, and next to them the Deputies of the People, who are divided into *Three Orders*, the *Order* of St. *Jago*, of *Calatrava*, and *Alcantara;* and these, together with the *King*, have all the Affairs and Interests of the Government under their Inspection and Determination. The Kingdom of *Poland* is a Mix'd State, made up of all the Three Forms of Government. It consists of *King, Nobles,* and *People.* But then by the People are to be understood, the Nobility of the Lower Orders, the *Knights* and *Gentry*. In this *Commonwealth*, there is a Strict Union and Alliance between all the *Three Orders;* so very Strict, that the *King* can do no Publick Act of Government, without the Advice and Authority of the *Senate*, nor the *Senate*, in like manner, do any Thing without the *King* and the *Nobility*. Hence it is, that the Laws of *Poland* are in their full Strength and Vigour, and all *Orders* are solemnly Sworn to Keep, Observe, and Retain them. So that with us any Attempt to alter or invalidate the Established Laws of our Country, is always looked upon and resented, as a most Daring and Heinous Impiety. This *Oath*, which is mutually Administered to every *Order*, and by which they are Bound to the Observation of the Laws, and the Maintenance of

the

the Liberties of their Country, is in the *Polish* Language called, *Captur*, That is, *a Covering for the Head:* For as such a Covering defends the Head from all the Assaults of Frost and Snow, Storm and Tempest; so is this *Oath* a Sure Covering and Defence for the Publick, against all Attempts upon its Laws, Liberties, and Happiness. In the Maintenance and Support of these Publick Blessings, there is no Good Man, who will not venture his Life and Fortune, against Tyrants and Usurpers, and all other Invaders of the Common Rights, Liberties, and Happiness of our People. For these Reasons it is, that the *Polish* is really and truly a Free Nation, under the Influence and Direction of this One Maxim, That True Freedom consists in not Thinking or Doing what is contrary to Law, and in Living up to the Rules and Precepts of it, in every Particular. A *King* of *Poland*, in the Administration of his Government, is obliged to make the Law, the Sole Guide and Rule of his Conduct. He cannot govern according to his own Will and Pleasure, nor make War or Peace, without the Advice and Consent of the *Senate*. He cannot go beyond, or break in upon their Decrees, nor exceed the Bounds, which They and the Laws have set him. What follows from such a Constitution, is plainly this, That a *King*, thus Limited in his Power, is so much the more Honourable in his Person. His authority is not only Dreaded, and his Name held in Esteem; but He is really Venerated, and almost *Deified*. And for this, there is very Good Reason: For how can such a *King* be otherwise than Esteemed, Honoured, Obeyed, and Beloved above all Men, who in his Publick Capacity, and the Exercise of his Power, has no other Will than the Law, which is the Reason and Wisdom of a Nation; who follows no other Advice, but the Dictates of a Wise and Venerable *Senate*, and who uses no other Authority, than what is Backed by the Assent and Concurrence of all the *Orders* of his Realm, and which is Enforced by the Love and Good Affections of his People? In short,

short, a *King* of *Poland* is such in Reality, as *Plato, Aristotle, Xenophon*, and all the Great Philosophers and Legislators of every Well-constituted Republick, only imagined and described in *Idea,* and by Representation: Such a King as Nature intended, and such as *God* seems to require. The *Senate* is a Perfect *Aristocracy,* and have a Supreme Power and Authority lodged in their Hands. This Body consists of the most Prudent and Venerable Men, chosen out of the Order of the Nobility: Who, together with the *King,* have the Sole Right to Advise and Determine in all Affairs, relating to the Publick Administration of the Government. These *Senators* are with us, what the *Homotimi* heretofore were among the *Persians,* and the *Ephori* among the *Lacedæmonians.* The *Equestrian,* or *Lower Order* of the Nobility, are the Representatives of the People, and have their Part of Share in the Publick Councils: And this Order of Men is the Proper Nursery both of our *Kings* and our *Nobility. Britain,* now called *England,* is a *Monarchical State:* The *Senate* consists of a *Select Number* of the *Nobility,* and of *Certain Commoners,* Representatives of the People: And these *Two Orders,* together with the *King,* do constitute the Great Council of the Nation, which is called, *Parliament.* The *Republick* of *Venice* is Modelled and Formed very much after the same Manner. Under the Name of the *People,* or Citizens, are comprehended the *Nobles* and *Gentry:* And great Care is taken to prevent any of the Populace from interfering or mingling with these *Two Orders,* upon any Pretence whatsoever. None, but the *Nobility* are admitted into the Great Offices and Places of Trust, in the Administration of the Government. Hence it is, that their *Senate* makes up the Compleat *Aristocratical Form,* and is both the Head and Basis of their State. Out of this Body their *Great Duke* is chosen, having some faint Resemblance and Image of a *King.* No other Republick, no Monarchy whatsoever, has so long and so quietly remained in the Full Enjoyment of their First uninterrupted

Constitution,

Constitution, as the *Venetian:* But whether this is owing to the Good-will and Pleasure of *Providence,* to the Smiles and Bounty of Fortune, to their Strict Observance of Law and Justice, or to the Nature and Strength of their Situation, so happily calculated to prevent and Intestine Disorders or Seditions of their People, which might Interrupt their Peace, or prove Fatal to the Government; we do not at this Time, or in this Place, think it Proper or Pertinent to enquire. Let these Instances of Good and Well-formed Governments and *Commonwealths* suffice at present; and let us now examine, whence their Happiness arises, and to what Causes it is owing.

There are Three Things, which contribute chiefly to the Publick Happiness and Welfare: These are Magistracy, Law, and Civil Order, or Discipline. For without These, no City or Society of Men can remain long in a Regular and Peaceable Condition. It is the Duty of the Magistrate, to Preside over the People, and to Prescribe to them such Things as are Right and Good, Useful to the Publick, and agreeable to Reason and Justice. *Cicero* very Wisely and Elegantly observes, *That the Law is as much above the Magistrate, as the Magistrate is above the People;* whence it may be truly said, that the Magistrate is a Speaking Law, and the Law a Silent Magistrate. No Government can possibly subsist without the Magistrate. By his Prudence, Counsel, Fidelity, and Wisdom, it is kept Upright and in Good Order: And by his Conduct we know, how to Form a Judgment of the Happiness, Regularity, and Stability of any Government. A Ship overtaken and beset by a Storm, rises and falls, and reels to and fro, expecting Ruin and Destruction every Moment, unless timely preserved by the Care and Diligence of Those, who are appointed to Steer and Conduct her aright: And just thus it is with a Government, exposed every Moment to the Tempestuous Fury of Seditions, Tumults, and Civil Commotions; and which, unless the Magistrate interpose with his utmost Diligence and Good Conduct, must yield to the Evils that

that encompass it, and be Rent and Dashed to Pieces by them, as easily as a Wave is Divided and Torne asunder by a Rock. In our Natural Constitution we find by Experience, that our Body is governed by the Animal Part, and the Animal Part by the Mind or Rational Spirit. In the very same manner, every Body Politick, City, or Society of Men, must necessarily have an Animal Life, and this Life is the Law, because it dictates Justice and Honesty, which are the Perfection of all Human Life: And this Law, thus animated, must be also endowed with a Mind or Rational Spirit, and such is the Good Magistrate, when he governs with Wisdom and Prudence, which are the Noblest Fruits and Products of his Reason. Where there are neither Laws nor Magistrates, there cannot be so much as the Shadow or Appearance of any Human Society; and such a Country may be looked upon as forsaken both by *God* and *Man*. Right Reason is the Great Law of Mankind: For this every Wise Man looks into himself, and the People look up for it to the Magistrate, or to the Written *Tables* and *Laws* of their Country, being very Careful to avoid whatever is Condemned or Censured, not only by a Written External Law, but by the Internal Dictates and Rules of Right Reason. Those Men, therefore, who are eminently distinguished and noted for their Superior Wisdom and Conduct, and have more of the *Golden* and *Silver* Nature I before hinted at, in their Composition, than the rest of their Fellow-Subjects, whereby they are better fitted for Publick Use and Service, ought in Proportion to their Merit, to be Entrusted and Preferred by their Country. For by their Counsel and Wisdom, Cities and Provinces are as well Preserved and Defended against all Hostile Attempts and Invasions, as by so many Bulwarks and Fortifications; freed from all Dangers, and firmly established in Peace and Happiness. It is, in the first place, absolutely Necessary, that all Candidates, for any High Office in the State, should be well endowed with those Particular

ticular Vertues, which tend to the Promotion of the Publick Good and Welfare: In the next place, that They be Well-affected to, and True Lovers of the Constitution of the Government, in which they are to be employed, desirous to live quietly under it, without attempting any Changes or Alterations, in prejudice to an Old and Well-grounded Establishment: And in the third place, that They look upon the Power or Trust which is reposed in them by the People, to be intended for no other Use or Purpose, but to be employed in their Service, and for the Common Good. By which means they will Govern and Behave in their Offices, with so much more Honour to Themselves, and Benefit to Others; whilst the People under them will readily Obey, and Submit to them, with no less Pleasure and Satisfaction. Great Skill and much Wisdom are required in Him, who worthily Aspires to any High Office, or Share in the Magistracy: And let him consider, that it is not one House, or a Single Family, one Wife, or a Few Children, that are committed to his Care: But the *Commonwealth*, and his Country has entrusted him with the Government of Vast Multitudes, in their Minds, Opinions, Wills, and Affections, widely Differing, and often at Variance with each other; that by his Management and Conduct, they may be United and brought Together into one Harmonious State, and League of Love; and that as much as possible, there may be for the future no Difference, or Disagreement among them.

There are *Three* Sorts or Degrees of Power, or Magistracy in every *Commonwealth*. The *First* is possessed by the *King*, as *Supreme*, the *Second* by the *Senate*, and the *Third* by the People. Which of these Powers is most Beneficial to the Publick, remains now to be enquired into. The Great Vertue, Superior Wisdom, and Godlike Conduct of a Good Monarch, are set in a full and fair Light, and every where gazed at and admired. He is looked upon to be the Lord and Governor of his own Kingdom,

Kingdom, as his *Maker* is of the whole World: And for this Reason, he ought to behave in his Government, with Justice and Piety; because he is honoured and regarded as the Deputy and Vicegerent of Heaven, whence he derives all his Counsel, Wisdom, and Prudence; Vertues and Qualities, which are not to be considered as his own acquired Property, but as Gifts and Blessings bestowed and poured down upon him, by the *Great King* of the *Universe,* under whom he Reigns. But now, since no one Single Man, or Monarch, is by his Wisdom and Diligence equal to the Task of Governing whole Multitudes: For it belongs not to Man, but only to *God,* throughly to inspect and take perfect Cognizance of whatever passes in the World, and to direct it with a Just Unerring Hand: Hence it is, that all Wise States and Societies are obliged to call in to the Assistance of their Kings or Governors, certain Wise and Prudent Counsellors, to be Their Coadjutors in all Publick Affairs, and to Administer with and under Them in the Government of the *Commonwealth.* These Counsellors, being a Middle Order of Men, placed exactly between the Prince and his People, have in That Situation a full View and Survey on the One Hand, of the whole Kingly Office, and how it is executed; and on the Other, of the Privileges, Customs, and Manners of the People, and how they are disposed and tempered; and can therefore easily Foresee, and readily Provide against, any Attempt that shall be made on the Regal Power and Dignity; and as easily and readily Assist the People, whenever their Liberties, or the Publick Welfare, are in Danger. On this Account it is, that we look upon this Middle Order of *Counsellors* or *Senators,* to be the most Useful and Serviceable to their Country. A *King,* however Wise and Good, cannot of himself look into all the Affairs of State, and attend to all its Interests: And he is often liable to be tempted by the Love of Power, or some other Appetite or Passion, to go off from the Guidance and Dictates of his Reason. On the other hand,

hand, the People or Multitude, are, when left to themselves, a Headless Unthinking Body, void of Reason, or unable to form, or to follow the Best and Wisest Dictates. But now a *Senate,* or Order of Men called together, and elected out of the Best and Wisest of their Fellow-Subjects, and such as have distinguished themselves by some Great and Glorious Exploits; such a Number of so many Good and Wise Men put together, and Assembling in the Midst, between *King* and *People,* may from such a Station, as from a Watch Tower, look out carefully, and keep a Vigilant Eye upon the Publick and all its Affairs, and hold themselves always prepared, to guard against all Tumults, Seditions, and Dangers whatsoever, which may Threaten or Annoy their Country; always Ready to keep it in Safety, and to promote its Welfare and Happiness.

There hardly ever was a Government, or Commonwealth in the World, in which the *Senate* was not entrusted either with the Whole, or at least, with a very Considerable Part and Share of the Supreme Power. For though those Guides or Leaders, who heretofore gathered and drew together a Wild Savage People, dispersed and wandring up and down in Woods and Desarts; fixed and enclosed them in Towns or Cities, and formed them into Societies, had thereupon the Name of *Kings* given them, and did for a While keep the Sole Power and Dominion in their own Hands; Yet when these First Rudiments and Foundations were once laid, and the Fabrick began to rise and grow up to Perfection, it was too Great and Unwieldy a Work, to lie altogether under the Direction and Management of a Single Person. The People, weaned from their Infant-State, would by Degrees contract a more Manly Disposition; and shaking off their former Rude and Savage Temper, grow Polite and Refined, and by Art and Knowledge so far improved, that the Prudence and Authority of a Single Governor were by no means Sufficient to Guide and Direct, or to Awe and Restrain them. It became therefore absolutely necessary for every

every Monarch, to call to his Assistance certain Wise Men or Counsellors, and to make them his Assessors and Partners in Power, that by their Common Advice, and in the Joint Strength of their Wisdom, the Whole Commonwealth might be Managed and Conducted with so much the more Ease and Safety, Honour and Advantage. Such was the Wisdom and Policy of *Romulus*, when being throughly persuaded, that to Place or to Keep all Power in the Hands of a Single Person, was by no means Commendable, but either Odious, Dangerous, or Unjust, he chose out of the People One Hundred Men, Noted for their Wisdom and Experience, and thereupon gave them the Name and Authority of *Fathers* or *Senators*. His example was followed by *Theopontus* of *Sparta*, when he instituted the Order of the *Ephori*, took them to be his Partners in the State, and gave them a Share of the Supremacy. His Wife indeed censured his Conduct, and observed to him, *That his Children, when they came to Reign, would find the Regal Power Weakened and Diminished:* But the Monarch answer'd, that *They would find by what he had done, their Kingdom enlarged, and better secured than ever:* For it was his Opinion, that the Wisdom and Authority of a Senate, were the Support and Security of *Monarchical* Government. From these Instances it is evident, that the *Senatorial Order* was, in the Earliest Times, made Partaker with the First *Kings*, in their Dominion and Power, and had in such Esteem and Veneration by all Commonwealths, that they never looked upon any thing in the State as well secured and established, which had not been enforced by the Wisdom and Authority of the *Senate*.

When I make use of the Word *Senate*, I always mean by it an Assembly or Body of Men, with whom is entrusted the Supreme Power of Counselling, Advising, and Decreeing, in all Cases whatever, relating to the Government of the Commonwealth. According to this Description, a *Senator* is such a Subject or Citizen,

who

who is legally chosen and called up to have his Seat and Part in this Assembly, so appointed to Advise and Decree in all the Affairs of a Government. From which Account of the Nature and Dignity of this High Trust, it is evident, that no Care and Pains ought to be spared, in filling this Illustrious Order with such Citizens or Subjects only, as are most Eminent for their Wisdom, Prudence, and Nobility: Because there is no Society or Body of Men, so Savage and Barbarous, as to refuse their Choice of being Governed by such Men, or who will not think their Obedience to such Men, or in such a Case, truly consistent with their own Honour and Advantage. Now among the Multitude and Different Ranks of Subjects or Citizens, it is impossible to find a Character of Distinction for Wisdom and Vertue, more truly Glorious than that of the *Good Senator*. The Generality and Bulk of Mankind, either by their Youth and Inexperience, or by the Variety of their Circumstances and Uncertain Way of Life, or their own Natural Inconstancy, are Diverted and Turned out of the Track and Way, which leads to True Glory and Greatness: But the *Good Senator* is not to be Warped by his Affections, or Seduced by his Appetites. The Fire of Youth cannot lead him Astray; but he is under the Government of Reason, and the Guidances of his Own Counsel; and the Maturity of his Age makes his Experience Perfect. A *Senator*, or *Senior*, is One, who is grown *Old* in the Exercise of Good Sense, Right Reason, Counsel, Advice, and Judgment; who has subdued all the Passions and Unruly Appetites of Youth, and brought his Reason to a State of Maturity; in which State it really makes the Human Nature Perfect, and brings it near in Resemblance to the *Divine Image*. In every Work and Operation of Nature, there is (as some *Philosophers* have observed) a Majority, a Minority, and an Equality. Whatever is in the Middle, or in a State of Equality, is supposed to contain all

the

the Perfections of the Two Extremes: And thus the *Good Senator*, who Fills the Middle Station between *Prince* and *People*, may Engross the Perfections of Both to Himself; and whilst he is thus Posted, may plainly discern, How and in what Manner, *King*, *People*, and *Commonwealth* Behave in their several Places and Offices; how the Magistrate performs his Duty, and what Care is taken of the Laws and Liberties of the Subject; and as the Balance turns, he may Provide accordingly, and timely Prevent a Daring and Licentious *People* from running into *Anarchy* and *Confusion*, or an Ambitious *Monarch* from Aspiring to *Tyranny* and *Usurpation*. The Necessary Qualifications for the *Senatorial* Office, are Wisdom and Prudence in the Highest Degree, together with Long Experience, and a Thorough Knowledge of the World. It is his Duty to Wake, and be upon the Watch Day and Night, whilst Multitudes are at Rest, and in a State of Ease and Quiet. With him is entrusted the Care of making Many Safe, Happy, and Flourishing, Wealthy, and Abounding in all Good Things. And surely a Due and Full Discharge of this Trust requires such Talents and Capacities, as are easier to be found in the *Divine*, than in the Human Nature. *Scipio* very well observed, as we are told by *Cicero*, *That to the Steersman we owe a Happy Voyage, Health to the Physician, and Victory to the General: But to the Governor of the Commonwealth we owe the Happiness of Multitudes, their Wealth, Plenty, Reputation, and Glory, with the Increase of Vertue and Honesty;* all which Blessings none but the Best and Greatest of Mankind can Insure to his Fellow Creatures. Let us now examine, What are the First Exercises and Rudiments, which are the Foundation of that Excellent and Extensive Wisdom and Vertue, which complete the *Senatorial* Character: For when this Foundation is once well laid, we shall regularly Ascend Step by Step to That Exalted Height of Glory, the Crown and Reward of Vertue, of which the *Good Senator* justly stands Possessed.

It

It is for the Sake of the Citizen or Subject, that every Good Government or Commonwealth was at first formed and instituted: And therefore we may with good Reason insist, that every *Senator* ought to be a Citizen or Subject of That particular Nation or Government, over which he is to Preside. On this Account his Country may have come to have a Tye and Obligation upon him, so very strict, that he may not only look upon it as his Duty to have always the most Ardent Affection for her Safety and Interest, but think it Honourable, Honest, and Necessary, to venture his Life, and shed his Blood in her Defence and Service. The Love of one's Country is Superior to, and Stronger than, all other Passions or Affections whatsoever. It is almost impossible for a Man not to Love that Particular Spot of Earth, above all others, to which he owes his Parents, his Children, his Neighbours, his Friends, and his own Being; and which has freely and liberally bestowed upon him all that is Useful, Profitable, and Pleasant, in Life; together with a Name and Dignity, and That High Honour and Station, to which he is now advanced, and in which he has deservedly obtained so much Applause and Admiration. It is from Nature, that we borrow those Ardent Desires and Affections, which make the Love of our Country Perfect; for whose Sake, and in whose Defence, no Good Man, when duly called thereto, ever yet refused to Die with Chearfulness. Among the most Profligate and Abandoned Citizens and Subjects, there have been some found, who after they had impiously Conspired to overthrow and destroy a Nation, have upon recollecting that this Nation was their Native Country, Sweet and Delectable, that ought to be Dear to them above all things, happily Relented, and would not proceed to any Acts of Violence against her. Did not *Veturia*, when her Son *Martius* was just ready to invade *Rome* with a Formidable Army, stop his Career, and soften his Rage, by putting him in Mind of his Father's House, and

the

the Place of his Nativity? Conjuring him to remember, that he was approaching those Walls, wherein were the Houshold Gods and Seat of his Family, his Parents, Wife, Children, and all the Pledges of his Love: And charging him with the most Daring Impiety, in presuming to Violate his own Natural Mother, and Lay the Country Waste, to which he owed his Being, and all the Pleasures and Ornaments of Life? On this Occasion, great was the Love of *Veturia* to her own Country: And no less was that of *Martius,* when won by these Intreaties, he spared his Country, though during the Contests, which at that Time raged in the most violent Manner, between the People and their *Tribunes,* and the *Senate* or *Patrician Order, Martius* had been treated at *Rome* with a good deal of Ingratitude. *Sertorius,* as we read in *Plutarch,* made it his earnest Request to *Pompey* and *Metellus,* that by their Intercession, he might have Leave to come Home; assuring them, that he had rather live a Private Obscure Citizen in his own Native *Rome,* than be Exiled, and made a Prince or Emperor, in any Foreign Dominions. So True are those Two Lines in *Ovid:*

> *Our Native Soil to all her Sons imparts*
> *A Secret Instinct, to allure their Hearts.*

This Love of our Country is a Strong Tye and Bond upon the Soul, obliging us to give up ourselves, and all that we have, into her Power, as Pledges of the Sincerest Affection. *Pythagoras,* as we are told by *Plato,* being asked, *How a Man could so harden himself, as to become Ungrateful to his own Country?* very readily answered, *By trying first to become Unnatural to his own Mother.* Whatever Injuries our Country does us, we must heartily pass over and forgive. We can have no Resentment so keen, but the Love of our Country will turn its Edge, soften all our Passions, and stifle in us all Thoughts and Projects of Revenge. Let every
Senator

Senator, therefore, be chosen from among the Citizens and Natives of his Country, in Preference to all Strangers, Aliens, and Foreigners whatsoever. For their Counsels and Designs, in Matters of Policy, if they are not really Dangerous and Pernicious to the Publick, are at least liable to very strong Suspicions. For this Reason it was, that the *Athenians* would not admit Aliens and Foreigners into their City, much less into their Councils and *Senate*, as being persuaded, that their Attachment to another Government might incline them to attempt new Changes and Innovations; whereby the Good Old Laws, Manners, and Customs of *Athens*, might be altered; and these Alterations produce Seditions and Disorders in the State. We find the *Venetians* to be much of the same Mind at this very Day. For they are remarkably Cautious, how they admit any One, by a False Title or Pretence, into the Number and Rank of Those, who are entrusted with the Administration of the Government: From which all Strangers and Foreigners are utterly excluded. But now, what is to be Understood by the Word *Citizen*, and to whom That *Title is Applicable, very well deserves a more exact Enquiry.*

CHAP.

CHAP. IV.

The CONTENTS.

What a Citizen *or* Subject *is. The several Ranks and* Orders *of* Citizens. *How they stood among the* Romans. *The Differences between the* People *and the* Populace, *or* Mob. *Out of what Order of* Citizens *the* Senator *should be Chosen. What True Nobility is, and whence derived. The* Qualifications *for* Nobility. *Of* Birth *and* Vertue. *The several Sorts and Degrees of* Nobility. *Of* Military *and* Pacifick Nobles. *The Statesman Superior to the* Soldier. *Of* Private *and* Publick Vertue. *Of the* Goods *of the* Body, Mind, *and* Fortune. *Of the Strength of a Nation, and its* Standing Forces. *How they are to be Regulated. The Character of a* Good Soldier.

UPON the Question, What a *Citizen* really is, or How to be defined or described, Philosophers and Legislators are very much divided in their Opinions. Some take the Word in the Loosest Sense, and imagine, that all the Inhabitants of One and the same City are to be called *Citizens*, without any Distinction. Others will have it, that to make a Citizen, there must be a Descent in Blood from some of the Nobility or Gentry. Some again are of the Opinion, that if there be such a Descent by either of the Parents, it is sufficient to make a Citizen: Whilst others contend for Pedigree, and a Long Descent from many Noble or Generous Ancestors, as a necessary Qualification for this Title. And there are some who believe, that when a Man is received into the Community, and has his Freedom by Donation or Enfranchisement, he is fully and completely a True and

Legal

Legal Citizen. *Aristotle* defines a Citizen to be such a One, who is born of a Free and Generous Family, and capable of being admitted into any Office in the Magistracy. All these several Opinions, however different from one another, are easily Reconcilable. For since it is the Law or Custom of every Society, that makes a Citizen, it is not to be wondered at, that there should be such a Variety of Opinions concerning the Nature and Qualifications of a Citizen; since there is as great a Variety in those Laws and Customs, by which he is made. In *Popular* States or Cities, all the Inhabitants in Common are called Citizens, whether they be Good or Bad, Rich or Poor, Learned or Ignorant: All are alike Qualified for the Public Trusts and Offices; all are Peers or Equals, Servants and Vassals only excepted. Such heretofore were the *Athenians,* whilst their Government was strictly *Popular:* And such at this very Day, are the Inhabitants of the *Helvetick Cantons.* There are also many Towns in *Germany,* which are called *Free;* the Inhabitants being altogether Independent of the Nobility and Gentry, and sharing all the Power in common among themselves. In *Monarchies* and *Aristocracies,* those Subjects are called Citizens, who live up to the Rules and Precepts of Vertue. The Wisest and most Vertuous, are admitted into all the Offices of an *Aristocracy:* And in *Monarchies,* the First of this Character, has the Sole or Supreme Power, and is made Regent, that is, *Recteagent,* on account of his Superior Goodness and Excellency. A People of a Servile Nature, and Vicious Disposition, are not easily to be governed, but by a *Despotick Power;* that is, by such a Ruler, who treats all his Subjects as so many Slaves, and governs by no other Law, but his own Absolute Will and Pleasure. There is, however, a great Difference to be made, between a People of a Servile Barbarous Disposition, Ignorant of the Common Principles of Vertue and Justice, Slaves in short of Nature's Making, and such who are made Slaves, not by any

Vices

Vices or Fault of their own, but are oppressed and brought under by the Power, Ambition, or Avarice of Tyrants and Usurpers. We read of some reduced to this State, who by Killing or Expelling the Tyrant, have Freed both themselves and their Country; and when they could not succeed at such an Attempt, have readily given up their Lives as a Sacrifice to Liberty. In *Oligarchies* the Chief and Only Qualification for Power, is Wealth and Riches. In this State, they who excel in Wealth, are the only Persons who are called, or reputed Citizens. But such Citizens, by the very Nature of their Qualifications, are a Vile and Contemptible Order of Men, having no Regard to Vertue; whose Sole Study and Business it is, by all Ways and Means whatever, to add daily to their own Private Wealth, and in the Strength of this Single Recommendation, to grasp at the Highest Honours and Dignities of the State: In the obtaining of which, Money is always sure to have the Advantage in an *Oligarchical* Constitution, over Wisdom and Goodness.

Among the *Romans,* there were several Orders, or Ranks of Citizens. The *Latin,* the *Municipal* Order, and Those of the *Colonies.* For every Citizen held his own Rank and Order in every City, upon the same Conditions, upon which the City itself was made Free by the People of *Rome.* Of these Cities, some were called *Free,* in the Strictest Sense; others were called *Foederal;* and a Third Sort were only *Stipendiary.* Some were made Citizens with a Plenary Right, and in Full Privilege; as having a Vote, or Suffrage, and being capable of any Office or Dignity in the State. Others were only *Honorary Citizens,* being made Free, without having a Right to Vote, and wearing the Name of Citizens, only as a Title and Mark of Distinction. Such were Those of the *Equestrian Order* in *Campania,* as we are told by *Livy;* and such were the *Cerites,* as they are described by *Aulus Gellius.* But now in the Capital City of *Rome,* They only were accounted Citizens,

zens, who were possessed of a House in the City, and who were Enrolled and Rated in the Tables of the Censors.

From these Examples and Observations, it is very evident, that in all Commonwealths and Cities whatsoever, those Men, who have a Right of giving their Opinion and Vote in all Matters relating to the Publick, and are capable of being made Magistrates or Officers, in the Government or City, to which they belong, have the Best Claim to the Name of Citizens. Whilst all their Fellow-Subjects under them, who cannot justly claim the same Privileges, are rather to be called Inhabitants, or in the Roman Language, Clients, than True and Undoubted Citizens. There are other Qualifications, which contribute to the making up and perfecting the Character of the Good Citizen; and these are Vertue, Birth, Wealth, and Nobility. But in the Judging and Determining of these Qualifications, great Regard must be had to the Particular Laws and Customs of every Society. Since every Commonwealth consists of Two Orders of Men, the People properly so called, and the Populace, or Inferior Multitude; we may accordingly reckon Two Orders only of Citizens, the Noble and the Plebeian. Cajus, a Noted Civilian, says, that the Word People includes all Citizens whatsoever, and takes in Patricians, Nobles, and Senators; whilst all beneath these are comprehended under the Name of Plebeians. Those of the Nobility are Citizens, Strictly and Properly so called; whilst Those of Inferior Ranks are Citizens only in Resemblance and Similitude. We would have the Senator be of the Former of These Orders, and partake of That True Nobility, which has its Rise and Foundation from Vertue. This True Nobility is of Two Sorts, either Proper and Personal, or Derivative and Hereditary, as being Originally founded in the Vertues and Superior Excellency of Honourable and Wealthy Ancestors, and by them Transmitted to their Posterity. They who are alike Noble and Honourable, on account both of their own

Personal

Personal Vertues, and those of their Ancestors too, may very justly claim the Preference, and have a double Title to Publick Esteem and Veneration. Goodness and Vertue often run down with the Blood, and it is Natural for Children to resemble their Parents. The Famous *Lyrick Poet*, has touched upon this Subject, with much Elegance and Veracity.

> *Heroick Sons their Father's Worth proclaim;*
> *Their Features, and their Vertues, are the same:*
> *Horses and Bulls their Gen'rous Race improve;*
> *No Eagle e'er produced a Tim'rous Dove.*

To the Forming and Finishing the Full and Complete Character of the Truly Noble, or Generous *Citizen*, *Three* Things are requisite, according to the Opinion of *Aristotle*: And these are, Birth, Wealth, and Vertue. Whoever is happily possessed of all these Three Advantages, may be truly said to be *Noble*, in the Highest and most Perfect Degree. Such Men as these are always to be Esteemed and Honoured, as the Best and Noblest Citizens: But since it very rarely happens, that all these Qualifications fall to the Share of any one Single Subject, it is therefore the Particular Privilege and Undoubted Right of Vertue, that by herself, and in her own Strength, she can Ennoble Mankind, without any other Qualification. Birth and Wealth are Undoubted Ornaments of the Noble and Generous; but when Vertue is wanting, they serve rather to the Debasing and Degrading of Mankind. Where there is Title without Vertue, Men are a Stain and a Blemish to their Name and Family; and the most Renowned Ancestors are Obscured and Disgraced by the Vices and Follies of an Infamous Posterity. *Tully* hath very well observed, That *it is much better to Rise in the World by our own Personal Vertues and Achievements, than to depend upon the Character and Opinion the*

World

World has of our Forefathers: Or, in other Words, To live in such a Manner, that we may be the Founders of Nobility, give Rise to an Illustrious Family, and set Posterity an Example. The Offspring and Descendants of a Noble House, are on that Account, Honourable, and Worthy of Esteem, if they take Care to Surpass, or at least to Live up to the Glory and Renown, which their Predecessors, by their Actions, have acquired. For who can forbear Commending and Extolling such Conduct, which reflects new Honours upon a Family, and preserves the Fame and Renown of Great Ancestors, from being concealed or buried in Oblivion, by the Vices and Misbehaviour of their Posterity? There was a very Just and Commendable Law among the Rhodians, by which all Wicked and Vicious Sons, who lived in a Professed Opposition to the Vertues of their Parents, were cut off, and deprived of their Inheritance; which, upon the Exclusion of the Profligate and Obnoxious Claimants, descended to the Next in Blood, who was of an Honest and Vertuous Character: For our own Life and Behavior are the Test and Explicit Declaration of our Legitimacy and Piety, by which Posterity is convinced of our Respect and Gratitude to the Memory of our Forefathers; when we take Care to behave in such a Manner, as to approve ourselves the Heirs, not only of their Real and Personal Estates, but of their Vertues, Glory, Religion, and Fidelity to their Country; which are the Best Estate and Effects, and the Noblest Inheritance, of which we can possibly come to be possessed. According to what Juvenal has very well observed, It is not a Long Pedigree, or a Hall filled with Pictures and Images, but Vertue only, that gives Rise and Being to True Nobility.

Statues and Pedigrees are all in vain;
For only Vertue can Ennoble Man.

Nothing but Vertue can Raise a Man above the Condition of his Birth and Fortune: And Vertue is the same to all her Admirers. She refuses None, and opens her Arms to all her Lovers, in the same Free and Hospitable Manner. *Cleanthes* was at first only a Drawer of Water; and Vertue did not find *Plato* Great and Honourable, but really made him so. We read of many Men, who from Slaves have been raised to be Monarchs; and of many Kings, who have sunk and dwindled into Slaves. Time, and its several Changes, have turned the World upside-down, and occasioned these Strange Revolutions. What was *Agathocles*, but a *King* made out of a Potter? What at first were *Romulus, Tullus, Hostilius, Tarquinius Priscus*, or indeed, the whole *Roman* Race and Offspring in general? *Juvenal* gives us the Best Account of their Original.

> Rome *from an Infamous* Asylum *rose,*
> *And no Great Fame to her Forefathers owes.*

Whom shall we Look upon and Esteem as a Person of a Truly Noble and Generous Stock, but the Man who is Naturally Disposed and Inclined to Vertue? There is, in the Opinion of *Boetius*, nothing in Nobility truly and substantially Good, but the Natural Necessity and Impulse, by which Men are withheld and restrained from Degenerating, and Falling away from the Vertues and Dignity of their Forefathers. There being Various and Different Kinds of Trials and Exercises, which are the Test and Proof of our Vertue, this Vertue must consequently produce Various and Different Kinds of Nobility. There is a Nobility of a Private Nature, which may be properly called, *Philosophical:* And this belongs to the Vertuous Retired, who give themselves up to Solitude and Contemplation. There is also a Civil or Publick Nobility, which is obtained by the Glory of

Conducting

Conducting the Affairs of a Government, or of Administring to the Welfare of one's Country; or by fighting her Battles, and carrying her through all the Difficulties of an Honourable War, with Success and Advantage. Courage, Encounters, Bloodshed, Wounds, and Scars, gotten in the Publick Service, are the Sure Testimony and Marks of this Kind of Nobility: The Glory of which is Great and Durable; and its usual Rewards, Statues and Pedigrees, together with the Memory of Scars and Wounds Honourably received, are transmitted to Late Posterity, exciting them to a Pious Imitation of the Vertues of their Ancestors, or to the Glory of Surpassing and Excelling them. There is therefore nothing in Blood and Ancestry, but this Privilege and Prerogative of Nobility, which is an Image and Monument of Primitive Vertue and Excellence, remaining with a Family, as a Pledge of their Good Behaviour in Life, as a Provocative to Emulation, and a Spur to prick them forward in the same Track of Glory, which is marked out for them, by the Footsteps of their Forefathers.

In every Commonwealth or Government, there are Two Critical Seasons, a Time of *War*, and a Time of *Peace;* and accordingly there are Two Sorts or Orders of Noble Citizens, the *Warlike* and the *Pacifick*. Of the *First* Order are Those Citizens, who by their Courage and Conduct have either Defended their own Country, or Enlarged its Territories and Dominions: And of the *Second* are Those, who by their Wisdom and Counsel distinguish themselves in the Peaceable and Prosperous Administration of the Affairs and Interests of a Government. Where both these Characters, of the *Counsellor* and *Warrior*, are happily United in One and the Same Minister, his Administration will consequently be so much the more Advantageous and Useful to the Publick. For according to common Observation, without Counsel and Wisdom, there can be no Great Undertaking; and without Conduct and Action, it can never be Successfully Finished or Executed.

Executed. They, who in Times of Peace preside over the *Commonwealth*, and by their Good Management, preserve it in Peace and Quiet, and in a Prosperous and Flourishing Condition, are Preferable to, and more Useful than those Other Citizens, who by their Arms and Conduct either Save or Defend, or Enlarge its Dominions. As the Soul is Preferable to the Body, Peace to War, and a State of Ease of Tranquillity to the Tumults and Disorders of a Campaign, so is the Counsellor or Statesman, proportionably Preferable to the Soldier or General. *Homer* introduced *Agamemnon* speaking to this Purpose; *That he could much sooner make himself Master of* Troy, *if he had Ten such Men as* Nestor *and* Ulysses, *to Advise and Counsel him, than if he had Ten such Men as* Ajax *and* Achilles, *remarkable only for their Personal Courage and Bravery.* Of much the same Mind was *Pyrrhus,* when he freely acknowledged, that *Cyneas,* by his Wisdom and Eloquence, had taken more Cities, than ever himself had subdued by his Valour and Prowess. They, who in Both Capacities are alike Useful to the Publick, and by their Skill in the several Arts, both of Peace and War, can do their Country Double Service, may justly Claim to have an Undoubted Right to more Honour and Respect, than the rest of their Fellow-Citizens. For the more a Man excells in Vertue, the more he ought to excell in Dignity and Honour. It is also much to be wished, that in every *Commonwealth*, the *Good Senator* should not only be a Good Citizen, but a Good Man too: For there is a Wide Difference between the Vertues requisite to Adorn a Private, and those which Adorn a Publick Life. The Private Citizen makes those Vertues his chiefest Aim and Study, which serve to furnish out a Life of Honesty and Goodness: Whilst the Citizen of a Publick Character attends altogether to the Observation of those Laws, by which the Publick Welfare is Secured and Promoted. It often happens, that a Good Artificer or Mechanick, may be a very Bad Man: And

And just so a Citizen, who in his Private Character has very little Regard to Justice, Temperance, and Fortitude, may yet in his Publick Capacity be truly Good, and by his Counsel and Cunning, his Diligence and Bravery, be of Great Use and Service to his Country. Something of this Sort was to be found in the Character of *Julius Cæsar*. His Private Life was perhaps Unblamable, and he might be allowed to be a Good Man; but he failed in his Publick Character, and was certainly a very Bad and Corrupt Citizen. The *Good Senator* must take Care, that his Character may not be liable to the same Charge and Imputation.

The Felicity or Happiness of every *Commonwealth*, is to be measured by the Felicity or Happiness of the Subjects or Citizens, who are the Members of it. For such as are the Manners and Reputation of the Citizens, such will every City or Society be in its Reputation and Character among Men. The Happiness of Mankind in general, and of every Society of Men in particular, is derived from one and the same Original, is enforced by the same Reasons, and depends upon the same Vertues, which make Men Happy, both in a Private, and in a Publick, or Social State. To this Happiness, whether of Particular Persons, or of Communities and Publick Bodies, Fortune must concurr as well as Vertue. A *City* or *Commonwealth* is then truly Happy, when it is perfectly Good. Now of *Goods* there are Three Sorts: The *First* and Noblest are Those of the *Mind:* The *Second*, those of the *Body:* And the *Third,* are Wealth and Riches, or the Acquisitions and Favours of *Fortune*. Of the Goods of the Mind, Vertue is the First and Chiefest, or rather the Sum and Substance of them. For it is Vertue only that makes a City or Government Wise and Courageous, Temperate and Just. A City may be then said to be truly Wise, when it is governed by Good Counsel and Prudence, which have their Rise from Arts and Sciences, from Good Discipline, and a Thorough Knowledge of Men and Things: For by these,

these, all Publick Wisdom is Established. Such Accomplishments are not to be found in Artificers and Mechanicks, but in Men of a Civilized and Generous Education, formed and disposed by Nature, for Vertue, Renown, and Glory. From Subjects and Citizens thus accomplished, arise Princes, Senators, Judges, Commanders, and Governors; and from them the Character of Wisdom is derived upon a Whole Nation. On the other hand, a Government is soon liable to a Charge of Weakness and Ill-Conduct, when its Governors and Ministers are Unwise, Unskilful, and Unlearned. The Courage and Bravery of a State are seen in its Generals, Officers, and Soldiers; by whose Industry, Valour, and Skill in the Art of War, a Nation comes to be Renowned, and Formidable for its Strength and Military Reputation. Such Commanders and Forces are a Terror to all Foreign Enemies, the Defence and Safeguard of their Country, where any Danger is near, and serve to preserve it in a State of Peace and Tranquillity.

The Publick Fortitude or Strength of a Nation consists in the keeping on foot a *Standing Force,* Well skilled and Disciplined; by which Means the Subject is Protected in Ease and Quiet, and is under no Apprehension of any Terrors from abroad, or any Tumults or Insurrections at home. It is absolutely necessary, even in Times of Peace, that the Soldiery should be well-trained and Exercised in the Military Art, and that they should always employ their Arms in the Cause of Vertue only, and not in the Wild Sallies of Rapine and Violence. To draw the Sword upon a Fellow-Subject and Citizen, or in any Case prejudicial to one's Country, is an Impiety unworthy the Name and Character of a Good Soldier, or even of a Good Man. It is the Highest and most Distinguishing Glory of the Military Order of Men, to behave with Gentleness, Clemency, and Humanity, towards their own Countrymen, and to reserve all their Rage and Fury only for their Enemies. When the Storm of War arises, and the Invader is out

upon

upon the Hunt, watching an Opportunity to make a Spoil and Prey of his Neighbour's Possessions, the Safety, Religion, Honour, Credit, and Liberties of a Nation, are all deposited in the Hands of the Soldiery; their Country depends entirely upon them, and from their Bravery expects the Deliverance and Preservation of its People. Whoever, therefore, aims at the Glory of being esteemed a Good and Gallant Soldier, and Defender of his Country, must take particular Care never to indulge himself in Sloth, Idleness, and Domestick Luxury; but give himself entirely up to the Sword and Spear, to Labour and Fatigue, and all the Arts and Exercises of War. No Good Soldier will ever engage in any Private Broil or Mutiny, or make himself a Party in a *Civil*, or a *Social* War, and will take Care always to be in Readiness, when his Country calls him forth to her Defence, upon any Sudden or Dangerous Emergence. The Young and Vigorous are Skilful enough in spreading the Toils for the Deer, the Bear, the Boar, and the Hare; and can train up their Dogs to the Chace of the Wild Beasts of the Field and Forest: Why then should they not be as Skilful and Diligent in Measuring out a Camp, Marshalling and Leading on an Army, and in giving Battle and Chace to an Enemy? Whoever is Unskilful in these Arts, let him make War in the Woods: But whilst he is forming Designs, and laying Snares for the Life and Possessions of his Neighbour; or whilst he passes his Time ignobly in Sloth and Idleness, or in Tumults and Seditions, he is no longer to be accounted a Soldier, but a Sluggard; and from the Height of True Nobility, sinks down into the Mob and Scum of Mankind. His life and Character are a Disgrace to his Station and Dignity, and he dwindles to a Slave and a Vassal. Suppose a War to be proclaimed, and then consider with yourself, that you undertake it in behalf of your Country: Be always Ready and Prepared for her Defence, lest by Unnecessary Delays, and even before you have earned your Pay, the Enemy escape, and retire,

laden

laden with the Spoils of your Fellow-Subjects; whilst your Country's Cries to you for Help come too late, in whose Defence you could not have been too Quick and Vigorous; since by your Lingring and Slow Advances, you have Exposed her to Rapine and Devastation. Suppose there be no Established Pay for the Army, let not this Delay or Discourage you: For it is better to be a Brave and Voluntary, than an Inlisted and Mercenary Defender of That Country, to which you owe your Life, and all the Honours, Wealth, and External Blessings, that render it Sweet and Delectable: Whilst no other Return or Pledge of Gratitude is required at your Hands, but only This, that you Love your own Country, above all Things, and keep yourself always in Readiness, as her Faithful Soldier and Volunteer, to appear in Arms for her Defence, without any View or Regard to the Mercenary Reward of your Services. Far be it from You to imagine, that Money is the only Thing, which Ennobles and bestows Honour upon Vertue; or that you are to approve yourself, not as the True and Faithful Soldier of your Country, but as a Hireling and Stipendiary, entirely devoted to Self Interest and Covetousness. Whilst there is Peace, it is the Duty of every Good Soldier to make himself acquainted with the Art and Exercise of Arms, and to train and qualify himself for War; and he may be Worthy of the Name and Title of a Good Soldier. Among other Things, he must take Care to behave towards his Countrymen and Fellow-Citizens, with Justice and Equity, not Domineering or Setting himself above those whom the Community hath made his Equals; not using his Arms, or flying out into any Acts of Rapine and Violence, by which the Honourable Peace and Quiet of his Neighbours may be Disturbed or Interrupted. What was it you ever Fought for, but only Peace? And when this Blessing hath been happily obtained, why should you make War at home, and break in upon the Common Tranquillity? It is certainly the True Interest of every

Government,

Government, to restrain the Violences and Disorders of their Soldiery, by the Strictest Laws, and the Utmost Severity; to confine their Armed Men to an Honest and Orderly Way of Life, and to Deterr them from offering any Affront or Injury to their Fellow-Subjects: For when Injustice is once in Arms, and has gotten the Sword in her Hand, there is not a more Formidable and Outrageous Monster upon Earth. Unless the Daring Insolence of the Soldiery be kept within Bounds, by Severe Laws and Proper Restrictions, it will soon break loose, and fly out into the most Exorbitant Excesses; to the Overturning of the Constitution, and the Reducing all the Good and Well-behaved Members of the Community, and even the Laws and Justice itself, to the Miserable State of being Trampled upon, and Enslaved by an Army. History assures us, that this was often the Case among the *Romans:* With whom it was a Custom of a good many Years standing, for the Soldiery to make Choice of their own Commanders, and even their *Emperors;* the Consequence of which Privilege was this, That the *Commonwealth* came thereby to become so entirely Subservient to, and at the Mercy of the Army, that neither the *Senate,* the *People,* nor the *Laws,* were able to put a Stop to, or restrain the Outrages and Violences of the Soldiery. But enough hath been said upon this Subject; and my Excursions, like those made by the *Light Horse,* have perhaps taken up too much Time, and added an Unusual Length to my Discourse upon the Military Duties and Offices: In the Prosecution of which, I have been animated by my Subject, and have made Use of the same Freedom and Boldness, which is Inseparable from the Character of a Soldier.

I return now to my former Arguments. A City or Commonwealth may be then said to be truly Temperate and Just, when the Superiors or Governors, and the Subjects or Inferior Members thereof, do in their Lives and Actions conform to those Rules and Precepts,

Precepts, which Temperance and Justice have set them. Now this Conformity is not to be obtained but by Good and Wholsome Laws, which serve as a Direction to Mankind, not only how to Live, but how to Live Well. To this Purpose are all those Particular Laws, commonly called *Sumptuary*, by which the Diet, Provisions, and Cloathing of the Subject, are duly Regulated, and all Luxury and Intemperance are Restrained or Prohibited in a *Commonwealth*: And with these are to be Reckoned those other Laws, which relate to *Justice* and *Judgment*, and by which the several *Courts* and *Tribunals* of a *State* are kept in due Order, and do therefore serve to the free and open Exercise and Administration of *Justice*; a Vertue by which we are taught to Render unto every Man what is really his own. When the Subjects or Members of the Body Politick are Sound and Healthy, Robust, Lively, and Courageous, Rich and Honourable, Illustrious and Glorious, it is then most certain, that a *Commonwealth* may be truly said to abound in all the Blessings which attend the Body, and in all the Goods and Acquisitions of Fortune. But of These we shall Treat more at large towards the End of this Work. Thus we have hitherto shewn at large, what is the True Happiness of a City or Commonwealth, and wherein it consists. It now follows in course for us to enquire, what it is, that makes the several Subjects and Members of the Community truly Happy: After which it will be an easy Matter to Discover, what Arts and Sciences, what Exercises and Employments, are necessary to Form, and Furnish out the *Accomplish'd Senator;* whereby he may be made Perfect and thorowly Possessed of all the Blessings and Happiness, both of Private and Publick Life.

CHAP.

CHAP. V.

The CONTENTS.

Three Things required to make our Nature Perfect. *The Origine of all Human Imperfections. How They are to be Repaired. Of the Use and Benefits of* Philosophy. *Objections commonly made to* Philosophy. *Some* Philosophers *unfit to be* Statesmen. *Of* Speculative *and* Recluse Philosophers. *Of the* Middle Class *or* Order. *What Sort of* Philosophy *most Proper for the* Senator. *His* Genius *and* Natural Disposition. *The* Education *of the* Senator. *Of* Academical Discipline. *The Advantages and Defects of it. Of* Classical *Learning. Of* Philosophy *in all its Parts and Branches. Of* Natural *and* Mathematical *Knowledge. Of* Speculative *and* Practical Philosophy. *Of* History *and* Travel. *The Dignity and Usefulness of* Schoolmasters *and* Tutors. *Which* Sect *of* Philosophers *the most Excellent. The Benefits of* Eloquence. *The Manner of* Speaking *in the* Senate. *Of the Study of the* Law, *and the Abuses of it.*

Ccording to a received Opinion of the Old *Sages* and *Philosophers*, there are *Three Things* requisite to the making of Mankind Perfect; and these are, *Nature, Manners*, and *Reason*. It is by no means in our Power to make ourselves Happy by *Nature*. This is a Peculiar Gift and Blessing bestowed upon us by our *Maker:* For it is of his Good Pleasure only, that Men are endowed with a Natural Disposition, and Propensity to Goodness, Prudence, and Wisdom. It also frequently happens, by a Lucky Turn and Accident, that as Men are generated by Men, and Beasts by Beasts, so Good and Wise
Children

Children are very often descended from Good and Wise Parents. This is certainly the Regular Course, and what Nature always intends; but the Reason why She is sometimes Obstructed and Diverted in her Course, is plainly this, Because She is Depraved and Corrupted, has her Work often Spoiled by a Bad Education; and to speak in the *Christian Style*, is Tainted by the Original Corruption and *Fall* of our *First Parents*, who were Diverted and Sunk from their Primitive Perfection, by the Wiles and Artifices of the *Malicious Deceiver*. Hence it came to pass, that nothing was left behnd us, of our First Natural Integrity and Purity, but certain Glimmering and Dim Fires, which serve to Light us in our Search after Knowledge and Vertue: So that the Defects, which are now in us, must be happily supplied by Reason and Good Manners, or, in other Words, by Art and Exercise, before we can regain our Primitive Perfection. It is therefore the Great Aim and Daily Duty of Mankind, to conform as much as possible to the First Unfallen Nature, that is, to *God* the Author of it, and to Address to him, for the Renewal and Restoration of our Lost Perfection and Happiness. It is the First Great Precept and Law of Human Nature, that Every Man should own himself to be the Workmanship and Offspring of *God*, from whom he derives his Reason and Understanding; by which he is made like unto his *Maker*. But now since this Reason of Mankind is Obscured and Wrapped up in the Folds and Coverture of the Body, and is Shut up and Enclosed therein, as in a Prison; by which means it cannot easily come at the True Knowledge of itself; there is a Necessity of its being set Free, and delivered out of this Prison of the Body, before it can throughly Discern, Know, and fully Contemplate, its own Being and Excellencies, or attain the Perfect Glory of Resembling its *Maker*. For then is a Man truly Worthy of the Name and Dignity which he bears in the World, when he lives in Conformity to that Part of his Being, which is Rational, and rejects

the

the Gross and Bodily Part, or will by no means Gratify and Indulge it. There is therefore a Necessary Discipline, which every Man must Undergo and Inure himself to, before his Reason, which is to him a *Deity,* can be made truly Perfect. Nature is certainly Maimed and Imperfect, when any of the Good Things are wanting, which Necessarily serve to complete its Happiness. And in like manner, the *Chief Good* and Happiness of Mankind are Imperfect and Deficient, whenever Reason is Maimed or Obscured. For Reason is to Man the same as Nature, Law, Vertue, the *Chief Good,* and *God* himself. Whence it follows, that there is a certain Discipline, which every Man must undergo, before he can attain the Full Knowledge of *God* and Nature, of the Laws and Vertues, and of the Good Things and Happiness of Life. This is that True Philosophy, the Gift of *God* Eternal and Immutable, which conveys to us the Full and Complete Knowledge of all Things, both Human and Divine. By this we are brought acquainted with the Nature of the *Deity,* and of the several Vertues and Vices, with the Principles, Operations, Origine, and Effects, of all Beings whatsoever. And when we look into This, as into a Faithful Glass, we there see the Forms, Images, Species, and Ideas, of the several Beings of the Universe, and our Two Parts, both Soul and Body, drawn and painted as it were to Perfection. *Tully* hath very well observed, *That this Universal Philosophy and Knowledge of all Things is the Guide of Life, the Sure Searcher after Vertue, the Great Enemy to Vice, an Infallible Remedy, and Lasting Health to the Soul.* There is Nothing in the Whole World, whether it be Thought or Action, no Incident or Proceeding in the *Commonwealth,* the *Forum,* or *Courts* of *Judicature,* whether it be in a Great Matter or a Small, but Philosophy takes Cognizance of it; that Philosophy, which is the Parent and Conductor of all Counsels, Undertakings, and Resolutions whatsoever. If you take Care to be led and governed by this Divine Principle, in all

your

your Words and Actions, whatever you Say or Do, will be truly Wise, Prudent, and in every respect Perfect and Heavenly. No Wars, Seditions, or Tumults, no Intestine Feuds and Animosities, no Violent Attempts of the Wicked and Turbulent, can ever prevail in That *Commonwealth,* in which the Governors are either Philosophers themselves, or are led by such Counsels, as Philosophy dictates and prescribes.

But here now I can imagine some one of the Multitude assembled in the *Forum,* starting forth, and boldly Remonstrating, in the following Terms: "What art Thou, O *Philosopher* ! who
" pretendest to make thy Subtle Airy Knowledge a Sufficient
" Foundation, whereon to build the Happiness of the Publick,
" and the Counsels and Wisdom of *Kings* and *Princes.* Thy
" Whole Art is nothing but *Jargon,* and a Heap of Noisy Con-
" tention and Wrangle, instead of teaching us the True Way to
" Happiness. Dost thou still go on to Introduce such an Art as
" this into the *Commonwealth,* which in all likelihood will be rather
" Fatal than Beneficial to the Publick? Would'st thou Rend and
" Distract a Government, with Civil Broils and Sedition, as thou
" hast filled the *Schools* and *Academies* with Dispute and Conten-
" tion? There indeed you may Scold and Dispute on, without
" coming to Bloodshed. But you cannot Play the same Game
" in a Nation, without engaging your Fellow-Subjects in Slaugh-
" ter and Confusion. How can you *Philosophers,* whose Opini-
" ons are so Various and Different, and very often so Contrary to
" one another, ever pretend to agree in Settling the Welfare and
" Happiness of a Government? What Part must a Nation take
" on this Occasion? Must they adhere to the *Epicurean,* the *Peri-*
" *patetick,* or the *Stoick Hypothesis*? Do not all these *Sects* differ
" in their Notions, about the very Sum and Substance of True
" Happiness, as well as about the Terms, Conditions, and Limi-
" tations of it? Is not the Whole Body of *Philosophy,* a Wild Un-

"certain

"certain Scheme; since the Masters of it are not yet agreed, even
"in their Notions of the *First* and *Greatest Good?* And when
"they know not what this is, how can they Prescribe to us the
"True Way and Discipline of Life? Let such Masters and Tea-
"chers of Vertue as these are, who adhere to one Favourite
"Scheme, and make That the Sole Resting-Place, and Taberna-
"cle of Life, be thrust out and driven from the Community, ra-
"ther than well-received and encouraged, as the only Dictators
"of True *Policy.* Suppose there be a Consultation and Debate
"upon the Great Articles of *Peace,* or *War,* the Making of
"Laws, and the Putting of them in Execution; how will a Sett
"of Philosophers deliver themselves, or behave on this Occasion?
"Whilst a *Senate* is gravely Debating the Great Business of War,
"they will perhaps imagine themselves assembled in a Council of
"*Cyclops* or *Giants,* just ready to take Arms, and fly out upon
"some Desperate Expedition. What Law can they be supposed
"to Make, or what Measure of Obedience will they Prescribe,
"who have no other Law worthy their Notice, but what they
"carry within their own Bosoms? For their own Reason, or ra-
"ther their own Private Opinion, is the only Law they make Use
"of, or believe they are Bound to Obey. Look on a Wretch of
"one of these Sects, and see him walking abroad with his Staff
"and Lanthorn, lighting himself at Noonday, coasting the Streets
"in quest of an Honest Man, striking Some, and abusing Others,
"and looking upon All those of his own Species as so many Brutes,
"his own dear Self always excepted! Such are the Mad Gambols
"and Frolicks of many of the Gang and Herd of *Philosophers,*
"whom you so much boast of! What else was *Diogenes, Zeno,*
"*Epictetus,* and many Others? And would you now Appoint
"such *Philosophers* as these, to be Princes and Governors, Keepers
"and Conservators of the Liberties of a People?"

To

To all This we Answer very Briefly and Effectually, that there are Two Sorts of *Philosophers,* whom we look upon as utterly Unfit and Incapable to preside in the Government of a *Commonwealth.* Of the First sort are They, who have only just wet their Lips, and Tasted of the First Elements of *Philosophy,* without going through the whole Discipline and Institutions of True Wisdom; whereby the Thirst of our Inordinate Desires, and the Fires and Violence of our Vicious Lusts, are Effectually Allayed and Extinguished. Such Men as these are, give into a Way of Life entirely opposite to all the Rules and Precepts of *Vertue* and *Philosophy:* And the Reason of it is this, Because *Philosophy* has not entered far, or taken deep Root in them. Had it done so, it would have made them Learned and Good; Learned, in the Acquisition of Wisdom and Prudence; and Good, in the Practice of Justice, Temperance, and Fortitude. For there is nothing in all Philosophy more Noble and Excellent, than the Institutions and Precepts of These Vertues; of which, whoever makes himself a Complete Master, is thereby entitled to all the Blessings and Happiness of Life. Besides This, there is Another Sort of *Philosophers,* quite different from the Former, who from their very Childhood have made Philosophy their whole Study and Delight, their Rock and Resting Place, to which they are Chained down, and upon which they have fixed their Residence. Their Speculative Notions and Contemplative Way of Life, not having any Regard to the Civil and Common Good of Societies, are therefore of no manner of Use to the Publick: And this Sort of Men, however they may be justly reckoned Men of Learning and Ingenuity, yet because they are Inclosed and Wrapt up in one Single System of Philosophy, and never bring forth their Learning for the Use and Benefit of the Publick, are therefore deservedly looked upon as Unfit for Business, and Unqualified to meddle in the Affairs and Interests of a State. *Plato* is of Opinion, that such of these Solitary and Recluse *Philosophers,*

who

who are in their own Nature Civilized, and Well-turned for the Business of the World, and capable of being brought to do their Duty in a Publick Station, to their own Glory, and the Advantage of their Country, should be compelled to come out of their Retirement, and obliged to take some Publick Trust upon them. Because he looks upon them to be well Qualified for the Government of a City, and capable of appeasing any Tumults and Seditions, or of Keeping the People Easy and Quiet. But for Those, who are of a quite different *Genius,* he gives them up to the Enjoyment of their Solitude and Recluse Life, and leaves them and their Philosophy to grow old together. In the mean time, we are clearly of Opinion, that neither They, who have only made a Small Progress in Philosophy, nor They, who have gone too far, and are wholly Immersed and Swallowed up in Speculations, should at any Time be admitted into a Publick Station and Office in the Government. Not the Former; because they have not yet obtained that Honest and Vertuous Way of Living, which Philosophy prescribes: And by no means the Latter; because they Imagine they have attained to more Happiness, than what is to be met with in the Civil or Political Life, and that Solitude is the only State of Bliss, which is the same to them, as the *Fortunate Islands,* or *Garden of the Hesperides.* This however is certain, and Plato agrees with us in the very same Opinion, that Mere Philosophy prescribes such a Way of Life to Mankind, as is by no means compatible with the Duty and Office of a Good Magistrate, and disposes us to look upon all High Stations and Dignities with Contempt and Indignation. Hence it is, that we are under a Necessity of Looking out for a Middle Class and Order of *Philosophers,* particularly fitted and well-qualified for the Administration of Publick Affairs: And such are they, who, in all their Philosophical Studies and Enquiries, have no other View and Design, but the Attainment of such Rules and Institutions, as are Conducive

to

to the Happiness of Human Society, and the Good Government of the *Commonwealth*. This is that Particular Sort of Philosophy, of which we would have the *Accomplish'd Senator* take Care to make himself a Master; whereby he will be fully instructed, how to govern and bear Rule in his own Country, and will approve himself a Common Friend and Publick Blessing to Mankind.

It is above all Things requisite, that the *Good Senator* should be by Nature Well-turned and Disposed for Vertue, Well-inclined to Temperance and Justice, readily capable and fond of Instruction. True Philosophy can never take Deep Root, and bring forth the Proper Fruits in him, unless he has Memory and a Good *Genius,* is of a Teachable Disposition, and of a Strong, Free, and Lively Spirit, being naturally Just and Temperate, and a Lover and Admirer of Truth. Nothing but a Good Education can Improve upon This Stock, and bring it to Perfection; and such an Education every *Good Senator* ought to have, from the Earliest Years and First Dawning of his Childhood. For (as *Plato* very well observes) *A Good Education is the Source and Fountain of all Knowledge; by which we are brought up together with our Fellow-Creatures, and made as it were Companions and Playfellows in every Kind and Improvement of Vertue.* The *Good Senator* must be trained and instructed from his very Infancy, in the Due Use and Exercise of his Passions; so that all his Joys, and all his Sorrows may be regulated and restrained by the Proper Rules of Justice and Vertue. It is Vertue only that can Instruct us, when, and on what Occasions, we are either to Rejoice or be Sorrowful; and herein (according to *Aristotle)* consists the True Notion of all Good and Vertuous Education. As it is the Real Interest of every *Commonwealth*, to make all her Citizens and Subjects Good, that She herself may be so too; so is it particularly Incumbent upon her, to take Care, in what Way and Manner they should be all brought up and educated. The Good Husbandman and Gardener keep a
Watchful

Watchful Eye over the Tender Shoots and Branches of their Trees, and provide in Time for their Quick and Early Growth. Just so should a *Commonwealth,* the Nurse and Parent of her own People, be remarkably Careful and Diligent in the Education of all her Youth, and in Training them up betimes to the Laws and Precepts of Vertue. The *Lacedæmonians* had among them a Particular Order of Magistrates, chosen on Purpose to take Care of the Education of their Youth; and to this Office they Elected none but the Gravest and most Prudent of all their Citizens. These were called, the *Publick Præceptors,* or *State-Schoolmasters;* and it was certainly owing to this Wise Institution, that the *Lacedæmonians* were, of all other *Grecians,* the most Renowned for Vertue and Warlike Exploits, and had every where this Character given of them, That They were the Great Masters of Fortitude, and the Sole Tutors and Directors of the Art of War. We read in *Plutarch,* that when *Diogenes* returned from *Sparta* to *Athens,* and was asked *Whence he came?* and *Whither he was going?* The Philosopher readily answered, *That he came from seeing Men, and was now going to make a Visit to Women.* By which *Sarcasm* he plainly hinted at the Reigning Effeminacy of the *Athenians,* who on this Account had made themselves Ridiculous, not only to the *Lacedæmonians,* but to all the Other Republicks of *Greece.* Hence it was, that when a certain *Athenian,* in a Conversation with *Agesilaus,* King of *Sparta,* was boasting of the Height and Strength of the Walls of *Athens,* That Monarch very readily answered, *That such a Fortification very well became their City: For where Women were to be shut up and enclosed, the Highest and Strongest Walls were always judged to be of absolute Necessity.*

But from this Digression let us now Return to our Former Subject of *Education.* A Subject of no small Importance, though very much Neglected in the Present Age, when we see so little Pains bestowed in an Affair, which necessarily requires, and really

deserves

deserves so much. Parents are now grown Careless and Negligent, and as the Custom is, we see them Shifting off the Charge and Concern of bestowing a Vertuous and Liberal Education upon their own Children, and giving it away into the Hands of Strangers. Nor is this all; but the Heirs of a Noble or a Generous Family are delivered over into the Custody and Management of a Wretched *Pedant,* or Unskilful *Pedagogue.* The Care and Diligence of *Cato,* in the Education of his Son, is never to be enough Commended. He would by no means suffer his own Wife to Wash and Bathe him, or to Swathe and Dress him, unless himself were present to Oversee and Assist her. He had then in his Family one *Chylo,* a Grammarian, a Man well enough versed in Learning, and with whom he had entrusted the Education of his Child: Yet still he thought it an Indignity to have a Servant Revile and Reproach, Insult and Domineer over him, or whenever he was Tardy and in a Fault, give him Bodily Correction. He knew how great a Benefit the Instruction and Education of his Son really was, and he scorned to be Indebted for it, to the Pains and Care of a *Pedagogue.* When he was fit to be Instructed in Literature, and in the Laws and Customs of his Country, the Father himself would have the Sole Care of him. None but he must teach him how to fling the Javelin, to go through the Whole Exercise at Arms, to understand Horsemanship, with the Manner of Fighting hand to hand, or in Close Combat, the Whole Art of Swimming, and all other Achievements, by which Youth are inured to the Bearing of the Two Extremes, both of Heat and Cold. Besides this, it is also said, that *Cato* wrote a *History* in a very Large and Legible Character, for the Use of his Son, on purpose to bring him acquainted with the Acts and Exploits of his Forefathers, and with the Art and Method of Presiding in the Affairs of the *Commonwealth.* Whenever his Son was Present, the Father would never suffer any Obscene or Filthy Discourse, or Conversation, or let an Expression

slip

slip, which had the Least Savour either of Rashness and Anger, or of Vice and Folly; being on this Occasion altogether as Cautious, as if a *Priest* or a *Vestal Virgin* were at that Time in Company. Such was the Behaviour of the Great *Cato,* and such in general the Good Conduct of all the *Romans,* in the Care of their Families, and the Education of their Children! Among the several Nations and Republicks of *Greece,* there was the same Care used in the Training up of their Youth. For which purpose, Publick *Schools* and *Academies* were opened by their *Philosophers,* and the Discipline observed in them, is by History brought down to our Times; the Memory and Glory whereof will no doubt endure for ever. From these Philosophers of *Old Greece,* the True Knowledge of all Human Vertues, and the several Arts and Sciences, by which the Whole Universe is displayed and made known to us, are handed down to the Present Generation. These were the Great Masters and Teachers of That Useful Knowledge, which shews us the Way how to Live well and happily, in a Private Station; and in what manner Publick Societies and Communities of Men are to be Governed. We of the Present Age have, like the *Old Grecians,* our *Academies,* or *Universities,* the Seminaries of Learning and Vertue, whither our Youth resort, as to a Plentiful Harvest, in order to go out from thence, laden with the Fruits of a Learned and Vertuous Education. It is the General Wish and Desire, that the *Rulers* and *Governors* of these *Seminaries* would be more Careful to Instruct their Youth in the Art of Living well, than in the Art of Controversy and Disputation; and instill into them True and Sound Philosophy, instead of *Jargon* and *Wrangle,* and the Little Friskish Arts of Sporting and Playing with Words. Were this the Case, we should soon see their Scholars come to be more truly Useful Members of the State, and Promoters of the Welfare and Happiness of their Fellow-Creatures. Among the Ancients, their young Students in Philosophy were for

a good

a good while *Hearers* only, and not suffered to *Speak* in their Schools. But now the Custom is, to bring them forward betimes, and to encourage them in Noise and Clamour. By which means they soon come to be *Orators* indeed, but without a *Meaning;* and *Philosophers,* without *Wisdom;* whilst the Good Discipline and Vertue, which sound so loudly from their Lips, never sink Lower, or take deep Root in their Hearts. Their *Tutors* and *Governors* are sometimes weak enough to commend them, for this very Spirit of Wrangling, to promote Contentions of this Sort among them, and to encourage their Pertness and Boldness in Disputation; whilst no Notice is taken of the Vertues of Modesty and Humility, of Prudence and Good Behaviour, or of the Love of Honour and Justice. But now the Governors of our *Academies* or *Universities* ought certainly to know, that their *Schools* were intended for the Propagation and Improvement, not of a Sleepy, Dreaming, and Speculative sort of Knowledge, but of that Civil Science and Wisdom, the Glory of which consists in Thinking Rightly, and in Doing Well. The *Old Academies* of *Greece* were the Seminaries of their Republicks; out of which, as out of the *Trojan Horse,* came their Best *Kings,* and most Renowned *Generals* and *Governors. Alexander* and *Scipio,* Two of the Greatest Commanders that ever lived, with many Others too Numerous to be recounted, had their First Rise in Glory from an *Academical Education:* And in the very same Way should all those Citizens be Trained, and throughly Exercised, who would learn the Two Arts of Living Vertuously, and of Governing Wisely. Hence it comes to be a National Concern; and it is certainly the Duty of every Government to have *Publick Schools* and *Academies,* so well Instituted and Ordered, that they may be as Storehouses and Repositories, out of which the State may be Furnished with all the Vertues that adorn Mankind.

Before

Before the *Good Senator* can be throughly Formed and Accomplished, he must have a Genius and Natural Disposition to Good, as well as a Liberal and Vertuous Education. When Human Nature is Turned and set upon Evil, it can never be Mended or Improved by Philosophy; but on the contrary, is rather in Danger of being made still more Vicious and Corrupt, and may perhaps sink to the Lowest Degeneracy. For since of ourselves we are naturally Inclined to Evil, if this Natural Inclination, instead of being Reformed by Vertuous Precepts, is really Strengthened and improved by the Craft and Cunning of Philosophy, we shall only Learn thereby, how to excell in Wickedness, and to be Vicious with so much the more Ingenuity and Success. The Best Knowledge, when it falls to the Share of the Worst of Men, loses all its Value; and from a Blessing, is turned into a Curse, serving only to instruct Men how to perpetrate the most Execrable Villanies. There is a *Brutal Force* in every Bad Man, which Art and Intense Thinking may easily carry forwards into something perfectly Savage and Barbarous; as we see a common Fitt of Anger, by the Improvement of the Subtle Spirits, insensibly raised to downright Frenzy and Madness. These therefore are Undoubted Truths, That a Genius and Disposition to Good may, by Vile Arts and Bad Instructions, come to be exceeding Evil; and a Bad Genius and Disposition to Evil, may grow still worse and worse, and fall at last into the most Horrid Impieties, by the Abuse of Good Instructions, and of the Best and Noblest Education. For all Good whatsoever, when it passes over into the Opposite Extreme, is soon changed into the Worst of Evils: Just as Good Seed, when it is cast into a Bad Soil, loses its Former Nature, and brings forth nothing but Noisome Weeds. There is therefore an Irresistible Force in Education, by which the tender Minds of our Youth are Bent this Way or that Way, just as they take the First and Earliest Impressions. *Diogenes* being asked, *What Method a Man ought to take, in order to attain a Life of Ease and Tranquillity?*

quillity? gave this for an Answer, *That he must, in the* First place, *Reverence the* Gods, *for they only can make Men truly Happy; that he must, in the* Next place, *breed up his Children to Vertue; for a Vicious Education will make them the Worst of all Enemies to their own Parents; and that, in the* Last place, *he must take Care to be always Grateful to his Friends:* For it was a Good Saying of the *Oracle,* That an Ungrateful Man was a Common Nuisance, and an Abomination to all the World.

In the Progress towards a Complete Education, the Young Pupil must be Well-Instructed in the Art of *Speaking,* both Properly and Gracefully, and must be set to work with all Diligence, in Searching and Enquiring after Truth. At his First Setting out upon this Enquiry, there are three Arts necessary to be Acquired, *Grammar, Logick,* and *Rhetorick.* For these Arts are as it were the Portals and Avenues to the Palace, wherein True Wisdom resides. From these are to be learned the Rules and Art of Speaking and Conversing, which must be Confirmed and Improved by Use and Exercise, and by reading the Works of the *Classick Orators* and *Poets.* When the Young Student has made a Progress thus far, let him no longer Content himself with these Trite, Vulgar, and Ordinary Attainments; but let him soar aloft, and early grasp at much Higher and Greater Improvements. The Rational Soul will now begin to look more narrowly into itself, and to exert all its Faculties, in quest of that more Durable and Substantial Food, with which alone it can be well Nourished, and fully Satisfied. Now *Philosophy* is not only the Proper Food, but the True Medicine of the Soul; by which all its Maladies and Sorrows are healed, and by which Man is made truly and perfectly Happy. We are Raised and Elevated, Spurred on and Excited, by the Desire of Attaining still Greater and moe Excellent Accomplishments, when once we have shaken off these Earthly Impediments, and Clogs of the Body, and are pursuing our Enquiries up to those Celestial Regions, whereunto our Soul is always Aspiring. The most we can at present

sent attain to, is first to Search into the most Obscure and Abstruse Secrets of Nature, and to Contemplate and take a View of the Whole System of the Universe: And then to look into the Life, Actions, and Ways of Men, and to see how Families are Ordered, and in what Manner Cities and Commonwealths are Governed and Established. In the Former of these Enquiries, *Natural Philosophy, Metaphysicks,* and *Mathematicks,* are our Chief Guides: And in the Latter, *Moral Philosophy, Policy,* and *Economy.* Both these Sorts of Philosophy have but one and the same End and Design in View, or at least there is here but little Difference between Speculative and Practical Knowledge. For as in the Contemplation of Heavenly Things and Operations, or the Ways and Works of our *Maker,* the Soul is as it were Separated from the Body, and Endeavours, in its own Strength, to make itself Happy, and so far Like unto *God:* So in a Life of Honesty and Goodness, where the Soul is armed and surrounded by all the Vertues, and is in Full Practice, and a State of Activity, it must in order thereto shake off all the Allurements, Filth, and Dregs of the Body: And when once the Soul hath, by both these Methods, shaken off the Body and all its Incumbrances, it may then truly Resemble its *Maker,* and in its own Right lay claim to Happiness. But now these Two abovementioned Parts of Knowledge differ in this Particular, That One of them is entirely consistent with a State of Ease and Leisure, whilst the Other is altogether conversant with Business, and always in a State of Activity and Employment; though still the *Divine Similitude* may, in either of these States, be retained by Mankind. Hence it is, that all Happiness is of Two Sorts, either Private or Publick. They, who repose all their Happiness in an Active Life, or in the Exercise of all the Vertues, are always to be esteemed the most Beneficial and Useful Members of the *Commonwealth.* For every Good Thing, by being communicated to many, does thereby gain so much a greater Addition to its own Real Worth and Intrinsick Value.

lue. And accordingly the Happiness, which diffuses and Extends itself to Multitudes, is certainly preferable to that Narrower and more Contracted Felicity, which a Single Person engrosses wholly to himself. And yet still it must be confessed, that a Life of Speculation is First in Order, and more Honourable than the Other, because Speculation always precedes Practice, and gives Life and Dignity to the Best and Noblest Actions. It is the Great Privilege of the *Divine Being*, to remain Unmoved and Unactive, and to pass away Eternity in Contemplation, and in the Oversight and Providential Survey of the Universe. By whose Example some Philosophers have preferred a Life spent in the Contemplation of Heavenly Things, to a Life of Activity, and to all the Blessings and Happiness, of which Human Nature is capable.

But now since the *Good Senator*'s Happiness, and all his Knowledge and Wisdom, are entirely Conversant with a Life of Activity and Business; because he is certainly such a One in his Character, who knows how to measure all his Actions by the Rule of Honesty and Right Reason, who is well Qualified to manage all Affairs both Private and Publick, and who understands how to Govern a City by Counsel and Wisdom, how to Found and Establish a Constitution by Wholsome Laws, and how to Reform it by a Regular Execution of Justice; it must follow, that he ought to make himself acquainted with that Part of Philosophy, which gives out the Rules and Precepts of Vertue, which are the Bounds and Limits of all Human Actions, and contain the Whole Art and Science of Behaving well, in a Publick or National Administration. Whatever relates to Manners and Good Conduct, he must be sure to understand throughly, and to put in Practice with the utmost Exactness, because upon this depends the Art not only of Living, but of Living well, and of giving Good Advice to others, and Governing them with Wisdom and Discretion. How shall That Man lead a Life agreeable to the Rules of Strict Vertue, who

really

really knows not what True Vertue is? And how shall He be able to set a *Senate* right in the Great and Fundamental Duties of Justice, Prudence, Temperance, and Fortitude? Or how shall He Undertake to appease a Tumult, or quell a Sedition; to Dispense or Expound the Laws, who is Ignorant of the Common Principles and Precepts of Justice and Prudence? Can such a One as this be able to give his Advice about a *War* or a *Peace*, a *League* or a *Treaty*, and to give it Well and Wisely, who really knows not when a *War* is Just or Unjust, a *Peace* Honourable or Dishonourable, and a *League* Dangerous and Fatal to the State, or Wellmade, and fit to be kept Sacred and Inviolable? It is the *Senator's* Duty throughly to Understand all the Obligations to Honesty in their Full Force and Utmost Extent, and all the Vertues. To know them not only by Name, or just as the Sounds reach his Ears, when they are mentioned or called over, but to comprehend their True and Real Nature, and to keep and retain them in his Mind. The Sum and Substance of all this Useful Knowledge is not to be obtained, but by Consulting the Works of the most Approved Authors and Writers in *Moral Philosophy, Policy,* and *OEconomy.* For out of these Treasures we may make a Collection of all the Vertues, and of all the Arts of Government, and be able to tell, how Men are to behave in their own Moral Character, and in what Manner they are to Order and Direct their own Families. By applying ourselves to these Studies, we shall be well Instructed to Form a Right Judgment upon all the Transactions the Affairs of Life, and to Discern between Honourable and Dishonourable, Good and Evil.

But besides this, there is another Sort of Learning, necessary to the Accomplishment of the *Good Senator,* by which we are brought acquainted with, and obliged to Retain in our Memories, the most Remarkable Sayings and Exploits of Those, who have gone before us in the World, just as they are delivered and brought down

down to us, in the Memorable Relations and Traditions of our Forefathers. The True and Perfect Account of all these Things, so well worthy of Note, is no where to be met with, in so Full and Ample a Manner, as in the Monuments and Remains of Faithful *Annalists* and *Historians*. What *Tully* observes, is certainly True, and very much to the Purpose, when he call history *The Witness and Evidence of Past Times, the Torch-bearer and Guide of Truth, Human Nature's Remembrancer, the Leader and Conductor of all our Actions, and a Messenger and Envoy sent to us by our Forefathers*. I would gladly ask, from whom shall we learn True Fortitude, Fidelity, Justice, Temperance, Frugality, and a Thorough Contempt of all Pain and Sorrow, and even of Death itself, but only from the *Cornelii, Valerii, Fabritti, Curii, Decii, Mutii,* and Other Heroes of Antiquity? And what shall I say of the Great Examples of our own Age and Nation, eminent in every Degree of Vertue and Glory? Shall I mention the *Lechian, Piastian, Boleslaian,* or *Jagalonian Families,* shining and eminent in every Degree of Vertue, by whose Example the present Age is not only improved and edified, but gives out their Well-spent Lives, the Worth and Dignity of their Character, and their Good Conduct and Honest Behaviour, Worthy of Eternal Praise and Commendation, as a Pattern fit to be copied by all Succeeding Generations? From such Principles, and such Examples, the *Good Senator* may easily learn, What the Precepts of Vertue really are, which he is obliged to conform to; and what are those Examples of Vertue and Fortitude, which it is his Duty and Interest to follow.

To this Stock of Learning and Knowledge, many Additions are to be made, before the *Good Senator* can be throughly Accomplished. He must take Care to be well acquainted with the Customs of his own Country, and the Manners of his Countrymen, their Way of Living, their Temper, Disposition, and General

neral Behaviour, their Sentiments and Opinions concerning the Present Posture of Affairs, and all the Remarkable Occurrences, and Passages of Publick Life. Besides this, he must be sure to make himself a Master of that truly Useful and Necessary Knowledge, which completes the Character of a Wise Statesman. He must throughly Understand the Laws of his own Country, and how, or in what manner, they are Made and Enacted. He must be well acquainted with the True Nature of War and Peace, what Quarrels and Enmities his People are engaged in, and what Leagues and Treaties are Subsisting between them and their Neighbours: What Taxes, Duties, and Customs, are already Imposed, or Necessary to be Demanded: What the Rights of the Subject are, and what the Proceedings of the Ministry: What Discipline is Observed, or in what Manner the Laws are Executed: What are the Dispositions of the People, and how at present they stand affected: What are their Discontents or Differences, and how they are to be Allayed and Pacified: What is the Present State of Morality: How the Youth of his Country are Educated and Employed: What Principles, Customs, and Rules of Conformity, are necessary to be Introduced, in order to Reform or Moralize a People; and what is the Present State of Religion, and the Publick Worship of GOD. Nor must the *Good Senator* be Ignorant of what passes among the Allies and Confederates of his own Country; what are their Rights and Demands, and what Agreements and Conventions are Subsisting between his own People and their Neighbours. He must in short be acquainted with all the Reasons and Ends of Government, understand all the Customs and Usages of his People, the Proceedings of all the Courts of Judicature, and all Publick Assemblies. Neither is it fit he should be altogether a Stranger to whatever daily occurs in the Publick Administration, or in Judicial Proceedings, or to the Examples and Characters of all about him, and to the Desires and Expectations

pectations of All his Fellow-Subjects. *Anthony* seems to me, to have given a Full and Lively Description of a Good Counsellor or Governor, when he says, *He is such a One, who well Understands, and always Adheres to, whatever may Contribute to, or Promote the Establishment and Welfare of a State; or Add to, and Increase its Happiness.* Such Counsellors and Senators were the *Lentuli*, the *Gracchi*, the *Metelli*, the *Scipio's*, and the *Lælii*, of *Old Rome*. But now in These our Times, such Examples are Uncommon enough: For we often see Men crowding for Honours and Offices, and making themselves Candidates for the *Senatorial* Dignity, and Government of the *Commonwealth*, without bringing along with them to the Place of Election, the Necessary Qualifications of Wisdom, Knowledge, and Experience. If here and there a *Candidate* of a more Exalted Character appears in Publick, yet still perhaps his only Recommendation is a Single *Campaign,* or the Services of *One Year,* or it may be a Little Smattering in the *Law,* or the Greatness of his *Wealth,* or the Popular Clamours of his *Followers* and *Dependents;* whilst he has nothing beyond all this, or at least but a very Slender Acquaintance with the Best and Noblest Arts, or with all those Vertues which are necessary to the Formation of *the Accomplish'd Senator;* the Perfection of whose Character consists in this, That he be always ready and well resolved, to Think and Act aright; That he look upon it as Dishonourable to follow the Opinion of others Servilely and Implicitly; That he behave as if he were always a Candidate for the First Place in the Court of Wisdom, and labour to attain the Utmost Glory that Good Counsel and a Good Life can give him, to adorn and make his Character Perfect; and, That he never look upon any thing as truly Just and Right, Worthy of Praise, and Agreeable to Sound Wisdom, but what is dictated to him by the Precepts of Vertue, the Laws of his own Country, and by Right Reason. The Knowledge of Men and things is certainly the Rise and Foundation

dation of all True Wisdom, which can never be attained, but by a Thorough Acquaintance with the Best and Noblest Arts and Sciences; and without these it is Impossible for any Man, much more for a *Senator,* to Think, and Speak, and Act upon all Occasions, either Well or Wisely.

For the Greater Improvement of his Knowledge, and the Perfecting of his Character by Wisdom and Prudence, it may be Necessary for the *Senator* to become acquainted with the Laws and Customs of other Countries, besides his own, and the Ways and Manners of their People. This Sort of Knowledge is to be attained by *Travel:* And accordingly *Homer* speaks thus of *Ulysses;*

> Muse, *Sing the Man, who sail'd from* Phrygia's *Shore,*
> *Through various Realms, their Manners to explore,*
> *Their Cities, and their Laws.*____

The Great Benefit to be made of *Travel,* arises from our Observing carefully upon the Good Behaviour, Manners, and Civility of Those abroad; and upon such of their Rights and Customs, as are Laudable and Worthy of our Imitation; and from Noting and Censuring their particular Follies and Vices, which we must be alike careful to Avoid. The Laws of Foreign Nations, their Jurisdictions, Liberties, Way and Manner of Living, their Civil and Military Discipline, with the OEconomy and Management of their Domestick Affairs, the Situation of their Country, their Clime and Soil, their Publick Buildings, their Ornaments and Fortifications, are also well worth our Notice, and deserve the Particular Enquiries and Inspection of the Judicious *Traveller.* Besides this, it may be of Use to know the True and Real Character of every Prince, whose Dominions we Visit; and to enquire, what Opinion the People have of him, and how they are affected towards his Government. If there is a Senate or Great Council? How are they

they Chosen, and what are the People's Sentiments of their Prudence and Conduct? How, and in what Manner is Justice Administered? What is the National Genius of the Country? What the Temper and Disposition of the Inhabitants? What particular Men have they among them, Eminent for their Wisdom and Learning, and what Great Generals and Commanders? These are the Proper Enquiries to be made by a Wise and Judicious *Traveller*; and besides these, he may perhaps be artful enough to make some Useful and Advantageous Discoveries, which he may Retain and Bring home with him; and when a Proper Opportunity offers itself, they may be Produced to the Advantage and Improvement of his own Country, or in order to do her Service upon some Critical and Necessary Emergence. But then Great Caution ought to be used on this Occasion, and we must be very Sparing and Wary in our Attempts to introduce any Strange and Foreign Customs into our own Country, lest we thereby Infect our People with the Itch of Novelty, and Corrupt their Minds by Softness and Effeminacy; whereby they will be soon brought to forget the Rigid Vertues and Plain Honesty, with the Manners, Laws, and Customs, of their Forefathers. For the Populace are in their own Nature changeable enough, and over-fond of Novelty; and nothing is more Fatal to a Government, than Dangerous and Pernicious Innovations. But when we meet with any Thing, which is truly Honest and Laudable; any thing that is Agreeable to the Manners and Temper of our Countrymen, Useful and Beneficial to the Publick, and Well-fitted to the Clime and Soil in which we live; Every thing of this Sort we may safely borrow from Strangers, and bring home with us: And beyond this any Attachment to Foreign Fashions, Modes, and Customs, is by no means fit to be Endured. Many of the Greatest and Wisest Men of Antiquity, took Particular Delight in Travel. Thus did *Nestor, Menelaus*, and *Alexander* the *Great:* And it is a Remarkable *Epitaph* Extant in *Diodorus Siculus*,

Siculus, which was once Inscribed upon the Monument of *Osiris*, King of *Egypt:* "I am That Osiris *the* King, *the Eldest Son* " *of* Saturn, *who leave behind me no Spot of Earth, which I did* " *not once Visit; thereby Learning All that is Necessary and Useful to* " *Mankind."*

If a Youth, who intends to Qualify himself for the *Senatorial Dignity*, has no Opportunity of Travelling, let him supply this Defect, by Reading over the Best and most Approved *Cosmographers, Geographers,* and *Historians:* And let him be always Careful to lay in such a Stock of Knowledge, as may preserve him from That Low and Childish Behaviour, which is the Necessary Result and Effect of Ignorance. In that Part of Philosophy, which treats of the more Obscure Operations, and Abstruse Secrets of Nature, I would not have him entirely Unskilful: But then he may be very Sparing of this Sort of Studies; and to run too far into them, or with too much Eagerness, is neither Pleasant nor Profitable. The Way of Life, to which he is destined, does by no means require an Universal Knowledge. Wisdom has a Large Field to range in, Boundless and Unmeasurable. The Sciences must be Cantoned out and Parcelled, since no one Single Person can possibly make himself a Master of them all. Whatever falls within the Compass of our Knowledge, may be divided into Three Parts, Things *Honest, Pleasant,* and *Profitable.* The Knowledge of what is Honest and Pleasant, serves rather to Sweeten and make Life Agreeable, than to Qualify us for the Affairs of Government; that when the Mind is almost Spent and Tired with the Business of the *Court,* the *Rostrum,* and the *Tribunal,* it may Retire, and Collect new Strength and Vigour, Refresh and Recreate itself, by Indulging for a Time in Lawful Ease, Softness, and Delicacy. It is not to be denied, that this Sort of Philosophy may possibly do the Publick a Good deal of Service, especially if its Followers do really Love a Civil Life, or Life of Business, and take more Pleasure in
coming

coming abroad into Publick View and Conversation, than in hiding and immuring themselves in Cells and Solitude. But if their Want of Health, or any other Impediments and Avocations; if their Incapacity for the Execution of any Publick Trust or Office, will not permit them to appear in any Higher Station; let them go down among the Lower Classes of our Youth, give into Dress and Gayety, or go back to the Schools, or frequent the Publick Assemblies, and Places of Resort for Diversion or Exercise. There is a Private and Retired Sort of Philosophy, which yet is of Great Use and Service to the Publick. For we are not to look upon Them as the Only Philosophers, who know how to Manage and Direct the Affairs of a State or Commonwealth: Since besides These, there are Others, to whose written Labours and Immortal Works we are Indebted, for the Remains and Monuments of True Wisdom and Learning. And there is also a Third Sort of Philosophers, whose Business it is to Instruct those under their Care in the Rules of Vertue, and in the Art of Government; from whose Lectures and Labours we borrow all our Knowledge in Law, Morality, and Government, and in the Way and Method of attaining True Happiness. These Men certainly deserve well at our Hands; because of their Leisure and Retirement we are Instructed in Business, and taught to come abroad with Reputation and Advantage. The Ancients had many Philosophers of this Order: Such were *Theophrastus, Heraclides* of *Pontus, Dicæarchus, Socrates,* and *Pythagoras*: And it is remarkable, that the Book which *Dicæarchus* the Philosopher wrote upon Government, was by a Decree of the *Spartan Commonwealth*, ordered to be Read publickly once a Year, and that all their Youth should be Assembled together, to attend to, and hear the Lecture.

 The Proper End and Design of True Philosophy, is to Manure and Cultivate the Mind, to Plant in it the Seeds and Principles of Vertue, and not to Grate or Tickle the Ears with Contentions,

tions, Wrangle, and Disputation. All Ill-Language, Scurrilous Contumelious and Passionate Expressions, all Noisy Combats and Contentions about Words, seem to me to be Unworthy of the Name of True *Philosophy*. And it is certainly downright Folly to imagine, that Vertue and Philosophy are only Empty Sounds: For Constancy, Fidelity, and Probity, which make the Sum of all Philosophy, are Real and Substantial Vertues. All other Arts and Sciences are not (properly speaking) *Vertues*, but are the Instruments and Ornaments by which Vertue is Attained and Perfected. There are also Various *Sects* in *Philosophy*, but these Differences ought by no means to disturb or distract the Minds of its Followers. Let *Epicurus* be Banished out of our *Gardens*, or at least out of our Minds: For that Sort of Philosophy, which Patronizes Pleasure, ought never to be Admitted into the Presence of the *Good Senator*, whose True Character we are in Search of; nor be received by him, who is destined to preside in the Councils and Government of his Native Country. I have by no means the same Aversion to the Sect of the *Stoicks*. Let them however be Quietly dismissed, as Unfit Companions for the *Good Senator:* Because (as *Tully* informs us) they Maintain and Believe, that all those Men, who are not Truly Wise, are no Better than Slaves, Robbers, Common Enemies, Barbarians, and Madmen; whilst at the same time they are not throughly agreed among themselves, wherein to fix the True Notion of Wisdom. Now certainly it must be a very Great Absurdity, to Elect such a Man into the *Senate,* who is firmly persuaded, that all his Assessors and Companions in the same Trust, are such Men, as really have no true Notion of Wisdom and Liberty, and are Unworthy of the Name of Citizens. There have been Great Contentions between the *Stoicks* and *Peripateticks*, concerning the *First* or *Chiefest Good*. But the *Peripateticks* are That *Sect* of *Philosophers*, which I should most readily follow, because they set out the several Vertues in the Best Order, and

enforce

enforce them by the Strongest Arguments. Truth seems to have been the Chief Aim of all their Enquiries; and out of their *Schools*, as out of the *Trojan Horse*, have come forth Citizens, Commanders, Kings, and Philosophers, of the Best and Noblest Characters.

When the *Good Senator* hath once made himself Master of all These Arts and Sciences, and This Immense Stock of Knowledge, the Attainments he is possessed of will Shine forth, and become so much the more Conspicuous by Eloquence, which is the Ornament of Wisdom. Where this is wanting, all his other Accomplishments, let them be never so great, will insensibly Dwindle and Fall away in Obscurity. Eloquence, or the Art of Speaking Wisely and Finely, will enable the *Senator* not only to Support his own Dignity, but to Defend the Rights and Liberties of many other Private Persons, and the Cause and Interests of the *Commonwealth*. By this the Minds of Men, when Ruffled and Raised to an Undue Ferment, are easily Composed and Pacified. By this, when they are Lulled and Becalmed, they are as easily Raised and put in Agitation; and This has done more Sure and Fatal Execution, than the Sword or the Spear. Whenever the *Senator* rises to Speak, let him Speak with all the Force of Reason and Wisdom, and with all the Graces and Ornaments of Rhetorick. Let his Speech be Well-weighed and Composed, and yet seem to be *Extempore*; and let the Dignity of Action and Gesture always accompany whatever he has to Deliver. Next to Eloquence, let him endeavour to make himself a Master of the *Civil Law*, the End and Design of which, is to preserve a Just and Exact Equality in the Distribution of All Things. For who is so well qualified to decide the Causes and Controversies of his countrymen, to suppress Tumults and Seditions; well and wisely to defend the Laws of his own Nation, or the Customs, Rights, and Liberties of the People, as the Man, who is really a Master of Law and Equity?

It

It is a Well-known and very True Saying, *That the House of a Good Lawyer is the City Oracle.* *Anthony* describes the Good Lawyer as One, *Who well Understands all the Accusations, Pleas, Defences, and Cautionary Proceedings, which, by the Laws and Customs of his Country, are in Use among Men, in their Contentions and Controversies with one another.* But the *Lawyer* I would Exclude from the *Senate* is such a One, as is a Notorious Brawler and Tongue-Pad. For this Sort of Creatures are of a Low Vulgar Order, Servile and Mercenary, capable of being made the Ministers of Falshood and Injustice: Wretches, who often bring their Tongues and their Minds too, Well-armed and Instructed, into a Court of Justice, and there Employ them in the Defence of Wrong and Oppression. It is indeed hardly possible for That Man to be a Sincere Lover of Truth and Equity, who will Prostitute his Eloquence, and let out his Tongue to Hire. But now on the other hand, it is Part of the Office and Duty of the *Good Senator*, to preserve the Proceedings of Judicature from all Corruptions of Fraud and Deceit; to become a Voluntary Accuser, and Strenuous Adversary of all Wicked and Traitorous Subjects, and a no less Hearty and Zealous Defender of the Good and Vertuous; not having any View or Regard to his own Private Profit or Interest, but being wholly Actuated by a Just Sense of his own High Dignity, a Sincere Love of Justice, and a General Good Will and Affection for his Fellow-Subjects. Such was the Behaviour, and such the Principles of the Wisest and most Noble *Romans*, that ever sate down in their *Senate*. History is full of Instances to this Purpose: But from this Digression, I return to the Prosecution of my First Design, and am now to speak of the Nature of *Civil Wisdom* or *Discipline*.

CHAP. VI.

The CONTENTS.

Of Civil Wisdom *and Discipline. Of Bodily Improvements and* Exercise. *What are the most Manly* Exercises. *Of Good* Generals, *and Good* Senators. *The* Romans *remarkable for These Two Characters. Of* Good Laws *and* Statutes. *An* Encomium *on the* Greek Commonwealths. *The Length of* Art, *and Shortness of* Life. *The End and Aim of every Man's Accomplishments. The Grounds and Foundation of the* Polish Policy. *The Perfection and Happiness of the* Golden Age. *The* Fall *of* Man, *and* Rise *of* Philosophy. *Which Sort of* Philosophy *deserves the Preference.*

CIVIL Wisdom or Discipline is nothing else, but the Art of Directing and Conducting our own Lives, and the Lives of all our Countrymen and Fellow-Citizens, according to the Rules and Precepts of Vertue and Justice. The Philosophers call That Man truly *Civilized*, who has all the Faculties and Vertues necessary to the Due Administration of Power: As they call him *Kingly* and *Royal*, who is qualified in the same manner for the Highest Place, or Supream Power, in a State; or (as they sometimes add) has Authority to make Laws, for the Better Regulating of Private Life, in all Vertue and Honesty. The End and Design of all Civil Discipline, is the Good of the Community, or in other Words, the Strict Administration of Justice: For herein consists the Welfare of the Publick. *Plato*, in his Institution of a *Commonwealth*, hath prescribed Two Sorts of Discipline; One for the Motions of the Body, and the Other for the Powers of the Mind. He calls *Musick*, the Discipline of

the

the Soul, and *Exercise* the Discipline of the Body. By *Musick* he understands, That Harmony, Concent, and Concord, which is between the Soul and Vertue, when they readily Answer to, and Agree with each other. This Agreement is not to be procured, or brought about any other Way, than by Philosophy and the Laws; for by these Two we are taught to Distinguish between Honest and Dishonest, Just and Unjust; what is to be Loved and Chosen, and what to be Hated and Rejected; as also how we are to Behave towards our Friends, our Parents, and our Governors. By *Exercise* he means all those Motions of the Body, which serve to the Improvement of our Strength, and the Increase of our Fortitude. Such are *Dancing, Racing, Wrestling, Hunting, Riding,* and *Flinging the Javelin,* both with the Right *Hand* and the *Left:* For by the Mismanagement of *Nurses,* the Strength of these Two Limbs is very much Impaired, or rendered vastly Unequal. In short, whatever tends to the Improvement of Man's Body, either in the Art Military, or in any Lawful Sport or Diversion, may be comprehended under the General Term, or Name of *Exercise.* There is nothing whatsoever, which is of Greater Use and Service to Mankind in general, and especially to Those of the *Civil* or *Senatorial* Character, than to join the Exercises of the Body, and those of the Mind together, and to add Temperance and Fortitude; that by this Last Vertue they may learn not to Despise what is Below them; and by the Former, not to Aspire to what is Above them; and by both these Vertues in Conjunction, may be Restrained from the Excesses of Fear and Boldness. Fortitude will Instruct us, how to Resent and Guard our Selves against any Publick or Private Injury; and Temperance will preserve us from offering any Injury to Others. Fortitude will make us in Love with Goodness and Honesty: And Temperance will make us Averse to whatever is Base and Ignoble. *Musick* and *Exercise* (to Speak in the *Platonick* Way) are Great Helps

Helps to us in all Cases of this Nature. By the Former, we are made Temperate, and Accomplished in every other Vertue: And by the Latter, we are Improved in Fortitude, both of the Mind and Body: And there is Good Reason, why these Two Accomplishments should be joined together: For *Exercise*, without *Musick*, is apt to Sour our Nature, and make us Cruel and Savage: And *Musick*, without *Exercise*, is alike apt to make us Soft and Effeminate. But when Both meet together in a Man, they render his Character and his Vertues Perfect.

The Way and Method, by which every *Senator* may attain True Glory, and in the Attainment of which he ought always to Exercise himself, is by Wisdom and Good Counsel, in Times of Peace; and by Fortitude and Good Conduct, in Times of War. For These Services, by the very Condition of his Birth, his own Country may justly Claim at his Hands. It was a Noble Institution and Custom among the *Romans*, worthy of the Praise and Imitation of all Posterity, for the Sons of their Noblemen and Citizens of the First Rank, to be bred in such a Manner, as that they might attain the Two Glorious Characters of being *Good Senators* at home, and Brave *Generals* and Commanders abroad. Hence it was, that no other Nation or Republick could ever Boast of so many *Senators* and *Generals*, so truly Wise and Courageous, as were at one time inclosed within the Walls of *Rome:* And on this Account it was, that *Cyneas* the Ambassador of *Pyrrhus* to the *Romans,* was pleased to call *The Senate of* Rome, *an Assembly of Many* Kings.

Some Philosophers have been of Opinion, that a Good Part of *Civil Discipline* consists in Reforming and Moralizing the Whole Body of the People. For the Good Citizen is not only to be Instructed, how to Govern, but also how to Obey; and not only to Obey the Magistrate, or Those in Authority over him, but to Reverence and Love them. Now since this is to be brought about

by

by Enacting Good and Wholsome Laws, the *Senator* must on this Occasion exert all his Best Faculties, and Labour to approve himself a Wise and Skilful Legislator. For Obedience to the Magistrate, and to the Laws, is the First Step towards an Honest and Vertuous Life: All Law being nothing else but Vertue and Honesty, reduced to a Fixed Standard, and to a Certain and Orderly Regulation. When *Theopompus*, King of *Sparta*, was told, that the Reason why the *Lacedæmonian* Commonwealth Flourished and Prospered in so extraordinary a Manner, was This, Because they had Kings and Rulers well versed in the Art of Government: He readily denied it, and gave This as the Best Reason, *Because the Subjects were as well versed in the Art of Obedience.* The *Lacedæmonian* Discipline, (according to the Testimony of *Plutarch*) consisted chiefly of these Particulars: They knew how to Obey the Laws and the Magistrates: They could firmly endure any Labour or Fatigue: They understood the Art of War, and were always Prepared either to Conquer or to Die. Almost in Every Government and Commonwealth of *Greece*, there were Common Rules and Principles of Discipline, generally allowed and agreed unto, by which their Youth were daily Trained and Exercised, and were thereby fully Instructed, how to Govern their own Country in Times of Peace, and how to Defend it in Times of War; and whenever they Retired from Publick Business, how to Behave in Private Life, Vertuously and Honestly, and with Pleasure and Contentment. They had their *Schools*, their *Games*, and *Exercises*. *Musick*, and *Painting*, and *Swimming*, were their ordinary Diversions: And of such whom they had a Mind to Ridicule for their Want of Sense and Good-Breeding, it was usual for them to say, *That they could neither Read nor Swim.* A *Theban* being asked, *By what means the Constitution of a Kingdom or Commonwealth might be Preserved?* Answered, *By Justice, and the Observation of the Laws; and above all other Things, by Training their Youth to Good Discipline,*

and

and Preserving their Old Men from Covetousness. The Power of Good Discipline is certainly very Great, and especially of That Discipline, properly called *Civil*, by which the Members of every Society are trained up, and fitted for the Reception of every True and Perfect Vertue.

By the way, we must by no means pass by a Well-known Truth, which stands Confirmed by Common Observation, That there have been a Good Many Men in the World, who never had the Least Tincture of Learning, or any Acquaintance with the Arts and Sciences, who never tasted of the Rudiments of Philosophy, or perhaps ever heard of its Name; and yet by their Conduct have approved themselves Wise Men, Prudent, Good, Just, and Courageous, and have Executed the Offices of the *Commonwealth* laudably and worthily. The Truth of this Observation, and the Examples of these Men, seem perhaps to require of us some other Account of Philosophy, than what we have already given, to Reject all that we have hitherto said upon this Subject, and to give it as our Opinion, that True Wisdom is not to be attained by Study, or by Length of Years. For according to That Well-known *Proverb* used by Physicians, *Art is Long, but Life is Short*: And the Opinion of *Plato* is very remarkable, who never would Pronounce a Man truly Happy, till by Old Age and Experience, and upon the Last Declension and Verge of Life, he began to Form his Sentiments of the World, and his Notions of True Wisdom. For it is Experience only, that can Improve and make us Better, and nothing but Time and Age can add to our Prudence and Wisdom. These most certainly are Great and Noble Accomplishments; but it is a Sad and Melancholy Consideration, that before we can Arrive at These Attainments, there are many Difficulties and Obstructions laid in our Way, by the Uncertainty of our Lives, and the Frailty of our Nature. There are many, who are but just arrived at the Middle Stage of Life,

when

when Death meets them half way, and cuts them off from Proceeding any further. And Others there are, who give themselves up to follow the Lusts of the Body, rather than the Dictates of the Mind, and hate a Life of Vertue and Wisdom, as too Rough and Ruggid, and more to be avoided than *Scylla* or *Charybdis*. What shall I say of Those Men, who for want of a Natural Genius and Capacity, can never Think or Act as becomes Philosophers? All these Impediments tend very much to the Cutting us off from all Hopes of attaining True Wisdom and Sound Philosophy; yet we must not therefore be Dejected, or let our Minds be cast down, or over-run with Despair. The Happiness of Life is not to be reckoned by the Length of Time, or the Number of our Years, but by our Growth and Proficiency in Vertue. Without Vertue, our Life will be unavoidably Short, Wretched, and Miserable, though it should exceed the Age of the *Phoenix*, or the Number of Years that *Nestor* reckoned. Where is the Disadvantage of Dying Young, if after Death, Vertue shall give us New Life and Immortality? When *Silenus* the Poet was taken Prisoner by some Scouts and Maroders belonging to *Midas*'s Army, and was by them brought into the King's Presence; for want of Money to Redeem himself, he begged leave, instead thereof, to make the King a Present much more Valuable than either Silver or Gold, and accordingly Presented him with these Two Short Sentences, telling him with as much Gaiety as Truth, *That the Greatest Blessing the Gods could bestow upon Man, was, Not to bring him into the World at all: And the Next to this was, To take him out of it as soon as possible.* When by a good many Reasons and Arguments he had Supported and Established these Two Principles, the King ordered him to be well Rewarded, and readily Dismissed, and gave him his Liberty. I would now only ask this Question, Which Life of the Two is the most Happy and Preferable? Whether a Life of Corruption, Frailty, and Misery; or That Glorious, Happy

Happy and Immortal Life, the Possession of which is Ascertained and Secured to us by Vertue? We Live but to Die; and why then should we not chuse to Die, that we may Live? All our Studies, and all our Labours ought to be freely Expended in the Search and Acquisition of Vertue; and Philosophy is the Parent, the Nurse and Nourisher of Vertue, by which if we are not Raised to the Highest Dignity and Station in Life, yet we shall be so far Elevated, as to have vast Numbers and Multitudes at a great Distance beneath us. There is an Honest Ambition, which, if it cannot carry us up to the First, may at least Fix us in the Second or Third Rank of Mankind. *In the Race of Glory* (as *Tully* well observes) *it is Great to come in Second, and Honour enough to stand next in Precedence to the First and Best Characters in Life.* In War, if we cannot reach the High and Exalted Renown of an *Achilles*, we shall be enough Heroick, and far above Contempt, if we can at least copy the Example of an *Ajax*, or a *Diomed:* And surely That Man is by no means to be Censured for his Want of Skill and Learning, or to be pulled down into the Lowest Order of Philosophers, who cannot vie with the Wisdom of a *Plato*, a *Solon*, or a *Lycurgus*.

There are many Men (as I have already hinted) who have acquired a very Large Stock of Wisdom, and have made themselves Masters of the Art of Government, without Consulting the Books and Writings of Philosophers, and without any other Assistances, but the Institutes and Precepts of their Forefathers, the Examples of their Wisdom and Goodness, Use and Experience, Paternal Instruction, and Domestick Discipline, the Laws, Customs, and Manners of their Country, a Happy Well turned Genius, and a Natural Capacity, upon which they Grafted some few Improvements and Advantages of an Honest and Liberal Education. In every Nation and Commonwealth, there have been many Instances of Men of this Character, who borrowed all their Civil

Discipline

Discipline or Wisdom, from the Publick *Forum*, and had no other Masters or Tutors, but the Laws and Customs of their Country, and the Precepts, Manners, and Example of their Forefathers. *Demades*, a Man of great Prudence, and well versed in Publick Business, being one Day asked, *From whom he had learned all his Wisdom, and who had been his Tutor or Preceptor?* Readily answered, *The* Tribunal *of* Athens: For he looked upon the *Forum*, and upon Experience in Publick Affairs, as far Preferable to the Institutions and Speculations of Philosophy. The *Old Romans*, in the Strength of their Natural Genius and Capacity, and without ever Consulting the Books and Writings of the Philosophers, drew out that Fine Scheme and Well-formed Constitution of a *Commonwealth*, which they bequeathed to Future Generations. And what shall I say of our own Forefathers, who raised the Fabrick, and drew out the System of a Constitution, not much unlike the *Roman*, for the Use of Us their Posterity? The Old *Polanders* were by no means acquainted with the Discipline of *Plato, Solon,* and *Lycurgus*, or with the Works of *Aristotle*, and other Philosophers and Legislators of the First Note and Character. Instead of Books, they looked into Themselves, and by their own Natural Genius and Vertues, raised themselves to Glory and Happiness. Their First and Greatest Wisdom, was to make Vertue their Sole Guide and Leader, whom they were resolved to follow; and to whose Dictates all their Thoughts and Actions were exactly Conformable. They had very little Business or Employment for their *Kings* and *Senate*, in composing Feuds and Differences, or in putting an End to Strife and Contention, by Judicial Decrees and Sentences: But those High Offices were altogether taken up with the Important Concerns of Setting People a Rule and Example of Vertue, or Leading them on to War, for the Safety and Defence of their Country.

The

The First and Purest Times, by the Poets called, *The Golden Age*, produced a Sett of Men, perfectly Wise, and truly Good. Well might they be called so, since in those Clear Dawnings of Unsullied Nature, and those Unmixed Rudiments of Life, Vertue shone forth in full Lustre, and had the Sole Dominion and Power over All: Whilst Vice and Folly had not yet shed their Pernicious Venom, and Infected and Corrupted the World. Men were then easily Allured and Drawn into the Love of Vertue and Right Reason, Truth, Justice, Honesty, and Sincerity: Because to follow These, was the same Thing as to follow Nature: By whose Impulses and Instinct, they were Led and Directed into All Good, and Restrained and Preserved from All Evil. And certainly there could be no great Difficulty in avoiding Vice and Folly, at a Time when the very Names of them were not so much as Known or Heard of in the World. *Ovid* hath very Elegantly Described this State:

> *The First Pure Age, with Gold Unsully'd flow'd;*
> *When Man, without a Law, was Just and Good.*
> *No Judge they had, no Summons to the Bar,*
> *And as they had no Guilt, they knew no Fear.*

But soon after this Bright and Glorious Morning, the Sun of Righteousness and Vertue began to decline from his Meridian Lustre, and set at last in a Thick Shade, and brought on a Gloomy Night of Vice, Ignorance, and Folly. Upon this Great Change the Minds of Men were Warped and Turned, and ran down violently into quite Another Channel. They were now grown as Fond of Vice, as ever they had been of Vertue. They forgot and forsook their First Love, and grew fond of this New Mistress, though all over Corruption. They not only Slighted and Neglected Vertue, but heartily Hated, and Armed themselves against her.

To

To live by Rapine and Injustice, and by Injuring and Oppressing Others, was thought Heroick and Glorious: And their Reason was of no Use to them, but as they Prostituted it to their Lusts, and employed it in the carrying on of the most Wicked and Villanous Designs. Hence the same Author goes on in this Manner:

The Iron Age *was Last, replete with Vice;*
When Faith and Truth were banish'd to the Skies:
Whilst in their Stead, Fraud and Oppression reign;
The Lust of Empire, and the Love of Gain.

This Gulph and Deluge of Vice and Wickedness had certainly Swallowed up and Overwhelmed Mankind, if Reason and Nature, after the Great Shock and Defeat so suddenly brought upon them, had not Sounded a Retreat, and collecting their Scattered Forces together, Retired and taken Shelter under the Patronage and Protection of a Few Men, willing and able to Retrieve their Losses. These Happy Few were the Nobler and Better Part of Mankind, who still maintained and carried on the War against Vice, and when their Fellow-Creatures were almost turned to Savages, and gave into a Roving, Wild, and Brutish Way of Life, endeavoured to Reclaim them and bring them back to their Former State of Humanity, by their Learned Arguments and Discourses, and, by Writing as well as Speaking, to Instruct them in the Offices, Vertues, and Dignities, by which the Honour of Fallen Nature might be Restored to its Former Lustre. These Men founded Cities, and gave out Laws, which are Sure Guides of Life. These Reduced all the Vertues to certain Rules and Precepts, and the Manners of Mankind to certain Offices and Duties. Upon These they Wrote at large, and made this sort of Learning the Subject and Burden of many *Volumes.* Next to them came Others, who not only treated of the Moral Duties and Offices of Mankind,

Mankind, but of the Nature and Works of the Universe. This Knowledge both of Human Nature and of Universal Nature, was by the *Greeks* called in one Word, *Wisdom*; and the Masters and Professors of it were called *Wise Men*. But this Title appearing afterwards to be too Lofty and Ostentatious, *Pythagoras* was the Occasion of changing so Hateful a Name, for the more Humble and less Invidious Appellation of *Lovers of Wisdom*, or *Philosophers*. By these means it was, that the Light of Nature, which had been so long Clouded and Obscured by Vice and Corruption, began to shine out again: And thus the Knowledge of Things Human and Divine, was Conveyed and Handed down to us by *Philosophy*. Through her Beneficial Aid and Assistance we are enabled, in some Degree, to recover the Primitive Vertue, Simplicity, Innocence, and Happiness of Life, which we had before Lost and Forfeited. Whoever among the Ancients was throughly resolved to live Honestly, to free himself from all Manner of Vice, and to make an Acquaintance with Vertue, and Delight himself therein; there was but one well-known Method for such Men to take, which was, to apply themselves to the Writings and Lectures of the Philosophers, and to receive their Instructions, as being distrustful of their own Natural Propensity to Vice, and justly Fearful and Diffident, lest Ill Arts and a Bad Education, Darkness and Ignorance, Sloth and Idleness, Ease and Delicacy, Leisure and Wantonness, False Opinions, Wicked Customs, and Vicious Habits, should spread their Early Infection, and by Degrees Taint and Corrupt them. 'Tis Philosophy therefore, that revives the *Golden Age*, and brings Man back to his Primitive State and Way of Life, the Fulness of his Nature, and the Completion of his Happiness: And when we learn from Philosophy, That *Humane* Way of Life, which was in fashion during the *Golden Age*, and all the Vertues and Rules of Honest and Good Behaviour; we are then fully accomplished, by the Acquisition

sition of Civil Wisdom and Prudence, and put into the Possession of True Felicity and Happiness.

There are but Two Ways of attaining to Wisdom and Prudence, without the Help of Education and Discipline, or any the least Proficiency in *Philosophy*. The First of these is by a Participation, or Infusion of a certain Divine Nature, enlightening the Mind, and enabling it to Comprehend, Foresee, and Understand all Things, without Labour or Study. The Ancients Imagined, that *Theseus* and *Cecrops*, among the *Greeks*, and *Romulus* and *Numa* among the *Latins*, were thus Divinely Illuminated; and that their Great Skill and Knowledge in the Art of Government did by no means come from the Ordinary Precepts and Instructions of Certain *Sages* and *Masters* of *Philosophy*, but were infused into them by a *Superior Genius*, and took their Rise from the Inspiration of certain *Celestial Beings*, whom they called the *Muses*. The other Way of attaining to Wisdom, is by Custom and Use, by a Long Attendance upon the *Forum* and the *Courts*, and by a Course of *Practice* in the Several Proceedings of *Law* and *Justice*; by which Men are trained to the Knowledge and Arts of Government: And if such Men, so trained, are in their own Natural Disposition Good and Vertuous, and make the Laws of their Country the Rule of their Behaviour, and the Sole Measure of their Conduct, in the Discharge of any Publick Trust or Office, they may easily attain a Good and Laudable Character: Though with all their Prudence it will be Difficult, and almost impossible, for them to avoid some Slips and Mistakes; and their Conduct will be liable to many Turns and Alterations; whilst their Character, far from being Perfect, will very often be in Danger of a Forfeiture. On the other hand, if such Men prove to be of a Wicked and Corrupt Disposition, they will (by Practice) add daily to their Impieties, and by Degrees fill up the Measure of them, and of their own Folly and Disgrace: There being no Greater Scandal, Bane, and Plague,

to

a Nation, than a *Minister* or *Magistrate*, Daringly Wicked, and Grosly Ignorant. *Mitio*, in the *Comedy*, says very well, *That Want of Knowledge is the Sure Forerunner of all Injustice*. An Ignorant Statesman, or Publick Officer, who understands not the True Measure and Rules of Government, and imagines perhaps, that a Little Skill and Experience, in some one *Court* or *Tribunal*, is the Sum and Completion of all *Civil Wisdom* and *Discipline*, is really better Qualified to Foment Differences, and raise Tumults and Seditions, than to find out the Proper Reasons and Arguments to suppress them; to understand the Political Art and Management, or to give out the Good Counsel and Advice, by which Publick Grievances and Common Evils are effectually Healed, or happily Prevented. How can he Advise or Assist on these Occasions, whose Hands are Weakened, and whose Understanding is Darkened by Ignorance, That Gross Profound Ignorance, which is the Parent of all Vice, and the Root of all Evil?

Since then it is very Evident, that Mere Nature is not of herself a Competent, and Sufficient Guide, to lead and direct us in our Search after Truth and Vertue, Wisdom and Happiness; Because the Mind, which makes this Search, is Retarded and Overburdened by the Pressure and Dross of the Body, and the Whole Man is perverted in his Nature, and fatally Curious to make an Acquaintance with Evil, not being able in its own Strength to maintain a Life of Innocence and Vertue, such as was Common enough in the First and Purest Age of the World: Hence it must follow, that there is a Necessity of our looking out for a New Method and other Principles and Counsels, whereby to free ourselves from this Bondage and these Incumbrances of Flesh, in which we are at present Entangled; from the Dominion and Power of Vice, and from the General Contagion and Corruptions of the Present Age: Whereby we may recall That First and Purest Age of Primitive Innocence, in which the Life of Man was perfectly agreeable

to

to the Dignity of his own Nature, and nearest in Resemblance to the Divine. There are but Two Ways of Accomplishing this Great Work, which can never be completed but by Art and Exercise: The Latter of these Two is perfected by Labour, and the Former by Philosophy. That Immense and Extensive Body of Knowledge, which takes in the *Ideas* of all Things Human and Divine, which comprehends all Arts and Sciences, the Description of all the Vertues, all Schemes and Systems of Government, and in short the Whole Universe, as it stands limited by the Well-known Boundaries of Earth and Heaven, is comprized and briefly denoted by the one Single Name of *Philosophy*; which sets the Mind free from its Imprisonment in the Body, subdues all the Lusts and Unruly Appetites, and teaches us how to Advise and Govern, both Ourselves and Others, that we all may Live Well and Happily. Let the Candidate for the *Senatorial Dignity* follow this Great Mistress, and listen to all her Dictates and Precepts: And let him not affect a Life of Solitude and Retirement, or Walk by himself, in the *Forum*, the *Temple*, or the *Courts* of *Judicature*, when there is no resort to those Places: Let him not shun the Sight and Conversation of his Fellow-Citizens, or Retire to a Dark Cell, and a Life of Idleness and Obscurity. But let him Delight himself in Society, and in a Free and Open Communication with those of his own Country, and with That Publick Body he is bound to Defend and to Adorn. There is no Lustre in Vertue, Good Sense, and Wisdom, when they are Shut up and Confined to Darkness and Solitude. Let them come forth, and appear upon the Stage of Business: For Wisdom, when Retired and in Obscurity, is of no more Use, than the Treasure of a Miser, whilst it lies buried under Ground. They are Both as Unprofitable, as when we really are without them. Nothing appears with more Grandeur and Lustre, than Vertue, just risen from her Cell, and coming abroad in the View of Mankind, Disdaining her Former Obscurity,

curity, and shewing herself openly to the World, that all Eyes may be fixed upon her Beauty, and all Ears open to her Precepts. It is in fact hardly possible for the Best and most Judicious to know, when a Man is truly Excellent, unless they have made a Trial and Experiment of his Vertues: The Course and Barriers are the Place of Trial for the Race-Horse: The Ring, or the Stage, for the Wrestler and Combatant: And the Good Senator can never be truly Known, but by his Actions and Exploits.

CHAP. VII.

The CONTENTS.

Of the Manner of Electing *the Senator. All* Canvassing *Unlawful. The Ways of attaining to* Honours *and* Offices. Avarice *fatal to a State.* Honours *ought not to be Sold. All* Elections *ought to be under one Established Rule.* Magistrates *should set the People a* Good Example. Mal-Administration *the Ordinary Cause of all* State-Revolutions. *Out of what Order of Subjects the* Senator *should be* Elected. *The* Manner *of* Electing *as different as the Forms of Government. Of* Elections *by Lot. How the* Greeks *Elected their* Senators. *How* Candidates *ought to be* Qualified. *Who ought to be* the Electors. *The Ill Practices of* Ambitious Candidates. *The* Mob *excluded from all* Elections. *Of the Interest of the* Crown *in* Elections. *How the* Romans *Elected their* Senators.

Hitherto we have been Treating of That Particular Discipline and Manner of Education, which are Necessary to Qualify the *Accomplish'd Senator*, for the Attainment of True Happiness in Private Life, and of the Happiness of his Country, by a Publick Administration. And we Flatter ourselves, that Enough hath been said upon this Subject. But since Nature, in her own Strength, is not able to furnish us with Knowledge sufficient to make us truly Wise and Happy: And since these Great Ends are to be attained only by Study and Exercise; we must pursue our Improvements to the Utmost, and still Study on, at least whilst there is any thing Remaining, of which we are Ignorant: Or, in other Words, the Words of *Seneca*, We must Study so long as we Live, or so long as we find any Benefit or Advantage by what we Learn. By this we may certainly know, when we have made a Good Progress in Vertue, if we find our Lusts and Unruly Desires Quelled and Subdued within us, by the Superior Force of Reason and Vertue; that All is Calm within us; and that without us, our Life and Actions are exactly agreeable to the Rules of Justice, Prudence, and Temperance, and nearer Resembling a Heavenly than an Earthly State. I proceed now to Enquire into the Form and Manner of Electing the *Senator* to his High Trust and Office: And on this Occasion, the Strictest Equity, and the most Exact *Decorum*, ought never to be Omitted.

Of all the Benefits and Advantages, which contribute to the Preservation both of the Being and Happiness of a *Commonwealth*, there is none Greater, or more for the Glory of a State, than what accrues to it by a Timely Care and Wise Provision, not to admit any to a Publick Trust or Office, but those, who are most Eminent for their Prudence, Wisdom, and Vertue: And in all Publick elections, to make Choice of such Men only, who are Recommended by the Laws, and their own Private Good Character; by the Dignity of their Station, the Weight of their Example, their Modesty, and other Well-known, Vertues and Accomplishments: And not pushed into Power, by Force and Violence, or by Ambition and Bribery. The Dignity of the Magistracy is a Concern of the Utmost Consequence to a State, and requires the Nicest and most Critical Discernment. For the Generality of the People are easily induced to believe those Men to be Wise, and Good, and Honourable, whom they see Preferred and Entrusted with Power; and Behave towards them, and Address to them as such. Indeed Power and Magistracy are a Sort of Private Tribute, or Acknowledgment, paid to a Particular Person by his own Country, in Return for his Great Vertues and Eminent Services. It is therefore the Duty of every Good Man, and every Good Citizen,

tizen, in his Pursuit after any Perferment, or when he stands for any Office in the Magistracy, to have always in View the Safety and Honour of his Country, rather than his own Private Power, or the Advancement of his Fortune. The Examples of some of the Old *Romans*, such as *Sylla, Cinna, Carbo, Marius, Pompey, Cæsar*, and Others, are by no means to be followed by the Modern *Senator*. For by their Ambitious Designs, and their Factious, Tumultuous, and Seditious Proceedings, they brought on a Civil War, and Overturned the Constitution of the *Commonwealth*. What *Lucan* says of *Cæsar* and *Pompey*, is well worth our Observation:

> *Good Fortune to the Utmost Height will Soar:*
> Pompey *could bear no Equal in his Pow'r,*
> *And* Cæsar *no Superior.* ———

It would be much for the Publick Interest, if a Law or Laws were made, for Restraining Ambition, and for Preventing the Common Practice of Soliciting and Canvassing for Places and Offices in the State. Such a Law was wisely Contrived by the *Romans*, at that very Time, when their Commonwealth was in the most Flourishing Condition. For among them to Canvass openly and publickly for any Place or Office in the State, was Punished with Banishment. This is That Sort of Ambition, which I look upon as justly Culpable and Worthy of Censure; whereby Daring Men, not having any Regard to the Publick Laws, or to Common Honesty, are tempted to aspire to the Highest Honours and Offices of a Government, and to attain the Possession of them, by Force and Violence, by *Doles, Largesses,* and *Entertainments*, or by any other Indirect and Dishonest Practices. There are many Candidates, who in a Professed Distrust and Diffidence of their own Vertues and Due Qualifications for an Office, set up for

Honours

Honours and Dignities, to which they have no other Pretensions, but by Corruption and Bribery. And a more Fatal and Pernicious Pest and Plague than this is, cannot well break out, and spread itself in any Government whatsoever. Men of this Character have a Natural Aversion to Vertue and Honesty, and look upon Riches as the only Proper Means of Acquiring Honours and Preferments. All their Care is to add to their own Private, and not to the Publick Stock; because they imagine that Wealth, and not Vertue, has the Disposal of all Publick Dignities and Offices. In every *Commonwealth*, where such Men are in Power, it must follow in Course, that Covetousness, and the Inordinate Desire of Wealth, will most certainly prevail; and Luxury, Deceit, and Fraud, Strife and Contention, and a General Contempt of all Laws and Offices, Human and Divine, will be the Natural and Undoubted Offspring of such Foul and Unclean Parents. Whoever gives into this Sort of Principles, will always have an Eye to what is for his Interest and Advantage, without any Regard to what is Honest and Vertuous; and when he plainly sees that Vertue is really Disrespected, as well as Unrewarded, and that no Regard is paid to her in the Disposal of Offices and Preferments; he will set himself upon acquiring Power and Dominion over his Fellow-Citizens, and upon crushing those beneath him, by all manner of Fraudulent and Dishonest Artifices, or by Force and Violence. Whilst the Poor Oppressed Subjects are forced to bow down their Necks, to live in Misery, and in a State of Vassalage and Servitude to the Rich and Mighty; whom not Vertue, but Power, Luxury, Treachery, and Deceit, have set in Authority, and placed them above their Brethren. These are They, with whom Vertue and Honesty are of no Weight, when the Balance is set, and their own Private Interest is put into the Opposite Scale. And These are the Men, who can basely Prostitute the Laws, Rights, and Liberties of their Country, and even Publick Justice itself;

expose

expose them to Sale, or set them up to Auction. When there was but too great a Number of this Sort of *Senators* in *Rome, Jugurtha*, well observing the Corrupt State of the City, is said to have Exclaimed in this Manner: *O Venal and Mercenary* Rome! *How art thou Exposed to Sale, if thou could'st but find Buyers?* When the *Lacedæmonians* consulted the *Oracle*, about the Manner of Establishing and Perpetuating their Government, *Apollo* gave this Answer, *That Nothing but Avarice could be the Ruin of* Sparta: And to avoid the Ill Consequences of this Fatal Prediction, they called in all their Gold, Silver, and Brass Money, and forbad the Use of those Metals in their Coin: Instead of which, they gave out a New and Baser *Species* of Money made of *Iron*, much fitter to raise Contempt, than to give any Allurement, and of no Use, but to carry on the Ordinary Business of Trade, and to make Commerce circulate.

There is Nothing in which a Government can better employ all its Care and Caution, than in preserving its Honours and Dignities from being Prostituted and Exposed to Sale, liable to be Marketed and Exchanged for Money, instead of being made the Prizes and Rewards of Vertue. Nor is it easy to be too Strict and Rigorous in Punishing Those, who are Bribed and Hired to oppose and carry on a War against Vertue. Avarice is a Compendious Way of Ruining a State. For when the Rich and Wealthy have plainly gotten the Advantage and Ascendant over the Good and Vertuous, every Subject and Citizen will naturally make it his Whole Study and Endeavour, to improve his Fortune rather than his Character; and how soon then must a State be Over-run with Delicacy and Effeminacy, Fraud, Luxury, Covetousness, and all other Vices whatsoever? Where this is the Case, Vertue will soon be run down and trod under foot. The Piety of the *Priest*, the Bravery of the *Soldier*, the Prudence, Fidelity, and Diligence of the *Senator*, and the Civil Discipline of the Whole

Body

Body of the People, will be all set aside, to make room for Avarice and Self-Interest, for Shameless and Undaunted Impudence, for Violence and Oppression, Injustice, Luxury, and All, even the most Unclean, Savage, and Barbarous Vices. It is therefore absolutely Necessary, that an Established Form, and Regular Method should be always strictly observed in the Choice of Magistrates, as the ready Means to preserve Vertue in its fullest Lustre, and to secure the Interest and Elections of such Men only, who are, by their Wisdom and Goodness, best Qualified for a Publick Trust. As to the Way and Manner of Chusing Fit Persons to serve in the Lesser or Lower Offices of a Government, it is not (at least in this Place) much for my Present Purpose, to make a Particular Enquiry about them. The Proceedings and Validity of all such *Elections*, must be Regulated and Ascertained, by the Laws and Customs of every Society. But since the *Senator* is the First of all Magistrates, and the most Important Officer of the State, with whom is entrusted the Sole Power of Advising in all Publick Affairs, and upon whom all the Motions of Government Turn; no Care and Pains should be omitted, in the orderly Conducting of such Elections, in which a Whole Nation, both as to its Safety and Welfare, is so very nearly Interested. When a State is unhappily placed under the Direction of a Sett of Corrupt and Wicked *Senators*, its Affairs can never be Well and Duly Administered; and it will be very Difficult to trace the Footsteps of Common Justice and Equity, or to discover so much as the Least Remains, or perhaps the very Form of Religion, in such as a Government. Fraud, Treachery, Injustice, and a Contempt of every thing that is Sacred, will soon take hold of, and infect the Populace; when once their Superiors set them a Bad Example, and lead them, like Beasts following the Track, into all Vice and Corruption. The Vices and Corruptions of those in Authority, have very often been the Occasion of Political Changes and Revolutions, and of turning a

State

State either upside-down, or quite out of its First Commodious and Regular Channel. *Limited Monarchies* have been changed into *Absolute*, or the *Unlimited Dominion* of a Single *Tyrant: Aristocracies* into *Oligarchies*; and *Democracies*, or *Popular States*, into the Wild and Confused Ravages of the *Mobb* and *Rabble*.

For the Better Preventing of these Mischiefs, and the more Orderly Conducting of all *Senatorial Elections*, Three Things are chiefly to be Considered. *First*, Out of what Order of Men the *Senator* is to be Elected: *Secondly*, By whom he is to be Elected: And *Thirdly*, After what Manner and Form the *Election* is to be made and perfected. To the *First* of These Questions I have (as I conceive) already given a Sufficient Answer, in that Part of my Present Work; in which I have shewn at large, that He ought to be Chosen out of the *Order* of the *Nobility*, or of the *Gentry* of the First Rank and Condition. To the *Second* Question, Who are to be the *Electors?* we are now to give an Answer: And before we can do this Effectually and to the Purpose, we must once more consider a little the Various Forms of Government, and their Laws and Customs: After which it may be easily seen, what Method of Electing is most agreeable to the Constitution of every Particular State, and which of all the Several Methods is the Justest and most Perfect, whereto a Wise and Well-ordered People should always take Care to Conform.

In the Choice of all Magistrates of all Orders and Degrees whatsoever, and especially in the Choice of *Senators*, the People of every Nation under Heaven have *Three Things* chiefly in their View; and These are Liberty, Riches, and Vertue. Which of These *Three* is First in their Affections, and whereto they pay the Greatest Regard, a Short Enquiry will Determine. They, who live under a *Popular Form* of *Government*, are always most Fond of Liberty, which is their Chief Good and Greatest Delight; and no wonder they look wholly to this in all Elections, since the very
Constitution

Constitution of their State is founded thereon. The Liberty they are so much in Love with, does (as they imagine) consist chiefly of the Two Alternate States, and Conditions of Governing and Obeying: And according to their Notions of Justice and Equity, no one Private Subject has more Right to the Sovereign Power than another; which Power, because it cannot be in the Hands of All, at one and the same time, every Member therefore of the *Commonwealth*, ought to take it in his Turn, when to Govern, and when to be in Subjection. Hence it was, that in the Choice of their Magistrates, they always made Use of *Lots*, and no One was Excluded from the Right of Drawing, or of being a Candidate. But certainly Rash and Unadvised Chance had more of Interest in this Affair, than Reason and Good Counsel. The Whole Design of this Institution was only to Preserve Liberty, Sacred and Inviolable: For since they looked upon themselves as a Body of Men in every respect Equal, they appealed to Fortune in the Decision of all Differences between them, on purpose to prevent the Poor from having Dominion over the Rich, the Learned over the Unlearned, the Strong over the Weak, and the Wise over the Ignorant: Lest by their Wealth, Learning, or Wisdom, they should Impose upon their Clients, or Those under them; and in a little Time perhaps, some Single Person should make Seisure of the Common Liberties, and Subject the Whole Republican Constitution to his own Absolute Power and Dominion. The Advocates for this Form of Government, always take it for granted, that a Whole Multitude will be much more Zealous and Hearty for the Preservation of the Liberties and Welfare, and the Improvement of the Happiness of the *Commonwealth*, than either a *Few Select Governors*, or a *Single Person*, or *Sole Monarch*. In such a State as this, the Condition of all the Subjects is exactly One and the Same; and there is no Difference between the Rich and Poor, the Wise and the Ignorant, or between any other Orders and Cha-

racters

racters of Men, but only between the Freeman and the Slave. In an *Oligarchy*, the Case is quite otherwise: For there a Few Noted Men, for their Wealth, Wisdom, and Good Conduct, Superior to the Rest, have the Whole Administration of the Government put into their Hands. But in States strictly *Popular*, the Ignoble, the Poor, the Mechanick, the Husbandman, and Hireling, have the same Pretensions to Power, and are capable of being Elected into the Highest Offices.

Among the *Old Athenians*, there were at Two several times Two Distinct Forms of a *Commonwealth*. Under the *First* of These, the Supreme Power was entirely in the Hands of a *Select Number* of Men, eminent for their Wealth or Wisdom: And under the *Second*, the Supremacy was shared in Common by the Whole Body of the Freemen, or Denizons of *Athens*. The *First* of these Forms was introduced by *Theseus*, who from a Wild, Wandering, and Savage Way of Life, drew the People together into One City, and persuading the most Powerful among them, that a Popular State was Preferable to Monarchy, did accordingly Establish it in such a Manner, that the Supreme Power was entirely in the People, whom he made his Equals in every respect; the Rights and Titles he Reserved to himself, being only These *Two*, That He was to be the Keeper of their Laws, and their Leader and Commander in all Warlike Expeditions. He Instituted one *General Court* and *Council*, consisting of the Whole Body of the People, and made no Difference between the Nobles and the Commons, but only this, That to the Nobles should belong the Holy Offices and Care of Religion, the several Functions of the Magistrate, and the Administration of Justice: Though with this Restriction, and under these Limitations, That on no Account whatsoever they should Claim any Precedence, or any Honours or Dignities, Superior to all other Members of the *Commonwealth*, but remain in a Perfect State of Equality. This Great Founder of the *Athenian State*,

was

was not (as *Aristotle* witnesses) Ambitious of a Kingdom, but Behaved as one of the People, and Instituted a Government, which was always looked upon, as Agreeable in every Part, to Justice, Equity, and the Happiness of Mankind. The Administration of his Government, was not carried on by Force and Popular Violence, but calmly Directed by Reason and Judgment; and the People were made Happy by the Best and Noblest Means, the Honesty of their own Private Lives, and Obedience to the Publick Laws and Magistrates. To this Original Plan of Government laid down by *Theseus*, some Additions were afterwards made by *Draco*, during his Administration. He found it Necessary to Introduce Penal and Sanguinary Laws: And after him *Solon*, (as we are informed by *Plutarch*) when the *Athenians*, by their many Seditions and Tumults, had Narrowed and Contracted their State to the *Oligarchical Form*, gave them New Laws and Offices, not much different from their First Institution and Introduced the *Cense-Books* and *Tax-Rolls* of their People. Besides This, there was a Later Form of Government, or rather a Second *Democracy* at *Athens*, the Founders and Contrivers of which were *Clisthenes*, *Aristides*, *Pericles*, and *Demosthenes*, during the Course of their several Administrations. These Men, over-fond of Popular Applause, reduced all Orders and Degrees of Citizens to a State of Perfect Equality. They increased the Numbers of the *Tribes*, and enrolled not only Slaves, but Foreigners, as Freemen and Denizons. *Clisthenes* brought in the Judgment and Sentence of *Ostracism*, to be inflicted on all Those, who, from the Opinion the People had of their Superior Wisdom, Prudence, and Vertue, might be suspected of a Design to Infringe upon the Common Liberties. *Aristides* permitted the Magistrates to be Chosen out of the Meanest and Lowest of the People. *Pericles* lessened the Authority of the *Senate*, and very much impaired its Lustre and Dignity. *Demosthenes* not only suffered himself to be Seduced

into

into an Opinion, favourable enough to the Licentiousness of the People, and to the Prevailing Notion, that the Supreme Power was wholly vested in Them; but to ingratiate himself still further, did, in a Set and Publick *Oration*, openly Defend their Supremacy, and Applauded their Licentiousness. *Aristotle*, and his Great Leader and Preceptor, *Plato*, with many other Political Philosophers, never Condemned the Popular Form, as an Absurd or Unjust Institution, provided the Laws of it were Good, and the People naturally Civilized, and Well disposed to keep and observe those Laws themselves had made. For who can find Fault with That *Commonwealth*, in which, though the People are the Legislators, the Lords and Makers of the Law, yet the Law, when once it is made, is to Them as a Sole Monarch and Absolute Sovereign, whom they are never to Disobey, and in whose Keeping are all their Liberties? I can readily grant, that such a Constitution is of all Others the most Desirable, if it could be Secured from those Tumultuous and Seditious Disorders, and those Turns and Changes, which in Governments strictly Popular are almost Unavoidable. The Multitude are well known to be a Changeable Uncertain Body, apt enough to Abuse their own Just Liberties, and to run them into Excess and Extravagance. When they are Uppermost, they are the Worst of all Tyrants; and when they are kept Under, the most Abject Slaves. Give them but a Tattle of the Sweets of Liberty, and they will greedily take down deeper Draughts, till they are Surfeited and Intoxicated with it. If by their Exploits and Behaviour, they have gained some small Power or Reputation, they presently grow Proud and Insolent, claim Precedence of all their Neighbours,, and will hear of no Rivals or Competitors in Glory. By these means they Contract a General *Odium*, raise Feuds and Animosities, grow Turbulent and Seditious, and by the Intemperance of their Ambition, are at last carried away into all manner of Confusion and Disorder.

Disorder. Out of which, sometimes arises that Fleeting Short-lived Form, or Shadow of a Government, which the *Greeks* call *Oclocracy*, or the Insolent Dominion and *Tyranny* of the *Mobb* and *Rabble*.

In other *Commonwealths* of a Different Make, it often happens, that the Subjects or People, dazzled with the Lustre of Riches, and too much Addicted to Covetousness, are thereby tempted to make Choice of such Governors, who have no other Recommendation, but their Wealth; to imagine, that only such Men are to bear the First Honours, and Execute the Highest Offices of State, and to make them the Keepers and Conservators of all the Publick Liberties. This Sort of Government, wherein the Supreme Power is lodged in a Few Hands, the *Greeks* call an *Oligarchy*, in which the Rich and Wealthy are always at the Helm, and have the Sole Administration in their own Hands. In all *Oligarchies*, the *Senators*, and other *Magistrates*, are chosen either out of the Whole Body of the People, or out of a Select Number of Candidates, either by Lot and Balloting, or by the Votes and Suffrages of the Electors. But when Riches are the only Qualification for Power, and all Honours are made Subservient to Wealth, the Subject will be sure to Lay out all his Pains and Study in the Improvement of his own Private Fortune, rather than in the Attainment and Increase of True Vertue. And in every State, where Wealth is had in such High Veneration, and almost Deified, Avarice will soon come to have the Sole Dominion: Sanctity, Piety, and Religion, will be thrown down and demolished, to make room for the Setting up of this *Idol*; to whose Fatal Influences are owing, all the Plagues and Disasters, which can possibly Visit and Infest a *Commonwealth*.

Monarchies and *Aristocracies* are indeed the only Forms of Government, in which the Greatest Regard is paid to Vertue in all Publick Elections, as the Surest Guide to Happiness, and the

Great

Great Promoter of the Good and Welfare of all Communities and Societies of Men. In the Choice of a King, whether the Electors proceed by Lot and Balloting, or by Votes and Suffrages, their Way is to fix upon such a Candidate, who by his Sanctity, Prudence, and other Great and Heroick Accomplishments, is remarkably Distinguish'd, and more Excellent than all his other Competitors. The same Method is to be Observed in the Choice of Many, or of a Select Number, where the *Aristocratical* Form is looked upon as preferable to the *Monarchical*, or when they chuse rather to be Governed by a *Few* than by a *Single Person*. Such Electors will not look upon the *Lot* and *Ballot*, or what Blind Uncertain Fortune shall please to Determine, as the sure Proof and Testimony of that Good and Just Character, which alone can recommend a Candidate to the First and Highest Offices of State: But, with more Safety and a better Assurance, will Depend altogether on the General Judgment, the Fixed and Established Opinion, and the Experience which the Best and Wisest of their Fellow-Subjects have of a Man's Character: And when they are agreed in their Judgment, they may very easily agree in their Choice. This General Voice is the Noblest Testimonial, and the Best Recommendation to Power: And accordingly the Poet, when he would describe a Patriot in full Glory, supposes Him walking in the Publick Streets, and says,

> *The People point, and shew him to each other,*
> *And cry, That's He.* ———

An Established Character, which is well supported by the Prevailing and Concurrent Testimony of the Best and Wisest Members of a Society, is the very Height of Glory, and the Noblest Qualification for all the Honours our Country can bestow upon us. Whilst the Popular *Urn*, or *Ballot-Box*, is only one of Blind
Fortune's

Fortune's Tools and Implements, by which She deals out Honours and Offices in a Loose Uncertain way, and Scatters them at random, without Reason, and without Judgment: Whilst Vertue stands by unregarded, and has no Share in the Disposal of these Favours. There are indeed some *Free States*, in which I do by no means Condemn the Use of *Lots*, either before, or after the Publick have passed their Judgments, upon the Good and Vertuous Characters and Qualifications of the several Candidates. For in many such Societies, there may possibly be Great Numbers of Wise, and Good, and Vertuous Men; and the Superiority or Difference between them may not easily be Determined, without appealing to Fortune: In which case the Use of the *Lot* is not only Allowable, but the only Way of Deciding an Election justly and impartially. And besides the Judgment a Candidate is supposed to have formed, of his own Worth and Qualifications for the Place or Office in Question, when he has also the Concurrent Judgment of his Fellow-Citizens, and can at last obtain the Judgment of Fortune in his own Favour, he is then Fully and Rightfully Chosen. Hence a Magistrate *Elect*, was by the *Latins* said to be *Allotted to his Office*, thereby intimating, in what Manner he was Chosen. The *Lot*, or *Ballot*, is still in Use among the *Venetians:* And in the Choice of the *Senate* of *Fifty*, the same Method was Prescribed by *Solon*, when he compiled the Laws of *Athens*. Among whom the Way and Manner was, to take down the Names of certain Persons, chosen out of Every *Tribe*, well approved and qualified for the Senatorial Dignity, in Particular Rolls, which were put into a Box provided for that Purpose: In another Box were put as many *White Beans*, as there were Names or Rolls in number, and as many *Black:* Out of which *Boxes* when the Name of a Candidate was drawn, with a *White Bean* drawn against it, such Candidate was duly elected a Senator; and They, against whose Names a *Black Bean* was drawn, were Dismissed and sent Home, as

having

having no Interest in That Election. Hence *Thucydides* calls the *Athenian State, The Council of the Bean.* Among the *Romans,* once the Lords and Masters of the Universe, the Manner of Electing their Senators was Various, according to the Various Turns and Revolutions, which at different times obtained in their Commonwealth. Their *Kings, Consuls, Dictator, Tribunes, Censors,* and *Emperors,* had in their several Turns, and in the Different Stages and Periods of their Government, the sole Power of chusing their Senators. But the *Lot* or *Ballot* was never in Use till *Augustus*'s time, when he restored and filled up the *Senate.* This, however, is certain, That in all their Elections to this High Dignity, they never regarded any other Qualifications, but Vertue and Honour, Renown and Glory, Birth and Blood, Order and Station, and the Credit and Reputation of having discharged the *Questor*'s, *Censor*'s, or other High Trust and Office in Government, Faithfully and Honourably.

As there certainly is nothing Greater and Nobler, more Illustrious or truly Divine, than Vertue; so can we not fix upon any one thing whatsoever, which ought to have more Weight and Influence in all *Senatorial Elections* and *Returns.* For nothing but Vertue can establish the *Senatorial* Character upon the Solid, Immoveable Foundations of Justice, Fortitude, and Prudence. It is indeed highly Convenient, that all Magistrates, in every well-regulated Commonwealth, of what Order and Degree soever they are, should be well accomplished in all these Vertues; but the *Senator* ought to be a Complete Professor, and a Perfect Master of them: Because the Custody of the Laws, the Arbitration of the Publick Liberties, and the Preservation of the Government, Whole and Entire, are entrusted in his Hands, and committed to his Care and Direction. From a Vicious and Corrupt Magistrate the People very easily take the Infection, and become Wicked and Debauched: Whilst on the other hand, by the Vertues and
Good

Good Example of the Magistrate, they are easily Reformed and Amended. When Men in Power give a Loose to any *Vice*, they are doubly Criminal; because they are sure to have many Followers. For in every Country, such as the Princes are, so will the People be: And whenever their Leaders and Governors change their Manners and Behaviour, the Subjects and Followers will take care to be in the Fashion. *Plato*, as he is quoted by *Cicero*, very well observes, and with a good deal of Wit, as well as Judgment; *That when the Masters of the Concert alter their Voice and their Notes, the* Chorus *naturally give into the same* Key *and Tune*. But certainly it is much more Pertinent to observe, that when Princes and Governors change their Morals and Way of Life, the Publick Manners, Rites, Customs, Institutions, and the Whole Commonwealth, are thereupon immediately altered. The Consequence of a Bad Example from our Superiors or Those in Authority, (the greatest Misfortune that can well befall a Nation) being plainly this, That when they are not only Bad themselves, but make others so too, they become answerable not only for their own Faults, but for the Vices and Corruptions of a Community; and are as wicked by Proxy, as they are in their own Persons. Such Men certainly deserve double Punishment, who add the Sins of a Multitude to those of their own Committing: And with what Face can they Exhort others to follow Vertue, when themselves have Forsaken it? or to Obey the Laws, which themselves have Broken? Among the *Romans*, *Scylla* was held in the Utmost Contempt, and became perfectly Ridiculous, because he was perpetually Exhorting his Fellow-Citizens, Adjuring, and even Compelling them, to be Sober, Chaste, Frugal, and Temperate; when at the same time it was very well known that Drunkenness, Luxury, and Intemperance, were his own Favourite and Peculiar Vices. *Lysander*, though he went into quite the Opposite Extreme, was altogether as culpable as *Scylla:* For he readily and openly indulged all his

Fellow-

Fellow-Citizens in the Habitual Commission of those very Vices, from which Himself most rigourously Abstained. *Lycurgus*, a Man far Superior to Both these, and well Worthy of the Name and Reputation he hath so justly Acquired, never Enjoined Others to keep and observe any Law or Precept whatsoever, but he kept and observed it Himself, and thereby set them an Example of Perfect Obedience and Conformity. It is therefore a Duty Incumbent upon all Citizens and Subjects, in all *Senatorial Elections*, and in the Choice of every Magistrate, who is to fill the Vacant Places or Offices of Publick Trust, to exert their Best Judgment and Utmost Prudence, in the free Exercise of That Right, with which, as *Electors*, their Country hath invested them: And they ought certainly to make Choice of such Men, who by their Capacity, Conduct, and Wisdom, by their many Vertues, Exploits, and Good Behaviour in Lesser Employments, have deserved well of the Publick, and gained a Just Pre-eminence over their Fellow-Citizens. The Way and Method of finding out such Candidates, and making an Acquaintance with their Characters, is not, as I conceive, by the Use of *Lots*, and *Balloting*: For whilst we think the Common Equality and Publick Liberties are best preserved by this Method, we thereby expose ourselves to much greater Dangers, and run the Risque of chusing such Men, who are not only Strangers to the Vertues, but Unworthy of the very Name and Dignity, of *Senators*. Let every Free-Subject therefore, in the Maintenance of this Common Right, keep the Publick Good always in View, and take Care how he Entrusts an Idle, Ignorant, or Unskilful Candidate, with Power, or gives him so much as the Chance or Alternate Turn, of Holding or Enjoying a Place or Office in the Commonwealth. For then are the Common Rights of the Subject secured to him in the Best Manner, when none but the Prudent, the Wise, and the Experienced Governor, can demand of him the Ordinary Returns of Submission and Obedience.

The

The only Best and most Rational Method of Electing *Senators*, is in my Opinion no other than this; To make those Members of a Commonwealth the Sole *Electors*, who by their Wisdom, Prudence, and Justice, have eminently Distinguished Themselves, and in the Strength of these Vertues, will not suffer the Least Vile or Scandalous Action that gives Just Offence, to pass Uncensured, and no escape being made a Disqualification for all Publick Trusts and Offices. In the *Republick* of which we are Members, and which is under the Direction and Government of *King*, *Senate*, and *People*, a Question may possibly arise, Whether the *Senator* is to be chosen by a *Few Select Electors*, or by the *Multitude*, or only by a *Single Person*? They who would have More than *One Elector*, do either admitt the Whole *Body* of the *People* to this Right, or only a *Select Order* or Number of them. Of the First Sort are They, who live under a *Popular*; and of the Second They, who live under an *Aristocratical* Form of Government. The Patrons of One of these Opinions must naturally Dissent from Those, who are of a quite Opposite Judgment concerning the Manner of conducting *Senatorial Elections:* And the Former Opinion is most agreeable to a *Democratical*, as the Latter is to an *Aristocratical* Form of Government. From This Contention between the Patrons of Both Opinions, may probably arise Tumults and Seditions; unless by laying aside their Mutual Discord and Contentions, Both Parties come to an Agreement, that Each in his Turn shall enjoy its own Right and Power of *Election*. But if such an Agreement were really made and established, to the General Satisfaction of Mankind, yet the Tumults and Disorders consequent thereupon, would be altogether as Great as Those it was Intended to prevent. For every Man naturally passes a Wrong Judgment upon himself, and is easily persuaded to believe, that he excells his Neighbours in Wisdom and Conduct, and has better Pretensions to their Favour, than any other Candidate.

date. He readily imagines, that he is Despised and Hated by the Opposite Party, and raises Feuds and Animosities to the Splitting and Dividing of the Body Politick. After this, he has no longer any Regard to Merit, but leaves all the Vertues behind him, and sets up for Power and Magistracy, by an open Avowance of his Ambition, and in Strength of his Power and Wealth, the Number of his Clients and Followers, and the Zeal and Activity of his Friends, resolves to gain, by Force and Violence, or by Bribery and Corruption, what his own Vertues would by no means Entitle him to. Such Methods of Attaining Power readily tend to the Enslaving of a Free Body of Good and Worthy Citizens, and often give the Worst and most Wicked Governors an Absolute Power and Dominion over them; whilst Vertue, Justice, and Prudence, are set aside; and Vice, Injustice, Fraud, and Treachery, are let loose to Over-run, and Lay Waste, a Government. It is certainly a very Dangerous Experiment, for a Commonwealth to trust the Choice of their Magistrates in the Hands of the Populace, or Mixed Multitude; who are by no means Competent Judges of the Worth and Qualifications of their Candidates. They are too apt either to Envy and Malign, or Implicitly to Favour those Men, in whose Hands they have, by any Former Grants or Trusts, already Deposited their Safety and Interests. Partiality is more likely to Sway with them, than Sound Judgment and Discretion: They are easily Flattered, and won by Submission and Intreaty; and are naturally led to Esteem and Reverence those Men in the Highest Degree, who submit to the Lowest Methods of Canvassing and Soliciting their Favour. In short, all their Resolutions and Determinations are formed, not upon a Regular and Judicious Choice, but Rashness and Inconsideration; and very often Force and Violence have the Greatest Share in all their Proceedings. *There is* (as *Cicero* hath well observed) *neither Counsel, nor Reason, nor Discretion, nor Attention*

tion in the Mobb or Multitude; and the Wisest of Men have looked upon their very Best Proceedings, rather as Tolerable, than Commendable. They are more eager to Chuse by Affection, than by Judgment; and they are oftener Allured and Enticed, than regularly Inclined and Directed, to give their Votes and Suffrages.

However, therefore, the Customs, Usages, and Laws of some Commonwealths may determine the *Rights* of *Election*; we can never allow the Mixed Multitude any the Least Share or Interest in these Rights; nor can we think their Interposition therein consistent with the Welfare of a Well-Constituted Government. We *Polanders* are clearly of Opinion, that the *Right of Electing Senators* ought to be entrusted wholly in the Hands of a Single Person; One, who by his Superior Vertue, Wisdom, and Prudence, is allowed to be the *First Man* in the State: Because it is much easier for him to guard against all the Above-mentioned Dangers and Evils, which unavoidably attend all *Popular Elections:* But then this Right or Power of Electing must be Vested in him by the Laws, or Delegated to him by the People: And he must not Claim it to himself, or attempt to Usurp it, by Superior Power, Force, and Violence, by any Arbitrary Incroachments, or by Bribery and Corruption. It is the Undoubted Right of a *Free People*, to Chuse those *Senators*, in whose Keeping they deposite all their Interests: But (in our Opinion) they would do well and wisely, to give up this Right in Trust, and committ it to the Care of a *Single Elector*, who may more effectually answer the Great Ends of This Institution. *Romulus*, the *Father* and *Founder* of *Rome*, was the *Sole Elector* of Those *Hundred Citizens*, who composed the *First Roman Senate:* And by this Precedent, the *Kings*, his *Successors*, reserved all *Senatorial Elections* entirely to themselves. When the Proud *Tarquin*'s Unsuccessful Tyranny was at an End, and with him was Extinct the Whole Race of the *Roman Kings*, the Power of *Electing* to the *Senatorial Office* did not

Devolve

Devolve to Many, but was retained only in a Few Hands; for the *Consuls*, the *Censor*, the *Dictator*, or (when their Government was changed into a *Monarchical Form*) the *Emperor*, did in their Several Turns chuse all the Members of their *Senate*. This *Roman Precedent* our Ancestors of *Poland* very wisely Introduced into their Commonwealth; and by giving up their Rights into the Hands of the *King*, made him the *Sole Judge* of every *Candidate*'s Vertues and Qualifications, and the *Sole Elector* of such Persons, who by the Laws of *Poland*, were for their Age and Experience, their Nobility, Wisdom, and Prudence, well Qualified for the *Senatorial Office*. Hence it is, that our Kingdom has gradually Increased in Reputation by the Vertues of its *Senators*, as well as of its *Kings*; and our *Senate* hath been called, not only the *Great Council of Poland*, but of all the *North*. Let the *King* therefore with us have the Sole Right of Chusing all the Members of our *Senate*; and in the Exercise of this Right, we Require at his Hands, the utmost Efforts of all his Prudence, Fidelity, and Wisdom; and that he never Admitt a Partner or Associate in his Government, who has nothing at Heart but the Acquisition of Wealth, the Increase of his own Private Fortune, or of the Fortunes of his Family, or is perhaps only Skilful in Architecture, or Fortification: And that he make Choice of such Counsellors only, who know how to make Laws, to Govern a Nation, and Protect and Preserve their Fellow-Subjects. When we are Sick, or out of Order, we readily Resort to the most Learned and Skilful Physician. In the Cloathing of our Bodies, and the Building of our Houses, and in many other Cases of the same sort, we employ the Best and Most Experienced Workmen in their several Crafts and Possessions. And why then should we not be as Careful in providing for the Welfare of a Nation, and the Good Government of the People, by looking out for, and electing such

Men,

Men, who, by their Wisdom, may Preserve a Community in Peace and Happiness? No Cunning, Wisdom, or Diligence, however Keen and Active, can be better employed, than in Finding out and Promoting Men of this Character. A *Good King* will not only Enquire into those *Senatorial Qualifications*, which we have already mentioned, such as Good Birth and Education, and the several Arts and Accomplishments, which Fit a Man for Publick or Civil Life; and to Improve his Natural Genius and Capacity, by enabling him to Govern a Commonwealth well and wisely: But will also Examine the Candidates other Qualifications, such as his Moral Character, his Reputation, Family, Age, and Vertues. Nor is This All: But a farther Enquiry ought to be made, Whether the Candidate hath borne any Office in the Magistracy? And in what Manner, or with what Fidelity, Prudence, and Diligence, he Discharged it? For they, who have gone through some such Office, are the fittest Persons to be made *Senators*. Such was the usual Practice among the *Romans*, with whom the Order of *Magistrates* was always a Seminary or Nursery for the *Senate*. In short, a *Good King* ought always to have the Good and Welfare of his People in View: And if this be his Chief Aim, he will easily learn to Distinguish those *Counsellors* and *Senators*, whom his Country stands in most need of, and to Judge of their several Talents and Capacities. What These Talents are, and wherein consists the *Senatorial Prudence*, so absolutely necessary to the Preservation of a State; and what are his several Duties and Offices, I shall now proceed to enquire; whence it will plainly appear, what Caution a *King* ought to use in the Choice of his *Senators*, and what Rules and Precepts the *Senator* ought to Observe and Retain, in the Administration of Publick Affairs.

But

But since my *First Design* is swoln to an Uncommon Bulk, and spun out to too Great a Length; I think it Convenient to deferr the Prosecution of it to a *Second Book*; wherein all these Particulars shall be explained at large. For I would not have the *Reader's* Mind Over-burthened or Perplexed, by the Weight and Intricacy of those Subjects which we have hitherto Treated of.

The End of the First BOOK.

THE
Accomplish'd Senator.

BOOK II. CHAP. I.

The CONTENTS.

The Connection and Argument of the Second Book. *The Senator ought to be Well-acquainted with the* Constitution *and* Laws *of his own Country. It is greater to* Preserve *than to* Found *a Commonwealth. Every* Polish Senator *is a Mediator between* King *and* People. *The Senator how Posted in a State. The Common Artifices of* Tyrants. *The Office and Duty of a* King. *How He ought to Regard his* Senate. *The Humours of the* Mix'd Multitude, *and Rise of all* Seditions. *The Mixture and Harmony of the* Three Estates *of a* Kingdom. *How* Tumults *and* Seditions *may be appeased. Every* Order *or* Estate *in a Government ought to be Zealous in maintaining the Rights of the* Other Two. *Of the* Doctrine *of* Equality. *The Rights of the* Subject. *Of* Demagogues, *and Alterations in* Religion. *Of the* Four Cardinal Vertues, *the Great and Necessary* Qualifications *for the* Senatorial Office.

WHAT are the first Rudiments and Institutions of the *Senatorial* Dignity; what the Various *Forms* and Models of a *Commonwealth*, or Body Politick; and which of them best deserves the Preference, we have shewn at large in the

First

First Book; and (as we conceive) to the full and entire Satisfaction of our *Readers*. Therein are laid the First Foundations of that General Good and Common Happiness, in which are comprised all the Blessings and Benefits, and all the Renown and Glory, which Man in a Civil State is capable of, or which Heaven can bestow upon Human Societies. We shall now, in this *Second Book*, proceed to shew, What those *Particular Vertues* are, by which the *Senator*, after he hath gone through the first Elements of *Policy*, may at last attain the Fulness and Perfection of his High Character; and may make himself a Master of all That Wisdom, by which the Arts of Government are Learned and Practiced, with the utmost Skill and Dexterity.

Here then, in the First place, the *Good Senator* must take particular Care to make himself acquainted with the Whole Frame and Constitution of That State or Government, in which he is appointed a Counsellor or Minister: He must know, what Temper and Disposition the People are of; what are their Laws and Liberties; what their Manners and Discipline; their Rights, Usages, and Customs: And he must not only have Abilities to discover, and make a Proper Use of all the Ways and Methods, by which a State may Preserve and Improve itself, or add to its Acquisitions and Reputation; but also to Foresee and Prevent all those Dangers and Evils, by which it may be lessened in its Interests and Character, or its Constitution Shaken and Disordered, or perhaps entirely Dissolved and Subverted. 'Tis not enough for a *Pilot* or *Master* of a *Ship* to steer a Well-known Course, and to bring his Vessel safe into Port, when the Winds and the Seas are all along Favourable to him, during the Whole Voyage; unless he is also acquainted with Storms and Tempests, understands the Nature of them, has tried their Utmost Force, can guard against all the Dangers of the Deep; and when his Ship has been well Tossed and Shaken by the Winds and the Waves, can carry her into Harbour, where she may

may be at Rest and out of Danger. The Case is exactly the same with the *Good Senator*. If in a Well-Settled State, where All is Quiet and Orderly, he behave with Prudence, and govern Wisely and Discreetly; it is no small Credit to his Administration: But his Highest Merit, and Greatest Glory will be, when the Blasts of Sedition are in their Full Roar, and the Waves and Floods of Dissension break in and beat hard upon a State; then to interpose, and smooth and becalm a Ruffled Nation, to restore the Wished-for Tranquillity and Quiet, and Pacify the Minds of the People, allay their Mutual Heats and Resentments, and bring all things back into the Right Channel of Order and Discipline. *Theseus* was enough Renowned, because by his Conduct, the Wild, Vagabond, and almost Savage *Athenians*, were reduced from a Barbarous to a Civilized and Social State, and had a City and Laws given them by their Founder. But the Glory of *Solon*, was still Greater, because by his Wisdom and Management, this City was restored to Order, and kept in Unity with itself, at a Time when it was almost Distracted and Torne to Pieces, by Sedition and Civil Discord, and had other Laws and Offices given them by their *Restorer*, more Effectual to the Confirmation of the General Peace, and Publick Tranquillity. When the *Gauls* had brought *Rome* to the very Brink of Ruin, it was surely as Great in *Camillus* to Save, as in *Romulus* to Build it. The *Fabii* approved themselves to Defenders of their Country's Liberties, by Finishing the *Vejentine* War, in the very Neighbourhood of *Rome*, with so much Glory and Reputation: But the Glory of *Cicero* was still Greater, who saved *Rome* itself from the Traiterous Conspiracy of *Cataline*. *Pompey* might very well be called a *Lover* of his Country; but *Cicero* was the *Deliverer* of it; which gave *Pompey* an Occasion of Saying, *That if* Cicero *had not saved* Rome, *himself had wanted a City to Triumph in:* And the Great *Orator*, in one of his own Speeches, very justly Glories in Saving *Rome*, by his Counsels, which Others, by

their

their Arms, had only Magnified or Enlarged. Take all the Vertues of *Cæsar* and *Pompey* together, and when they are compared with those of *Scipio Africanus*, how great is the Difference between them? They indeed fought many Battles, and by many signal Exploits advanced the Glory of their *Country:* But when *Rome* was Tottering, and in its Last Convulsions, when there wanted but another Day to complete its Ruin, and the Victorious *Hannibal* was just ready to make Spoil of all its Liberties, *Scipio* interposed, as a Mighty Deliverer, and by Saving his Country, added to her Former Power and Glory: So True is That Aphorism;

' Tis Greater to Preserve, *than to* Acquire.

The Glory of *Cyrus* consisted altogether in Subduing Kingdoms, and Enlarging the Territories of his Empire; but he was enough Unhappy in the Possession of what he had gotten. His Acquisitions were Many and Great; but he had not the Art of Retaining or Keeping, what he had Acquired with so much Glory. In the ordinary Accounts of Life, a Day of Deliverance is much more Lucky and Memorable, than the Day of One's Birth, and it is far more Meritorious to be Active in the Preservation, than in the Propagation of Mankind. Let the *Good Senator* therefore exert all his Prudence, not only in taking Care of things Present, but in looking to and providing against the Turns and Contingencies of Futurity: And let his Views extend to every particular Concern and Circumstance, which may any way affect the Publick Welfare. Let him weigh well, and narrowly look into, all the Changes, Chances, Hazards, Turns, and Tendencies, a State is Subject to; by which means he will always have it in his Power to guard against any Dangers which may threaten his Country, either by Averting an Evil he Foresees is coming, or by Plucking up and Extirpating a Publick Mischief, before it has taken too Deep Root, or is grown up to a too Formidable Height.

Height. Nor would I have the *Senator* unacquainted with the Various Forms and Constitutions of other States and Commonwealths besides his own. Their Examples may be of Use to him, and he may reap many Benefits, by looking narrowly into the Laws by which they are Governed, and the Manner and Customs which obtain among them, or which are Introduced for their Greater Security and Preservation; together with the Changes and Alterations, by which a State is Reformed or Amended. The Order and Coherence of each Particular Constitution, the Manner of holding its Great Councils, the Disposition and Dependence of all its State-Offices, its Liberties, Dignities, Authority and Jurisdiction, are all Subjects of Importance, and well worth the *Senator's* most accurate Enquiries.

Here, in our own Country of *Poland*, where the *Senator* is as it were a *Mediator*, and has his Post assigned him Exactly in the Midst between the *King* and the *People*, it is a necessary Part of his Knowledge, to be able to set out the true Legal Limits and Boundaries of the *Royal* Prerogative, Grandeur, and Jurisdiction; and of the Rights and Liberties of the *Subject*. Differences and Contentions will often arise between *King* and *People*; whilst one Party is pressing forward, and aiming at too much Power, and the other falling back into an Excess of Liberty. These Contentions, when carried on with Intemperate Heats, and a Spirit of Violence, have very often, and very sorely Afflicted our Government. The Issue and Consequence of every such Struggle being commonly This, That where the *King* prevails over the People, he soon commences Tyrant; and where the *People* are successful, we presently see as many Tyrants start up, as there are Heads and Leaders of the Multitude. Now the Arbitrary Power of *Many Tyrants* is much more Intolerable than That of a *Single Person*. Death soon puts an End to the Usurpations of a Single Tyrant, or his Lusts and Passions may be easily allayed, or worne out by Satiety: But the Tyranny and Licentiousness of a Multitude are Insatiable, and their

their Insolence increases by being Indulged. They spread abroad and scatter their Poison every where, and transmit the Contagion of it to Late Posterity. To prevent these Evils, the *Senator* must Interpose with all his Diligence, and use his best Endeavours to preserve the Just Undoubted Liberties of his Fellow-Subjects, in that Regular and Legal State, in which they are held in common by all the Members of the Body Politick. From the Mid-way Station, where he is properly Posted, he must look out constantly, and keep a Watchful Eye upon the Publick Welfare, and exert his Utmost Diligence, in preserving the *Commonwealth*, from whatever Dangers or Detriment it may possibly be Exposed to, either by the Ambition of a Few, who are Aiming at more Power; or the Seditions of a Multitude, contending for more Liberty. For the *Senator*, in his Proper Post, and by the very Nature of his Office, is really a Judge and Arbitrator between the Quiet and Peaceable, and the Violent and Unruly; between Liberty and Servitude, between King and People.

Many are the Artifices of *Tyrants*, by which they set themselves to Invade and make Spoil of their People's Liberties. As it is Natural for them to entertain a Jealousy and Suspicion of All about them, who are justly noted for their Vertue, Goodness, and Wisdom; so their First and Greatest Care is to remove such out of the way: And when they are removed, all other Opponents, either by Force and Violence, or by their own Cowardice and Weakness, are easily brought under and Enslaved; after which, all Law and Justice are soon laid aside, and the Will and the Lust of the Usurper are the only Measure and Rule of Government. Agreeable to this Artifice, was the Advice given by *Periander* to *Thrasibulus*, when he bid him *Trim his Harvest, and Lop off all the Ears of Corn that grew above the Rest:* Thereby intimating, that he should put to Death all the Choicest Nobility, and most Eminent *Senators* of *Athens*. *Sextus*, the Son of *L. Tarquinius*, had an Intimation

mation given him, much to the same Purpose: For he fled to the *Gabii*, under Pretence of being Banished, though he was privately sent by his Father, on purpose to betray and enslave that People. When he had enough Ingratiated himself, he dispatched a Messenger to his Father, intreating his Advice, *How to Behave, in order to finish his Design* ? The Old Tyrant gave no Answer, but took the Messenger into his Garden, and in his Presence cut off all the Heads of the Poppeys, which grew Uppermost in the flower-beds. Upon the Return and Report of the Messenger, the Son took the Hint, put the Principal Men among the *Gabii* to Death, and then, by Successful Rapine and Violence, seized upon the Government, and put an End to the Liberties of That Republick. Besides This, there is Another Artifice of great Use to Tyrants and Usurpers; which is, to prevent, as much as possible, all Commerce and Intercourse, between the Better Sort of Citizens; and to keep them from Forming Societies, Clubs, Meetings, and Assemblies, either for the Friendly Entertaining, or Mutually Conversing with each other: And by all means to Discourage the Study and Improvement of the Liberal and Useful Arts and Sciences. There is also another Stratagem commonly practised by such Men; and that is, to foment Factions and Parties to sow the Seeds of Discord and Contention in Abundance, to raise Jealousies and Suspicions amongst Brethren and Fellow-Citizens; that they may worry one another, and consume their Substance in Personal Broils and Private Quarrels: Then, when they are Poor, to lay fresh Taxes and heavy Burdens upon them, on a Pretence of some War, or Warlike Preparations: By which means they may be drained of their Wealth, pinched and enfeebled by Poverty; and That Generous and Noble Spirit humbled and brought down, which is so Necessary and Serviceable to a Free People, in the Defence of their Common Rights and Liberties. These, and many such-like Artifices of Tyrants and Usurpers, the *Good Senator* ought to be well acquainted with,

that

that he may always keep himself upon the Guard, and be able to Foresee and Prevent a Coming Evil, before it falls upon, and infests his Country.

It is also a Necessary Part of the *Senator's* Duty, to enquire narrowly into the Office of a *King*, the Nature, Limitations, and Extent of his Authority. He ought to know, that *Kings* were made, not for their own, but their People's Sake; and that in all their Councils and Undertakings, they should prefer the Joint and Common, to any Separate or Private Interest whatsoever. They Govern by, and under the Law; and the Great Design of their Government is, that the Rights and Liberties of their People may be Maintained and Preserved. The *Senate* have an Authority and Dignity concurrent with the *Regal*; and to this Body they owe a Proper Deference and Regard, and should always be in Readiness to Protect and Defend it. The Authority of *Kings* was intended as a Security for the Good and Vertuous, and as a Terror only to the Wicked. The Supreme Power was lodged in their Hands, as an Avenger of Wrongs and Injuries, a Keeper and Protector of Liberty, and a Judge to Decide between the Evil and the Good. A truly Excellent Prince has the same Care over his Subjects, which the Shepherd has over his Flock; and all this Care is to make those under him Happy and flourishing. *Homer* calls *Agamemnon* the *People's Shepherd*; and *Plato*, in Imitation of *Homer*, calls a *Monarch*, the *Pastor* and *Curator* of Mankind. As a Father governs his Children, so ought a Good *King*, to govern his People, and not as a Lord domineers over his Slaves. In the Execution of the Paternal Office, a Good *Father* will not only Admonish and Reprove his Children, and endeavour to win them by Gentleness and Kindness, but will sometimes lay about him with the Rod, and deal out the Wholsome Severities of Chastisement and Correction: And just in the same Manner will a Good *King* behave towards his Subjects: He will convince

convince them, that he chuses rather to Preserve his People, than his own State and Dignity: He will be Awful and Rigid, Gentle and Merciful, when a Proper Occasion offers, or as the Seasons of Government require; and will in all Things approve himself a Father to his Subjects, by Defending and Protecting them in their Just Rights, and by Promoting their General Good and Common Interest. The Difference between a *King* and a *Tyrant* is plainly this, That the One is altogether as Solicitous in securing his own Private Advantage, as the Other is in taking Care of the Publick. Whilst a *Tyrant* is altogether intent on Pleasure, Honesty and Goodness are the Delight of a *King*. The Love of Wealth is as sure a Mark of a *Tyrannical*, as the Love of Honour is of a truly *Royal* Disposition. A *King* is encompassed on every Side by Free and Faithful Citizens; but Mercenary Foreigners are the Body Guards of a *Tyrant*. When *Alphonsus, King* of *Arragon*, was asked, *In what Subjects or Citizens he took most Delight?* His Answer was, *In Those, who were more afraid of any Evil that might possibly happen to him, than they were of his Person or Power:* And in this he was perfectly Right: For wherever we Fear, we very naturally Hate too: And therefore every Good *King* will always Repose more Confidence in the Fidelity, Love, and Affections of his People, than in the Strength of his Arms, or the Number of his Forces. In short, a King ought always to be considered and revered as the *Great Administrator* of Wisdom and Counsel, the *Defender* of the Laws, the *Arbiter* of Right and Equity, and the *Preserver* of the Common Liberties of his People. And for the better Discharge of all these High Offices, let him constantly resort to his *Senate* for Advice and Direction, and always Love, Honour, and Esteem That Venerable Body, and treat them with a Filial Regard and Affection. *Trajan*, one of the most Excellent *Emperors* that ever reigned over Mankind, would often, and with great Prudence,

call

call the *Senate* by the Name of *Father*: For as a *Father* cautions his Son in all the Interests and Advantages of Life; so does the *Senate* advise and direct their *King* in the making of Laws and Ordinances, and in all the Methods and Measures of a Wise Administration; by which a State is preserved in Peace and Happiness. These Things, and whatever else is to be met with in the Laws, Usages, and Customs of a Country, which may in any sort relate to the Office of a *King*, the *Good Senator* must take Care to be well acquainted with, and must add all this to his Other Accomplishments in Learning and Wisdom.

In the mean time, the People, or Mixed Multitude, are to be considered as an Inconstant fluctuating Body, among whom the Diversity of their Years and Ages naturally produces as great a Variety in their Humors and Undertakings. For since the Old, the Young, and the Middle-Aged, are all mingled together in one Common Mass, hence arise Great Differences and Dissensions; every one follows his own Will and Pleasure, in virtue of their Undoubted Right, and in the Free Exercise of their Common Liberties. Because they are naturally Free, every one imagines, that the Modelling of his own Manners and Conversation belongs entirely to himself: And they are easily persuaded, that Liberty consists in a Man's doing whatever he has a Mind, or a Power, to do. As their Manners and Ways of Education are vastly Different, so are their Wills and Inclinations; whence arises as great a Difference and Variety in their Opinions, concerning the Laws, Liberties, and Constitution of their Country. These Differences readily produce Divisions, Feuds, and Animosities; Jealousies, Misunderstandings, Tumults, and Seditions. Whence it follows, that the Rabble are always variously Affected towards the Government under which they Live. They, who have had a good Education, and a tolerable Insight into the Liberal Arts and Sciences, or are naturally Well Disposed and Inclined to Honesty

nesty and Goodness: They who have got the better of their Passions and Lusts, and are Enemies to Effeminacy, Debauchery, and Voluptuousness; All such will take Care to conform themselves and their Actions to the Rules of Justice and Equity, of Peace and Civil Society; will never Depart for a Moment, or even in the Minutest Article, from the Good Principles of Vertue, Fidelity, Religion, and Honour, handed down to them by their Fore-fathers: But will keep and retain them as a Legacy or Inheritance, which the Founders of their State have Bequeathed and Entailed upon their Posterity. Such Men very well deserve the Name and Character of Good and Faithful Subjects: But there is another Class of Citizens, who are entirely devoted to Domestick Folly and Licentiousness. A Home-bred Generation, who never Looked or Went abroad, in quest of any thing truly Magnificent and Illustrious; and never Did, or perhaps Heard of an Action, really Great and Worthy of Renown. Such Subjects are the Common Ringleaders of all Seditions, and by their Craft and Subtilty, often prove a Grievance, a Pest, and Plague to any Government. They know not how to behave Prudently, Peaceably, and Modestly, or to take Example by the Good and Vertuous; and yet are willing to be Ranked and Numbered with the Best and most Valuable of their Fellow-Subjects. Rather than be looked upon as Idle, Useless Creatures, born to no Purpose whatsoever, they are perpetually Studying and Inventing some New Artifice or Stratagem, by which they may Distinguish themselves, and get a Name and Lustre among Mankind. Hence they go on by Chance, rather than by Choice, to set themselves up as the Patrons and Assertors of Liberty, to Harangue the Mob, to raise a Cry and Clamour, and without Distinguishing between what is Sacred and Profane, to throw all things into Confusion. If they happen to Excell those about them in the Volubility of their Language, or in the Natural Turn of

their

their Genius, always ready to Promote Sedition and Disorder, then they set themselves up for Leaders and Conductors of the Blind and Unskilful, and undertake the Correction and Amendment of the Laws, Religion, Faith, and Manners of their Fellow-Subjects. A Conspiracy is formed both against *King* and *Senate*, and against every Subject, who is eminent for his Vertue and Piety; whilst under their Management and Direction, the whole *Commonwealth* must undergo a New and Thorough *Reformation*. These Incendiaries are by the *Greeks* called *Demagogues*, and by the *Latins*, *Worshippers of the Rabble*. Under Pretense of Defending the Publick Liberties, they raise New Troubles, and attempt new Changes in a Government; only to screen some of their own Faults and Iniquities from Justice; or Stir the Waters and Sow Discord and Contention, only to gratify their own Natural Turbulency and Spirit of Discontent: Or else because their own Patrimony is wasted, and their Private Circumstances much involved, or utterly impaired, perhaps by Intemperance, or some other Vice of a Deeper Dye, they are therefore resolved to kindle a fire, in which others may be consumed as well as themselves, and to throw their own, together with the Fortunes of the Publick, into one and the same Common Heap of Rubbish and Ruins: For when there is a Necessity of Perishing, they are very willing not to Perish alone. In Ancient *Rome* there were many of this Character; such as *Gracchus, Clodius,* and *Cataline*. Such was *Clisthenes* at *Athens*, with many Others in other Nations and Commonwealths.

In the Republick or Nation to which we belong, the Body Politick (as I have already observed) consists of Three Ranks or Orders of Men, closely Connected and United with each other; and in this Temperament, Harmony, and Conjunction, consists the Security and Happiness of our Government. But if these Constituent Parts and Members of the Body Politick are

Displaced

Displaced or Rent in Sunder, the whole Constitution is presently Deformed, and Over-run with Misery and Confusion. Other Governments, whose Constitution is altogether Simple and Uncompounded, are liable therefore but to one Great Turn and Alteration. But because our *Commonwealth* is mixed and compounded of *Three* several Parts, it must consequently be always in Danger of as many Changes and Revolutions. For if the King abuses his Just Power, and exceeds the Proper Bounds of his Regal Office, we are then liable to be Enslaved by a *Single Tyrant:* If the *Senate* are false to their Trust, we are in Danger of having many *Absolute Lords* and *Masters* set over us: And if the Multitude or *Populace*, by open Force and Violence, get the Better both of the *Regal Power* and *Senatorial Authority*, we shall then be visited with a *Mobb* and *Rabble* of *Tyrants*, the greatest Plague that can befall a Society. Unless, therefore, in every *Commonwealth*, thus Formed and Constituted, the Office, Liberty, Jurisdiction, Dignity, and Authority, of each of these *Three Orders* be punctually set out, ascertained, and circumscribed, by good and wholsome Laws, made for that Purpose; and every Member of each *Order* be duly and effectually Restrained, not only by their own Fears, but by special Penalties, from all Vice and Injustice, and from the Breach of those Laws, which confirm them in their several Powers and Dignities; the Honest Well-Disposed Subject will in vain look for Rest and Quiet, and all the Happiness of Private Life, under such a Constitution. Here then must the *Senator* interpose, and look narrowly to the Execution of his High Office: *He must* (as *Cicero* speaks) *consider well within himself, that, by his Office, he is the Representative of a Whole City or Society, whose Publick Interests are entrusted to his Personal Care; that it is his Duty to support the Honour and Dignity of his Country, to look well to the Observation of the Laws, to assign to every one his Proper and Peculiar Rights, and to give a true and faithful Account*

count of whatever is committed to his Charge. In his Private Capacity, he must put himself upon a Level, and live in Subjection to the same Laws and Rules of Equity, with the rest of his Fellow-Subjects, behaving in such a Manner, as not to be Despicable and Below his Character, nor yet Insolent, Aspiring, and Above his Brethren; but in all things Careful and Studious, always to preserve the *Commonwealth*, in the Ways of Peace and Honesty. It is likewise his Duty and Interest, to be Cautious and Moderate in the Right Use of his Liberty; *That Temperate Liberty* (as *Quintius* calls it in *Livy*) which is Health to every Good Subject; not That *Exorbitant Liberty*, which is often grievous to others, and as often betrays those who assume it, into many Rash Enterprizes, and pushes them headlong upon their own Ruin.

Whenever an Unruly People, prone to Licentiousness, are breaking out into any Publick Disorders, the Severity of the Law must be let Loose to Quell and Suppress them: It being the Undoubted Interest of every Government, to preserve its Good and Faithful Subjects, from being Injured and Insulted, by the Wicked and Unruly. Every *Commonwealth* is the Sole Undoubted Property of the Good Subject only: Whilst the Wicked and Profligate have justly Forfeited all Right thereto. It is indeed impossible to secure a State from all Commotions, Disorders, and Seditions whatsoever; and the Observation made by *Hannibal*, and recorded in *Livy*, is certainly Just and True; *That a Great City, or Society, can never be long at Rest. If it has no Enemies abroad, it will soon find some at home; and like other Great Bodies, if it is safe from all External Injuries, its own Weight and Vigour will very often Depress and Incommode it. We are Men* (says the *Comick* Poet) and *Frailty and Humanity are inseparable Companions.* Let our Pretensions to Wisdom, Prudence, and Goodness, be what they will, yet Corrupt and Fallen Nature will press forward in the Smooth and Declining Ways of Vice, with much more Ease and Alacrity, than when

we

we are climbing the Steep Ascent, and Height of Vertue. Besides this, daily Experience convinces us, that in every Community and Society of Men, there is always a much greater Number of the Weak and Wicked, than of the Wise and Vertuous. Whenever therefore the Storms of Sedition arise, and threaten the Publick Peace, the *Good Senator*, who is embarked with all his People, in one and the same Vessel, which is the *Commonwealth*, now surrounded and tossed to and fro by an unruly Tempest, will do well to follow *Cicero*'s Advice, and by bearing patiently the first Onset, by complying with the Present Humours of the People, by softning and alluring the Disaffected, by confirming those in their Loyalty, who have not yet gone Astray, and by Appeasing and Allaying the Turbulent and Outrageous; he may possibly prevent the Worst, and preserve a State from falling into the Hands, or being at the Mercy of the Vilest and most Profligate of all its People. Dissimulation and Connivance are sometimes not only Lawful, but very Useful and Necessary Expedients, where a Body of Men are engaged in any Wicked Design, by Mistake and Unpremeditated Error, and not with any Desperate and Malicious Intention. Where the Case is different, and Attempts are openly and voluntarily made, to carry on some Black and Barefaced Villany, any Kindness or Mercy shewn to the Leaders or Followers in every such Enterprize, is utterly Unlawful and Pernicious, and can end in nothing else, but the Destruction and Overthrow of all Government whatsoever. In order therefore to Restrain and Appease the Disorderly and Unruly Wills of the Multitude, and to Quell their Rash and Headstrong Motions, and Tendencies to Sedition, the *Senator* must apply his Best Diligence and Utmost Wisdom; always observing the Two Excellent rules laid down by *Plato*, and recorded in *Cicero*; By the *Former* of which, He must be sure to take Care, that in Defending the Rights and Liberties of his Fellow-Subjects, his Conduct may plainly appear to be altogether

influenced

influenced by the Noblest Principles, the Love and Care of the Publick, without any Regard to his own Private Advantage: And by the *Latter*, that all his Concern and Endeavours must extend to the Whole Entire Body of the *Commonwealth*; lest by his Zeal and Forwardness in the Defence of one Part, or Member of it, he be suspected of a Design to Desert or Betray all the rest. Whoever is Over-Active and Solicitous, in Maintaining or Promoting the Particular Interest of any one *Order* of the Government, distinct from, and exclusive of the rest, will thereby open a Gap and Inlet for Popular Discontent and Sedition, the Two Great Evils that never Fail to Weaken or to Overthrow a Government. The *Good Senator* ought to be alike Zealous for the *Royal Interests*, as for those of the *People*; and as ready to Defend the Cause of the *People*, as of the *Nobility* or his *Fellow-Senators*. The Wise, and the Weak, the Rich, and the Poor, with all other Ranks and Degrees of Men, are to be maintained in their several Rights, with the same Disinterested Zeal and Impartiality. It was the Want of such a Publick Spirit of *Patriotism* as this is, that occasioned all those Broils and Contentions, which so miserably Rent and Afflicted the *Athenian State*, and brought on those many Seditions, Tumults, Revolts, and Civil Wars, which were the Scandal and Overthrow of the *Roman* Government.

To Prevent these Mischiefs, the right Way and Method is, to be always Strict and Severe in the due Observation of the Great and Fundamental Rule of *Equality*, by which the Safety and Welfare of a State, and the Mutual Love, Good-will, and Affection of all its Members and Subjects, are effectually Maintained and Preserved. Whenever this Doctrine and Principle of Equality is Disregarded, or not Well-attended to, Civil Feuds, Animosities, and Contentions, naturally follow, and infest That Government, in which Equals aspire to an Unequal or Superior State, and Unequals or Inferiors to a State of Equality. 'Tis a very Just, as well as Common Observation, that *Peers* and *Peers, Equals* and *Equals*, always agree very well together. They, who by their Birth or Wealth, are above their Brethren, must not therefore claim an Inequality or Superiority over them. Nor are they to be reckoned *Equals*, who enjoy the same Common Liberties. They indeed, who excell in Vertue, are on that Account Superior to their Neighbours; and yet in another respect, they are only their *Equals*; they are *Equals* by a Rightful and Judicial, or, as the *Arithmeticians* term it, by a *Numerical Equality*; but they are Superiors in Dignity, or in the Power of Giving and Bestowing Honours and Rewards, to which Vertue always has the Best Claim and Pretension. This Sort of *Equality*, because it cannot be truly Stated, or rightly Measured, but only by Strict Reason and Judgment, is therefore called *Geometrical*. But now the *Good Senator* ought always to be very Punctual and Exact, in adhering to this Doctrine of *Equality*, take it in either of the Two Senses, or Meanings already mentioned. In the Distribution of Law and Justice, and in the Preservation of the Common Liberties, he must have the same Regard to all his Fellow-Subjects; not taking from one, or giving to another, more than what is their Real Due; because in their Claim of Right and Liberty, they are entirely *Equal:* And it is very easy to find out, wherein this Liberty consists, and what are the True Bounds of it; because it is set out, defined and limited, by the Laws of every Nation, whereto every Man may resort, for a Full and Just Account of his Rights, and of all that he can claim as Due to him, either by *Written Statute*, by *Custom* and *Usage*, or by *Private Contract* and *Agreement:* And in the Judging and Determining of all such Cases, no Regard must be had to the Superior Influences of Wealth, Birth, or Power; but the Rich and Poor, the Noble and Vulgar, must be all treated alike, and have Justice administered to them with Utmost Impartiality. But now That other Sort of *Equality*, which cannot be well Stated

ted but only by Reason and Judgment, and which is consistent with the Claim of Vertue to Superior Honours and Dignities, lies much more out of the Way, and is not so easily Discerned and Ascertained. To Form a Right and True Judgment of the Vertues, the Intrinsick Value, Worth, and Wisdom of Others, seems to require a Divine, rather than a Human Intelligence and Penetration. We are often deceived by False Colours, and Fair and Specious Pretences; and we are by no means Competent, or at least, Infallible Judges of one Another. To pass an Unerring Sentence on these Occasions, is a Task of Uncommon Difficulty, and fit only to be performed by Omniscience. And yet such a Discerning Spirit is above all other Things most Useful and Beneficial to the Publick: For if we were thereby Enabled to make a Right Estimate of the Vertues and Dignity of other Men, when these are submitted to our Judgment and Censure; we should then be able to know, who were the Properest Persons to be entrusted with the Publick Interests and Offices, and whom we ought to reject and set aside; whom to Love, and whom to Hate; whom to Reward, and whom to Punish; and by making Choice accordingly, we should preserve our Country in Peace and Happiness: Whereas by a Bad and Erroneous *Election*, we expose it to be overrun by Vice and Corruption, and whatever may Spoil the Beauty, or Defile the Purity of the Body Politick. It is further to be observed, That in Popular Governments, where the Rude Unskilful Mobb and Multitude have all the Power, but without Reason or Judgment to direct them in the Right Use of it, the Way is, to leave the Distribution of all Rewards and Punishments to be decided by *Lots*; not without a Solemn Address and Application to Heaven, that the Choice may fall upon the most Worthy and Deserving. But since in the Use of *Lots*, Reason is set aside, and we depend entirely upon the Rash and Uncertain Decision of Fortune; we therefore dismiss this Blind Guide from all Share, in a

Matter

Matter of such Moment, and depend entirely upon Human Prudence and Wisdom, in determining and preserving a true and perfect State of Equality. The truly Wise and Prudent *Senator* will easily know, how to behave with Decency and Honour, on all these Important Occasions; and in order thereto, will follow the Good Conduct and Example of a Wise and Worthy Master of a Family, who having many Members of his Household Freeborn, and of a Liberal Education, treats one according to his Age, another according to his Proficiency in Vertue, and a Third according to his Present Condition and Circumstances. In just the same manner does the *Senator* treat his Fellow-Subjects, in regard to their Years, Vertues, Condition, and Manner of Life, and the particular Rank and Order to which they belong. Besides this, he will always have a due Concern for the Rights and Liberties of the People, who know very well, that their General Claim consists chiefly of these Particulars; That they are capable of all Offices in the Magistracy; That they have a Right to Interpose in the Making and Amending of all Laws; That they have a Vote and Suffrage in the Passing of all Publick Statutes and Ordinances, and in all Causes, where the Lives, Liberties, or Properties of their Fellow-Subjects are brought into Question; That they cannot be Seized and Detained, Impleaded, Imprisoned, Bound, Fettered, Tortured, or Executed, contrary to Law; That they cannot be deprived of their Wealth or Possessions unjustly, or without a Sufficient Cause, That no Tax or Tribute can be extorted from them, but for very good Reasons; That where the Magistrate commands any thing contrary to Law, they are not bound to obey him; That in such a Case they have a Right to Admonish him, and to Remonstrate against his Proceedings; That they are not in the least to be Injured and Oppressed, by those in Power; and, That they are Free to Think and Do as they Please, except only, where Law and Equity have laid them under a Restraint; That they have a Right to oppose Tyrants,

rants, in Defence of the Laws and Liberties of their Country; That they have a Share and Part in all Publick Councils whatsoever; and, That the Sum of all their Political Principles consists briefly in believing, that the Power of Commanding is entirely in the *King*, and the Power of Advising altogether in the *Senate*. For when the *Senate* is thus set at the Head of all Publick Councils, and what they Decree is well observed by all other Orders of the State; then is the Government well tempered and regulated; and then is the Great Law of Equality well observed among the Subjects, when the *People* enjoy their Properties, the *King* his Authority, and the *Senate* their Right of Advising; and when above all other things, there is a General Agreement and Resolution, that the *Laws* shall every where, and in all Cases, be duly Observed and Executed.

But in nothing more can the *Senator* display his Diligence and Care, than in preventing and suppressing all Seditions, which rend and distract the Body Politick, and expose the Lives of all its Members to Uneasiness, Misery, and all sorts of Calamities. Every thing Human and Divine, Sacred and Religious, is put out of Order, Perverted and Polluted by Sedition: And when this Deadly Poison has once taken hold of and infected a *Commonwealth*, its Vigour and Glory soon fade away, and its whole Constitution is easily Dissolved or Subverted. The Causes that give Rise to Sedition, are so many and various, that the Mind and Reason of Man cannot easily enumerate or account for them. And therefore the *Senator* ought always to be upon his Guard, and use his best Care and Endeavours, that the Malady, when it has once broken out, may not spread itself still farther and farther, and at last Infect the very Vitals of Government. Particular Care must be taken, to Reconcile all Differences, and Restore Amity and Concord among Those who are in Power and Authority: For their High Example very often enlists and draws after it the Whole Multitude, or at least the Majority of the People:

People: And it is well known by Experience, that the Greatest Turns and Changes of Government, have had their Rise from very small Beginnings, and the minutest and most trifling Incidents. In quelling therefore, and allaying all Seditious Commotions, Two Methods are principally to be observed: One is, to Enquire well, and Know perfectly, why, and on what Occasion, the People are uneasy? Whence, and from what Causes arise their Discontents? How are they Animated, and what puts them into Confusion and Disorder? For so it sometimes happens, that a sudden Heat or Fury, an Inordinate Appetite and Unreasonable Demand, a Panick Fear, a fitt of Anger or Resentment, or some such Unruly Passion and Affection, kindles the fire, and calls the Multitude to Arms. Sometimes they are Provoked and Instigated by Avarice, or a Thirst for Prey and Plunder; or by Revenge, and the Hatred and Contempt of their Superiors: And at other times, Religion is the Great Cause of the Quarrel, and Sounds the first Alarm to all their Tumultuous Motions. Such was the Case at *Rome*, upon the Introduction of the *Etruscan* Worship and Ceremonies: And within our own Memory, as great Disorders have happened on the very same Occasion in *Germany*, *France*, and *Bohemia*; where the State hath been miserably Rent and Afflicted, by the Attempts made to Innovate upon, or to alter the Established Religion. There are also other Causes, which give Rise to Sedition; as when one *Order* of Subjects aspires to a Place or Dignity in the State, which does not legally belong to them; and taking Advantage of some Successful Exploit or Enterprize, set themselves up above their Brethren and Equals; which was the Case of the *Council* of *Areopagus* at *Athens*, and of the *Nobility* at *Argos*, after they had been successful in War, against the *Lacedæmonians*, and thereupon attempted to alter the *Popular Constitution* of their Government. In the very same manner, the People of *Syracuse*, much elated by their Success against the *Athenians*,
changed

changed the *Democratical* Form of their Government into a Perfect *Oclocracy*, or *Mobb-Commonwealth*. Not unlike this, was the Case of the *Roman* State, wherein the People taking a Disgust to the *Senate*, openly Revolted from its Authority, and chose their own *Tribunes*; who, by Insolence and Outrage, soon got the better of the *Senate*, lessened and diminished its Power and Privileges, and by the many Tumults and Insurrections of their own raising, reduced the *Commonwealth* to the very Brink of Ruin. Another Way of Promoting and Fomenting Sedition, is by Suffering one Single Person to engross many Great Places or Offices in a State, and to hold them at one and the same time, in Conjunction. This is a most Pernicious Practice, in whatsoever Government it obtains: For by this means, others, who have as good Pretensions, are discarded and laid aside, as Unworthy of any Publick Trust or Honour. It is therefore highly reasonable, that every *Minister* and Officer of State should content himself with one Office at a Time: For by this Regulation, the *Commonwealth* will find its Advantage, in having so much a Greater Number of Faithful Stewards, always attending its Affairs and Interests, and of Diligent Labourers, always employed in securing and promoting the General Welfare and Happiness. In Petty States and Societies, it may perhaps be sometimes convenient to entrust many Offices at a Time in the Hands of a Single Person; but in Large and Populous *Commonwealths*, such a Practice is very often the Forerunner of Great Disorders and Seditions. But to prevent and put a Stop to every Commotion of this Sort, let the *Senator*, in all Cases, and on all Occasions, take particular Care, that the Laws and Customs of his Country be duly and punctually Observed; and let him be sure to oppose the first Efforts and Tendencies to Sedition, before it spread too far, and gather to a Head; lest it be then too Strong and too deeply Rooted, to be easily Quelled and Eradicated.

Eradicated. For 'tis a Just Observation, that every Evil is easily crushed in the Egg, but when Hatched, Winged, and Full-grown, it is not so easily Tamed and brought Under. Among other things, the *Senator* ought to be very Cautious, how he Listens, or gives Credit to, every Rumor or False Report, which is given out, on purpose to Amuse and Mislead the People. Such Tricks and Artifices are often made Use of in a State, by Subtle and Crafty Incendiaries, who have no other Design, but to flatter and Betray the giddy Multitude, and to blow up a Gale of Popular Breath in their own Favour; and who will attempt any thing that Courage and Confidence can inspire, in order to bring about a Turn and Revolution, which may be of Advantage to their own Particular Designs and Self-Interest. The Destruction of the Better Sort, or of the Good and Faithful Members of the *Commonwealth*, is what such Men chiefly Aim at, in all their Combinations and Conspiracies; and they raise a Popular Clamour, and a Tumultuous Dust and Cloud, only to Stifle and Conceal their own Private Faults and Particular Vices. The fire which is kindled by the Breath of their Nostrils, and blown into a flame by their Insolence and Fury, unless it is soon brought under, and in due time extinguished, will presently spread itself far and near, and lay waste the fairest Structure of a Government that ever yet was Erected. There is a Necessity of looking out in every Republick, for some One excellent Man, of more than Human Abilities, with whom All its Quiet, Safety, and Happiness, may be Deposited and Entrusted; and under whose Leading and Conduct it may escape all Tumults, Seditions, Contentions, Animosities, Changes, Alterations, and all other Dangers whatsoever; may always remain Happy, and in a State of Perfect Ease and Tranquillity. Such a Man, such a Hero, who would fully answer this High and Exalted Character, ought to make himself a

Perfect

Perfect Master of the Vertues of *Prudence, Justice, Fortitude,* and *Temperance:* For these are the *Four Cardinal Vertues,* upon which all others Turn and are Dependent: And all Words and Actions, all Human Affairs and Negotiations, are derivable therefrom, as from their Proper Source and Fountain.

CHAP. II.

The CONTENTS.

Of Prudence; *its* Excellencies, *and how far* Preferable *to the* Other Vertues. Prudence *Defined and Described. The Difference between* Speculative Wisdom *and* Prudence. Of Civil *and* Domestick Prudence. *This Vertue limited by* Truth *and* Justice. Honesty *and* Profit *the Scope of all Human Endeavours. The Two* Great Errors *of the* Imprudent. *Of* Laws, Good Examples, *and* Wholsome Exercises. *A Caution to be observed in making of* Laws. *Of the* Vigilance *and* Extensive Knowledge *of the* Senator. *They who Love not their own Country, are worse than* Brutes. *Of the Lesser* Vertues, *Attendant upon, and the Companions of* Prudence. *Of* Ingenuity, Docibility, *and a* Good Memory. *Of* Intelligence, Sensation, *and* Reflection. *Of* Circumspection. *Of the Use of* Standing Forces. *Of the* Administration *of* Justice. *Of* Human Foresight. *Of* False Pretences to Foresight. *Whence the* Senatorial Foresight *is derived. Of the* Good Genius. *Of* Example, Experience, *and* History. *Of* Caution. *Some Rules to be Observed in Speaking in the* Senate. *Of* Sagacity. *Of* Cunning *and* Artifice.

IN the Ordering and Conducting of all Human Actions whatsoever, the First, the Surest, and perhaps the Only Guide, is *Prudence*. Without This, we are so far from being able to conform ourselves in Practice to all the other Vertues, in a Complete and Exact Manner, that we cannot really attain the Full and Perfect Knowledge of their True Nature and Excellencies. Whence *Socrates* comprehends all *Vertue* whatsoever, under the

Name

Name of *Prudence*; though *Aristotle* differs from him in this Particular: And perhaps he might have said more truly and justly, that no Vertue was of any Long Continuance, or could keep its Ground, and Shine out in its full and proper Lustre, without *Prudence*. And therefore *Bion Boristhenius* gives the same Preference to *Prudence*, above all the other *Vertues*, as he does to *Sight*, above all the other *Senses*. But then he adds, That *Old Age* is the Proper Season for *this Vertue*, as *Youth* is for *Strength* and *Fortitude*. We do therefore recommend Prudence to *The Accomplish'd Senator*, as his First and Noblest Endowment. For without this, he will never be able to Speak and Act, as becomes his Age and Dignity; and all his Words, and all his Conduct, will be perfectly Vain and Insipid, unless they are Well-Seasoned with, and have the Strong Taste and Relish of this wholsome and excellent Vertue. But now in order to Define and Describe the true Nature of *Prudence*, it is necessary we should enquire, What it really is, and wherein it consists. The *Latins* derive *Prudence* from *Providence*, or *Foresight*, because the Mind is thereby directed to look forward upon future Things and Events, at the same time that it retains the Remembrance of Things Past, and Disposes of Things Present, in a due Order and Regulation. He, who never thinks of what is Past, must be ignorant of the ordinary Occurrences of Life; and he who has no Insight into Future Things, must be always Exposed to many Dangers; which, for want of Caution, he cannot easily avoid. *Prudence* (as *Cicero* describes it) *is tha Art of knowing Good and Evil, and the Difference between them; whereby we Distinguish between what is Desirable, and what is to be Avoided; and Regulate our Choice accordingly.* In *Aristotle*'s Opinion, *It is a Habit of the Mind, closely connected with* Right Reason, *and altogether conversant in* Action *and* Business, *and in all the Accidents and Events of Life, whether they be Good or Evil.* Speculative Wisdom differs from Prudence in this respect, because the Former never goes beyond

the

the narrow Bounds of Thought and Contemplation; whilst the Latter is wholly employed in Action, and in the Affairs and Negotiations of Human Life. Good Counsel and Good Fortune are necessary Helps and Auxiliaries to Prudence, in settling and securing the Just Bounds and Limits of That *Good* we are in quest of: But Speculative Wisdom wants neither Counsel nor Advice, because all its Enquiries terminate in Certain and Self-evident Truths. Hence it is, that *Geometers, Mathematicians, Natural Philosophers,* with many other Sages, who confine themselves and their Studies to mere *Theory,* have much better Pretensions to *Wisdom* and *Learning,* than to true *Prudence:* And *Diogenes, Zeno, Crates, Chrysippus, Carniades, Democritus, Metrocles, Aristippus, Anexagoras, Thales,* deserved the Character, rather of *Wise* and *Learned,* than of *Prudent* Men: For the Aim and Scope of all their Philosophy, was quite different from That of True Prudence. They confined themselves to Abstract Notions, and the Secret and Abstruse Parts of Knowledge, and had no Pleasure beyond this: They never meddled with the more Solid Part, or regarded any Enquiries that were immediately Useful or Beneficial to Mankind: Whilst *Prudence* has always the General Good and Publick Advantage in View, and holds all her Consultations, and Deliberates entirely upon that Single Subject. If indeed those Learned Men, laying aside the Natural Aversion they had to the World, and to the Ways and Customs of its Inhabitants, would have applied themselves to the Affairs and Government of their Country, there is no Doubt but they would have Excelled and Distinguished themselves by their *Prudence:* And of this we have sufficient Proof from the Great Examples of *Pericles, Solon, Lycurgus, Plato, Demosthenes, Cato, Cicero,* and many others.

True *Prudence* then has its Rise from Sound Reason, and when the *Senator* hath made himself a Master of it, either by the Study of Philosophy, or by Political and Civil Discipline, or by Long
Use

Use and Experience, he will then be able to Foresee and Guard against any Future Events, and to behave well and wisely upon all present Occasions and Emergencies: And when a Sudden and perhaps Hazardous Affair is undertaken, he will be always ready to give an Extemporary Good Advice, and by his Counsel to Expedite and Forward the Service and Welfare of his Country. A Prudent Man will soon attain the two Great Accomplishments of Human Life: He will have a Thorough Insight into all Affairs, and will know and Understand Himself. This therefore is that Great, Excellent, and truly Divine *Vertue*, in which the *Good Senator* ought always to abound, as his Best and Noblest Ornament. For without this, all the Reason of Man, all his Vertues, Actions, and Sentiments, are vain and unprofitable. The First Lesson that *Prudence* teaches us, is, as the Philosophers express it, *That a Man should be Wise for Himself.* A Prudent Man will in the First place take Care of himself, and be well Advised in the Management of his own Particular and Private Affairs. For without this, he is liable to the Imputation of Gross and Notorious Folly. *Prudence* includes the Care of our own Domestick or Family-Concerns, as well as the Art of making Laws for the Publick, or of Presiding in Council, or in Judgment. What we exercise at home, is, by *Cicero*, called *Domestick*, and what is employed in the Publick Service, is, by the same Author, called *Civil Prudence*. But in what Capacity, or on what Occasion soever, we are obliged to exert this Great Vertue in its full Force, we must still be careful to have all along a very strict Regard to Truth and Justice. For Truth is the Undoubted Property of the Prudent; and if we in the least deviate therefrom, all that we say or do, will have a Taint and Corrupt Mixture of Falshood and Impiety. He therefore, who justly weighs, and wisely considers with himself, what is True and Just, Decent, and Proper to be done, upon every Occasion,

and

and who is Quick and Acute, Speedy and Expeditious, in the Performance of it, does (in my Opinion and Judgment) best deserve the Character and High Title of a *Prudent Man*: But now in all his Searches after Truth and Wisdom, the *Senator's* Prudence must take its Rise from certain Principles, as from a Source or Fountain, whence it may trace the Issues and Progress of Truth; and these are *Honesty* and *Profit*. For whatever is Said or Done, either in a Publick, Private, or Mixed, Case and Capacity, ought always to have something, either Honest or Profitable, in View, as the Mark and Scope of all Human Endeavours and Enterprizes. Whatever we can comprehend by Thought, or express by Language, is briefly, but really and fully comprised within these Two Great Limits and Boundaries. But then it requires a very Acute and Penetrating Genius, to be able to Discover and to Distinguish exactly between what is *Honest*, and what is *Profitable*; Because the Mind is often Darkened and Obscured by the Lusts and Lower Appetites, and Man's Judgment is Depraved and Perverted, and his Reason Dethroned and Deprived of the Proper Dominion it ought to have over all his other Faculties. Whence it often happens, that we are deceived not only in our Notions and Opinions of what is Honest and Profitable; but are really so far Blinded and Besotted, as to grow doatingly Fond of the Vilest and Foulest Vices. To prevent our being thus shamefully Imposed upon, there are Two very Great Errors, which we must be careful to avoid. One is, that we never Presume to Know, or rashly and tenaciously Adhere to, any one Point or Principle, of which we are really Ignorant. And the other is, that we never give our Consent to any thing really Ill, or which is contrary to the Known Rules of Vertue, and the General Prevailing Opinion of Good and Wise Men. But now the *Senator* may easily and fully comprehend the Utmost Extent and Due Limits of whatever is *Honest* and *Profitable*,

if

if he will always keep a Fixed and Steady Eye upon the Good and Welfare of the Publick. For this is the Sole Aim and Scope of all *Senatorial* Prudence and Wisdom: From which there never should be any the least Deviation whatsoever. Neither his *God*, his Country, his Fellow-Subjects, nor the Laws of Prudence, require any thing more at the Hands of the *Good Senator*, than that he should, upon all Occasions, use his best Endeavours to promote the Welfare and Safety of the *Commonwealth:* And as I have already observed, then will a *Commonwealth* be truly Happy, when it is furnished with the Affluence of all Good Things; when its Members are Just, Temperate, Prudent, Brave, and Free; when they are Blessed with Health and Wealth, are at Peace and Unity among themselves, and entirely at Rest from all Divisions, Parties, and Factions, whatsoever. It is also a Part of the *Senator*'s Duty, to extend all his Care and Pains, not only to the making of his Country Happy, but also to find out and apply the Best and Properest Means, for Securing, Continuing, and Perpetuating its Happiness. For so it often happens, that a People, or Body of Subjects (and what People is there, whose natural Inclinations to Vice are not much stronger than their Love of Vertue?) will by Degrees fall away, and go aside from the Streight Paths of Honesty and Goodness; whilst Corruption gains Ground, and insensibly steals in upon them; till at last the Infection over-spreads the whole Body Politick; and draws after it a Train of many Evils; which, like a Tempest, surround, and shake, and toss it to and fro, and keep it always Fluctuating, and in a State of Uncertainty and Danger.

In order to prevent the Rise and Growth of all such Publick Mischiefs, a Timely and Effectual Remedy must be Provided by the Enacting of Good and Wholsome Laws. For the Law is a Bond and Tye upon every Officer and Magistrate, obliging and restraining him to the Exact Performance of his Duty, and is the Great Preservative

Preservative of every Subject's Vertue and Fidelity. Besides those Strict and Express Laws, which have Rewards and Punishments annexed to them, there are other Methods, highly conducive to the same Good Purposes; as by Prescribing and Encouraging Good Examples, by Introducing Useful and Laudable Modes and Customs, and by Promoting such Exercises and Entertainments, as may bring the People to be in Love with Vertue, to look on it as a Pleasure; and consequently to give themselves up, with so much the more Readiness, as its Zealous Votaries and Followers. Something of this Sort was attempted in the *Laconian State*, where many such-like Institutions and Ordinances were given out to this purpose, and had with them the Full Force and Authority of Established Laws. To this we must always be sure to add, the Right Use and Full Extent of *Discipline*; by which the Minds of the People, both in War and in Peace, are trained and inured to the Knowledge and Exercise of every Vertue whatsoever. There is one Way and Method commonly made Use of, by Good and Wise *Senators*, in the Framing and Compiling of Laws, which is, to Aim them rather at the Preventing, than the Suppressing of Evil; and thereby to cut off from every Subject all Opportunity and Occasion of Offending. This is a Commendable Practice, and Worthy of the Good *Senator*'s Imitation. For it is his Duty and Office, to heal and compose the distempered, or disordered Minds of the People, by Good and Wholsome Laws; just as a Skilful Physician heals and composes the Distempered, or Disordered Bodies of his Patients, by Good and Wholsome Medicines and Prescriptions.

Here by the Way I can by no means approve of Their Method, who upon the First Breaking out of any Publick Vice or Malady, set themselves immediately to suppress it by Penal Strictures and Severities: And I should rather chuse to trace and enquire into the Rise and Original of it, and to cut it off at the Fountain Head,

by

by Suppressing its First Causes, than by Pursuing it with Severity, through all its Effects and Consequences. In my Opinion, all our Counsel and Wisdom ought first to be employed in bringing Men to Justice, rather than to Execution. Suppose, for Instance, a State should be visited with a Dearth or Famine; would not That Magistrate be very Cruel and Inhuman, who should spend all his Time in punishing Theft with Death, and not rather employ himself chiefly, in finding out Ways and Means to supply his Country with Provisions; whereby all Occasion of Stealing would be taken away, or at least the Necessity of it Prevented? On the other hand, imagine a Country over-run with Luxury and Debauchery; would it not be much better to Stop the Inundation by Sumptuary, than by *Sanguinary* Laws? 'Tis an Excellent Prescription given out by *Cicero*, when he says, *That the Best Cure for Avarice is to Suppress Luxury, its Mother-Vice, by which it is brought forth and nourished.*

In short, the *Good Senator* must always keep a Watchful Eye upon whatever may be for the Advantage, or to the Prejudice of the *Commonwealth*. For unless this be done, and if he remains Careless or Ignorant of these Publick Concerns, whenever his Country is visited with any Political Malady or Distemper, or turns its Sword into its own Bowels, by Civil Discontents and Animosities, he will never be able to find a Proper Remedy for these Evils, or to use and apply it effectually. He must therefore be always Inquisitive, and look narrowly into the Lives and Conduct of his Fellow-Citizens, and observe how they stand Affected to the Constitution, and whether they are Punctual and Regular in their Obedience to the Laws, and Lawful Commands of their Superiors; how the Magistrates execute their several Offices, and the Trusts reposed in them; whether they are Active and Diligent, True and Faithful to their Country; or whether they are Covetous, Cruel, and Inhuman, or Just, and Good, and Merciful; what Instances

are

are to be given of their Prudence and Good Conduct, and what of their Skill and Experience in the Laws, and of their Justice and Impartiality in the Execution of them; and whether they proceed in Judgment upon the Known and Publick Laws, or upon any Private and Arbitrary Decrees of their own Making and Ordaining. He must likewise extend his Views to the Whole *Commonwealth* at once, and to all its several Parts and Members. He must be well acquainted with the Rights, Liberties, and Immunities of the People, and the Laws and Customs on which they are founded. He must (as *Cicero* very wisely Directs) *Be able to tell, what Defence a Nation can make for its self; what are its Forces and Fortifications; what its Treasure and Revenues; who its Friends, Allies, and Stipendiaries; and by what Terms and Conditions, they stand Bound and Engaged to the Commonwealth.* Lastly, he must understand in general, the Way and Manner of Decreeing in all Cases whatsoever; the Precedents of Former Times, and the Conduct and Examples of his Progenitors and Predecessors. This is the Sum of that Extensive Knowledge, which a *Prudent Senator* must take Care to be Master of, and always to keep and retain. For he is so Stationed, that the Eyes of all his Fellow-Subjects and of his Country are continually upon him, and to him they look up for their Common Safety and Security. If he is Careless and Ignorant, or Unwilling to do his Country Good, he is not only an Ill Man, or an Ill Subject, but an Infamous and Abandoned Traitor. Next to the Love of God, the Love of our Country ought to be the Strongest and most Vigorous Pasison of our Souls; and in Consequence of this Love, our Country may demand of us a Strict, Constant, and immovable Fidelity. He, who loves not his own Country, is perhaps little better than a Beast; and really not so good as some Creatures of the Animal World beneath us: For they have a Natural Desire and Affection for their Native Lands or

Fields,

Fields, which are to them particularly Sweet and Delectable, and will chuse rather to perish, than to be forced or driven out of that particular Spot of Ground, where they were brought forth and nourished, which is, in effect, their Country. If this Love of our Country were happily united to, and closely connected with True and Consummate *Prudence*, we should then be all of a Mind, and in a State of Perfect Concord: Nothing would ever be said or done in a *Senate*, that favoured of Malice, Partiality, Imprudence, or any other Iniquity; but all things would be strictly Weighed and accurately Examined, and after a Due Deliberation, and an alternate Debate, what was Enacted or Decreed, would be the Issue and Effect of true Solid and Unerring Judgment. Thus far then we see, what the Force and Power of True *Prudence* is, and what the Extent of its Influences. By *Prudence*, a Way and Inlet is opened to us, by which we have Access to all the other Vertues; and without this Support, every Vertue besides is Weak and Feeble, and cannot Stand out long, even in its own Defence. By the Aid and Assistance of *Prudence*, we are instructed and enabled, to become truly Just, Temperate, and Brave, and know when, where, and in what manner, these Vertues are to be duly Exercised and put in Practice.

Prudence is a Vertue of such Dignity, that She carries with her, and Draws after her, a long Train of many other Vertues, her Companions, Followers, and Attendants, who serve as a Guard to defend, and as an Equipage to grace and adorn her. By their Subserviency, She executes her High Office, and extends the Influences of her Administration much Farther and Wider. When all these Vertues are well fixed and rooted in the *Senator*'s Memory, and with all his Best Care and Diligence he hath entirely Devoted himself to their Service; he cannot fail of attaining the Utmost Praise and Glory due to *Senatorial Prudence*, whether it be displayed in *Action*, or in *Counsel*, or in the General Management and

Good

Good Conduct of Life. The *Senator* therefore must be Ingenious, Docible, of a Good Memory, and Understanding, Circumspect, Provident, Cautious, Sagacious, Cunning, and Crafty. For all these Vertues or Accomplishments, in the concurrent Opinion, both of the *Platonists* and *Peripateticks*, are the Necessary Attendants and Companions of *Prudence*.

Ingenuity is a Natural Power or Faculty, conjoined and superadded to our Reason, by which we are enabled to Invent and Discover all the Finest and most Secret Parts of Knowledge, that can possibly be attained unto, by a Human Understanding. Where there is no Great Assistance to be had from Industry, Docibility, and a Good Memory; or where little Use is made of these Helps, *Ingenuity* is of itself a very Shining and Valuable Accomplishment, and very often serves to recommend Men to Publick Notice and Favour, who have really very little Knowledge or Experience, in any one Art or Science whatsoever. Let the *Senator* therefore be well acquainted with the Strength and Extent of his own *Ingenuity*, and improve it in such manner, that it may be always Sharp and Quick, in the Invention and Discovery of Proper Matter, and Useful Topicks; Fertil and Elegant, in Explaining and Adorning them; and Firm and Constant, in Remembring and Retaining them. That particular Sort of *Prudence*, which is seen and exercised in our First Conception of Things, is entirely owing to a Quick and Acute *Ingenuity*, which is Increased and Improved by Docibility and a Good Memory: Of which they who are Masters, are commonly called *Ingenious:* And this is Confirmed and Established by Discipline, Use, and Experience. The Ingenuity most to be liked, and to which the Highest Commendations are due, is such, as is neither Volatile and Inconstant, nor Pert, Petulant, and Scurrilous, nor Slow, Dull, and Heavy; nor Light, Frothy, and Fallacious; nor Turbulent, Impudent, and Incorrigible: But is, on contrary, Solid and Constant, Sharp, Keen,

Keen. and Well-pointed; Candid, and Good-natured; Bright, and Clear; Pleasant, Elegant, Genteel, and Free.

Docibility and *Memory* are great Helps and Recommendatory Advantages to a Lively and Quick Ingenuity. By the *Former*, we are enabled to Understand, and to Explain, whatsoever we Learn or Borrow from others; and by the *Latter*, to Keep and Retain all Truths, which we have formerly Thought of ourselves, or which others have given out and delivered to us. In the Attainment and Exercise of these Accomplishments, the *Senator* ought to be doubly Diligent. For not to Retain or Remember, what we have Heard and Seen, is really a Mark and Proof of a very Mean and Low Capacity, if not of Downright Dulness and Stupidity. In these Attainments and Exercises, the most Eminent among the Ancients, were *Demosthenes, Alcibiades,* and *Mithridates.*

As *Ingenuity* is the Glory and Ornament of the *Senatorial* Character, so *Intelligence* or *Understanding* is as a Light and Guide to *Ingenuity*; and in virtue of this Capacity, we are enabled to apprehend and take Cognizance of all Things, or of their *Ideas,* as they are brought in, or conveyed to us, by *Sensation* and *Reflection*, and to Form a Right and Discriminating Judgment between Truth and Falshood. *Intelligence* is the Common and Universal Faculty, by which all Knowledge is Acquired, and by which we are directed how to distinguish between Vice and Vertue, and to assign Punishments for the One, and Rewards for the Other. To this Faculty the *Senses* are always closely joined and united, and they are the Messengers and Interpreters between us and the Things that are without us. As they are Fallible, we must take Care how we are Deceived or Misled by them, and must Endeavour to preserve them from Decay and Languishing, and from a State of Drowsiness and Stupidity. It often happens, that we are shamefully imposed upon by the Subtle and Artful, or by the False and Imaginary

ginary Appearances of Things; and are thereby enticed, and prevailed with, to offer Violence, not only to Right Reason, but even to Common Sense: Which Fallacy we must be very Careful to avoid, in all the Affairs and Interests of Life; but especially in those Important Moments of it, when we are called upon to Discern, and to pass Judgment, between Truth and Falshood, Good and Evil.

Circumspection is another Vertue, without which the *Senatorial* Character cannot be made Perfect. In the Practice of this Vertue, he ought to extend his Views, not only to his own Private and Domestick Affairs, but to the Common Good and Publick Welfare, and whatever may be Injurious and Detrimental to his Country. It is a Part of his Office and Duty, to look round upon all the Quarters and Avenues of a State, and to watch every Blast and Storm, that may be just Arising and Threatning any Danger; the better to provide for the Publick Safety and Defence. This Vertue, called *Circumspection*, is nothing else but a Wise and Accurate Consideration of what is proper to be done on every Important and Momentous Occasion, and serves to the best and noblest Purposes both in *War* and in *Peace*. In *War* it always goes before, and prevents the Malicious Interposition and over-bearing Sallies of Fortune, by prompting a Commander carefully to look round upon all the Various Way and Methods, and to chuse the Best, by which an Enemy may be Attacked and Defeated. It never enters upon any Undertaking or Adventure, in a Rash and Bold Manner, or reposes all its Confidence in Chance and Good Luck; but relies altogether upon Sound Reason, and Mature Counsel and Deliberation. *Fabius* was remarkable for this Vertue, and it is said to have saved the *Roman State* by a Wise and Premeditated *Delaying* and *Forbearance of Action*. The Conduct of *Flaminius* was quite of another Sort; who, for Want of *Circumspection*, and by too great a Confidence

dence in his own Strength and Personal Bravery, was set upon by *Hannibal*, drawn into an Ambuscade, and thereby entirely Defeated. I need not mention *Q. Cepio*, the Consul, with many Others, who miscarried in the very same Manner. But now in Times of Peace, the *Senator* must look out, with all the Eyes of *Argus* and *Lynceus*, and exert all the Powers of this Useful and Necessary Vertue of *Circumspection*, in all Cases, which concern the Peace, Unity, and Welfare of his Fellow-Subjects. Without this, it is impossible to Foresee and Prevent Seditions, Tumults, Wars, or any other Accidents and Misfortunes, which may disturb or overthrow a Government. There are some Members of a State so very Imprudent, or so blinded by the Dishonourable Love of Ease and Luxury, that they hardly Discern aright, what is really Present and in full View before them; much less are they able to look forward into the Future Events and Contingencies of Things, by which a *Commonwealth* may be Incommoded and brought into Danger. Such *Senators* ought to be Admonished and put in Mind of their Duty, or to be Removed and Dismissed from the Trust reposed in them; since they have so notoriously abused it, and are fit to be numbered only with the Useless and Unprofitable Citizens, who are more Intent upon Serving themselves, than upon Serving or Saving their Country. They can calmly and tamely behold a War hanging over their Heads, and threatning all around them: They see the Enemies making Incursions, carrying off the Spoil and Plunder of their People, and driving away their Countrymen into Slavery. Their Wives, Sons, and Daughters, are sold to Foreigners or Barbarians; their Towns and Villages are Burned and Destroyed, their Country Wasted, and the Temples of their Gods Polluted by Profanation and Sacrilege: In short, they behold their Native Kingdom exposed as a Mark to be Shot at, Pierced, and Wounded, by the Shafts and Arrows of Insolent and Savage Invaders;

Invaders; whilst for want of *Circumspection*, they are unable to provide a Proper and Effectual Remedy for these Evils, or know not how to apply it, in order to heal and allay the Sores and Calamities of their Country. At another time perhaps, they can in like manner, see their Fellow-Citizens running headlong into Sedition and Disorder, torne and crumbled, weakened and enfeebled, by Parties and Factions; the Liberties of the Meaner sort trampled upon by those in Power, the Publick Faith, and even Religion itself, despised and neglected; whilst themselves are Unconcerned at so direful and horrid a Spectacle. But then here the *Good Senator* interposes, and spreads out both his Arms to save and protect his Country. He endeavours, with all his Might, to Restore to her, Peace and Tranquillity, and to Secure and Perpetuate her Happiness. He provides against the Incursions and Outrages of Strangers, by a Strong and Sufficient Force, able to Guard and Defend the State, and to Repell the Insolence of the Hostile Invader; raises and repairs the necessary Fortifications; strengthens and secures the Frontier Towns, with good Works and Garrisons; reinforces the Strong Holds and Places of Retreat, and guards all the Inlets and Accesses, by which an Enemy may make his Approaches to Spoil a Country. It is also of great Use and Advantage to the Publick, always to have in Readiness a sufficient Body of Troops, well Armed and Disciplined, to watch and oppose the Motions of an Invader, and to secure and Protect their Fellow-Citizens. For when a *Commonwealth* is well provided with such able and faithful Defenders, and is guarded and surrounded by them, as by a Wall or Bulwark; it may then look upon all its Neighbouring and Foreign Enemies with Contempt, and defy all Attempts of an Invasion, to the Endangering of its Safety and Happiness. Such a Body of Defenders, was heretofore kept up in the *Lacedæmonian State*; and they very well deserved the Title usually given them, of being *The Walls and Fortifications*

tifications of their Native City. In the mean time, the Good and Happiness of the Subject is most effectually Preserved, by a due Administration of Justice, by keeping the Subject always in Temper and Well-affected to the State, and by a Strict and Impartial Execution of the Laws. The *Accomplish'd Senator* must be particularly Circumspect and Prudent, in the Prosecution of these Good Designs, and in the Attainment of these Publick Blessings. For to be Remiss and Negligent in Suppressing all Seditions and Disorders, and in Securing the Peace and Happiness of a Government, is not only a sure Mark of Folly and Ignominy, but a Proof of Gross Impiety and Treachery to the Publick. And where now shall we find any other Subject of the *Commonwealth*, but only the *Accomplish'd Senator*, who is Sufficient for these Things? He has his Post in the very Centre of the State, whence he has a Clear and Exact View of all the Rights and Liberties of his Fellow-Subjects, whether they concern their Lives or their Properties, and of all the Motions and Approaches of the Turbulent and Seditious: And he is thus Posted, as it were by Divine Appointment, that he may have a Full Prospect and Survey of all Things about him, may Form a Proper Judgment of all Present Occurrences; and by his Circumspection and Diligence, may Enlarge his Views, and make a Wise and Timely Provision even for Future Events and Contingencies.

As by a due and regular Precaution, the *Physician* guards against the ill Consequences of a Growing Distemper; the *General* against the Stratagems and Ambushes of an Enemy; and the *Master of a Vessel*, against a rising Storm or Tempest: In the very same manner, does the Good and Prudent *Senator* provide against all Dangers, Decays, Turns, Changes, and Accidents, that may befall a State, to its Prejudice and Disadvantage: He has an Eye not only to what is Present, but to what in all Probability will hereafter happen. This *Foresight* is That Power or Vertue, which

the

the *Latins* call *Providence*; and they who are Masters of it, are from thence Styled *Provident*, or *Prudent* Persons. Now *Providence* (as *Cicero* describes it) *Is the Art of foreknowing Future Things, long before they are Produced, or actually Subsisting.* 'Tis true that *Prescience*, or the *Foresight of Things to come*, is rather a Property of the *Divine*, than of the Human Nature. This Faculty is Peculiar and Essential to our *Creator*, and none but He can see clearly and distinctly, into the Dark Events and Secrets of Futurity. But since we are made after his Image, and are thereby in some measure Partakers of the Divine Wisdom, it may so happen, that in many Cases, we may be able to foresee and know some things which are to come, and before they really happen. There are Two Ways of doing this; One is by Divine Inspiration, or some Extraordinary Light, which *God* in his good Pleasure, condescends to give us. And the Other is, by our own Natural Capacity and Instinct. All I have to say upon this Subject of *Providence*, is to be Referred entirely to this Last Method of Foreknowing; it not being at all Pertinent to my Present Design, to take any Notice of those Discoveries, which are made by *Dreams*, by the *Inspection of Entrails*, by *Fortune-telling*, by *Prodigies*, or by *consulting the Stars and Planets*, or by Resorting to, or Conversing with *Necromancers, Conjurers, Augurers, Ariolers, Astrologers, Dæmons,* and *Apparitions*, or with the Works and Compositions of such-like Pretenders and Pretended Beings. Even the *Infidel* and *Atheist* will sometimes Undertake to Foreknow and Foretell what is to come: But let it only be granted me, that the Mind of the *Good Senator* may be so throughly Sanctified and Purified, and so entirely freed from every Vicious Stain and Tincture whatsoever, that the Body, wherein it dwells, may become a fit Receptacle of That Celestial Spirit and Divine Intelligence, by whose Assistance he may be endowed with the Gifts of Foresight and Prediction, and may See far into the Dark Recesses of Futurity: And we may then, and

on

on this Account, ascribe to the *Senator* a more than Human Understanding, a Perfect Unerring Foresight, immediately derived to him from his *Maker*. After which, he is no longer to be Regarded as only Wise, Prudent, and Provident, but as a Holy, Pious, Religious, and *Divine* Creature. The *Ancients* give us many Instances of some such Extraordinary Men, who were *State-Prophets*, and foretold things merely Civil and Political, when they were Inspired, and had Raptures put into them, by some Celestial *Nymph*, or *Virgin*, or by some One of their *Deities*. Of this Sort were the *Sybils*, and with them may be reckoned *Tiresias, Mopsus, Amphiarus,* and *Calchas*. How this Heavenly Gift of *Providence* is acquired, does not seem much for my Present Purpose to Enquire: It must be a Ray of Omniscience, streaming down from Heaven, and resting upon the Soul, whence it Reflects its Proper Light, with so much more Strength and Clearness, whenever the Soul is in a State of Secretion and Abstraction, from the Dregs of Flesh, and is wholly intent upon this Divine Emanation. From this Digression, I return to the Consideration of that Sort of *Providence*, which is confessedly Human; though even this, as it sometimes shews itself in its Effects and Operations, is not to be accounted for, without a Divine Impulse and Energy. For when a Prudent Man hath taken Care to Stock and Enrich his Mind with the Knowledge both of Men and Things, hath made himself acquainted with the Affairs and Transactions, both of Past and Present Times, and with the Motives and Principles, the Designs and Consequences, the Turns, Tendencies, and Changes of all such Affairs and Transactions: And hath likewise entertained in his Mind, a Perfect Notion, and Clear *Ideas*, of all things proper to be Undertaken and Done, which are under the Direction of Right Reason, or at the Certain and Regular Disposition of *Second Causes*, and the *Powers of Nature;* Such a Proficient in Wisdom, and in the Knowledge of

all

all Things, so fully Informed, and so well Versed in all the Parts of Private and Publick Life, and in all the Concerns and Interests of Government, by Exerting the Utmost Force, and the Keenest and most Penetrating Faculties of his Reason, may be able to look far into Futurity, and to have a Competent Share of Foreknowledge and Prescience; by which he may judge aright of Events and Contingencies, and of the Good or Evil of them, and the Frailty, Stability, Duration, and Certainty, with which they are like to be attended. It is indeed taken for granted, that there is something of a Principle truly Divine, or more than Human, in Men of this Exalted Character; which Principle has sometimes been called by the Name of a *Good Angel*, or *Genius*. Such a One was supposed to be constantly Resident in the Great *Socrates*, to whose Dictates he was always Conformable: Though I cannot think any thing else is meant by this *Angel* or *Genius*, than a Mind richly endowed with Wisdom, kept Chaste, and Clear, and Free from Vice, and constantly Exercised in Judging uprightly and impartially of all things Subject to its Enquiries and Cognizance. And in the Strength of this Faculty, a Man may come to know things Future and Contingent, and to Form a certain Judgment of them, upon very Slight Notices and Forerunning Observations. Example and Experience, to which the *Senator* ought always to have a very Great Regard, are also a Sure Means of attaining this Faculty, or Vertue of *Foresight* and *Providence*. Suppose, for instance, a Man had a mind to prognosticate, or foretell the Troubles and Confusions, which, in all Probability, would Plague and Perplex a *Commonwealth*, if an Attempt should be made to Alter or Subvert the *Established Religion*; how could he possibly Form his conjectures more certainly and effectually, than by looking back upon, and by considering the several Distresses, and Calamities, which on this very Account befell the several States and Kingdoms of *Germany*, *France*, *Bohemia*, *Hungary*, and *England:* By
which

which they were miserably Rent and Shaken, and brought to the very Brink of Ruin and Desolation? This Way of Judging of Things to come, and of Presaging and Foretelling Future Events, holds good in all other Cases of like Sort, or whenever we Judge of the Consequences of things, in any one Situation of Publick Affairs, or Critical Juncture whatsoever. In the Pursuit and Application of this Method, *History* and *Experience* are of very great Use to us; because *Examples* are Cogent and Prevailing Arguments, to set us right in our Attempts to Avert, or to Suppress any Impending Evil; and we naturally fly from That, which we are well assured hath been Dangerous, or Fatal to others. Let the *Good Senator* therefore, exert all his *Prudence* in a *Providential* Care of the State, and in Foreseeing and Guarding against all Evils, which may possibly threaten or annoy his Country. Let him Forego no Opportunity, and Spare no Pains, in preparing himself and his Fellow-Subjects for Action, in Warning them of their Danger, and in Consulting of Proper Ways and Means to guard themselves against it. For according to a Well-Known and Common Observation, we can never be wounded by the Dart or Javelin, which we see before-hand is directly aimed at, and coming towards us. When any Mischief or Evil falls upon us Suddenly or Unawares, we cannot so easily avoid it, and perhaps not without a considerable Loss and Damage to ourselves: For in these sudden Attacks and Onsets, we are Surprized and Overtaken, are Struck at once with a Panick Fear and Consternation, and have neither Time nor Power, sufficient to help ourselves, or to Work out our own Deliverance. When in the Maturity of our Judgment, we can see Danger coming at a Distance, we are then Precautioned, and can provide against it. But our Caution must be Well-timed, and Previous to our Danger, lest we Taste and Feel the Mischief that threatens us, and grow Wise only by our own Experiments. For when all that we apprehended, is really fallen

len upon us, and we have tasted of its Utmost Malice and Severity, to cry out, *Who would have Thought it?* Is the Low, Vulgar Expression, and Ordinary Language of Fools. When a Ship is Safe and in a Calm, or before a Prosperous Gale, then is the Proper Time for the *Master*, or the *Mariners*, to look about them, and provide against the Dangers or Desolation, which a Sudden Storm or Tempest may possibly bring upon them: But when the Sea is Swoln and has got a Head, and all the Furies of the Winds are let loose upon them, a Wise Foresight and Providential Care come too late, and are then to no purpose. In the very same manner, whilst All is Well, and the *Commonwealth* Safe and Quiet, Whole and Entire, not disturbed by any Intestine Broils and Commotions, nor threatened and surrounded by any Foreign Enemy and Invader; then must the *Good Senator* be upon his Guard, and keep his Eyes and Thoughts always Watchful, and Intent upon the Safety and Welfare of his Country. From what is Past, and from what we have already Seen, and Felt, and Experienced, it is much better for us to be Doubtful and Suspicious, than to be made Wise only by Future Trials and Experiments. For as a Certain *Author* very well observes, *It is much more easy to find Fault with what is Past, than to Correct and Amend it.*

After *Providence*, the next Vertue in Rank and Order, is *Caution*, her immediate Attendant and inseparable Companion. As *Providence* guards and secures us against *Future*, so *Caution* does against *Present* Evils, and all the Dangers that can possibly Beset and Surround us. We have a Natural Desire and Affection for whatever promotes our own Good and Welfare, and a Strong and Natural Aversion to whatever may Hurt or Incommode us. This Aversion to Evil, when duly Regulated and Conducted by Right Reason, is (properly speaking) *Caution:* And to this the Wise Man lays Claim, as to his Particular and Undoubted Property. The Great Benefits and Advantage of this

Vertue

Vertue are to be seen in every Thing we Say or Do; for to Speak what we Think, and to Execute what we Design, with *Caution*, is an Essential Part of the Character of That Man, who is Perfect in *Prudence*, who is a Master of Business, and of all the most Important Affairs and Offices in Life. The *Senator* therefore, in all Publick Speeches and Debates, must keep to the Rules, not only of Gravity and Brevity, but of *Caution* too, and must be, as *Horace* well expresses it,

Sparing of Speech, and Cautious in his Words.

For it very often happens, that by a Rash and Eager Way of throwing out our Words, Wildly and at Random, we are often brought to say those Things, which we may after be very Sorry for, and by some Unguarded Expressions, bring ourselves, and our Country, into Danger. This, especially, may be often the Case, when we are sent abroad, as *Envoys* and *Representatives* of the *Commonwealth*; if in our treating with Foreign States, or in any Consultation at home, upon Matters of the first and highest Importance, we should heedlessly let drop any Thing, or hastily discover any Secret, that the World ought by no means to be let into. *It is*, as the *Comick* Writer well observes, *very Idle and Ridiculous to Admit, or Take for Granted, what a Man may Cautiously Avoid, or Decently Deny.* Let the *Senator*, therefore, when he speaks in any Publick Debate, always keep in View the following Precautions. Let him take Care not to speak in a Fitt of Anger or Mirth, or in a Fright, and under the Apprehensions of Fear, or rashly, hastily, and in a Hurry; or without Forethought and Premeditation. For be observing these Rules, he will be sure to maintain the Character of a Wise and Able Speaker. Suppose he is in Treaty, or has any Affair to transact with the Enemies of his Country, with any Neighbouring State, or with their
Ambassadors

Ambassadors and Ministers, who, by the very Nature of their Office, are always prying into the Secret Councils and Designs of other States, and employ all their Art and Cunning, watch all Opportunities, of forming the Best Conjectures they can, and take Notice of every Sign and Token, every Incident and Appearance, that occurs to their own Observation, or which they can Wring or Extort out of others; in order to lay hold of some Secret of Importance. On this Occasion, the *Senator* must be sure to Arm himself with his Best Caution, to fasten and lock up his own Breast, to Guard and Secure it on every Side, and to keep so strict a Watch over all his Words and Gestures, the Motions of his Eyes, and the Features of his Countenance, that not the least Notice or Intelligence whatsoever may break out from any of these Quarters, to betray the Secrets of his Heart. There is also much *Caution* to be used, in giving Credit to the Reports and Informations brought to us by Other Men. For Incredulity is very often a Useful, Necessary, and Prudential Vertue. But then the contrary Extreme is as much to be avoided, and we must take Care not to be Over-difficult and Slow of Belief. On some Occasions, we may readily Come into and Applaud, what is Related or Disclosed to us by Others; always provided that our Credulity be consistent with the Dignity of our Station, and our Love and Regard for Truth. For an Unjust or Ill-grounded Assent is always against the Laws and Rules of Veracity. Taciturnity is no doubt a Vertue; but by affecting too much of it, we may give others an Occasion of Reflecting either upon our Capacity and Abilities, or upon our Courage and Manhood, and expose ourselves to Censure, as Weak and Unskilful, or as Easy to be Dashed and Daunted, by an Excess of Modesty; such as better becomes a Raw Girl or Maiden, than an Able and Experienced Statesman. There is a Regulation to be Observed and a particular Art in Knowing, When to Speak, and when to

be

be Silent. But of one Thing we must always be Cautious, which is, that we take Care to Hear, more than we Speak: For Nature, when she gave us Two Ears, and but One Tongue, did thereby seem to Dictate this Good Advice to us. To Know how, and when to be Silent, is a Great and Principal Part of Prudence. For in the Intervals of Silence, we may well weigh and consider before-hand, not only What, but How, and Where, and before Whom, in What Place, at What Time, and on What Occasion, we are to Speak; and may Direct and Frame our Discourse accordingly. *Caution* is also a very Useful and Necessary Ingredient in all Counsels or Consultations, for carrying on any State-Enterprize, or Affair and Undertaking of Importance. But then in the Use and Right Application of it, a good deal of Skill is required, in making the Proper Enquiries for our own Satisfaction, that such Undertaking is truly Honourable, and Conducive to the Public Welfare, and that we run no Hazard either of our own Reputation, or of the Safety and Interest of our Fellow-Citizens. All Good Counsel must on these Occasions be the Effect and Produce of Integrity, Foresight, and Prudence; and in tracing all the Parts of it, the *Senator* must exert all the Vigour of an Acute and Lively Invention, all his Sagacity and Caution, and (as I may venture to add) all his Cunning and Artifice. How Great and Necessary a Vertue Caution is, in all Military and Warlike Undertakings, I need not at present Mention; my chief Business and Design being to instruct the *Senator* how to behave in the *Commonwealth*, in the *Senate-House*, in the *Forum*, in the several Courts of *Judicature*, and to speak to him in his *Gown*, and not in his *Armour*. Let me only observe by the Way, that Wars are brought to a Speedy Conclusion much sooner, and with much better Success, by *Caution*, than by any other Vertue whatsoever. For by this Armies are Preserved, and the Designs

and

CHAP. II. *SENATOR* 193

and Stratagems of an Enemy Discovered and Defeated. So that let a Commander have all the other Military Vertues in Perfection, yet if he wants *Caution*, he can never Act up to the High Dignity and Character of a Great and *Accomplished General.*

Sagacity is Another Vertue, necessary to form the Character of an *Accomplished Senator*. Now *Sagacity* consists in a Quick, Ready, and Accurate Perception, and Apprehension, of the full Meaning, Drift, and Design, of whatever occurrs to us in the Way of Intelligence and Information, or in the Way of Counsel and Advice. *Sagacity*, in the Strictest Sense of the Word, is really nothing else but Sensation Quickened and Refined, to all the Nicety and Delicacy of which our Faculties are capable; whence this Vertue is sometimes Ascribed even to the Brute Animals that are beneath us. As our *Prudence* is shown in forming Good Counsels and Designs, of our own Contrivance; so our *Sagacity* is seen by our Readiness to Apprehend and Take, and by our Wisdom and Prudence, to form a Right Judgment of whatever is Offered or Proposed to us by Others.

Lastly, It is not enough for the *Good Senator* to be Acute and Quick-sighted in penetrating into all Publick Affairs, and in Judging of their Present State, and of their Issues, Events, and Consequences; but he must also be *Cunning*, and *Crafty*, a Master of Design, Artifice, and Stratagem, able to search out, and pry into, the very Thoughts and Intentions of his Fellow-Citizens, to know What are their Wills and Desires, what their Present Sentiments and Opinions, and what their Hopes and Expectations. For by knowing what they Intend and Design, he may be the better Able to keep them within the due Bounds and Limits of their Duty, and may have it in his Power to avert any Evils or Dangers, with which his Country

may

may be threatened. A Malcontent and Disaffected Body of Citizens will sometimes arise, and form Plots and Conspiracies against their Betters and Superiors, either out of Hatred and Malice, or in a sudden Fitt of Rage and Fury, or to shew their Bravery and Boldness, in Defence of their own Rights, when they imagine they are Oppressed, and held in Contempt by those, who have gotten the Sole Power and Government of the *Commonwealth* into their own Hands, and make no other Use of their High Titles, Great Riches, and Power, but to curb and restrain, to insult and trample upon their Subjects and Inferiors. From these Causes and Seeds of Discontent, arise open Hostilities, and a Resolution of Attacking and Subduing those in Power. Civil Wars, Tumults, and Seditions, readily follow: Death and Destruction are threatened and contrived; and if the first Stirs and Motions of such Malcontents, meet with Encouragement and Success, they care not if the Whole *Commonwealth* be thereby brought to the very Brink of Destruction. In order to a Timely Suppression of these Disorderly Motions and Tendencies to Rebellion, and for the effectual Quieting of the Minds of an Incensed and Ill-disposed People, the *Good Senator* must Interpose in Time, and exert not only all his Prudence, but all his Cunning, Artifice, and Subtlety. It may be in vain for him to imagine, that he can do any Good by mere Dint of Industry and Diligence, or by throwing himself into the Breach, and appearing openly in Defiance and Opposition to these Tumultuous Proceedings. His best Way will be to attack the Enemy in the Rear, or to break, and disunite his Forces, by annoying him at a Distance. At the same time he ought to omit no Persuasions, Admonitions, Intreaties, Remonstrances, Censures, or Chastisements, which may by Degrees reduce an Incensed and Disaffected People to a Softer, Gentler, and more Civilized Temper

Temper and Disposition. After which, he may freely throw in his Full Power and Authority, in order to avert the Evil with which his Country is threatened, and to preserve his Countrymen from ever entering upon the same or any such Wicked, Traiterous, and Execrable Designs.

CHAP. III.

The CONTENTS.

Of Consultation *and* Deliberation. *Of the Subject Matter of all* Deliberations. *Of Raising Money by* Taxation. *Of* Exports *and* Imports. *Of making* War *and* Peace. *Of the* Defence *and* Safeguard *of the* Realm. *Of* Trade *and* Commerce. *Of the Making of Good and Wholsome Laws.* Good Counsel *the Result of all Wise* Deliberations. *Of Things* Honest *and* Profitable, *and the Differences between them.* Fortune *ought never to be depended upon. Of* Subtle *and* Bold Undertakings. *Of* Rashness *and* Expedition. *Of* Preliminary Consultations. *Of Giving* Sentence *and* Opinion. *The Benefits of* Experience. *Of* True *and* False Oratory. *Of the Manner of* Voting *and* Giving Opinions. *Rules to be observed in* Speaking *and* Debating. *Of* Personal Attendance *in the* Senate. *The Perfection of the Senatorial Character. Of* False Patriots.

BY what Arts and Counsels, by what Ways and Means, the Peace and Tranquillity of a State may be Preserved or Restored, and all Factions, Tumults, and Seditions, may be Prevented or Suppressed; and all the Causes and Occasions, which gave Rise and Being to such Disorders, may be removed and taken away; is a Matter of the Highest Consequence, which ought to be again and again thought on, and well weighed, by the *Good Senator:* Because it is an Established Truth, that the Whole of his Duty is briefly comprehended in this, That he always take Care to preserve his Country in Peace and Security. The better to Forward and Perfect this Great and Glorious Design, the Pro-

per

per Means to be made Use of are, *Consultation* and *Deliberation*, the Ordinary and Natural Products of which are, Good Counsel and Advice, the only Proper and Salutary Medicines for a Distempered or Declining *Commonwealth*. In the Course and Progress of all Consultations, particular Care must be taken, that every Subject brought into Debate, may be well-weighed and throughly examined, in as Nice, Accurate, and Judicious a Manner, as Human Prudence, or Human Wit, can possibly Prescribe or Devise. All Consultations whatsoever proceed entirely upon such Matters only, as relate to Mankind, in a Publick or Social State, and to the Safety and Welfare of States and Communities. We are not to Deliberate or Consult upon such Affairs as are Proper and Peculiar to a Future State, and of Eternal and Immutable Duration. We are not to meddle with Impossible Events, with Natural Causes and their Effects, or with the Wild Rovings and Extravagances of Chance and Fortune. We are not to enquire into the Things of that World which is Above us, and out of our Reach, or into the Secrets of this Lower Subterraneous World, which are hid from us, and removed far out of our Sight. We are not to look for Hidden Treasure, or any other such Discoveries; of which there is not the least Sign or Token, to warrant the Probability of a Successful Enquiry: Neither are we to Dispute upon Trifles, and Things of no Consequence; such as a *Vacuum*, and the life; or upon what is already Past and Done, and which cannot be Altered: But all our Consultations must turn upon Future Events, or upon what may happen, either one Way or Other; and accordingly as it does happen, may thereby affect the Good and Welfare of our Fellow-Creatures and Fellow-Citizens. *Aristotle* has very justly reckoned up or enumerated Five different Sorts of Things, which are the Proper Subjects of Debate and Consultation; and these are, the Raising of Money by *Subsidies* and *Taxation*; the Proclaiming of *War*; and the Making of *Peace*; the Defence and

and *Safeguard* of the *Realm*; the Balance of the Several *Imports* and *Exports* in *Trade* and *Commerce*, and the Passing and Enacting of Good and Wholsome *Laws*. If a Consultation is to be held upon Ways and Means to raise Money, Enquiry must be made into the *Duties* and *Customs*, payable by a Country; that if they are too Small, they may be Augmented; and if too Great, they may be Lessened and Diminished: For no New Taxes ought to be Imposed or Collected, but upon a very Urgent and Necessary Occasion; because all such Extraordinary Impositions are grievous to the Subject; and how Just and Reasonable soever they may be, are often made the Occasion of Tumults, Seditions, and Civil Disorders. When the Emperor *Tiberius* was persuaded by some of his Friends, to Lay a New Duty or Tax upon the People, he very readily answered, *That a Good Shepherd had a Right to the* Fleeces *of his Flock, but had none to* Flay *and* Devour *them*. In the Disposition of the *Consumables* and *Provisions* of a Country, the Good *Senator* ought to advise the Keeping and Retaining of all such as are Necessary; and the Exportation of such only as a People can easily Spare, or are willing to Part with: And in Determining this Point Justly and Prudently, we must enquire into the Customs and Conditions of other Countries, as well as of our own; on which Occasion, *History* may be of great Use, and give us many Lights and Informations preliminary to all such Enquiries. In Deliberating upon the Two Great Affairs of *War* and *Peace*, it is first Necessary for us to know, what is the Present *Military State* of our Country; what, and how Numerous its Forces are; and how far they are capable of Reinforcement, or Augmentation; of what Sort the War is, which we are entring upon, and with what Enemy we Engage; whether with the *Turk, Tartar,* or any other Nation. A Strict Enquiry ought also to be made into the Forces and *Military* Strength of our Enemies; Whether their *Horse* or their *Foot*, are most Formidable;

whether

whether they are Disciplined and Exercised in the same, or in a different Manner from our own *Troops*; and whether they are a Match for us, or Inferior to us in Number and Strength; that we may Regulate our Conduct accordingly, and make *Peace* with those who are too Mighty for us, and *War* upon those who are Weak and Unable to resist us; the *Scheme* of which, and all its *Operations*, ought to be well Laid and Settled, upon the Best Principles of Prudential Foresight and Consideration. It may likewise be of Use to us, on these Occasions, to look over the Examples and Historical Accounts of Former *Wars*, their Rise, Progress, Issue, and Events. For Similar Instances and Parallel Examples always Illustrate and Explain each other. The Cause and Occasion of every *War*, and the Justice of it, must also be well assured, after many Trials, that the Matters in Difference, between us and another State, cannot be fairly Decided, but only by the Sword: For as the *Comedian* well observes, *'Tis a Wise Way of Proceeding, to try all Expedients for an Accommodation, before we come to Blows:* And an *Honourable Peace* is always Preferable to an *Unjust War*. In all Deliberations or Debates upon the Defence and *Safeguard* of the Realm, Enquiry must be made, and an Account taken, of what *Strong Holds* and Defensible Places, *Guards*, and *Garrisons*, are necessary for this purpose; and what is the Present condition, Order, and Discipline, of the *Standing Forces* and *Militia* of a Kingdom. And if the Debate be upon *Trade* and *Commerce*, and the *Exports* and *Imports* of a Country, it is in the First place requisite to Enquire, whether any Necessaries, of which the People are in Want, do ever go out of the Kingdom; and whether any thing is Exported or Sold to Foreigners, but only mere Superfluities, or the Residue and Overplus of what is spent at home. We must also take Care to make a Just *Estimate* and Calculation of the *Price*, and Value of all *Commodities*, sold to, or exchanged with Foreign Countries; and

and to *Balance* the *Difference* between *Profit* and *Loss*; that the *Publick Treasure* or *Current Coin* of a *Commonwealth*, may not be Lessened or Diminished: And we must likewise be Strict in prohibiting the *Importation*, or Use of all such *Consumables*, as serve to introduce or encourage Luxury and Effeminacy. But *Lastly*, the most Consummate Prudence is always requisite in the Making and Enacting of Good and Wholsome *Laws:* For therein consists the very Being, as well as Happiness of the Publick. On this Occasion, it is Necessary we should be well acquainted with the Whole State, Condition, and Circumstances of a Nation, the Present Situation of its Affairs; what *Laws* it Stands in need of; what New Ordinances will be well received by the People, or most effectually conduce to the Preserving and Strengthening of the Constitution, and the Securing and Promoting of the Common Good and Happiness. For the *Commonwealth* was not made for the Law, but the *Law* for the *Commonwealth*. And the better to inform ourselves upon this Subject of *Legislation*, it will be of great Use to us, to enquire into the Laws of other Countries, as well as of our own: Whereby we may know, how to guard against the Evils, under which our Neighbours labour; and to take Example by them, in all the Instances of Wisdom, and Good Conduct, for which they are Remarkable or Renowned. By the way it will be of great Advantage to us, in all Debates and Deliberations upon Matters of Moment, or of the First Consequence, not to depend altogether upon our own Judgment, but to Advise with Others, and to take them into all our Consultations. Because it is Impossible for one Single *Senator* to know every Thing, or to have more Wisdom than many *Counsellors*. It being an Undoubted Truth, that (as *Homer* observes)

Where Two *Advise,* One *must be Wiser made.*

The Natural Produce and Result of all Wise and Prudent Deliberations, is *Good Counsel*; whereby a Foundation is laid, for all Great and Noble Actions; and by this is seen the Superior Excellency and Utmost Perfection of the *Senatorial* Character. Now *Counsel* is nothing else but the Invention and Discovery of the Proper Means, Way, and Method, by which any Action, or Undertaking of Moment may be well Executed, or any Danger or Inconvenience avoided. It is a necessary Part of the *Senator*'s Office, to be ready, upon every Emergence, to give his Country good and wholsome Advice: And since in every Action or Undertaking, there are *Three* Things to be Considered, the *Counsel* that gives Rise to it, the *Method* in which it is carried on and conducted, and the *Issue* or Event of it; it is therefore as absolutely Necessary, that every such Undertaking should be preceded by a Wise and Prudent Deliberation, as that it should be followed by a Good and Prosperous Event: And as a *Gladiator* upon the Stage, well and wisely advises and considers with himself, when, and how, and where, to Attack and Wound his Adversary; in the very same manner, must the *Senator* look well to the Persons, Times, and Opportunities, whereto his Counsels are Aimed and Directed. There are (as *Cicero* observes) ----- *Three Sorts of Things upon which Men* Deliberate, *or Give and Take* Advice; *and these are Things Honest and Profitable, and the Differences that are between them, whenever they Interfere, or are Inconsistent with each other.* If in all these *Three Points*, the *Senator* is fully Instructed and Well-experienced, he can never be at a Loss, or unable to give good Advice, on any Occasion, or in any Affair of Publick Life. It is a High Degree of Wisdom, to judge aright of what is *Honest* and what is *Profitable*. And where Two Subjects of the same Sort offer themselves to our Consideration, it is a Mark of Uncommon Prudence to be able to decide, which of the Two is most *Honest* or most *Profitable*. Sometimes we are called upon to give an Extemporary

porary Advice, and are surprized into a Necessity of delivering our Opinion in haste, and at the very Moment it is demanded of us: But whenever, or in whatsoever Cases, we do this, we must never recede, or vary in the least Article, from the Two Main Points of *Profit* and *Honesty*; or, in other Words, we must always chuse the *Good*, and reject the *Evil*; and of Two Evils, where Both are Unavoidable, must be sure to make Choice of the Least. The Best and Readiest Way of forming Good and Wholsome Counsels, is to keep a Full and Steady Eye upon the *First* and *Greatest Good*, and to have it always in View, whether we are Deliberating upon Matters of Publick or Private Concern, of what relates to our own, or to our Country's Happiness. For from this First Principle all our Thoughts, Deliberations, and Counsels, ought to be Derived, and constantly Referred and Directed thereto. Unless the Publick Happiness be our Chief Aim in every Thing, all our Counsels and Deliberations are Vain and Fruitless. For how can the Mariner Steer a Right Course, when he knows not the Port to which he is Bound? In Debating within ourselves, what Advice is proper to be given, the Utmost Prudence is required; but in giving it out to others, the Utmost Sincerity and Fidelity. Bad Counsel is always most Fatal to those who take it, and Good and Faithful Advice their Greatest Benefit and Happiness. The *Senator* must also be Cautious, when he gives Advice, to leave as little Room as possible for *Fortune* to interpose, and play her usual Gambols and Feats of Extravagance. For Chance seldom brings about any Events, that carry with them Evident Marks and Resemblances of a Wise and Rational Contrivance. And as no Man is accounted truly Brave and Courageous, whose Courage depends more upon Good Luck and the Casual Success of it, than upon his own Deliberate Resolution; so neither can the *Senator* be truly and justly valued for Wisdom and Prudence, if in all his Conduct he depends more upon Chance and Fortune, than upon his own

Reason

Reason and Judgment. Let therefore all his Counsels and Undertakings, be the Effects of Prudence, Goodness, Fidelity, Mature Experience, Thorough Deliberation, Impartiality, and Freedom of Thought; without the least Stain or Mixture of Folly and Weakness, of Criminal Craft and Cunning, of Temerity and Rashness, or of Secret Malice and Ill-will to the Publick. Subtle and Artful, or Bold and Daring Undertakings, are to outward Appearance, Pleasant and Entertaining; they carry a Fair Face, and dazzle us with a False Lustre and Brightness; but 'tis a hard Task to Work them up and Prosecute them Aright, and they are often Pernicious and Fatal in their Consequences. Let the *Senator* also know, that nothing is a greater Obstacle to Good Counsel, than Eagerness and Temerity. For thereby we are often Betrayed into the Sad and Deplorable State, of a too Late and Unavailable Repentance. Many Instances might be given of this in some State Transactions, and many more of a much more Fatal Tendency in Affairs of War, and in the Management of Campaigns and Expeditions. But then on the other hand, whilst we are maturely Debating and Expediting any Publick Undertaking, we must have a Care how we use too many, or too long Delays. When our Scheme is well Laid, and throughly Formed, we may then be as Active and Expeditious as possible, in the Execution of it. There are many Affairs, which the *Good Senator* may with Decency enough avoid being Concerned in: But when once he is Engaged, he ought never to Desist, till they are happily Perfected and completed. We ought, as the Common *Proverb* directs, *To be Slow in Undertaking, but Quick in Execution*. The End and Design of what we Undertake is more to be Considered, than the Rise and Occasion; and all our Proceedings are to be Regulated and Justified, by the Great Law of *Necessity*. Every Commonwealth calls together its *Senate* and *Assembly* of Wise and Experienced Men, qualified by their Abilities, and obliged by their Office, to Deliberate

berate upon all the Affairs and Interests of their Country; maturely to weigh all Publick Designs and Projects, and to sit and ripen them for Execution. At all such Consultations and Meetings, such Men only ought to be Present, whenever Affairs come to be Treated of and Transacted, which are of the Utmost Consequence and Highest Importance to the Publick. It is, *Lastly*, of great Use and Service to a *Commonwealth*, to observe this Standing Rule, that the *Senate* never Enter upon any Business *within Doors*, but what has been before canvassed, and throughly examined *without*. For it is a Great Folly to imagine, that the most Important Affairs can be presently Dispatched, or require no more Consideration, than only of a short Hour, or a few Transitory Moments.

After Deliberation and Consultation regularly had and taken, nothing remains but the Giving our *Sentence*, Judgment, or Opinion, in any Affair of State, then under Consideration. Such *Sentence* is nothing more than the Open Declaration, or Signification of the Thoughts and Counsels of the Mind. The Voice and Speech are the Proper Instruments and Means of Conveying our Sentiments to Others, in order to make them acquainted with the Secret Designs and Intentions of our Heart. There is a *Judicial Faculty* implanted in us by Nature: For we often find some Men, who have no great Character for Learning and Wisdom, are yet very much to be depended upon, for their Judgment and Opinion, and in time come to be Masters of very Good Sense, Great Cunning, and Sagacity, by mere dint of Use and Experience, which are a Sure Guide and Introduction to True Prudence. Men of more Years, than Learning, are therefore very much to be relied upon for their Judgment; because Age and Experience have in Effect supplied them with a *Third* Eye, by which they are enabled to make a Survey, both of Past Transactions, and Future Events, as well as of the Present, with so much the

more

more Accuracy and Exactness. We really know not what a Man is, till we have been Witnesses to his Conversation; and till a *Senator* has delivered his Mind and Judgment, there is no Forming a true Notion, either of his Wisdom or Prudence. *Socrates*, one Day meeting a Youth, whom he had never seen before, looked for some time very earnestly upon him, and at last said to him, *Speak, that I may know what You are.* The very same Method must be used, and the same Experiment tried, before we can approve the Wisdom and Gravity of the *Good Senator*, or pronounce him duly Qualified for his High Station and Office. For Speech is the Indication, the Image, and Representative of the Mind: And by this, must the *Senator* give Proofs of his Judgment, and of the Force and Extent of his Capacity; always Directing all his Discourses to the Good and Welfare of the Publick; for this is the Great End and Design of all *Senatorial* Sentences and Opinions whatsoever. There are some *Orators*, whose Speeches are all Gloze and False Colouring, intended rather to Please and Tickle, than to Inform and Instruct. Their Words are all Tinsel and Feathers, Shew and Ornament; and they have more Regard in what they say, to Finess and Delicacy, than to Plain and Solid Truth. Were their Speeches to be taken to Pieces, searched and sifted to the Bottom, they would appear to be mere Froth and Emptiness, void of all Weight and Solidity, Fidelity, Veracity, and Sincerity. The Good *Senator*'s Rhetorick must never be thus Adulterated. He may display his Eloquence before the Wise and Eloquent, but he must speak Truth even before Fools. There is another Sort of *Speakers*, who are Swoln and Bloated with Pride, Malice, and Jealousy, enraged and incensed by some Private Quarrel and Animosity; and whenever they have gotten an Opportunity of Speaking in Publick, lay about them altogether with Personal Reflections and Calumnies. These Men are of no Use and Advantage to the Publick, and serve only to kindle a Fire, to infuse Jealousies and
Misunder-

Misunderstandings, and to ruffle the Peace of a Country, by introducing Parties and Factions, Hatred, Discord, and Contention. If they were really Good Men, or Good Subjects, they would Stifle or Conceal their Private Quarrels, Suspicions, and Animosities; and make it their Choice, as well as think it to be their Duty, not to trouble the *Commonwealth* with them, under Pretence of doing it Service. There is also a Third Sort of *Senators*, who for want of a Capacity, for Counsel and Abilities in Speaking, implicitly give into the Sentiments of Others, and always Tread in their Steps; whence the *Romans* commonly called them, *Pedarian Senators*. They who behave in this manner, are really not much to blame, unless they are obliged to it, by downright Ignorance and Stupidity. For it is of Use and Benefit to a State, to have the less Able and Skilful Members of its Councils, readily complying with, and assenting to the Sentiments and Advice of their Wiser and more Experienced Leaders. And sometimes it happens, that a *Senate* is Unanimous, and all its Members of one Will and one Mind: On which Occasion, it is much the wisest Way, readily to concurr in the General Opinion, and not to give any Opposition, only for the Sake of making a Speech, or to Spin out the Time, by Long and Tedious, or Bombast and Fulsome Harangues. Differences in Opinion will unavoidably happen, and must consequently occasion Various and Dilatory Debates and Altercations; whereby a *Senate* may be Split and Divided into Opposite Sides and *Parties*. In all Attempts to compose these Differences, and to bring all such Debates to a Good and Happy Conclusion, we must be very Careful to avoid all Indecent Language, all Excess of Passion, all Calumnies, Reproaches, and Personal Resentments; with whatever else may Interrupt the Course of a Regular and Wise Consultation, or Ruffle, or Alienate the Affections of our Brethren in the same Trust and Office. In order to put an effectual End to all such Debates, and the Divisions that follow

low thereupon, the *Majority* must always finally Determine the Matter in Dispute: For it is most Agreeable to Justice and Reason to think, that what a Multitude of Wise and Able Counsellors are agreed in, must be most for the Benefit and Advantage of the Publick.

The Way and Method of giving Opinions, or taking Suffrages, is very Different in some States and Nations, from what it is in others. In some Countries the Order is, that the *Seniors* should be first Heard in Delivering their Judgment; in others, the *Juniors* have the Preference, and in a Third Sort, the Way is, to call upon the Wisest, and the most Prudent and Experienced Counsellors, to give their Opinion before those of a Less Distinguished Character. Every Government must keep to its own Customs; and whatever hath obtained a Prescription of many Years, and is agreeable to the Prevailing Opinion and Constant Usage of a Nation, is thereupon to be received by the People, as Good, and Just, and Equitable, and for the Interest and Advantage of the Society. It is, however, a much better Way for the *Seniors* to deliver their Opinion first, that the *Juniors* may thereby have more Time and Opportunity of Deliberating upon the Question. And on the other hand, when the *Juniors* are first heard, what they say may very often occasion Differences and Divisions among the *Seniors*, and Puzzle or Entangle a Matter in Dispute, by a Multiplicity and Variety of Opinions. It may also be Convenient not to permit the *Members* to speak, when, and as often as they please, but to call upon them for their Sentence and Judgment; whereby Order and Decency may be Preserved, and Tumult and Contention may be Avoided. And on this Occasion, the *Members* may be at Liberty, to give in their Doubts and Scruples, which may be well excused by the Difficulty of the Question, and the Great Variety of Opinions thereupon; whereby a Well-meaning Mind is easily Perplexed, and cannot presently Resolve which Side to chuse. But then

then in complying with, or adhering to the Judgment of Others, we must be careful to avoid all Suspicion of Rashness and Precipitancy, and of Party or Personal Affection: And our Concurrence must be the Effect of our own Reason and Judgment. The Opinions and Resolutions of a *Senate*, are to be valued by their *Weight*, and not by the *Tale* or *Number* of *Voices:* And great Care must be taken, that the Best and Wisest Members of a Council may not be Borne-down, or Overpowered, by the Multitude or *Majority*. *Aristotle* permitts a Counsellor, deliberating upon any Affair of Moment, to be *Twice* in Doubt; but if after this, he could not come to any Settled Resolution, he was for that time to lose his Right of giving any Opinion at all. We must also be Cautious, how we Protract the Day, and spend too much Time in Debating a Question, without coming to any Resolution. For we are Guilty of a Double Fault, when we Tire both ourselves and Others, with Long and Tedious Harangues. *Cato* was once very severely Censured by *Cæsar*, for Trespassing upon the *Senate* in this very Particular. A decent Brevity is always to be observed in Speaking, as also an Honest Plainness, and a Clear and Open Sincerity, without Dawb and Flattery, without any Alluring and Enticing, or any Cloudy or Doubtful, Perplexed or Obscure Expressions. We must not be Over-eager and in Haste to Speak, nor lay any Snares for others, or mingle any little Trick, Artifice, or Fallacy, with what we Deliver. Every thing we say must have its Weight, and carry with it a Serious, Solid, and Important Meaning; and must be well Seasoned with Simplicity, Piety, Sanctity, and Truth. Perhaps too it may not be amiss, to have every *Senator* solemnly Sworn, before he gives his Opinion, that thereby the *Divine Being* may be called upon as a Witness to the Truth and Sincerity of the Heart. There is no very Material Difference between delivering an Opinion in *Writing*, or by *Word of Mouth:* The Surest and Concisest Way is to give it in *Writing*, especially upon all those Subjects, to which we cannot Speak so

justly

justly and fully as we ought, without being very Prolix and Tedious. In short, These *Three* Rules, laid down by *Cicero* in his *Laws*, ought to be carefully Observed by every *Senator*; *First*, that he constantly give his *Attendance* in the *Senate:* Because a *Full House* or Assembly, always gives so much the Greater Weight and Authority to all its Decrees and Resolutions. *Secondly*, That he Speak only in his Proper *Place*, or Turn, or when he is called upon: And *Thirdly*, that he Speak in such a Manner, as to keep always close to the Subject in Debate, without Sallying forth into the Infinite and Boundless Mazes of Prolixity and Impertinence. That *Senator*, who wilfully and carelessly Absents himself from the Publick Service, without a Just and Allowable Cause of such his Absence, ought (as the same *Author* enjoins) to be Censured and Punished as a Criminal. Neither is it Convenient that *Senators* should be permitted to leave the City in which such Assemblies are held, and to withdraw themselves into any Foreign Territories or Dominions; unless they are sent abroad by their own Country, to take upon them some Command of Consequence, or to execute an Embassy, or some other Commission of the like Nature and Importance: Lest by Thinning the *Senate*, or by the Members absenting themselves, some Detriment or Prejudice should unhappily befall the *Commonwealth*. The *Romans* took Care to prevent the Ill Consequences of such a Practice, by a Law made for that very purpose.

But after all, the Great and Fundamental Principle, which gives Rise to all the *Senatorial* Dignity, which crowns his Character, and makes it Perfect, is his Conformity in all his Words and Actions, and in all the Relative Capacities and Offices of Life, to the Strict Rules of Vertue and Piety, and by approving himself a Just and Good Man, and adorning his Station with a Suitable Conduct and Behaviour. It is not enough for us, that we are Wise and Prudent, unless we are Good and Vertuous too. For Prudence, without

out Justice and Goodness, dwindles to Craft and Cunning, and is commonly looked upon rather as a Vice, than a Vertue. Wise Men are Denominated from their Wisdom, but it is Vertue that gives the Good, the Just, the Equitable, and the Honest Man, his Proper Titles; and makes him to be in Character, what he is really called by Name: And Good Men take their Style from their Vertues, and not from their Wisdom. Who then is a truly Good Man, but such a One as is Described by *Plato, Who well Understands what Vertue is, who takes it into his Bosom, and Closest Embraces, and lives up to all its Strictest Commands and Dictates; and who chuses to die for the Sake of his Country, and to Save her from any Imminent Danger, or from falling into an Abject State of Servitude; or from being oppressed by the Arbitrary Dominion of Tyrants and Usurpers, or of Men eminent and remarkable only for their Baseness and Infamy.* Such *Patriots* will endure every thing, rather than see the Ancient Constitution of their Native Kingdom altered or overturned: For every Change or Alteration always turns out to the Prejudice and Disadvantage of the People. The *Senator* must therefore Use his Best Endeavours to approve himself an Example and Lively Instance, not only of Prudence, but of Goodness and Justice too: For Prudence is no longer a Vertue, than whilst it is coupled and goes hand in hand with Justice; and it is Justice that gives the Distinguishing Title and Character to all Good Men. There are some Men, raised to High Stations and Dignities in the State, who thrust themselves forward into Publick Business, by a Prompt and Easy Faculty and Fluency of Speaking, and by giving Proofs of a Lively Wit, and more than Ordinary Sagacity; whilst their Heart and Mind are full of all manner of Deceit and Subtlety. When such Men as these are engaged in Supporting the Laws, or in Defending the Liberties of their Country, no Orators whatsoever can Deliver themselves with a Better Grace, or with more Beauty and Elegance: But when their Speeches are
closely

closely attended to, searched and sifted to the Bottom, they are all Sediment and Corruption; Wrong and Injustice are the Lees and Remainder of all their Fluency; there is nothing truly Great and Noble in what they Say, nothing but Froth and Emptiness: For all their Pretences to Prudence are a mere Mask and a Vizor, and the Tongue that utters such Enticing Musick, is by no means in Concert, or has any Communication with the Heart. There is not a Greater Plague, or more Deadly Poison, that can possibly Visit or Infect the Body Politick, than a Sett of such Men, when lurking within the Bowels of a Government; especially, if by their Power and Authority they are so Stationed and Situated, as to be able to Distress and Incommode it. In this Class of Men, are to be Numbered all Those, who are of a Debauched and Licentious Disposition and Character; or who set themselves up for Men of Reach and Penetration, Artifice and Stratagem, or for Lovers of their own Interest, by a Readiness to committ all Manner of Oppression and Injustice, or by promoting Tumults, Seditions, and all other Publick Disorders. Bad as these Men are, in nothing is their Villany seen to greater Perfection, and at no Time is it more Successful, than when they can draw in their Countrymen to believe, they are really Honest, Good, and Faithful Subjects: For as Men in general, when raised to the Full Dignity and Highest Attainments of his Nature, is undoubtedly the Best and Noblest of all Animals; so when he falls altogether as Low, and as far beneath the Standard of Law and Justice, he is of all the Rest of his own Species the most Vile and Dangerous. In all our Addresses to Heaven, for the Safety and Welfare of our Country, it ought to be our First and most Earnest Prayer, that all such Citizens and Subjects may be utterly Destroyed and Rooted out. But till this can be done, the *Senator* is to Use his Best Endeavours, that all of this Character may be Reclaimed in Time,

and

and brought back into the Ways of Truth and Justice. Hitherto we have seen what *Prudence* is, the next Vertue to be enquired into is *Justice*; and particularly That Sort of Justice, which is an Essential Part of the *Senatorial* Character.

CHAP. IV.

The CONTENTS.

Of Natural Justice. *Of Mutual* Benevolence *and* Good-will. *Of* Piety. *Of* Self-Preservation, *or the* Justice *due to ourselves.* *Of* Divine Justice, *or the* Justice *which is due to our* Maker. *Of* Natural Religion. *Of* Publick Worship. *Of the* Christian Institution *and* Priesthood. *The* Danger *of attempting to Alter the* Established Religion. *How such* Innovations *come to be Fatal to a* State. Religion, *how far advantageous to a* Government. *Examples of the ill Consequences of* Religious Innovations. *Of the Character of* Sanctity *as annexed to the* Senate. *Of the Method of* Opening *every* Senatorial Assembly. *Of* Human *or* Civil Justice. *All* Justice *is founded in* Fidelity. *The Character of a* Faithful Man. *Of* Justice *in the Distribution* of Honours. *Of the* Ancient Method *of* Decreeing Honours. *How Those of a* Publick Character *are* Distinguished *by the* Moderns. *Of* Numerical *and* Judicial Equality. Dueling *condemned. Of* Executive Justice. *Of* Primitive Justice. *The* End and Design *of all* Good Laws. *Of* Idleness *and* Luxury. Industry *ought to be* Encouraged. *The* Old Laws *of a* State *ought rather to be* Amended *than* Repealed. *Every* Senator *ought to be* Punctual *in the Observation of the* Laws. *Of the* Judge's Duty. *Of* Severity *and* Moderation.

Whoever Surveys and Considers the General State and Condition of all Things both in Heaven and Earth, may easily find, that *Nature* observes a constant and regular Course, and hath established certain Firm, Perpetual, and

and Unalterable Rules, and Laws of Motion and Action, which the Beings around us are not of themselves able to break through; but are always Kept and Restrained to their own Proper Sphere, and within the Limits of one and the same Track and Circuit, from which they can never vary, and out of which they can never Deviate or Wander. The *Celestial* Orbs and Elements, the Several Orders of the *Animal* World, the *Volatile* and *Reptile* Species, have an Innate Energy, Tendency, and Instinct, bestowed upon them, not by Chance and Fortune, but by the Contrivance and Direction of an All-Wise *Creator*, the Constant Courses and Regular Effects of which, they have not the Will, or if they had a Will, they would still be unable to Alter or Supercede. What now shall I say of Man? Is it not Plain and Evident, that his *Maker* hath set before him Good and Evil, and hath annexed thereto Life and Death, Happiness and Misery, as a Reward and Punishment; and that the Ways leading thereto, the One on the Right-Hand, Narrow, Rugged, and almost Unpassable; and the other on the Left, Plain, Pleasant, and Easy of Access, Wide, and capable of receiving whole Multitudes of Travellers, are readily Marked out and Set before him? And that the Good and Pious are easily prevailed upon, to make Choice of the Narrow Path leading to Life, and the Vicious and Wicked as easily betrayed or enticed into the Broad Way leading down to Destruction? But to come still closer to the Subject we are upon, that is, the Art of Governing *Cities* and *Commonwealths*; If the Rule of Publick Life, and the Scheme and Method of Administration be Good and Perfect in its Kind, Firm, Certain, and Unalterable, agreeing in every Part with the Law of Nature or Right Reason, or in other Terms, with the Law of *God*, every Body Politick, under such a Direction, and constantly adhering thereto, will be Lasting and Perpetual; and whenever it departs from this Rule, will dwindle and fall away into a State of Weakness

ness and Corruption. To enter into, and go over every Particular Instance, were an Endless Task: But in general it is certain, that all the Beings which our Senses can discover, or our Understanding search into, were by Nature made Perfect in their Kind, complete in every Part, and put under one and the same constant Regulation. Hence it was, that to live up to the Dictates of *Nature*, was by the *Stoicks* looked upon as the Sum and Perfection of Human Happiness. For *Nature* is our Great Mistress, the sure Unerring Guide of Life; and in Following and Obeying her, we Follow and Obey the *God* and Author of *Nature*. The General Agreement therefore, the Consent and Harmony of *Nature*, may very properly be called *Justice*. For Justice is a Vertue that directs us how to maintain those Rights, Compacts, and Agreements, which Nature hath Established or Assented to. So that whatever is agreeable to *Nature*, is really and truly Justice; and Injustice consists in Crossing upon, or in Deviating from this Principle. They who live as *Nature* directs, and are obedient to her in every thing, ought therefore to be Reputed as strictly Just. For not to Think or Do any Thing that may Offend *Nature*, or *God*, or *Man*, is the very Height and Perfection of all *Justice*. And hence it is, that they who treat of Justice, do commonly divide it into *Three* Parts, Natural, Divine, and Human.

Natural *Justice* has its Rise from the First Principles and Dictates of *Nature*, which has kindled up Certain Lights in us, whereby we are enabled to discern between the Good we ought to Chuse, and the Evil we ought to Shun and Avoid. 'Tis the Great Law of Equity, that we abstain from all Injuries; and never Contrive or Attempt any thing, which may be Hurtful or Displeasing to Others. Mutual Benevolence or Good-will to Mankind, is that Great and Fundamental Vertue, by which Men are drawn together, and united in one Common Body, or Publick Society.

Society. In the First Pure Age, which the *Poets* call *Golden*, Justice bore so absolute a Sway, that no Fraud, Violence, or Injury could approach to hurt, or to interrupt the Peace of Human Societies: No Seditions, Tumults, Parties, or Contentions broke in upon the General Tranquillity. But Mutual Confidence, Love, and Benevolence, were every where seen in the Utmost Perfection; and Mankind, without the Assistance of a Legislator, Judge, or Advocate, knew how to Discern and to Chuse what was Good and Right, and were as Studious to promote the Ease and Interest of their Brethren and Friends, as to Secure and take Care of their own. This Vertue prompts and directs us, how, and in what manner, we ought to Love our Parents, Children, and all others who are in any degree Allied or Related to us. The Justice due to our Parents, is commonly called *Piety*; and for this Vertue the Daughter of *Cymon* was so eminently Remarkable, that when her Father was Condemned to be Starved, she fed him with her own Milk, through the Grates of his Prison, and thereby Returned him the Life he gave her, and gave herself an Immortal Reputation. The Doctrine of Self-Preservation, is a First Principle, common to us and all other Living Creatures whatsoever, and is the Immediate Result of Natural Instinct. There is a Debt of Justice which we owe to ourselves, and in Consequence of which, we are bound to Maintain and Support ourselves in Life, to Defend and Preserve our own Beings, and to look well to the Conduct and Good Government of all our Actions: Whilst they, who by Want, and Famine, or out of a Wilful Neglect and Contempt of Life, offer Violence to themselves, and destroy their own Being, are to be Censured as Notoriously Unjust, and as Professed Enemies to Human Nature in general. We are also obliged by Nature to take Care of our Friends, and to promote their Interest and Welfare; and by Preserving and Keeping up our own Families, to Preserve Posterity, and to Keep up and Strengthen the

next

next Generation. In short, they who follow Nature are truly Just, and whatever is Unnatural is consequently Unjust. For Nature has an Abhorrence to what is Evil, and dictates nothing but what is Right and Good. This Natural Justice the Scholars and Followers of *Socrates* did accordingly Define to be *The Science or Knowledge of what is Right and Good, and most Agreeable to Reason.* He who exercises this Vertue in Private Life, and makes it the Chief Guide of all his Actions, may be truly called a *Good Man*; whilst He who communicates the Fruits and Effects of this Vertue to the Publick, is alike Entitled to the Character of a *Good Citizen:* Because he is a Common Benefit, and does Good to others as well as to Himself. This sort of Justice, which consists in Living up to the Dictates of Nature, is not only the Glory and Ornament of the *Senator*, but of every Private Person whatsoever. They, however, whom Nature hath happily Distinguished, by bestowing on them a Larger Share of her Best Gifts and Endowments, ought in Proportion to Distinguish themselves, by a more Regular and Eminent Practice of this Vertue. And above all, the *Good Senator* ought to be most Eminent for this Vertue, in regard to the High Station in which he Shines, and in Gratitude to Nature, who gave him the Abilities that Qualified him for his Office. 'Tis his Glory to Excell and Outshine others in Justice; and it is his Shame and Disgrace, if others Outshine him in Vertue, who are Inferior to him in Dignity. These Rules and Precepts, relating to Natural Justice in general, which I have here laid down, are of Use to all Mankind, in the Ordinary Affairs, Conduct, and Intercourses of Life.

Divine Justice, or the Justice due to our *Maker*, is an Obligation laid upon us by Nature to Acknowledge, to Worship, to Fear, to Love, and to Reverence Him. This is a Privilege, as well as Duty, peculiar only to Man. For Nature, in the Formation of all Living Creatures whatsoever, took Care, that the

Notion

Notion of a *Deity* should be Fixed and Implanted only in the Mind of Man. To our *Creator* we look up, whilst the Animals beneath us are Prone and Intent upon the Earth, and Stoop down to their several Pastures, for Food and Nourishment. Man therefore, of all other Animals, in their several Kinds and Orders, is the only Being in the World, with whom Nature hath Entrusted the High and Honourable Office of Worshipping and Adoring his *Maker*, and of giving him the Reverence and Honour due unto his Name. The Natural Notion of Religion, is of such General Prevalence and Extent, that the World never yet produced a Nation, that did not Acknowledge some *Deity* or other, and think it Just, Reasonable, and Necessary, to Institute and Keep up an Established Form of Publick Worship and Adoration. There is a Communication and Intercourse between the Divine and Human Nature, which is Cemented and Strengthened by Natural Necessity and Benevolence, and can never be Interrupted or Torne in Sunder, so long as Man is the Offspring and Child of *God*, and is therefore obliged to look up to, and to Honour and Reverence him, as the Common Parent and Father of all Mankind. The Worship of the *Deity* ought always to be under the Strictest Regulation of Order and Decency, and to be kept up in Sanctity, Purity, and Piety; that we may thereby Serve our *Maker* both with Heart and Voice, and with a Mind Chaste and Upright, and free from Stain and Corruption. All our Sanctity and Piety, and our whole Duty towards *God*, is briefly summed up and contained in this Single Word, *Religion*, which consists in performing the Services, in giving the Honours, and in making the Return of Gratitude, due unto our *Maker*, with a Heart full of Purity and Holiness. Hence they are called *Saints*, or Holy and Religious Men, who are Commissioned or Appointed to draw the Body of the People together, and to Order and Prescribe the Forms and Regulations of Divine Worship. Such are the several *Priests* and *Bishops* in the
Christian

Christian Commonwealth, who are Authorized and Empowered from above, to Propagate Religion, and to Instruct Mankind in all its Doctrines and Precepts; at whose Hands we are taught to expect the only True and Perfect Method of Worshipping and Reverencing our *Maker* aright. These Men are the *Forerunners* and Harbingers of the *Almighty*, sent before him to Proclaim and make Known his Name to the World; whom we are to receive, as if our *Maker* himself were present. They are the *Interpreters* of his Laws, and the *Officers* appointed to give us Notice of his Good Will and Pleasure. As in all Religious Enquiries, the First and Principal Thing to be Regarded, is fully to Know and Understand, Who, and What, our *God* really is, what He requires of us, and in what Way he would have us Worship him; for without this Knowledge, we can never be so Just to Him, as in Duty we are bound to be; so in the Fulness of this Knowledge, and in our Conformity thereto, consists the Whole of all Human Happiness: And for Happiness we were Ordained, at the very Time when our *Creator* made us.

Jesus Christ, the Son of the Only True *GOD*, is That *Saviour*, who hath Enlarged our Knowledge of Heavenly Things, and Revealed to us the Whole Will and Pleasure of his *Father:* He hath given his own *Kingdom*, that is the Church, a Perpetual *Law*, of Divine Authority; hath Instituted a New Spiritual *Magistracy* or *Priesthood*, and hath laid down Certain Precepts and Rules of Government, which carry with them Plain Marks and Indications of their Heavenly Original. The Priests, or Spiritual Magistrates and Officers of his Kingdom, are by his own Deputation invested with High Power and Authority, are in effect his Vicars and Viceregents, and in virtue of their Delegation made Partakers in some Measure of his Divinity; at whose Hands we are to expect a Sure Judgment and Decision in all Religious Disputes and Controversies, and to attend to them as the Keepers and Interpreters, not only of of the *Old Decalogue*, but of the *New Commandments* and *Institutions* superadded to the *Law of Moses*; in so Full and Ample a Manner, that all They who would be well and throughly acquainted with True Religion, and know in what Way their *Maker* ought to be Worshiped, with Justice, Sanctity, and Piety, should resort to these only, and to no other Guides or Directors whatsoever: The Great and Divine *Lawgiver*, having expressly Forbidden, by a Law of his own, that we should not listen to any other Guides or Teachers, but those commissioned by himself, and appointed to be the Interpreters of the Divine Will and Justice, and Promulgators of the Laws and Decrees of Heaven. As therefore in the Civil State, or Commonwealth, we Resort for Justice to the Publick Magistrate; so in the Spiritual or *Christian* Commonwealth, of which we are Members, we Resort to the *Spiritual Magistrates*, the *Priests*, and *Bishops*, for Decision in all Matters of Religion, Faith, Piety, and *Justice* towards *God*. They who assume to themselves a Right of Judging and Determining in Spiritual Affairs, and will not be Determined by the Proper *Magistrate* appointed for that very purpose, but treat him and his Authority with Hatred, Despight, and Contempt, are no better than Traitors and impious Promoters of Sedition; corrupt and unworthy Members of the Body Politick, and justly liable to the Severest Punishments, Infamy, Banishment, and Death. What then shall we say of those Men, who fly from their own Country into some Foreign City or Commonwealth, for the Sake of Embracing some New and Strange Religion; whilst they Reject and Despise the Laws, the Faith, Piety, and Holy Institutions of their own *Church* and *Nation*, wherein they were Born and Educated; and had rather remain as Exiles in a Strange Country, than Stay at home and retain the Honourable Names of Countryman and Fellow-Citizen? Such Behaviour, and such open and barefaced Violence offered to Religion, is utterly Unjustifiable and without Excuse. A Change of Religion is the worst Plague that

can

can Infest a Government, and the most likely Means to Overturn or Subvert it. *Tully* hath very well observed, That *Religious Broils and Commotions are always attended with Changes and Revolutions in the State.* And for this very Good Reason may be given; for since every Government owes its Preservation to the Good will and Favour, the Care and Oversight of Providence: And since no State can plead a Title to this Favour, but only on the Account of Religion, which binds and obliges us, and is as it were a League and Covenant, between Us and our *Maker*; the Conditions of which are plainly these, That we on our part shall Serve and Worship him, and He on His shall Defend and Protect, Bless and Prosper us in all our Undertakings; it must follow, that upon every Change of Religion, there must be also a Change in the Worship of *God*, and upon the Alteration of the Publick Worship, the Minds of Men will be altered at the same time, and run out and wander into a Variety of Opinion, always Wavering and Unsettled, and Rambling to and fro in a Confused State and *Chaos* of Religions; the Natural Consequence of which is, a General Prevailing Contempt of the *Deity*, whereby he cannot but be justly Angry, and highly Incensed at the Change he finds in his People, provoking Him to give them Proofs of his Indignation, by exposing them to the Fatal Consequences of their own Novel Humors, by leaving them to themselves, or pushing them down the Precipice, upon which they stand Tottering and Unguarded. Faith and Piety are the Favourites of Heaven; and by these Vertues a Nation is Exalted and made Happy. Every thing goes well, and prospers with those, who serve *God* faithfully; and every evil Thing is the Portion of those, who are at Enmity with him. Besides this, the Power of Religion is really so very Great, and has such an Influence upon the Minds of Men, that together with Religion they readily believe themselves fully Possessed of all the Vertues belonging to Human Nature, and under the most Sacred Obligations, both of Duty and Constancy, to Keep and Retain them. He who truly

truly Fears and Worships his *Maker*, will always find in himself an Harmonious Agreement and Concurrence of all the Vertues, firmly Established and ever Increasing, True and Genuine, Lasting and Unchangeable. The several Vertues of *Justice*, *Prudence*, and *Temperance*, are always included in the True Worship of *God*, and are so closely Bound up and Interwoven with Religion, that it is impossible to Divide and Separate between them. Constancy in Religion is the sure Means of Perpetuating the Laws, Customs, Vertues, and Constitution of a Government. But when Religion is Altered, Mankind are Altered at the same time, and all the Laws, Customs, and Vertues of a Country, are immediately Changed and Subverted. Whence follows a General Disorder, and Confusion of all things in Human Life; and Seditions, Tumults, Animosities, Contentions, Wars, and Bloodshed, are the Natural Consequences of such a State, and hasten the Destruction and Final Overthrow of a Government. For how can we imagine, that the Wicked and Unjust, the Lovers and Promoters of Sedition and Discord, should be duly Qualified to become Mediators, or to treat of Peace and Amity, of Justice and Religion? And what Justice can we expect to find in a City or Commonwealth, or what Fidelity, or Social Agreement among Men, when Piety and Religion are once set aside? How shall he, who is Unfaithful to his *Maker*, be True to his Brethren and Fellow-Subjects? And how shall the Man, who is always Unstable and Wavering in Matters of Religion, come to be Fixed and Settled, or to Behave with Uniformity, in all his other Actions, and with a Steady Adherence to all his Compacts and Promises? We all wish for Peace in our own Country; But what Peace can be expected from those Men, who are always at War with Faith, Religion, and their own Consciences? Our First and Greatest Wish ought ever to be, that the True Religion may be Settled among us, in all Sanctity and Purity; and then, that it may be firmly Established, and remain Unalterable. Every Change

Change in a Well-settled Government, is carefully to be avoided; but of all other Changes, a Change in Religion is the most Fatal and Dangerous.

How many States and Kingdoms does History give us an Account of, which, on Account of Altering the Established Religion, have been miserably Mangled and Afflicted, or finally Ruined and Destroyed? When the *Grecian* quarrelled with the *Latin* Empire, and fell into Schism and Dissension, it soon lost not only its Religion, but its Liberty and Language too; and is now reduced to a State of Abject and Ignominious Slavery under the *Turk*. With our own Eyes we have seen Countries wallowing in Blood, and are Witnesses to such a Scene of Calamities, as we had much rather Pity and Deplore, than attempt to Describe in its Proper Colours and Circumstances. Other Nations have engaged in War for the Defence of their Religion, but the *Grecian* Empire, by taking Arms against Religion itself, reaped no other Benefit from the Quarrel, but to see herself Stained and Contaminated with her own Gore. I say nothing of *France* and *Flanders*; both which Countries are hardly yet recovered of the Wounds they received in a Religious War. And I willingly pass over many other States and Kingdoms, who, in attempting to change the Established Religion, have suffered in an Exemplary Manner, and brought such a Yoke and Burden upon their Necks, as they are not yet able to shake off. In general, there is nothing that so effectually Blinds the Minds of Men, or sooner Infatuates them, and sets them a Madding, than the Rash and Headstrong Enterprize of Altering an Established Religion, when once the Giddy Multitude have set their Hearts upon it. And therefore every Good Magistrate, and especially Those of the *Sacerdotal* Order, can never be enough careful to Guard against all Innovations and Changes in Religion; and whenever any such are introduced into a State, to call them immediately into Judgment, that they may

be

be Censured and Condemned, and together with the Guilty Authors of them, may be utterly Abolished, Rooted out, and Exterminated.

Let therefore the *Good Senator* be Well-settled and Confirmed in his Religious Judgment and Sentiments, and let him not Waver or be Doubtful and Sceptical in his Opinion. For Constancy in Religion is the Foundation of True Wisdom, Vertue, and Honour. An Unstable Man, and one of Unsettled Notions in Matters of Religion, ought by no Means to approach the *Senate-House*. For in the Great Council of a Nation, nothing ought to be Transacted or Decreed, which is contrary to Sound Faith, and true Religion; but every Debate and Determination therein, ought to be the Effects of Constancy and Perseverance in the Principles of Sincerity, Sanctity, Purity and Religion. Hence the Name of *Senate* had always the Additional Title of *Holy* or *Sacred*, annexed to it, because the Matters there Treated of and Decreed, were looked upon, not only by the Eyes of the Subject, but of God *himself*, as truly Sacred and of Divine Authority. For this Reason it was, that the Place in which the *Senate* assembled, was always esteemed as *Holy*, and the *Senators* assembled therein, out of Regard to this supposed Holiness, thought themselves obliged to abstain from all Counsels, which Savoured of the least Guilt or Impiety. When the *Romans* held a *Senate*, they opened the Assembly with offering of Frankincense, and a Sacrifice to That God, in whose Temple they met. By a *Christian Senate* quite a Different Method ought to be taken; and before they Proceed to Business, Supplications and Prayers ought to be made to the only True *God*, with all Piety, Sanctity, and Religious Devotion. For a *Senator* therefore to entertain any false or erroneous Opinions in Religion, is not only Indecent, and Unbecoming his Character, but Impious, Sacrilegious, and Abominable.

They who are conversant in Philosophy, generally make Choice of the *Peripatetick* Scheme above all others, and adhere strictly thereto, in all their Writings and Disputations; because it really contains the Justest and Clearest Way of Reasoning, and the Noblest Sentiments and Rules for all the several Offices and Institutions of Human Life. In like manner, the *Good Senator* will be well advised, if he takes the Exterior Form and System of his Religion, not from the *Greeks* or *Latins*, two Nations more renowned for the Polite Arts and Sciences, than for Sincerity and Purity in Religion, but from the *Primitive Church*, whose Authority stands Attested by God Himself, and Adorned with the Examples of Multitudes of *Saints*; whose Succession from the *Apostles* is Clear and Uninterrupted; and whose Truth, Purity, and Sanctity, are Approved and Allowed by the Unanimous Consent of all the National Churches upon Earth. They who are Contrary to this Institution, and frame to themselves New Models and Devices of a Novel Invention, are not only liable to the Just Censures of the State, but are really Professed Enemies both to God and Man. In the mean time, we ought heartily to Address ourselves to Heaven, and to Beseech the *Almighty*, that after so long a Trial of his Faithful Worshipers, and so many severe Punishments inflicted upon the Unsteadiness and Inconstancy of Revolters and Spiritual Delinquents, they may at last Return into the Bosom of the Church, and that all Nations and Commonwealths may tread in the Good Old Paths marked out for them, and learn to be Faithful, Religious, and Just, from the Precepts and Example of their Forefathers.

Enough hath been Hitherto said of *Divine Justice: Human* or *Civil Justice* is not so easily Described, as being a very Abstruse and Intricate Science: For though we are by Nature instructed in the first Principles and Rudiments of this Vertue, whereby as well in the Theory, as in the Practice, it seems to be an Easy Attainment,

tainment, Well-known, and Common to all Mankind; yet the Full and Complete Knowledge and Exercise of it, belong to such Men only, as are of a more than Ordinary, or even Human *Genius*, and have been throughly Conversant in all the Other Vertues, and in all the Arts and Accomplishments that are of Use and Benefit to Mankind. Before a Man can be a Perfect Master of this Vertue, he must be truly Wise and Learned: And it is not Chance and Fortune, or Necessity and the Want of a Livelihood, but his own Free Choice and Design, his own Reason and Resolution, must make him a Voluntary, Assiduous, and Unwearied Follower and Promoter of Justice. Such a Mind, so Exalted, and so Well Prepared and Instructed, ought always to be found in the *Good* and *Accomplished Senator*. Civil *Justice*, in its Uses and Influences, comprehends and takes in all the Publick Affairs and Interests of Government, and is exercised partly in the Maintenance and Support of Human Societies, and partly in the Decision of such Causes, as are brought into the *Forum* or *Courts* of *Judicature*. Justice is of all other Vertues the most Useful and Beneficial to the Publick, and contributes most to the Stability, Preservation, and Reformation of a Government. All the other Vertues are confined within much narrower Limits, and may be fully Exercised and Displayed even in Private Life, and apart from all Society whatsoever. But Justice extends itself to Communities and Bodies Politick, and is chiefly employed in the Defence and Security of Social Life; whence it may very truly be called the Great Reconciler and Conservator of Mankind. Whatever Things are Base and Odious, Indecent or Inhuman, fly before the Face of Justice, and can never stand in her Presence; whilst Things Fair and Honest, Gentle and Peaceable, are her chief Delight, and always under her Protection: All her Aim, and all her Endeavour is, to preserve Mankind in Peace and Unity, and to fasten them together in the Bonds of Mutual Love and Benevolence;

Benevolence; to restrain them from Rapine and Violence, from Discord, Hatred, and Sedition; and to oblige them to Give to every one his Due, and not to Covet or Desire what is not their own. In this Vertue the *Good Senator* ought particularly to Excell; that he may thereby be Qualified and Enabled to Distinguish himself as a Defender of his Country, a Promoter of the Publick Good, a Protector of the Innocent, an Instructor of the Weak and Ignorant, a Supporter of the Lovely and Humble, a Tamer of the Proud and Lofty, a Lover of the Good and Pious, an Avenger of the Wicked and Vicious, a Friend to Truth, and an Enemy to Falshood and Impiety. The Foundation of Justice is *Fidelity*, and *Fidelity* (as *Cicero* defines it) *is a True, Constant, and Exact Observation of Whatever a Man assents to by Word, Promise, Agreement, or Contract*. The truly Just *Senator* will Confirm and make Good every Thing he says, without Scruple or Ambiguity, will punctually perform all his Promises, will readily stand to all his Contracts and Agreements, chearfully answer for whatever Securities he has given, and make a full and clear Return of whatever is Deposited or Entrusted with him. His own Word, Will, and Consent, will be as a Law to himself, obliging him to keep Faith with the whole World, and there will be no Occasion to call Witnesses, or to remind him of any Publick Law, or of his own Deed, Honour, or Oath, in order to force and oblige him to be Honest. When he is called away from his own Particular Friends and Private Affairs, to any Publick Assembly or Court, he will by his Counsel, Advice, and Interposition, take the best Care he can, to keep out Injustice from making Head, or gaining Ground in the State; and will preserve the Publick from being Harassed and Oppressed by the Powerful, or Impoverished and Beggared by the Covetous and Selfish Plunderer. He will use his best Endeavours, that none be admitted into the Magistracy, but such as are Worthy of it, and Promoters

of

of the Publick Good; and that Those Men may be turned out and Disgraced, who are Unworthy of the Trust reposed in them, or who, by their Vices, are become Careless even of their own Private Interest. The Honours and Advantages usually bestowed upon those, who by their Vertues and Merit have Signalized themselves in the Service of their Country, he will, by his Suffrage and Interest, give only to such, as by their Integrity and Conduct have really deserved them. He will readily Promote the Rewarding of the Brave and Valiant, and the Punishing and Restraining of the Idle and Vicious: For by the due Distribution of Rewards and Punishments, a Nation is both Preserved and Exalted.

In the Conferring of Honours, a Strict and Rigorous Observation of *Justice*, is of the Utmost Consequence to a State. And whatever Honours are at any time bestowed, they should always be Proportioned to the Vertues and Merits of Those, to whom they are given; so that the Greatest Merit may always be Entitled to the Highest Honours. Every Free Government ought to set a Rate and Value upon its Honours; For these are the Rewards of Vertue; and a truly Good *Patriot* will always Measure the Honours he receives, by the Merit of his own Conduct and Exploits. Nothing worse can be said of any State or Government, than that its Honours are given at random and promiscuously, without making a Difference between the Vertuous and Vicious, the Wise and the Foolish. It would be well for the Publick, if the Proper Marks and Distinctions of Merit were to be set out and described, by some Particular Law or Statute, with a Provision, that no Honours should be Conferred, but where the Vertues and Conduct of the Person for whom they were designed, stood approved and allowed of, by the General Voice and Concurrence of all Good Subjects and Citizens. Among the *Ancients*, Statues, Triumphal Arches, Sepulchral Trophies and Monuments, Publick Orations, and Panegyricks, with many other Honours of the same Kind,

were

were bestowed in a Solemn Manner, and by a Publick Decree of the State. But then in the Ordinary Intercourses of Life, and in the Mix'd Assemblies of our Equals and Fellow-Subjects, the chief Marks of Distinction are, on the Account of Age, Degree, and Condition; and in giving the Preference, we must learn to make a Difference between the Talents, which are perhaps Necessary to make a Man's Station, or are become Familiar to him by Use and Practice, and those Superior Advantages, which arise from Personal Merit, and from a Distinguished and Extraordinary Conduct. They, who are Well-born, and of a Good Family, or of a Fair and Vertuous Character, or are in Place, Office, or Authority, or are Rich and Wealthy, ought to have a more than ordinary Respect paid, on Account of their being Serviceable and Beneficial to the Publick. On the same Account it is, that we Rise up to the Aged and Experienced, and give them Honour, Place, and Precedence. Mankind are Valuable for Three Sorts of Advantages in Life, the Perfections of the *Body*, the Accomplishments of the *Mind*, or the Endowments and Acquisitions of *Fortune*. To each of these we must have a Particular Regard, for our better Direction how to proportion our Respect and Deference to those about us. We must look in the First place to the *Mind*, then to the *Body*, and in the Last place to the Goods and Advantages of *Fortune*. If we Alter and Invert this Order of Things; as for Instance, if we preferr Riches to Vertue, we shall then be Partial and Unjust, in our manner of giving Honour to those, to whom Honour is due. And these Differences and Distinctions are necessary to be observed, not only in giving Private and Personal Honour, but in conferring the Publick Honours and Offices of the State. The Benefits we receive from others, ought to be repaid according to their Worth and Value, and there is an Honorary Tribute justly due to those, who have been Serviceable to their Country.

With

With these Things the *Good Senator* ought to be throughly Acquainted, and so far as he is concerned in the Distribution of all Honours, Preferments, and other Publick Advantages, he ought to adhere Strictly to the Great Rule and Law of *Equality:* For this is the *Weighing-Beam* and *Scales* of *Justice*, in which every one's Behaviour, Vertues, Actions, and Merit, are tried and examined, and their Full Weight and Value are taken and adjusted. But then we must be careful, that we do not put more into One Scale, than into the Other; whereby our Judgment and Estimate of the True Weight and Value of Mankind, will come to be Partial and Unjust. They, who Attribute too much to the Undeserving, and too little to Men of Real Merit, are Guilty of a Double Fault and Injustice. Whence it is, that this Sort of Justice is by the *Philosophers* defined to be, *A Habit of the Mind, disposing us to assign to every Man his Proper Worth and Dignity, so far as it is consistent with the Publick Safety and Welfare.* Equality or Equity is one of the First-rate Vertues, that contributes to the Preservation of a Government, and is a Constant Attendant upon, Assistant to, and Follower of Justice, from whose Dictates and Directions she never Varies the least Point whatsoever. There are Two Ways and Methods by which she Forms a Judgment and Estimate, both of Men and Things: One is the Vulgar and Ordinary Way of Discernment, by Number, Weight, and Measure: The other more Uncommon and Difficult to be Adjusted, is by a Rational Judgment and Computation. Of this Latter Method, the Best and only Masters are They, who are Renowned for their Wisdom, and have been long Conversant in the most Weighty and Momentous Affairs. The Former is well known to every One, who is employed in Buying and Selling, and in the Ordinary Commercial Contracts and Occupations of Life: But now the *Good Senator* must be Perfect in his Knowledge of that particular Branch of *Equality*, which consists in the Judicial and Rational Estimate and Computation

Computation of the True Worth and Value, both of Men and Things; by which he may be able to give to every one his Due, may discern aright, when, and upon whom, and what Honours, Largesses, Preferments and Offices, are to be bestowed, or conferred by the Publick; may judge of Time and Place, Men and Things, and Determine accordingly, what is Right, and Just, and Good, Fit and Proper to be done, and most agreeable to the Prescriptions of Wisdom and Prudence. The True Discernment of Merit, is a Matter of the Utmost Consequence, and highly Necessary to the Doing of Justice to Mankind, and to the Promoting of the True Interests of a Government. For Want of this, some States, as well as Men, have betrayed Great Weakness and Folly, and fallen into many Dangerous Errors and Mistakes; and for Want of a more Regular Decision, Men have been Prompted and Pushed forward to try their Merits by *Duel*, and put the Decision of them upon the Casual and Uncertain Issues of Battle and Combat. Which Practice is not only Prejudicial to Particular Governments, but to Human Society in General. Thus much may Suffice for explaining the true Nature of that Sort of *Justice*, which is in Use and Practice among Men in a Social State, apart and distinct from that other Sort, which is altogether Conversant in the *Forum* and *Courts* of *Judicature*.

This other Sort of Justice, very nearly Resembling and Related to the Former, is altogether employed in *Judicial Proceedings*, has the Laws and Customs of a Country for its Rule and Measure, and depends upon the Sentence and Decision of Wise and Upright Judges. In the First Pure and *Golden Age* of the World, there were (as I have already observed) no written Laws, but every Man's own Heart was a Law unto himself, without resorting to the Books and Writings of the Counsellors and Legislators. The Chaste Unsullied Virgin, *Justice*, had then a Habitation and Commerce among Men; and in those early Times, gave out the Rules and Ordinances

ces of Living Honestly and Uprightly, with great Plainness and Sincerity. Whilst She stayed upon Earth, and presided in the Assemblies of Men, no Deceit, Injustice, or Wickedness, was heard of among them. But soon after this, when the World was Sated with Vertue and Justice, and Men grew weary of being Honest, they presently crossed over into the quite Contrary Extreme; grew Covetous and Desirous of what was not their Own, were Injurious and Violent to their Neighbours, claimed more than was their Due, seized upon every Thing that came in their Way, would make no Return or Restitution, and took delight in these Arts of Rapine and Injustice. Hence grew Hatred and Contention, Jealousies, Animosities, War, and Bloodshed, together with the Invention of all manner of Martial Instruments, designed and contrived for the Annoyance and Destruction of Mankind. To all these Violences, not only *Justice*, but even *Heaven* itself was forced to give Way: till at length the Goddess was Terrified and Dismayed at so many horrible Spectacles, and leaving the World to follow its own Lusts and Licentious Way of Living, took Wing and returned back to *Heaven*, where next to *Libra* and *Leo*, the *Scales* and the *Lion*, she chose for herself a Perpetual Seat and Habitation. So that to Heaven we must Resort, for all that Wisdom and Good Counsel, which is necessary to Government and the Administration of Publick Affairs. For in our Present State, tainted as we are with Vice and Folly, we cannot, without the Assistance of Heaven, truly know, what Justice is, or learn to Practice it in Perfection. What *Homer* says of Kings and Counsellors, Wellskilled in the Art of Government, *That they are the Sons of* Jupiter, is very much for our Present Purpose: For to Heaven we must apply ourselves, in order to be fully Instructed in all the Rules and Precepts that *Justice* dictates, and obliges us to observe, before we can bring back and restore those Blessed and *Golden Times*, in which our Forefathers lived; and before we can govern Nations, and

preserve

preserve the Peace of Societies, in the same Manner, as the Chaste and Spotless *Goddess* was wont to do, when she Resided among Men. To Heaven we must apply ourselves, before we can call her down once more from thence, and prevail with her to Stay and make her Abode with us. When our own Reason is too Weak and Short-sighted, to guide us into the Ways of Justice, Piety, and Sanctity, the Stern and Awful Goddess ought to Interpose, and oblige us to the Performance of our Duty, by the Force of her Laws, by Admonition, Exhortation, and Correction, and by Setting out the several Rewards due to the Good and Vertuous, and the Punishments due to the Wicked and Unrighteous. For as *Ulpian* has well observed, *It is the Unalterable Will and Constant Endeavour of those, who are truly Just and Honest, that every Man should have, and enjoy, what really and rightfully belongs to him.*

The First Projecting, Forming, and Enacting of all Laws and Statutes, is the Proper and more Immediate Business of the *Good Senator*, and a Necessary Part of his Office and Duty to the Publick. Thus it was in the *Lacedæmonian, Roman*, and many other States and Commonwealths. What *Plato* prescribes, ought always to be observed in the Making and Passing of Laws, *Which should ever be Enacted, out of a Particular Love and Affection for the People, and in order to do them good;* and not thrown out among the Vulgar, as the Personal Projects of Arbitrary and Lordly Tyrants, who affix to the Walls of their Palaces, their own Devices for Laws, backed with Frightful Menaces and Penalties; whilst the Laws of their Country are what themselves have very little Regard for: And no Reason is to be given for their own Edicts, but what is contained in this Imperious Style, *So would we have it;* or *Such is our Will and Pleasure.* On the other hand, a *Good Legislator* will always take care, that his Laws should rather appear as Precepts and Persuasions to Good Manners and Discipline, than in a Prescribing and Mandatory Form. The End and Design of all

Laws

Laws is, to make the People Good and Happy, and agreeable to this, ought the Mind and Intention of the Legislator always to be. For the Punishing of Delinquents is rather a Case of Necessity, than of Choice. Hence *Justinian* the *Emperor* observes, *That the* Law *has* Three *Great Ends or Designs in View, The* First *is, That the Subject should live honestly; The* Second, *That he should be secured from all Wrong and Injury; And the* Third, *That every Man should have and enjoy what is really his Own.* For it is certain, that where Laws take their Rise only from Right Reason, the Chief and only Design of them, will necessarily be the Encouragement and Promotion of Vertue, without the least Deviation whatsoever; because they are in themselves as so many Rules and Schemes of Vertue, Honesty, Reason, Nature, and a Good Life; from which, whoever varies, is so far Criminal; and whoever Despises and Tramples the Laws under foot, does in Effect openly Despise both Vertue and Reason, Nature and GOD. It was well observed by *Heraclitus* the *Ephesian, That every Free Subject ought to be as Zealous in defending the* Laws *of his Country,* as in *defending the* Walls *of his City.* For a *City* may stand without *Walls,* but without *Laws* it can never be of any long Continuance. To the Laws therefore every Subject ought to pay a Strict and Punctual Regard, and to resort to them for Directions, how to behave in Life, wherein to correct and reform his Manners, and to make a Right Discernment, between what he is obliged to Chuse and Follow, and what to Reject and Avoid. *Solon* and *Lycurgus*, are both commended for Enacting such Laws, whereby the Subject was not only Instructed what to do at present, but was put upon Guarding against any Future or Distant Evils. The same Care may very well become the *Good Senator*; and it is worth his while to consider and find out, what Studies, Employments, and Exercises, are fit to be Encouraged by the State, in order to make the Subject Good and Useful to the Publick, and Conformable in his Behaviour to the Great End and Design of Civil or Social Life. By these Means every one will be brought to follow that particular Employment, for which Nature hath Qualified him in the Best Manner; he will look upon it as his Glory to Excell therein, and when Vertue has the proper Rewards annexed to it, will Strive and Labour to Distinguish himself above all other Competitors. There is hardly any thing too difficult for a Man to Undertake, when he has a Sure Recompence and Crown of his Labours in View; and the Proposing of such Kind of Rewards, is the ready Way to prevent Laziness and Idleness, and to drive out of the Commonwealth the Parent and Nurse of all Vice whatsoever. Daily Experience convinces us, how easily Men perish and are lost through Idleness and Luxury; and very true is the Saying of *Cato, That by doing* Nothing, *we are soon brought to do* Mischief. *Diodorus* speaks of a *Law* among the *Egyptians*, by which every Subject was obliged to give in his Name to the Proper Magistrate, and to Specify what Way of Life he was in, what Business, Study, or Employment he followed, how he Lived, and by what Art, Profession, or Occupation. If he gave in a False Account, or was notoriously Negligent and Careless in his Profession, he was punished with Death. *Draco*, observing the Loose and Wanton Lives and great Idleness of his Fellow-Citizens, made a Law to the same Purpose, by which this Crime was declared *Capital:* And though *Solon* thought this Law too Harsh and Severe, and accordingly softened the Penalty annexed to it, yet the Punishment he introduced for Idleness, was no less than *Publick Disgrace* or *Infamy*. By the *Imperial Laws*, all Idle and Lazy Persons were deprived of what they possessed, or according to the Degrees of their Crime, were ordered to be Scourged, or were Condemned to the Publick *Works, Mines,* or *Edifices*. Let every Commonwealth therefore provide Employment for its People, either by Study and Exercise, in the Arts of Peace or of War: For Study and Exercise, like the *Trojan Horse*, have poured forth Multitudes of Good and Useful Men,

Senators,

Senators, Judges, and Priests, Generals, Centurions, and other Commanders, who have been eminently Serviceable to their Country. Let this Method be taken, and a Commonwealth will never want a Sett of Men, able and well-qualified, to lead out the People to War, and to govern them in a Time of Peace; to Administer to them in all their *Sacred* as well as *Civil* Interests, to defend them from the Incursions and Treachery of their Neighbours, and to enlarge their Territories and Dominions, by the Conquest of their more *Savage* and *Barbarous* Enemies.

 When an Attempt is made to alter the Laws of any State, great Care and Caution must be used on this Occasion; lest by such Alteration, the Good Old Manners and Honest Disposition of the People, be also Altered at the same time. For the People are but too much addicted to Novelty, and when once they see one Alteration made, they will readily Push for a good many more, and, it may be, discover an Inclination, to have the whole Body of the Laws abolished at once: Whereby all Law will soon come to be had in Contempt; and then Tumults and Seditions naturally follow, and perhaps Changes and Revolutions in the Government. The Old Laws of a State, ought therefore by all means to be kept up, Sacred and Inviolable. They may be prudently Corrected and Amended, but they cannot be totally Repealed and Abolished, without some Hazard; and every Change in a Government, though of Matters seemingly of no great Importance, is a Dangerous, and may be a very Fatal Experiment. It was a Custom in the *Locrensian* State, that when any One proposed a New Law, he came into the *Senate-House* with a Halter about his *Neck*, and there publickly Recited his Proposal: If it was not Received, or was adjudged to be Hurtful and Pernicious to the Public, he was immediately Seized and Strangled. Remarkable is the Saying of *Periander, That Fresh Diet and Stale Laws were always the most Wholsome.*

It

It is also much to be Wished, and much for the Interest of a Government, that *Senators*, or they who have a Share and Trust in the *Legislature*, should be Careful to observe the Laws of their own Making, with as much Exactness, as they expect they should be observed by others. For there is nothing the People are more Inquisitive after, or look more narrowly into, than the Lives of their Superiors; and they Endeavour to Conform thereto, as to a Written Law. When *Seleuchus* had passed a Decree against Adultery, condemning those who were taken in it, to lose Both their Eyes, and his own Son afterwards found Guilty of this Crime; though the Whole City interposed, and desired that the Punishment might be Remitted, yet he would by no means consent thereto, but lost One Eye himself, and took another from his Son, whereby he chose rather to be Punctual in the Observation of the Laws, than to set his People a Precedent for Disobedience, and for bringing the Stricture and Authority of the Laws into Contempt: For he looked upon what the Law commands, to be of much greater Force and Weight, than the Commands of a Single Prince or Potentate.

The *Two* Great Ends proposed by every *Legislator* in the Passing and Enacting of Laws, are *First*, the Establishing a Due and Regular Course of Justice in the State; and *Secondly*, the Enforcing and Executing of Justice, in the Course so Settled and Established. The First of these Designs is, what the Legislator has in View, when he Enacts such Laws as are Necessary to set the People right in their Notions and Practice of Vertue; and the Second is, what belongs to the Judge and Magistrate, who have the Keeping of these Laws, and by the due Execution of them, restrain the Inordinate Lusts, and put a Stop to the Crimes and Ill-Practices of Delinquents. It is *Aristotle*'s Opinion, *That every* Judge *should take the Laws and Statutes which he is bound to Execute, only from the* Legislator: As well because it is most likely to find more Prudence and

and Wisdom in him, than in a Multitude of Judges and Magistrates; as also because the *Legislator* looks entirely to the General Good, and to the Lasting and Future Happiness of a State, and is free from all Perturbations of Mind and Influences of Passion, which a *Judge* cannot so easily avoid, who has to do with Present Things and Persons, brought before him in Judgment, and who consequently is most liable to be drawn aside, and misled by his own Appetites and Affections. As it is entirely for the Interest of a Government, that Good and Wholsome *Laws* should be Made and Kept, so it is altogether as Necessary, that an End should be thereby put to all Controversies and Contentions among Men. Offences are Unavoidable, and Doubts and Disputes will arise in Matters of Right, which it is the Proper Business of a *Judge* to Decide and Determine. In every Commonwealth, there are of necessity certain *Judges* Commissioned and Appointed, for this very purpose, to put an End to all Strife, and to administer Justice to the People; whose Office is of the same Consequence to Mankind, as the Soul is to the Support and Well-being of the Body. Every Judge is a Mediator between Man and Man, that whatever is in Difference or Unequal between the Contending Parties, may by his Determination be composed and reduced to an Equality. When a *Line* is cut and divided into Unequal *Parts*, by taking what is Over and Above in One Part, and adding it to what is Short and Deficient in the Other, we presently reduce the Whole to an Equality. And this is a Lively Emblem of the Proceedings and Behavious of a Good and Upright Judge, who is the Life and Soul of the Law, and the Living Oracle of every Society and Commonwealth. It is the Proper Business of every such Magistrate, to be the Interpreter of the Will and Mind of the Legislator, and the Minister of Justice, whose First and Greatest Accomplishment it is, to Know and Discern what is Truth and Right. The Laws of a Country are his only Guide and Direction, to which he ought strictly

strictly to Conform himself, in all his Proceedings, Opinions, and Sentences: From these he ought never to vary in the least Point whatsoever, and to give Judgment always as the Law directs, or according to the Well-known Principles of Justice and Equity. To this every Judge ought to be Solemnly Sworn, that when he is in Judgment, he may always have GOD before him, as a Witness to his Proceedings, and stand to the Appeal of his own Mind and Conscience, That *Oracle* implanted by GOD in every Man's Breast, as the Evidence to, and Controller of all his Actions. Anger and Passion, Hope, Love, and Affection, Hatred, and Malice, and every the least Shadow and Suspicion of it, ought to be Banished far off from every Tribunal and Court of Judicature; together with Bribery and Corruption, Fear and Terror, Adulation and Flattery, and whatever may Obstruct or Pervert the Regular Course of Justice. For when a *Judge* is Weak or Wicked enough, to give Way to any of these Temptations, *Justice* will soon take her Leave of him, and be Banished out of his Mind, as well as out of the Court in which he Presides. Most certain it is, that no one Order of Subjects whatsoever, has contributed more to the Promoting of Sedition, Strife, and Oppression in the Commonwealth, than a Sett of *Judges* who are of a Mercenary, Corrupt, and Adulterous Disposition. On the other hand, by a due and regular Course of *Justice*, a Commonwealth is preserved in Peace and Unity. Love and Good-will to Mankind, are every where promoted; Complaints and Grievances, Hatred, and Contention, Animosities, Wars, and Tumults, cease and are no more, and a Commonwealth is raised to that Pitch of Happiness, that it can never want any Good Thing whatsoever; and nothing Evil can ever come near, or approach to hurt it.

This Particular Sort of *Justice*, which is altogether conversant in *Judicial* Matters, is of such Benefit to the Publick; that it never suffers any one Evil whatsoever to remain long in a State, without

out being effectually cured, and utterly rooted out. For when all Wrongs are Redressed, and all Criminals are duly brought to endure what they have Deserved, a Stop will be soon put to all Fraud and Violence, wrong, and Injustice, and to all other Rash, Impudent, and Daring Impieties. Among the Statues and Pictures of the Ancients, *Justice* was represented as a Pure, Lovely, and Chaste Virgin, but with a Rough, Stern, and Formidable Aspect, Eyes Bright and Piercing, and Features full of Modesty; but at the same time Grave, Rigid, and Severe. The Design and Signification of which Image and Representation was plainly this, That every *Judge* ought to be of a Chaste and Incorrupt Mind, but of a Severe and Rigid Behaviour in Judgment, in Discernment Acute and Sharp-sighted, Searching out and Prying into every thing, Grave and Steady, Constant and Inexorable. *Chambyses*, King of *Persia*, condemned an Unjust *Judge* to be Flay'd alive, and his Skin to be affixed to his Judgment Seat, that his Successors, by his Example, might learn to behave Faithfully and Uprightly, in the Execution of their Office. And here, by the way, the *Good Senator* ought to be put in Mind, that He, above all others, should be most Tenacious of Justice, because the Influence of his Example is of such Wide Extent, and because he is under Double Obligation to be Just, as well in the Enacting, as in the Executing of Laws for the People. It would be Notoriously to his Shame and Disgrace, if he should refuse Obedience to the Laws, of which himself is the Maker and Keeper. The same Power and command which he has over Others, the Law ought to have over Him: That *Law* which is not only Written, and hung up in *Tables* of *Brass* or of *Wood*, but that *Living Law*, which is Inscribed on the Heart, and contains the Dictates of Right Reason and Natural Justice. *Solon* being asked, *How a City might preserve itself in Safety and Tranquillity?* Readily answered, By *Keeping the Magistrate in as Strict Obedience to the Laws, as the Subjects were kept in their Obedience to the Magistrates.*

Magistrates. Bias was also of Opinion, *That every government is Safe, in which every Subject stands in as great Awe of the Laws, as of an Arbitrary Lord or Tyrant.* It is Unhappy for a Commonwealth, when its Laws are like a *Spider's Web,* in which only the Poor and Weak are Taken and Entangled, whilst the Rich and Powerful break through and Escape the Snare. The *Good Senator* ought therefore to be particularly Cautious, in guarding against all Incroachments of this Kind, and diligent and indefatigable in the Study and Knowledge of the Laws of his own Country, which ought to be his Sole Delight, and the Scope and Measure of all his Actions. For nothing tends more to the Completion and Perfection of the *Senatorial* Character, than a Full Knowledge of the Laws, and a Strict and Regular Execution of Justice. It does by no means become him to be too Severe and Cruel, in the Performance of his Duty: For according to a Vulgar Observation, the Extremity of Law is the Extremity of all Wrong and Injustice: And in all his Conduct he ought to take Care, that his Fellow-Subjects may regard him rather as a Stern and Rigid Judge, than as a Barbarous and Merciless Executioner. There is a Wholsome Severity, *Which* (as *Cicero* says) *has much the Advantage of an Hypocritical and Specious Clemency.* Cruelty belongs only to Tyrants and Barbarians, and a Fouler Vice cannot well be Devised or Imagined; nor any thing invented, more Monstrous, Odious, and Detestable in itself, or more Fatal and Pernicious to Human Society. Let the *Good Senator* therefore make it his Particular Study and Endeavour, to be Mild and Courteous, and not of a Brutish and Savage Temper: And let him not, for fear of this, go over into another and worse Extreme, and expose himself to Contempt, by means of a too great Lenity and Indulgence. For there is sometimes a Fault in Punishing, much Greater than the Punishment itself. Among the *Romans* there were *Eight* several Punishments, or Penalties appointed by the Laws, *Loss of Goods, Bonds, Stripes, Retaliation,*

Retaliation, Ignominy, Banishment, Servitude, and *Death.* In the Assigning and Affixing of All, or any of these Punishments, we must exactly Conform ourselves to the Laws, as the Sole Guide and Measure of all our Proceedings: And these Laws may be Moderated and Alleviated, but ought not to be Overturned and set Aside: They may be Restrained and Softened, but should not have the Sting taken out of them, which is wholly aimed at the Avenging of Wrong, and the Suppression of Vice and Wickedness. The Laws ought always to be in Charity with Mankind, and at Enmity only with their Faults and Vices. And this should always be a Rule of Behaviour, proper and necessary to be Observed by Men in Power, that the Greater their Power is, the Greater ought their Moderation to be, in the Use and Exercise of it.

CHAP. V.

The CONTENTS.

Of the Vertues *attending upon* Justice. *Of* Piety. *Of the Great Obstructions to* Piety, Heresy, *and* Superstition. *Of* Goodness. *Of* Innocence *and* Integrity. *Of* Affability, *and how it ought to be Tempered with* Gravity. *Of* Benignity *and its Concomitant Vertues,* Humanity, Condescension, Lenity, Clemency, *and* Moderation. *Of* Clemency, Mercy, *and* Pity. *The Doctrine of the* Stoicks *condemned. Of* Liberality, *and the Rise of This Vertue. How it ought to be Regulated, and the Extent of it. Of* Magnificence, *and how it differs from* Liberality. Luxury *ought to be Restrained by* Legal Penalties. *Of* Friendship *and* Amity, *and how these Affections ought to be Formed and Regulated. Of* Hospitality. *Of* Concord.

JUSTICE has an Influence and Command over all the other Vertues, and makes Use of, and calls them to her Assistance, in all Affairs necessary to the Support and Welfare of Human Societies. Hence she is usually called the *Queen* of all Vertues, and accordingly Retains in her Equipage more Attendants and Followers, than belong to any other Vertue whatsoever. The First of these is *Piety,* and the next in Procession are, *Goodness, Innocence, Affability, Benignity, Clemency, Amity,* and *Concord.* Of all which Vertues when a Man is fully Possessed, and is Well-furnished and Adorned therewith, he will then approve himself a Master of the most Consummate and Perfect *Justice.*

By a Strict and Regular *Piety,* the *Good Senator* will not only Preserve to himself the Favour and Good Will of Heaven, but the

Love

Love and Esteem of Men. This Vertue will establish his Credit, and oblige those about him, to pay an Uncommon Regard both to his Word and Example. No Vanity, Folly, or Deceit, will ever be expected from Him, who is so nearly Related to, and so much the Favourite of his *Maker*, and whose whole Conduct is Squared and Regulated by the Laws and Precepts of Religion. When *Numa Pompilius* undertook to settle a Religion among the *Romans*, the better to establish his Credit with the People, in a Shew of Sanctity, and on the Pretence of a Vow, he withdrew himself, together with the Nymph *Egeria*, his Supposed Wife, into a Place of Retirement, sacred to the *Muses*, and there conferred with the Gods, and took directions from them, concerning the Form and Model of Religion, which was then to be Introduced among the *Romans*. What he had before in vain attempted to bring about by Authority and Intreaties, was now by this Pious Fraud and Pretence happily Accomplished, and the People were Allured and Prevailed with, to receive That Religion, and Conform to That Way of Worship, which was of *Numa's* own Invention. False and Fictitious as this *Piety* was, it had however its wholsome Uses and Effects; What then may we not expect from the True, Holy, and Sincere *Piety* of the *Religious Senator?* It is by no means Proper for me, in this Place, to enter into a Particular Detail of Those Rites, Ceremonies, and Sacred Institutions, which fall immediately under the Cognizance of the *Good Senator*, when the Religion of his Country is to be Established or Reformed: Because I have already touched upon this Subject, in what hath been said concerning *Divine Justice;* and because I take it for granted, that every Subject in a *Christian Commonwealth,* is already sufficiently Instructed in the Principles and Precepts of True Religion. There are Two Extremes, which the *Pious Senator* must have a Care of falling into, One of which is *Heresy*, and the Other is *Superstition*. For these Iniquities disturb and infatuate the Minds of Men, and are at utter Variance with True and Unfeigned Piety. By the way we must
Remember,

Remember, that *Piety* lays us under an Indispensable Obligation of Love and Obedience to our Natural Parents, to whom we are by Nature Indebted, and own them all imaginable Returns of Duty and Affections, Good-will and Reverence. When they are grown Old, or are Sick and Infirm, we are bound at our own Expence, or by our own Labour and Industry, to Support and Maintain them; to Assist and Defend them in all Dangers and Adversities, and to Help and Succour them, whenever they stand in need of our Aid or Protection.

Goodness is also a Necessary Part and Ornament of the *Senatorial* Character: And *Goodness* is not to be Attained, but by a General and Uniform Practice, and Display of all the Vertues, in our Lives and Actions. The *Senator* will then approve himself, as a Truly Just and *Good* Man, when he hath raised his Mind to so Perfect and Sublime a State, as not only to Forbear the doing of any thing that is Evil, but to Forbear it in such a Manner, as if it were really out of his Power, and perfectly Unnatural to him. Of such a Man it ought to be said, as was said by certain Rusticks, or Vulgar Fellows, who (as we read in *Cicero*) when they had a Mind to Extoll a Particular *Patriot*, much Esteemed among them for his Goodness, were pleased to Describe him as so very Bright a Creature, *That his* Goodness *was discernable at Midnight*. Let then the *Good Senator*, through the Whole Course and Conduct of his Life, always make Choice of Vertue for his Guide; because in following her, he will never Slip or Tread awry, or Deviate one Step from the Glorious and Shining Track, which Justice and Probity have marked out for him.

Innocence, or Integrity of Life and Manners, is another Vertue, than which nothing more effectually contributes to the Perfecting of the *Senatorial* Character and Renown. By this he will rid his Mind of all Malice and Ill-Will, will learn never to be an Enemy to any Man, and never to Fear any Man who is an Enemy to him; will lead a Quiet and Happy Life, free from all Terror, Jealousy, and Suspicion, and all Dread and Apprehension, either of Fraud or Violence; whilst Sincerity, Purity, Veracity, Candour, and Generosity, will Blaze and Shine out, as the Graces and Ornaments of all his Words and Actions. The *Senatorial Innocence* ought to take its Rise and Foundation from a Principle of doing all the Good he can, and of doing no Wrong, and giving no Offence to others. This Vertue joins Simplicity to Prudence, and admits of no Hypocrisy, Dissimulation, or Deceit, and no Fiction, Disguise, or False Colouring whatsoever. It excludes from the *Senate* all Sycophants, Hypocrites, Dissemblers, Lyers, Informers, and Promoters of Scandal and Detraction. It makes a Man Free and Open in all his Actions, and sets him above the Low, Servile, and Mean Practices of Flattering and Dissembling. There is no Moderation, either in Innocence, or in Dissembling. He only is *Innocent*, who Abstains from every Thought and Appearance of Wrong; and he is certainly a Dissembler, who will allow himself in that Vice, or any the least Occasion, or in any Trifling Affair whatsoever. Over the Entrance to the Temple of *Ceres Eleusina*, was the Inscription; *Let no one Enter here, who is not Conscious of his own* Innocence. For none but the *Innocent* were to be admitted into that Sacred Place. The *Senate-House* is in like manner Sacred, and is, as it were, the Temple of Truth and Justice; which none should Approach, but such as are of a Clear and Upright Character, Blameless and Unspotted in their Lives. Let the Mind of all who sit therein be Open and Free of Access, Clear and Transparent, that the Purity and Sincerity of the Heart may be seen to the Bottom, and not appear Dark, Muddy, and Obscure; or Winding, Intricate, and Deceitful. Let not the *Senator's* Mouth utter more or less than what is in his Heart: Let his Tongue be the Interpreter of his Mind: Let his Looks, Gestures, and Features, give out the Signal, and exhibit the Marks of his Inward Native Sincerity; and let them not be Strained and Distorted, or Armed

with

with an Artificial Disguise, on purpose to Deceive or Impose upon Others. Such little mean Tricks and Artifices are fit only to be practiced by *Mimes* and *Strollers*, in a *Farce* or *Interlude*, or are the Low Ordinary Attainments of Rude Savages and Barbarians, who know not what Goodness is, who are a Scandal to the Shape, as well as to the Dignity and Offices of Human Nature, and have consequently a very Slender, if any Title, to that General Trust and Confidence, which we are all obliged to repose in one another. To these Vices the *Good Senator* must always be an Entire Stranger, and whilst he keeps himself free from them, he must also be careful to preserve others from falling into them; and treat those who are guilty of them, with the utmost Disregard and Contempt. Neither in Publick, nor in Private, must he ever join himself to, or take Part with those Men, who are of a Light, Vain, and Unsteady Temper, and must remain as great a Stranger to their Conversation, as he is to their Faults and Follies.

The next Vertue necessary to the Accomplishment of the *Senatorial* Character, is *Affability*, or a Sweet and Courteous Way of Speaking to, and Behaving towards all those, who are of an Approved and Established Reputation, and are at Peace and in good Esteem with their Fellow-Subjects. The *Accomplish'd Senator* will approve himself to all Such, as a Man Free and Unreserved in Conversation, always ready to Hear and give Attention to others, easy of Access, and having his Doors and his Ears open to the Approaches of his Fellow-Subjects, and to all their Addresses and Complaints. He will be Careful to avoid all those Ways of Speaking, Motions, and Gestures, which favour of too much Petulancy and Severity, or of Levity and Scurrility, however Disguised and Recommended, under the Specious Titles of Facetiousness and Pleasantry. Mirth and Humour, Jest and *Banter*, are such Entertainments as a *Senator* ought never to Make, or to be very Sparing and Frugal in bestowing them. It is not the *Senator's* Business

ness to shew his Wit, but his Wisdom; not to provoke Laughter by his Discourse, but by Grave and Serious Reasoning to Instruct and Reform. Affability and Gravity ought always to meet together in the *Senatorial* Character; not a Haughty Swelling and Insolent *Gravity*, but such as is Tempered with Modesty, Gentleness, and Good-Will to Mankind.

How necessary a Vertue *Benignity* is, and how much it contributes to a Just and Upright Life, Heaven itself has set us an Example. For to the Benignity and Good-Will of our *Maker* it is entirely owing, that we are Just in our Actions, and Happy in our Lives. And as he is *Benign* and Gracious to us, so ought we to be to one another. For according to a Well-known and very Just Observation, *It is the Duty of every Man, to be as a* God *to his Fellow-Creatures*. Under *Benignity* are to be Ranged the Private Vertues of *Humanity, Condescension, Lenity*, and *Gentleness*, in our way of Addressing and Behaving to others; and the Two Publick Vertues of *Clemency*, and *Moderation*, in the Exercise and Execution of *Justice*. Let the *Good Senator*, therefore, display his *Benignity* among his Brethren, and in all the Parts and Offices of Social Life, by being Humane, and of a Sweet and Courteous Behaviour, and by avoiding That Harsh, Sower, and *Cynical* Disposition, which can only become a *Timon*, a *Misanthrope*, or Man-hater; and let his Humanity have that good Effect upon him, that he may thereby Shew his Love to those about him, and be always ready to Assist and to do Good to his Fellow-Subjects. For as *Piety* and Religious Worship are what we owe to GOD, so Love and Good-Will are what Mankind may with Justice demand at our hands.

Clemency is a Vertue, the Observation of which properly belongs to Those, who are Entrusted with the Magistracy, whereby, in the Punishing of Offenders, they are Occasionally induced to shew Mercy and Compassion. Opposite to these are, Rigour and Cruelty, together with that Blood-thirsty Temper and Savage Delight, which

which some Men take in Torturing and Afflicting their Fellow-Creatures, and which are Familiar to Tyrants and Oppressors, who have no Fellow-feeling or Sense of Humanity. *Draco* was one of these Savages, who punished Idleness, as well as *Parricide*, with Death; and being asked, *Why he inflicted the same Punishment both upon Great and Lesser Crimes?* very readily answered, *That Those Little Crimes deserved Death; and for the Greater, he knew not how to Invent an Adequate and Sufficient Punishment.* The Saying of *Scipio* was much Milder, and more Agreeable to Humanity; who publickly declared, *That he had rather Save One Citizen, than Destroy a Thousand Enemies.* Clemency is of all other Vertues, the Greatest Ornament of Human Nature: And this Vertue (as I have already observed) ought particularly to shine forth in the Conduct and Character of a *Good Magistrate*. For Power, when Annexed to it, is so much the more Wholsome and Salutary, it being against Nature, and only Justifiable by Necessity, that a Man should have Authority to Inflict Pains and Penalties upon his Fellow-Creature: And it is as great a Disgrace to the *Magistrate* to have many *Executions*, as it is to a *Physician* to have many *Funerals*. The Lenity of the Governor makes the Subject Moderate, and Cautious of Offending. But then *Clemency* and a Placable Disposition ought to be under Proper Restraints. The Commonwealth must not be neglected, nor Severity with-held in the Proper Place, without which, no Government can be of any Long Duration, nor any Administration Lasting and Well-Established. Mercy and Pity are nearest and most closely adjoining to *Clemency*, and these are nothing else but the Pain and Uneasiness, which we find in ourselves, at the Sight or Apprehension of what others Suffer and Endure. The *Stoicks* were of Opinion, that no Sensation of this Kind could possibly reach or affect a Wise Man, and looked upon it as a Mark and Indication of a Low and Pusillanimous Spirit, that was easily cast down at the Shadow and Appearance only of

what

what Strangers suffered. They considered this Vertue, as Common and Familiar to the Worst of Men, and as the Usual Property of Weak Women, who will Spare no Tears and Complaints, in order to deliver the Worst of Criminals from Imprisonment or Death. Mercy, as They say, has a Regard only to the Person and his Present Condition, and not to the Cause of his Sufferings. Whence it is, that they allow of *Clemency*, as a Rational Principle, but condemn *Mercy* and *Pity*, as Defects, rather than Vertues. With their Controversies and Disputations we shall by no means Intermeddle, but shall give it as our Opinion in general, that *Mercy* and *Clemency*, when Exercised upon Proper Subjects and Occasions, are True and Real Ornaments of the *Senatorial* Character.

 Human Society receives a good deal of Advantage and Support, not only from those Good Actions, which naturally Result from a Just, Sincere, and Merciful Disposition, but from those Good Things, with which Fortune supplies us; among which are to be reckoned Money, Wealth, and Riches, whereby either in Giving or Receiving, we contribute to the Support, Maintenance, and Comfort of our Own, or of the Lives of Others. Whatever Nature has produced for the Use and Advantage of Mankind, was really intended to be in Common, but not so, as that no Man should have any Property therein, but should by Dividing, Parcelling, and Giving it out to Others, make it to be as much in Common, as the Nature of Things would allow of; whence follows a Necessity of Combining and Agreeing together; because we really stand in Need of, and have Occasion for one another. From this State of Affairs, the Vertue of *Liberality takes its Rise;* by which we are Directed, How, and When, and What of our own we are to Dispose of to those about us. *Liberality* is so called, because it really becomes a Free and *Liberal* Man, and requires a Free and *Liberal* Heart, in the Performance and Exercise of this Vertue. But then,

since

since there are many Degrees of Relation and Affinity in a Commonwealth, and some of these are Preferable to the rest; we can never perform this Duty aright, unless we first take Care to be most Liberal and Munificent towards Those, who are nearest to us in Relation and Affinity. Upon this Occasion we ought always to Conform to the Order of Nature, to preferr our Parents and Children to all others, our Kinsmen to those no ways allied to us, our Domesticks to Strangers, and our Countrymen to Foreigners. Neither can we be Punctual in our Observations of the Due Course and Regular Proceedings of *Liberality*, unless we take Care not to give more than our own Faculties and Circumstances will allow of, and not to give less than is consistent with our own Station and Abilities, and with That Humanity and Courtesy which are due to our Neighbour. They who never Stint their own Munificence and Generosity, are really Prodigals; and they who give nothing at all, are Covetous and Uncharitable Misers. Whoever would avoid these two Extremes, (and who is there, that would not avoid them?) let him first consider with himself, What, and to Whom he gives, How and in What Manner, at What Time, and in What Place: For to give to him, who does not Want it, or to give a Little, where More is Wanting, is really an Act of Injustice; for which there can be no Manner of Pretence, but the Outside Shew and Glory of Munificence. Every Man ought to be acquainted with the Real Value and Uses of what he bestows upon Another. We must not give a Shield to a Priest, a Library to a Soldier, or a Robe to a Rustick. Whatever we bestow upon Others, must be of such Things, as are in the *First* place Necessary, in the *Second* place Profitable and Advantageous, and in the *Third* place Pleasant and Durable. The Chief Reason for our *Liberality*, ought to be the Honesty and Good Character of the Persons, upon whom it is Bestowed; lest the Fruits of our Liberality are Expended by Ill Persons, and upon Ill Designs. For, as *Ennius*, quoted

by

by *Cicero*, very well observes, *All Benefactions, when Ill-timed or Mis-placed, are really Criminal, and a Prejudice and Detriment to the Publick*. He who only Rewards the Meritorious, is his Own, and not Another's Benefactor. There are some Men, who are rashly and intemperately Liberal, and who have no other Inducement to this Vertue, but a certain Natural Force and Impulse, which is not to be resisted. The Benefactions bestowed by such Men, do by no means deserve Thanks, because they are not disposed of, or bestowed, by Judgment and Deliberation; neither is there any Regard had therein, to the Publick Advantage or Convenience; and such Donations are very often made to the Vain, Foolish, and Undeserving. These Mistakes the *Good Senator* ought always to avoid, and to be very Careful, in what Manner he Exercises his *Liberality*. For there is no Vertue that contributes more effectually to the Establishing of Benevolence and Good-will among Men; by which we Shew ourselves to be Useful and Assistant to Others, and give them Proofs of the Justice, Munificence, and Sincerity, of our own Hearts. *Liberality* is nothing less than an Imitation of the Divine Being. And as GOD is Good and Liberal to us, so ought we to be to our Brethren. But then we must take Care, that what we lay out in Acts of *Liberality*, be not a Part of the Spoils and Plunder, which we have Heaped together, by Rapine and Oppression. *Liberality*, at the Expence of other Men, can be no Vertue in us, and is really no better than downright Injustice. What we Give, ought to be of our own Acquiring, by Fair and Honest Means, or by the Help and Assistance of Others: And we must give to those, who in all Probability are like to be made Better by our Liberality, and either in their Civil or Military Capacity, have been some way or other Useful and Serviceable to their Country. *Liberality* is chiefly Exercised in Relieving the Poor and Needy, in Paying Money for our Friends and Acquaintance, where they stand Engaged, or Indebted to Others; in Placing out

and

and Providing for their Children; in Redeeming those, who are taken by Pyrates and Robbers, from Captivity and Slavery; in Assisting and Helping our Neighbours to Improve and Increase their Fortunes; and in other Acts of Charity and Generosity, too Many to be easily Enumerated. Of all the Mistakes commonly made by Men of a *Liberal* Disposition, the most Fatal and Pernicious, are Those that proceed from Ignorance, or from our not being able to know, How to Bestow, or How to Receive a Benefit. We must make Choice of Proper Persons, and Objects for our *Liberality*, and consider well their Behaviour and Character, what Station of Life they are in, and how they Stand Related to, or Affected towards us: For without being Just, it is Impossible for us to be *Liberal*. Neither does *Liberality* consist altogether in Parting with our Money: For to some we may be Useful in their Particular Business and Occupation, to others by our Credit, to some by our Favour, to others by our Counsel and Advice, to some by our Protection and Patronage, and to others by our Mediation and Interposition; and by many other such like Ways of assisting and doing Good to those about us. All which Acts of Munificence, are by much the most Splendid and Honourable, and Best befitting the *Senatorial* Character and Dignity: Because they are not Supplied by the Purse, but by a Fund of Vertue, which is not to be Exhausted. Among the many Vertues that Shone out in the Character of *Scipio Africanus*, this was most Remarkable, That whenever he went abroad, he would not return home, till by his *Liberality* and Generosity, he had added One to the Number of his Friends. *Titus*, the Son of *Vespasian*, would often tell those about him, *That he had Lost a Day*; whenever a Day passed, in which he had done no Good to Others. It is also the *Liberal* Man's Duty, to make a Return of whatever Benefits himself Receives; a Return not only in Kind, but with ample Interest and Advantage. The Two Great Rules to be observed in Giving and

Receiving

Receiving, are these, That he who bestows a Benefit, ought presently to Forget it, and he who receives One, ought always to Remember it. To put another in mind of the Good we have done him, is no better than an Exprobration; and on the other hand, Ingratitude is a Vice justly Detestable and Odious, in the Sight both of GOD and Man. We must also be Careful to avoid all Grudging, Sowrness, and Churlishness, in the Way and Manner of Doing Good to Others; that we may not seem to do it by Compulsion and Unwillingly, or with Pain and Grief to ourselves. We must give Freely, Chearfully, and Voluntarily: For whatever we bestow either in Money, or other Things of Value, is not properly Speaking a Real Benefit, but is rather a Mark, Proof, and Token, of a Beneficent and Generous Spirit. What a Man gives, is not so much to be Regarded, as the Willing Mind with which he gives it; and all Benefits are to be Weighed and Measured, by the Intention and Good-Will of the Benefactor. Whence a Certain Person, who had received a Benefit at the Hands of an Unwilling and Churlish *Miser*, was pleased to call it, *A Morsel of Bread made of a Stone.*

The next Vertue to Liberality, is *Magnificence*; which is chiefly seen in a Splendid way of Living, and in Publick Largesses, and Donations. *Magnificence* differs no otherwise from Liberality, than as Liberality is altogether Conversant about Things and Persons of Lesser Note, whilst *Magnificence* is wholly employed about Men and Matters of much greater Figure and Consequence. The *Magnificence* of the *Ancients* appeared in their Generous *Doles* and *Largesses* to the People, in Building of Temples, and in Furnishing and Adorning them, for the Honour of their Deities; in Erecting Cities, Towns, and Villages, and in such other Works and Edifices, as were either for the Honour of Religion, or for the Use and Service of the Publick. But then in the Exercise of *Liberality* and *Magnificence*, there is a *Decorum* to be observed, and a

Consideration

Consideration ought to be had of Persons, and Things, Times, and Places; before the Limits of this Vertue can be rightly Settled and Adjusted. There is no greater Folly, than for Men to make a Shew of Grandeur and *Magnificence*, without Judgment and Sufficient Abilities, to bear them out in it. 'Tis a Vulgar, but a very Just Observation, *That our Expences ought never to Exceed our Income:* And though Parsimony is said to be a very Valuable Merchandize and Commodity. yet we may easily come to be too Sparing and Penurious, and by Degrees to be Covetous, Sordid, and Miserable, or to be Indolent and Careless, both of our own, and the Interest of our Neighbours. We must not Brood over our Wealth, or be Over-solicitous in filling our Bags, and accumulating Treasure to ourselves, only for the Sake of Gratifying a Luxurious Heir, with That, which might be of Service to our Parents, our Friends, and our Country. Avarice is an Incurable Distemper, that (as *Salust* observes) *Weakens and Enervates both Soul and Body:* And every Miser is Intent only upon Two Things, The Keeping of what he has Gotten, and the Getting of all that he Can. There is a *Moderate,* as well as a Profuse Way of Disposing of our Money. For the Use and Service of Good Men, or for Honest and Laudable purposes, we may be Free and even Lavish of it; and we really ought to Keep and Hoard it up, only for the Sake of our Friends, and in some Cases (as the Vulgar Expression is) for our *Physician* and our *Enemy*; but above all, for the Use of our Country, whose Necessities ought to be regarded, before those of any Private Consideration whatsoever. They, who are foolishly Profuse of their Wealth, and Expend it altogether in Luxury and Gluttony, in Sports and Pleasures, and such Delights as are Short-lived and Transitory, the Relish of which seldom or ever outlives a Day, deserve no better Character, than that of being Voracious Devourers and Consumers, not only of what is their Own, but of what might serve to the Uses and Advantage of the Publick.

Such

Such Light, Vain, and Unthinking Creatures, are as Prodigal and Profuse of their Credit, Reputation, and Honour, as they are of their Money: And it would be well, if the State would lay them under a Restraint, and by a Publick Law, prevent the Abuses and Misapplication of Private Property, and the Consumption of it, in a Way perfectly Vile and Infamous. Among the *Romans*, there was a Law, that no *Senator* should run in Debt above such a Sum. *P. Rufinus* was expelled the *Senate* by the *Censors*, for Keeping too much Money by him: And on the other hand, *Æmilius Lepidus* underwent the same Fate, for being too Prodigal and Expensive in his Way of Living. Let the *Good Senator* therefore manage his Affairs in such a Manner, as that he may have enough to bestow in Acts of Magnificence and Liberality towards *Good Men*; and let him be ready, not only with his Money, but by his Credit, Counsel, Advice, and other such-like Ways and Means of Expressing his Benevolence, to Succour, Relieve, and Assist his Brethren and Fellow-Subjects: For these Two Vertues of *Magnificence* and *Liberality*, serve to Sweeten and Reconcile the Minds of Men, and to promote Amity and Concord in the World, which are the very Bonds of Unity, and the Cement that holds together all Commonwealths and Societies whatsoever.

Nature hath so Ordered and Directed the Course of Human Affairs, that there is no living without *Amity* and *Friendship*, in the midst of all the Affluence that is Necessary and Commodious for our Subsistence and Well-being. Man is naturally a Civil and Sociable Creature, that can, on no account whatsoever, submitt to be Deprived of the Comforts and Conveniences of Conversation and Commerce, with those of the same Species. Hence arise those Natural Friendships, which are Founded in *Marriage, Consanguinity,* and *Relation:* For Nature is a Friend and Lover of Mankind, and Collects and Knits them together, by the Ties and Bonds, not only of Good-Will and Benevolence, but of Blood too. We plainly see,

see, that the Chief Care of all *Legislators* and Founders of Commonwealths, in marking out Laws and Statutes for the Use and Government of the People, is, That they may be thereby Knit and United together in Love and Friendship. For when the Laws of Friendship are duly observed, it is impossible that Malice and Hatred, Contention and Sedition, can have Strength and Vigour enough, to throw out their Poison, and do Mischief in the World; whilst Concord, Peace, and Tranquillity, are in Full Force and Power, and effectually Contribute to the Publick Happiness. The Sun is not more Necessary to the Chearing and Enlivening of the World, than Friendship is to the making the several States and Kingdoms of it truly Happy and Prosperous. Every Government must certainly know, that This is its First and Greatest Good, and where This Prevails, all Discord and Dissension must immediately Vanish. By the Strength and Attraction of this Amiable Principle, whole Multitudes of Subjects and Citizens will be drawn together, as a Nation and Body of Lovers, and (as *Pythagoras* speaks) *Will be made One.* For such is the Power of Friendship, that it brings Infinite Numbers of the same *Species*, to be of One Soul and of One Mind. Whence *Lælius* defines Friendship to be, *An Agreement made by Love and Benevolence, in all things both Human and Divine.* Now there are many Sorts and Degrees of Friendship; among which may be reckoned the several Friendships made by the several Nearnesses of Blood, Relation, and Affinity: But *Civil* or *Political Friendship*, which is an Agreement or Contract between Strangers, founded altogether in Vertue, is not so easy to be Traced and Described. For there is a Great Variety in the Tempers and Dispositions of Mankind, which hinders even Good Men from coming too hastily and rashly into a Contract of this Kind; and nothing but Time and Custom can make it Binding and Durable. The Minds of Men are often Changed, upon every Turn and Alteration in their Circumstances, and by the sudden Approaches

ches either of Good or Bad Fortune, or by the Differences of Age, or by the Acquisition of New Honours or Offices, or by such Disputes as may occasionally arise, on Account of Private Injuries and Worldly Interests. All these things serve to Obstruct or Interrupt a Course of Friendship. On the other hand, we must not be too Forward in rushing into a Friendship at once, with every one we meet, or who makes us an Offer and Tender of his Affection; but as the Vulgar Saying is, *We must eat a Measure of Salt together, before our Love can be Settled.* We must look well to the Honest Character and Good-Disposition of a Man, before we make him our Friend, and be fully assured of his Fidelity and Good-Will towards us. *Philosophy* is the Best Foundation and Cement of Friendship. For Similitude of Thoughts and Manners is the First Principle of Love and Unity: And the same Studies naturally Produce the same Will and Desires in Mankind. Hence arose that remarkable Friendship, which was between *Theseus* and *Perithous*, *Achilles* and *Patroclus*, *Pylades* and *Orestes*, *Damon* and *Pythias*. And so great was the Love and Affection between these Two last-mentioned Friends, that *Dionysius* desired to make himself a *Third Party,* in the League and Contract that was between them. The Mutual Improvement of Vertue, is what ought chiefly to be regarded among Friends; and we should be so far from making a Friendship with Persons of a Vicious and Profligate Character, that the very Sight of all such ought to be Offensive to us. Friends should always be Few in Number: For there is no Contracting a Strict and Intimate Friendship with a Multitude. We may have many Familiars, but these are rather our Companions and Partakers with us in the Common Offices of Kindness and Affability, than (properly and strictly speaking) our Friends. We ought to behave with Civility and Courtesy to All our Acquaintance, but a Friend is something more than an Acquaintance, and is chosen by us, as the Constant and Inseparable Companion of our Life. *Epaminondas*

nondas would often say, *That he never came from the* Forum, *without making some one Man his Friend:* But then this is to be understood, rather of a General Good-Liking and Acquaintance, than of a Particular Intimacy and Friendship. In the Course and Progress of Friendship, we must be sure never to do any thing for our Friend, which is not strictly Just and Honest: For Honesty ought always to have the Advantage over Personal Love and Affection. The *Three* Great Benefits of *Friendship* are, the Increase of Vertue, the Laws of which ought always to be kept Sacred and Inviolable; the Improvement of our Pleasures, which are Heightened by the Sweet and Delectable Intercourses of Intimacy and Familiarity; and the Security and Enlargement of our Worldly Interest and Advantage, which are often Increased and Redoubled upon us, by the Assistance and Good Offices of a Friend. When *Pericles* was desired by his particular Friend, to join with him in giving False Evidence against an Adversary, the Good Man readily answered, *That he was his Friend, no farther than was Consistent with his Honour and Religious Obligations;* thereby intimating, that no Friendship ought to bind us in Opposition to the Rules of Justice and Equity, and the Duty we owe to the Supreme Being. We ought rather to Rescue and Divert our Friend from any Evil Purpose or Design, than to Aid and Assist him in the Execution of it. Disputes and Contentions will sometimes arise among Friends; but when Both Parties are not alike ready and mutually agreed to do each other Service, or when One insists upon more than the Other is able to perform, all Friendship will soon be broke off between them. Of every thing like this, we ought to be very Careful, and nothing ought to be required of us in Friendship, which it is not in our Power to comply with. On this Occasion the same Rule is to be observed, by which we are directed, How and in What Manner we are to Honour our *Maker*, our Parents, and our Preceptors. It is certain, we can never pay them Honour enough, or be too

Grateful

Grateful in our Returns for the Benefits they have conferred on us: But whoever is willing to be Grateful to them, and does all he can to express his Gratitude accordingly, hath thereby fulfilled the Obligations he is under, and his Honesty and Piety are no longer to be questioned. Lastly, we must be careful not to make a Friendship with the Weak and Foolish. For all Familiarity with such Men will soon bring us into Contempt. These are the Rules which the *Good Senator* ought to observe, in all Contracts and Leagues of Friendship, and in the common Intercourses and Affairs of Life. He may possibly collect together many other Directions to the same purpose; but in general, he must Behave so in all his Friendships, as never to depart from the Laws and Precepts of Strict Justice; and must take Care, that his Country may always have the Largest Share in his Affections, as a Pledge and Security for the Public Safety and Happiness. There cannot be a more Agreeable Spectacle, or Pleasant Prospect in a State, than to see the Governors thereof united to each other in Love and Affection, and treating one another as Equals, Companions, and Friends. What Peace, Agreement, and Concord, can we hope to find among the People, when their Leaders are at Variance, and always Dissenting and Contending among themselves? Though there was a Constant and Well-known Enmity between *Aristides* and *Themistocles,* yet when those two Great Men were sent abroad upon an *Embassy* or Command, the Moment they approached the *Athenian* Territories, they presently forgot their Former Animosities, and laid them wholly aside, never to be Reassumed or Rekindled, till after they Returned home, and a fresh Occasion offered itself for Renewing the Quarrel. Men of a Generous and Noble Disposition will easily bring themselves, not only to Forget an Injury, but to Contemn and Despise it; and whenever they do this, for the Sake of their Country, their Name and Character for Justice and Goodness is so much the more Glorious and Remarkable. Not to be able

able to lay aside our Hatred and Animosity, and to involve even our Friend in our own Priate Quarrels, is a Sure Mark of a Rustical, Brutish, Savage, and Inhuman Disposition. Friendship ought to be Perpetual, but Enmity Mortal and Short-lived. To Friendship we must also add *Hospitality*, by which we are obliged to Receive, and Entertain, and to Treat in a Kind and Benign Manner, not only our Friends and Acquaintances, but even Strangers and Foreigners: By which means we shall be sure to Acquire not only Credit and Reputation, but Honour and Dignity. The Laws of *Hospitality* were so very Sacred among the *Romans*, that they would never break them, even with their Enemies, nor lift up a Hand that had been once joined in Hospitality to another, either to Strike or Offend a Guest, till the League was broken off between them. Let the *Good Senator* therefore take Care, not only to preserve the Friendships of his own Making, with Truth and Sincerity, but to preserve and confirm Those Friendships, which are Made and Contracted between other Men. Friendship is of great Use to the Publick, and altogether as Beneficial, as perhaps even Justice itself. *Plato*, who was of Opinion, That no other Vertue whatsoever contributed more effectually to the Publick Happiness, has therefore, in the Institution and Plan of his *Republick*, reduced all the Laws and Customs thereof to this one Single Principle of *Friendship*, and has laid down a Scheme of holding all things in Common, as a Means to keep Men together in Society, and make them Hearty and Vigorous in the Defence of it; Exploding and Banishing out of the State those Two Litigious Words, *Meum* and *Tuum*, as being the Causes and Occasion of all Dissensions and Changes in Government.

Next after *Friendship* follows *Concord*, which in other Words is nothing else but *Friendship Civilized*, or *Publick* and *Political Amity*. Now *Concord* consists in a General Agreement and Combination of all the Orders of Men in a State, for the Defence of the Laws and Liberties

Liberties of their Country, and of the Justice, Publick Faith, Religion, and Tranquillity of the Government. *Concord* gives a Nation the only Sure Hopes of Security and Self-Preservation; and by this the People are obliged to be of One Mind, at all Times, and upon all Occasions, and firmly to Unite together, as well in Council as in Strength, for their own Welfare and Safety. This therefore the *Good Senator* ought always to Promote and Encourage: For Discord is Poison to a State; whereas, if the People are United and closely Linked together, no Attempts made, by a *Tyrant*, *Tetrarch*, or *Imperious Lord*, can ever prevail to Break and Subdue them. *Concord* is much better than any Muniment or Fortification. Whence it was, that the *Roman Senate* was always held in the Temple of *Concord*, thereby intimating, That a *Senator* ought never to encourage Discord, Sedition, and Turbulency, but in every thing to promote Peace and Unity among his Fellow-Subjects. *Agesilaus*, King of the *Lacedæmonians*, being asked, *Why* Sparta *was not, like other Cities, surrounded with Walls?* bid those who asked him, look to the Citizens of *Sparta*, and to the State of Unity and Concord, in which they lived; and then told them, That *These were the Walls of* Sparta. When *Silurus* of *Scythia* was upon his Death-bed, he called his *Eighty* Sons about him, and gave them a Bundle of Arrows to break; which when they looked upon as an Impracticable Task, he took out each Arrow, and broke it by itself; thereby instructing his Children, that if they Agreed together, they would be truly Happy and Formidable, and perhaps Invincible. *Mycipsa* (as we are informed by *Salust*) when he was at the Point of Death, admonished his Sons, with all the Affection and Tenderness of an Indulgent Father, that they should always be at Peace and Amity with one another, bequeathing to them this *Golden* and Ever-Memorable Sentence, *That by* Concord, *Little Things are Increased; and by* Discord, *Great Ones are Diminished.* All *Senators*, therefore, ought to be aware of Strife and Contention

tion within their own Body, lest by their Example they Infect the Whole Mass of the People. It is a Shame for Men of this Order, to spend their Time in Wrangle and Ribaldry; and nothing so well becomes them, as Love and Peace, Concord and Benevolence. There is an End of That State, in which the *Senate* is wholly Employed in Broils and Contentions. How shall They settle the Publick Peace and Tranquillity, who are at Variance with One Another? On this Occasion, a Reconciliation ought to be Attempted, or They, who preferr their Own Private Animosities to the Publick Peace and Tranquillity, ought to be Removed from the *Senate-House;* into which Nothing should be admitted, that has any Tendency to Hatred and Malice, Dissension and Sedition. These Things we thought proper to be observed, in discoursing of *Justice* and *Concord*.

CHAP. VI.

The CONTENTS.

Of the Third Cardinal *Vertue,* Fortitude. *Its Excellency and Usefulness. How far Superior to the other* Vertues. *Private and Publick* Fortitude. *Of Military* Fortitude. *Of the Vertues accompanying* Fortitude. *Of* Magnanimity. *Of* Ambition, *and the Acquiring of* Honours. *Of* Constancy, *and the Love of* Truth. *How we ought to Behave, towards* Superiors, Equals, Inferiors, *and* Enemies. *Of* Perseverance. State-Secrets *ought to be kept. Of* Patience, Civil *and* Military. *Of* Confidence, *and of the* Good *and* Evil Genius. *Of* Security. *Its Faults and Advantages. Of* True Heroism. Military Men *ought to be Encouraged. Of* Despair, Anger *and* Fortune.

SINCE the Condition of Human Life is such, that it stands Tottering upon a very Narrow and Uncertain Pinnacle, and is daily Exposed to Innumerable Perils and Dangers, Afflictions and Evils of various Kinds and Degrees; against which we must either bravely Defend ourselves, or as bravely Endure and Support ourselves under them: And since *Fortitude* is that Safeguard and Armour of the Mind, by which we are enabled to Withstand all the Attacks of Fortune, and to Bear up, in the midst of our own Weaknesses and Infirmities; it remains, that we now speak of the Nature and Uses of this Great and Excellent *Vertue*.

We all naturally desire Ease and Quiet, and to pass away Life in a State of Peace and Tranquillity, without Fear, and without Danger; Secure from all Evils, and Undisturbed by any Inconveniences, Dangers, or Terrors, that may possibly Surround or Overtake

Overtake us. We are well and justly persuaded, that Vertue is our greatest and only Security; and that to her we owe our Ease and Quiet, our Freedom and Deliverance from all Trouble and Vexation, Care and Solicitude, Sorrow and Anxiety. But now Those Men are (in my Opinion) very much mistaken, who imagine, that it is in our own Power to make our Lives perfectly Pleasant and Happy, to keep ourselves in a continued Calm and Undisturbed State, without ever being Ruffled or Disturbed by any Terrors or Apprehensions, either of Imaginary, or of Real Evils. Nature hath marked out for us quite another State of Things, and Scheme of Life; hath stationed us at a very Honourable Post, hath set us in the Midst of Danger, and exposed our Minds to as great Trials by Trouble and Anxiety, as our Bodies are by Toil and Pain, by the Sweat of our Brows, and the Labour of our Hands. And indeed, we should never come to have a true Taste and Relish, either of Vertue, or of Happiness, if we never had any Knowledge or Experience of Pain and Misery: For when the Struggle is over, and we have gotten the Better of our Afflictions, the Sweets of Life do then return upon us with a greater Gust, and are doubly Delicious. Vertue really disdains a Solitary Unactive Life, is always in quest of Adventures, delights in Toil and Labour, glories in Distress, rejoices in Trials and Temptations, and triumphs in the midst of Danger. Hence *Hercules* is represented by the *Ancients*, as making Choice of the Narrow, Arduous, and Rugged Way of Vertue, and as turning his Back upon the Broad and Smooth Way, that leads to Pleasure and Vice. And certainly, whoever is a Sincere Follower of Vertue, and a Lover of True Happiness, ought to look upon Pleasure with Contempt; not to over-value the Things of this Life; to hate Idleness and Inactivity, and to banish Fear and Cowardice, as Base and Abject Passions. In our Way to Vertue, we must Surmount and Break through whatever Difficulties lie cross our Passage: Much more

when

when we have Acquired, and are the Masters of it, must we Exert all its Powers and Faculties, in Bearing for a while, and Combating with Dangers, Difficulties, and Distresses, till we have Subdued them under us, and are Victorious and Triumphant. Vertue is at all times, and in every Affair of Life, our Firm Support, and our Sure Defence: To her we owe all our Power and Strength, our Constancy and Courage. There is no Adventure so Dangerous and Difficult, but by her Assistance we can happily Finish it; nothing we can Hope for, truly Good and Great, but in Time we may be able to Attain it. *Fortitude* is an Exalted Strain, an Elevation and Excellency of the Mind, an Affection of the Soul, that in Obedience to, and at the Command of Vertue, enables us to endure the Greatest Toils, and to perfect the Noblest Undertakings. This alone is the Grace and Ornament of all other Vertues. *Prudence, Justice,* and *Temperance,* are, in their own Nature and Operations, too Soft and Delicate, and even Weak and Effeminate, unless Raised and Strengthened by *Fortitude.* To think and do Well, is the utmost of their Attainments: But to think and do Bravely, Courageously, Constantly, and like Men, are the proper Fruits and Effects of *Fortitude.* This Vertue is therefore Worthy of the *Good Senator*'s Notice, and of his Best Endeavours to attain it. Without This, he can never Act, or Speak any thing, that is truly Great and Noble, Famous and Memorable. The Extremes that lie on each Side of this Vertue, and which we must be careful to Avoid, are on the one hand, *Self-Confidence, Pride,* and *Temerity;* and on the other hand, *Idleness, Effeminacy,* and *Cowardice.* The truly Brave Man is so well Affected to Vertue, that for her Sake he will always ready to undertake any Enterprize, and to withstand any Dangers; always depending upon his own Reason and Judgment, rather than upon Chance and Fortune: And will never be hurried into Action, by a Wild, Rash, and Intemperate Boldness. The Great Glory of *Fortitude*, is particularly seen and displayed,

displayed, either in the Affairs of Domestick, or of Publick Life; and more particularly in what relates to *War* and Military Discipline. Domestick *Fortitude* is the Ornament of our Lives, and the Security of our Happiness. It removes far from us all Uneasiness and Perturbation of Mind, all Inordinate Desires, Unnecessary Fears, Inward Pains and Anxieties; all Love of Pleasure, Rage, Anger, and the Excesses of all the other Passions and Affections; and keeps us in a State of Tranquillity, Lasting and Durable, and Consistent with out Character and Dignity. *Military Fortitude* serves to carry us through all Toils, Dangers, and Difficulties; and is chiefly seen in our Contempt of Death, whenever we are engaged in an Honest Cause, or in the Service and Defence of our Country. The Brave and Courageous *Senator* will look upon it as his Duty, not to be dismayed at the Appearance of any Danger, nor to shrink at the Difficulty of any Undertaking, which Vertue puts him upon, or Honour requires at his Hands. It is the Property of a truly Great and Valiant Mind, not to fear any thing, to despise whatever belongs to this World, and to be persuaded, that no Difficulty can be flung in his Way, which he is not able to surmount. Let this Vertue rouze and animate the *Good Senator*, and let him take Care that all his Parts and Faculties, and all the Endowments and Vertues of his Mind, may have a Savour and Tincture of *Fortitude*, and may be Well-tempered and Seasoned therewith. All the Vertues without *Fortitude*, like Meats without Salt, are Tasteless and Insipid. *Fortitude* is an Impenetrable Armour, both within and without, and defends the Body, as well as the Mind, from the Adverse Attacks and Shifts of Fortune. By this we learn to be Easy and Quiet in *Prudence*, Constant in *Temperance*, and in *Justice* Unshaken, Firm, and Invincible. Let therefore the Mind of the *Good Senator* be always Strengthened and Supported by *Fortitude*. Let him be Steady and Resolute in the Undertaking of any Difficulty, Magnanimous in the Contempt of any

Danger,

Danger, and Intrepid and Unwearied under any Affliction that shall befall him. This Vertue of *Fortitude* has many other Vertues for its Followers and Attendants: These are *Magnanimity. Constancy, Patience, Confidence*, and *Security*.

In the Practice of every Vertue, whatever things are of a more shining Excellence and greater Renown than others, it is the Proper Business of *Magnanimity* to find out; and when they are known and discovered, to conform ourselves thereto, with the utmost Exactness. This Vertue is chiefly seen in the Acquisition and Attainment of Honours, and looks with Contempt upon all such, as are not Commensurate with, or the Adequate Rewards of Vertue. There is no Approaching of Rising to Honour, but by the Scale and Steps which Vertue has marked out. When *Marcellus* built a Temple to *Honour*, out of the Spoils and Plunder which he had gotten at *Syracuse*, he contrived the Portal or Entrance in such a Manner, that there was no Approaching thereto, but by Passing first through the next adjoining Temple of *Vertue*: Whereby he taught us this Lesson, That *Vertue* has the Only Title and Best Pretensions to *Honour*. This the *Good Senator* ought always to have in Remembrance, whenever he Solicites, or is a Candidate for any Honours in the State. Whilst he is upon any such Canvass, he ought to Despise all little Vulgar Reports, and groundless Calumnies and Reproaches, which a Man of Secure and Exalted Vertue will be far above, and will depend on his own Smooth, Level, and Shining Character, upon which Envy and Malice can never fix any Flaw, Spot, or Blemish whatsoever. Whether Fortune Smiles or Frowns, a Brave Mind will be always the same, and remain Unaltered and Unshaken; his Fortitude will shew itself, and shine out, in Times of Danger and Difficulty; and will go boldly out, to meet an approaching Danger, though Death itself stand in the Way. For it is always to be considered, that an Honest and Honourable Death, is a Sure Passport to a Glorious Immortality.

Sweet

Sweet is the Memory of *Codrus*, and never to be Obliterated, who freely gave himself up to Death, in order to save the *Roman* Army. And the Fame of *Curtius* and *Scævola*, will never be forgotten: *One* of whom readily flung himself into the Gulph, in order to save his People from the Pestilence; and the *Other* burnt off his Hand at the *Altar*, for the Sake of convincing his Enemies, that a *Roman* dared to do any Thing, in Defence of the Honour and Safety of his Country. It is also the Duty of the *Magnanimous Senator*, to be True and Constant in all his Judgments and Determinations concerning the Publick, and not to follow the Vulgar, who judge of every thing only by Chance, and just as their present Inclinations lead them. He will always be a Ready and Voluntary Patron and Defender of Truth, and for the Sake of Truth and Vertue, will have a natural Aversion for those who are guilty of Vice and Falshood; unless in such Cases, and at such Times, when Concealment and Dissimulation are Necessary, on Account of the Persons we are to deal with, or of the Present Exigency of Affairs. He must also be ready to conferr Benefits upon others, and to receive those that are due to himself, with Gravity, Modesty, and Humility. In all Acts of Gratitude we are to observe what *Hesiod* says, *That our Returns ought to Exceed what is Given or Bestowed upon us:* For the Giver is always Superior to, and more Noble than the Receiver. *Taxilis*, one of the many *Princes* of *India*, who (as *Plutarch* relates the Story) went out to meet *Alexander* the *Great*, saluted him in the following Manner; "I Chal-
" lenge Thee (says he) not to Battle, or to single Combat; but
" to a Trial of Skill, in a much Nobler Way. If Thou art In-
" ferior to us, take a Benefit at our Hands: If Superior, bestow
" One upon us." To whom the *Conqueror* returned this Answer;
" The Question (says he) between us is This; Which of the Two
" shall be the Greatest Benefactor to the Other." —— Here he paused, and broke off abruptly, ran and embraced the *Prince*,
gave

gave him back his Kingdom, and very much enlarged its Dominions and Territories. The *Magnanimous Senator* will also take Care to give Proofs of his Benign and Equitable Disposition towards All who are near, or about him, and especially towards Those who are the Proper Objects of his Liberality. With such as are of an Equal or Superior Order to his own, he will take upon him the Proper State, and insist upon the Privileges due to his own Dignity: But towards those Beneath him, and with the Humble and Lowly, he will behave with Humility and Condescension. This Sort of Conduct will procure him Honour and Esteem; and the Contrary to this will provoke others to Hate and Contemn him. In the Prosecution of Quarrels and Animosities, he will always take Care that his Cause be Just and Good; and he will pursue an Enemy openly and fairly, and not treacherously, and under Cover, or in Disguise. For it is more Noble and Generous to express one's Resentment publickly, than to conceal the Bitterness of the Heart, under the Sweetness of a Smiling and Hypocritical Countenance. *Magnanimity* will teach him, not only to forbear the doing any Injury to Others, but to despise the Injuries done by Others, and to trample them under Foot. He will, in a particular Manner, very easily pass over whatever Injuries are done to Himself: For to despise Injuries, is as sure a Proof of *Magnanimity*, as to despise Danger. To be easily Provoked, and when we are Provoked, to be Violent, Furious, and Implacable, is a Mark rather of Effeminacy than Manhood. Lions and Elephants, when they meet any of their Fellow-Creatures of an Order much Inferior to themselves, and see them crouching in an Humble Suppliant Posture, will generously pass by, and not hurt them. In general, the *Good Senator* will make Honesty his chief Study, and will use the Conveniences and Necessaries of Life, with Frugality and Moderation: Will Depend upon none but Himself, in the Choice and Manner of his Life: Will follow the Advice of his
Friends

Friends, rather than the Example of Strangers: Will entertain no Ill Thoughts of Others: Nor speak ill of them, or Listen to Those, who make a Practice of Calumny and Detraction: Nor be Angry without a Cause; which is a Low and Servile Passion: For what *Ovid* observes, is very True;

> *The Brave and Noble easily are Pleas'd,*
> *And Gen'rous Minds are always soon Appeas'd.*

There are some Men, who by Pride and Arrogance, assume so much Splendor to themselves, that their own Just and Natural Lustre is thereby Obscured and Extinguished. They who are guilty of this Fault, are most commonly such Persons, as make a very undue Estimate of their own Vertues, Value, and Dignity; and arrogate more to themselves, than becomes Men of Real Goodness and Prudence. This Sort of Weakness the *Senator* must Guard himself against, and must always Remember what *Tully* says, *That the Greater our Dignity is, the more Conspicuous ought our Humility to be: For Arrogance is a Vice, justly Odious and Hateful, in the Eyes of all Men.* But then on the other hand, Care must be taken, not to fall into the Opposite Extremes, the Low Groveling Vices of Levity and Pusillanimity. For they who take no Notice of any Contumelies, or Injuries whatsoever, and do this either out of Fear or Negligence, are of an Abject and Slavish Temper. And at the same time, they who in the midst of a Good Character for Vertue and Prudence, are careless in their Attendance upon the Highest and most Important Duties of their Function, merely out of Laziness and Idleness, or out of a mean Distrust of their own Abilities, to assist their Friends, or serve their Country, are to be Condemned as Guilty of Sloth and Folly.

In whatever a *Senator* Says and Does, and in his Manner of bearing with Afflictions and an Adverse State, *Constancy* is a Sure Guide

to

to him, a Director of his Conduct, and an Ornament to his Character. A Changeable and Unstable Mind, never Consistent with itself, and liable to more Turns and Shapes, than (as the Vulgar say) ever *Proteus* was, is as great a Blemish to his Character, as Fraud and Deceit. Reason and Judgment ought to have their Share in all Generous and Laudable Undertakings; but unless there be Constancy and Perseverance in the Prosecution of them, they will certainly end in a Foul and Shameful Defeat. Every Action should not only be Just and Honest in itself, but Followed and made Perfect by Constancy, and by a Steadiness in Council, that never leaves Unfinished the Design it has once Undertaken. The Constancy of *Aristides* is well worthy to be Recorded, who, when *Dionysius* asked of him his Daughter in Marriage, gave this Brave and Honest Answer, *That he had rather see his Daughter Dead, than Marry her to a Tyrant:* And after himself had Slain her, and was again asked, *Whether he was still of the same Opinion?* as readily answered, *That he Gloried in what he had Said, but was Sorry for what he had Done.* Who is there, that does not Applaud the Constancy of *Cato?* For who ever saw him Changed or Altered, in the midst of all the Troubles and Calamities, which in his time befell the Commonwealth? His Colour, Countenance, Looks, Motions, and Gestures, were always the same, as well when he was *Prætor* and Governed a Province, as when he was under an Accusation, and in Disgrace. In the *Senate*, in the *Army*, even in *Death* itself, and when *Pompey* lost the Day, and *Cæsar* by his Victory, and with an Armed Force, took Possession of the Liberties of his Country, he still continued Steady, Unshaken, and Uniform, in all his Behaviour. *Xantippe* was often heard to say of her Husband *Socrates*, *That he always brought Home the same Countenance, with which he went Abroad:* For so Great was his Soul, that neither Prosperity nor Adversity could in the least Shock or Discompose it. Whatever Evils or Dangers do at any time befall or threaten

threaten us, we ought to bear them with a Firm and Steady Resolution, and rather to endure any thing, however Grievous and Afflicting, than to part with the Firmness and Stability of an Upright and Constant Mind. The *Roman Regulus* has set us an Example; who readily exposed himself to a very Severe Punishment, rather than his Country-Men, who had been taken by the *Carthaginians*, should be surrendered and given up to a State of Vassalage and Misery. When *Anexagoras* was Scourged by the Command of *Nicocreon*, Tyrant of *Cyprus*, he is reported to have expressed himself in this Manner: *You may Tear, and Wound, and Mangle my Body: But my Mind is Invulnerable; and with all your Powers you can never shake its Constancy*. This, however, the Good Senator must be very Cautious of, That he be not too Tenacious, or too Resolute and Persevering, in what others take to be really Wrong and Unjust. *Constancy* ought to be the Inseparable Companion of Vertue. A Pertinacious and Obstinate Adherence to our own Judgment and Opinion, in Opposition to the Established Sentiments of all Good and Wise Men, and a Resolution to be Solicitous for, and to persist in the Defence and Support of a Bad Cause, is by no Means a Proof and Argument of our Constancy; but is rather the Effect and Produce of a Perverse, Positive, and Obstinate Temper; and favours more of Folly and Rashness, than of Sound Judgment and Discretion. Even in the Choice of the Frame and Model of our Lives and Conduct, a good deal of Constancy is required; and in Adhering to, and Retaining what we have once made Choice of. They who are Wavering and Instable on this Occasion, can never be suspected of overmuch *Constancy* in any Affair whatsoever. *Constancy* is the Preserver of all Good Counsels and Actions; For in vain do we Form to ourselves Good Projects and Designs, if the Wholsome Counsels we Give or Take, Ebb and Flow like a River near the Sea, and never run down in one Steady, Regular, and Constant Course.

The

The most Remarkable Instance and Trial of our Constancy is, when we are able to keep and retain the Secrets of a *Senate*. For in every *Senate*, there are some Debates and Proceedings, which, at least for a Time, ought not to be Divulged or made known to Strangers, not even to our own Country-Men and Fellow-Citizens. To betray any Secrets of this Sort, or to tell what passes in the *Senate-House*, is a Sure Proof of Weakness and Instability. And therefore the *Romans*, whenever they held a Consultation upon any Matters of the First Weight and Consequence, would not suffer any *Pedarian Senators* to be present at these Consultations, nor admit even the *Scribes* or *Clerks*, whose Office was supplied by some of the *Senators* themselves, chosen for that Purpose. At one Time indeed, the *Senate-House* was always open to any of the *Patrician Youth*, or Noblemen's Sons: But after the Famous and Memorable Exploit of *Papirius*, this Privilege was Occasionally taken from them; lest by their Levity and Inconstancy, Faults too common and familiar to Youth, they should at any time betray the Secrets of the State, the Knowledge of which might be Dangerous or Detrimental to the Publick. The Case of *Papirius* was this: When there had been one Day a very long Debate in the *Senate*, and upon his Return home, this Noble Youth was asked by his Mother, *What the* Senate *had been then Doing, and why they sate so Late?* He with a good deal of Art and Dissimulation very readily answered her, *That the* Question *that Day was, Whether it were most for the Publick Benefit, that a Man should have Two Wives, or a Woman Two Husbands.* Patience, or the Art of Enduring any Hardships or Calamities, that may possibly befall us, is another Vertue always Attendant upon, and Assistant to *Fortitude*. *Tully* hath defined *Patience* to be a Vertue of the Mind, *By which we are Enabled, for the Sake of Honesty or Profit, Freely, Constantly, and Contentedly, to bear whatever Load is laid upon us, either by Adverse Fortune or our own Engagements in any Difficult or Arduous Undertaking.* In all

all the Progress and Events of War, *Patience* is of admirable Use, and the *Military Man* is obliged to expose his Life to many Dangers, and to bear innumerable Toils and Fatigues, for the Sake of his own Honour, and his Country's Good. The *Senator* ought also to have his Share and Proportion of this Vertue, when the Weight of Publick Business lies heavy upon him, and his Country is under any Difficulties, or in any Distress. For every State is liable to many Troubles and Calamities; and a Due Portion of these is what the *Good Senator* must expect to endure. When *Coriolanus* lost the *Consulship*, for which he was a Candidate, had his *Patience* stood that Shock in a better Manner than he did, and had he abated something of that Pride and Insolence, which were but too plainly Visible in his Character, he had prevented all the Disasters and Calamities of the Latter Part of his Life. It is Commonly and very Truly said, that Patience is *a Remedy for all Diseases*. It is in vain to complain of what we cannot Help or Alter; but it may be easy for us to Bear it. When a *Senator* hath made himself a perfect Master of this Art of Sufferance, he will soon Contract such a Wholsome Habit and Temper of Mind, that all Pains and Calamities, whether of a Publick or Private Nature, will, like a Bitter Potion, be swallowed and taken down, and pass through him as Easily, and with as little Regard, as if they had never been. He who cannot bear Affliction, unmans himself by Softness and Effeminacy: But he who Endures and Perseveres, till he has Conquered all Difficulties, is a truly *Patient Man*. This Caution, however, is by the way necessary to be observed, That we never let the Multitude or Extremity of our Sufferings provoke us to any Intemperate Outrages, or Excesses of Fury: For *Patience*, throughly abused, will turn to *Fury*; unless we take Care to prevent it by Lenity, and a Temper of Mind not to be Ruffled or thrown into Convulsions. It is really our Duty to bear all necessary and unavoidable Evils; and if we

bear

bear them as we ought to do, *Patience* will at length give us the Victory.

Confidence is another Vertue of the Mind, which contributes much to the Strengthening and Improving of our *Fortitude*, and is a Well-assured Expectation and Presage or Prospect of Success, in any of our Designs or Undertakings of Moment. This Vertue is called *Confidence*, because the Mind that is Possessed of it, *Confides* entirely in itself, and depends wholly upon its own Lively Hopes, of reaping some Considerable Advantage, from whatever Projects or Schemes of Action we are at present Engaged in. *Prudence*, Good Counsel, and Hope, give Rise and Being to this Vertue. For when we have a perfect Knowledge of what we Undertake, and a good Opinion of the Issues of it; which Opinion is founded in Reason, and not Rashly taken up and Entertained by us; we are then *Confident* of Succeeding in our Honest Designs, and we go on with Courage in the Execution of them. For the Truly *Confident* know not what it is to Fear. When *J. Cæsar* met *C. Crastinus*, a Youth of very great Hopes, in the Battle of *Pharsalia*, and asked him, *What he thought of the Event of That Day?* The young Hero, stretching out his Hand and the Sword that was in it, gave him this Answer; *I know,* Cæsar, *that the Day is yours; but whether I live or die, you shall be sure to speak well of me.* What he said, came presently to pass: For he died bravely in that very Field, and *Cæsar* graced his Funeral with an Oration, or *Panegyrick*. *Aristotle* says, *That Confidence arises from a Habit and Custom of Conquering, and a Course of Success in whatever we Undertake.* But we may certainly Attribute it to several other Causes besides this. *Plutarch* speaks of a certain *Egyptian Philosopher*, with whose Company *Anthony* was very much delighted, and who undertook to tell any Person's Temper, Dispositions, Fate, and Fortune, only by his Face and Features. This *Sage* would always speak well of *Anthony*'s Fortune, but would

would set *Octavius Augustus*'s far above it, and intreat *Anthony* not to contend any longer with so Formidable a Rival; because *Octavius* had a Superior *Genius* always attending him, and for Proof of what he said, he gave this among many other Instances, That at all youthful Sports whatsoever, *Dicing, Cocking*, and the like, *Octavius* was always Lucky and Victorious. Great Men, Kings and Princes, are indeed supposed, from the very Time of their Birth, to have a *Genius* assigned them, as their Governor, Tutor, and *Guardian*, and as their faithful Monitor upon all Occasions, and in all the Great Enterprizes and Exigences of Life. What *Homer* and *Plato* call a *Genius*, other *Ancients* reckon in the Number of their *Lares, Lemures*, or *Dæmons*; and we at this Day call our *Good Angel*, an Invisible Being, that Admonishes us of all Dangers, and is always Present with, and Assistant to Military Men, in the Day of Battle. Some are of Opinion, that there are *Two Angels* assigned to every Man, one *Good*, and the other *Evil*. And here now, let me particularly Address myself to his *Present Majesty* of *Poland*, and put him in mind of what we so often read of in *History*, that when his Great Ancestor *Ulidislaus* was engaged in the *Prussian War* against the *Germans*, he saw a *Genius* in Armour standing by him, whom he ever afterwards mentioned with Reverence, and called him by the Name of DIVUS STANISLAUS; at whose Appearance he was Animated with such *Confidence*, that he easily obtained a Complete and Signal Victory, and delivered *Prussia* from the Yoke that then hung over its Neck. On the other hand, *Plutarch* speaks of the *Evil Genius* of *Brutus*, that as he sate in his Tent meditating upon the Projects and Events of the War he wa engaged in, appeared to him in a Form of Uncommon Magnitude, and being asked, *What he was?* said, *Thy Evil Genius*, Brutus, *whom thou shalt again see at* Philippi. Accordingly he there made him a Second Visit, and Foretold to him the Event of the Battle, and his own Death. It was

indeed

indeed Customary with the *Romans*, to *Confide* very much in their *Genii*; and we often see of their *Coins*, bearing an Inscription of this Sort, *To the* Genius *of* Augustus! *To the* Genius *of the* Senate, or, *of the People of* Rome. Whence *Ovid* says,

Our Watchful Genii *always Guard the State.*

But after all, the Best and Surest Foundation, upon which to build a Just and Well-grounded *Confidence*, is to be had only from Good Counsel and Prudence. With these Principles of an Honest Assurance, let the *Senator* arm his Mind, and he will then be able to Undertake the Greatest Designs, and to Execute them with Unquestionable Courage and Bravery. All other Foundations and Supports of *Confidence*, may possibly Fail, and miserably Deceive us. It has been Observed, and is certainly most True, that nothing is Safe, which is not Honourable and Vertuous: For the Surest foundation of a Lively Hope, is always laid in Vertue. But then we must be very Careful, that our *Confidence* does not betray us into Intemperate Boldness, Rashness, and Despair; which are Vices, that under a False Shew and Appearance of *Fortitude*, serve only to Swell and Blow up the Mind, and push us by our Imprudence upon the most Desperate Attempts, and the most Unsurmountable Enterprizes.

Security is the End and Attainment both of Living well, and of Behaving with *Fortitude*; and consists in a Rest and Tranquillity of the Mind, when Freed from all Care and Solicitude. They who are perfectly *Secure*, are (as *Cicero* speaks) *in the same Easy and Unconcerned State, in which they were, before they were Born.* For Security is nothing else, but a Deliverance and Freedom from all Trouble and Sorrow whatsoever; in which State the *Philosophers* were of Opinion, that all True Happiness consisted. For the Sake of this Happiness, *Democritus* and *Homer* travelled as far as *Egypt*,

CHAP. VI. *SENATOR* 279

Egypt, Babylon, and *Persia,* that from the Wisdom of those Nations, they might collect together such a Stock and Treasure of Knowledge, as might arm their Minds with *Security,* make them Perfect in Happiness, and consequently Contented with their present Condition. *Security* is of great Use and Benefit to the Publick: For when all Things are Quiet, and in a State of Peace and Tranquillity; when no Fears or Dangers, Murmurs or Complaints, Tumults or Disorders, are so much as heard of in a Government, the Publick Felicity is then at the Height, and incapable of any Increase or Improvement. But now we must be very Cautious, that our *Security* be not built upon an Uncertain, False, Light, and Sandy Foundation; and that it be not owing only to our Sloth, Negligence, and Idleness. When *Pompey* had raised a very Formidable Army against *Cæsar,* and was thereupon perfectly *Secure,* telling those about him, who had a Just Suspicion of *Cæsar's* Diligence, and who advised him not to be too Careless and Negligent, *That they might go Home and Sleep soundly*; this *Security* was the undoubted Cause of his Overthrow: For he lost the Day, and was miserably Defeated by *Cæsar.* It is sometimes the Fate of too many Commonwealths, that after a Long and Established Peace, they are easily betrayed into too Profound a *Security,* which ought more properly to be called *Sloth* and *Languor, Ease* and *Idleness.* Because in such a State, we see all Things Neglected and run to Decay, which should be constantly kept up, for the more Prudent and Wise Administration of the Publick Affairs, for Guarding the State against Approaches of Danger, and for Training the People to all the Arts and Institutions, necessary to Improve them in the practice of *Justice* and *Fortitude. Rome* had Raised, and very much Enlarged, her Empire, by no other Vertue but *Fortitude* only. She had carried her Laws, as well as her Arms, into many Remote Parts and Provinces. And these Arms she never laid down, from the Time of *Romulus,* to the Reign of *Augustus.*
But

But the World being Subdued, and the Empire settled in Peace and Tranquillity, *Augustus* was the *Second* after *Numa*, who (according to the Custom of declaring Peace) shut up the Temple of *Janus*, and thereby gave the City Rest from all the Toils and Commotions of War, *Rome* was then in Perfect Security; and we no where read of the Temple of *Janus* being Opened by any Succeeding *Emperor*. The People, instead of their former Rough and Military Life, now ran into all imaginary Ease and Luxury; till by Degrees the several Kingdoms, Cities, and Provinces, which had submitted to the *Roman* Yoke, withdrew their Necks from under it, and Bravely regained their Former Liberties. By little and little, *Rome* was Stript of its Former Strength, left Naked and Defenceless, and at last became a Prey to the Rough and Barbarous *Goth*. There is therefore no other *Security* in a State, which the *Good Senator* may safely give into, but such as is Consistent with a Wise Foresight of Danger, and a Timely Caution and Provision against it. Happy is That Government, which is always Intent upon, and Provided for a War, even in the Times of a Profound Peace!

There are some other *Principles* proper to be taken Notice of, as Contributing very much to the Vertue of *Fortitude*, and as Spurs and Incitements to the Minds of Men, especially of Those, who are Engaged in a *Military Profession*. There is never wanting in the World a Sett of Men, of such *Heroick* Honesty and Vertue, that they will readily and freely expose themselves to all manner of Hardships, Wounds, and Dangers, and for the Sake of their Country, their King, or their Friends, will rather lay down their Lives in Battle, than forfeit their Courage and Resolution. It is the Just and Well-known Character and Glory of our own Nation, that Honesty and Vertue are their Chief and Only Leaders in all the Wars, in which we have been hitherto Engaged. In the *Histories* of the Wars and Exploits of the *Romans,*

mans, Macedonians, Persians, Assyrians, Germans, and *Gauls,* we find that their Generals and Commanders, when they led their Men on to Battle, made use of Various Arguments to Instigate and Encourage them. Sometimes they put them in mind of the Strength and Number of their Forces, and sometimes of the Bravery and Experience of their Officers: At other times they Reminded them of the Glory of their Ancestors, and very often they Animated them with the Hope and Near Prospect of Plundering, and Glutting themselves with the Spoils and Wealth of their Enemies. But our *Polish Commanders* have ever had but one Way of Encouraging their Men, which was, to put them in mind of their own Native Honesty and Vertue, and of the Resolution always taken by their Countrymen, either to Conquer or to Die. They then, who are thus affected, and governed by these Generous Principles of Honesty and Vertue, will never Start at Danger, or Decline engaging in any Honourable Enterprize; will make Bravery their Choice and Judgment, and thereby Deserve the Title and Character of *True Fortitude*. With these are to be reckoned the Hero and Honourable *Volunteer,* who serve for the Sake of Praise and Glory, the Two Noble Principles that inflame and push them forward upon the most Arduous and Renowned Adventures. The Actions and Exploits of such Men, every Government ought to take a Proper Notice of, and to see that they are Gratefully and Honourably Rewarded. The Gentlemen of the Sword are indeed chiefly taken up with the Arts of War, and they are employed rather in Destroying their Enemies, than in Governing their Fellow-Citizens. But where any of this Order have distinguished themselves by their Wisdom and Prudence, they will deserve to be Advanced to the *Senatorial Dignity*. They who have served long and faithfully, and by many Toils and Fatigues have suffered much in the Cause of their Country, should at last exchange the *Sword* for the *Gown,* and enjoy the

Fruits

Fruits of a *Civil* and Honourable Tranquillity. Among the *Romans*, they were always chosen into the *Senate*, who could produce any Considerable Trophies, or Spoils taken from an Enemy, or were entitled to the *Civic Crown:* And no one was capable of any Office in the City-Magistracy, till he had served *Ten Years* in the *Army.* When *Regulus* was at one time expelled the *Senate*, and very much resented the Indignity then offered him; but was Unable to produce any just Pretensions, or make good his Title to that High Honour; at length Tearing his Robe asunder, he laid his Breast naked, and Pointing to the many Scars he had gotten in Defence of his Country, and Enumerating the many Services in which he had been wounded, was thereupon, by the other *Senators,* restored to his Place among them.

There are some Men, who have so little Regard for their own Lives, and so great a Contempt of Death, that in a False Shew and Imitation of True *Fortitude*, they rush desperately into all manner of Dangers, and whatever is the Event, have this Saying of the *Poet*, for their Excuse and Consolation:

The Vanquish'd find their Safety in Despair.

The *Numantines*, rather than be reduced to make Trial of the Clemency of their Enemies, destroyed themselves: And (as we read in *Livy*) the same was the Fate of the Citizens of *Saguntum.* But now we ought to be Cautious of Undertaking any thing in a Desperate Manner: For Despair is a Revolt and Departure from True *Fortitude*, and is commonly the Last Refuge and Resort of Men, whose Spirits are Tired and Broken with Adversity; and in this Condition they fly, in a Cowardly Manner, to Death for Ease, and for a Speedy and Effectual Deliverance out of their Troubles and Afflictions. The Truly Brave and Valiant make it their Choice and Judgment to despise
Life,

Life, and enter upon Danger, with a Rational Boldness, not as Men without Hope, but because they think it both Honest and Necessary to Behave with Intrepidity, and chuse rather to Die, than to prolong their Lives by any Base or Dishonourable Action. For a Death with Honour, is better than a Life with Infamy.

Anger is by the *Peripateticks* called the *Provocative*, or *Whetstone* of *Fortitude*, whereby the Mind is made Keen and Acute, and has a Fresh Edge set upon it; or from a Gentle Kindling and Inflammation, is Raised and Instigated, till it Bursts and Shines out in some Adventure of Difficulty and Renown. But then we must be Careful not to let our Anger fly out into any Excesses of Brutal Rage and Fury; lest we be thought rather Mad and Frantick, than Truly Brave and Courageous. The most proper Restraint we can lay upon it, is to make Use of *Anger*, only as a Follower and Companion, and not as a Leader and Fore-runner of *Fortitude*. It is a Disgrace for any Man, much more for a *Senator*, to enter upon any Affair of Consequence, in a Fit of *Anger*. This is a Practice becoming Brutes, rather than Men, when their Present Rage or Appetites prompt them to Revenge. In all Actions and Enterprizes of Note, we must let Honesty and Reason have the Command and Presidence, and make Use of *Anger* only for an Auxiliary. This Passion is by *Plato* called, *The Nerves of the Mind*, by which it is stretched and strained to Excess, or gently relaxed and abated. They who fight in a Rage, or when the Excesses of Anger and Resentment are upon them, may indeed give Proofs of a Brutal Force and Rage, but have no Good Title to True *Fortitude:* Because they are Prompted to Action, not by Honesty and Reason, but by an Impulse and Agitation of the Mind, common to Savages. *Epicurus* very well observes, *That Immoderate* Anger *is the Parent of Frenzy*,

which

which we must be Careful to avoid, for the Preservation of our Health and Intellects, as well as of our Temper.

There are many Men, who attribute so very much to *Fortune,* in the conducting of all Affairs whatsoever, that if they have but *Fortune* on their Side, they are apt to Triumph, even before they have gained the Victory; and in the Strength and Assurance of her Aid, can boldly venture upon any Undertaking, though never so Difficult and Unpromising. This is a very Prevailing, but a very Great Error. For though the Influence of *Fortune* is very Strong, especially in the Events and Issues of War, and extends chiefly to those Things, with which Reason has very litle to do, yet we must be far from submitting to her in so Servile and Implicit a Manner, as to Reject the Necessary Aids and Uses of Wisdom and Good Counsel. *A Good General* (as a certain Author well observes) *will not be under the Leading of* Fortune, *when his own Mind and Reason have the Sole Command over him.* When *Hannibal* applied to *Scipio* for Peace, he is said to have addressed him in this manner: " At " present (says he) I am in Adversity; and but very lately I " was in Prosperity: From Both which States I learn, that Rea-" son, and not Fortune, ought to be the Proper Guide of all " our Actions." Fortune is very apt to desert Those, who, in distrust of Good Counsel and Wisdom, throw themselves entirely upon Her. She is as Remarkable for her Weakness, as for her Fickle and Inconstant Humours; and is often obliged to make Men as Blind as herself, in order to preserve her own Power and Dominion over them. Let the *Senator* therefore be the Maker of his own Fortune. Let Reason and Counsel govern all his Actions, and *Fortune* will then Interpose, to Grace and Adorn them; and will follow him in all his Conduct, as a Shadow does the Substance. 'Tis a remarkable Saying of *Xenophon*'s, That *Good* Fortune *and Good Men, and Bad* Fortune *and Bad Men, are insepa-*
rable

rable Companions in War. The many Successful Exploits of *Alexander, Scipio,* and *Hannibal,* are not properly to be imputed to their *Fortune*; but to their Wisdom, Prudence, and Vertue. Every Man of this Character will make use of *Fortune*, when She offers him her Service, and will direct all her Turns and Windings to his own Advantage: But unskilful Men, when any thing happens out luckily, and to their Mind, do well to ascribe it to *Fortune*. For *Fortune* is to *Fools*, what *Chance* is to the *Brute Beasts* beneath us; whilst no Good or Wise Man will ever chuse such a Blind Being, for the Guide and Conductor of all his Actions. But it is Time we should proceed to an Examination of the Last Great *Cardinal Vertue* of *Temperance*.

CHAP. VII.

The CONTENTS.

Of the Fourth Cardinal *Vertue,* Temperance. *Whence this Vertue has its Rise. Of the Two Sorts of* Pleasures. *Wherein* Temperance *consists. How far Beneficial to a* State. *The Mischiefs of* Avarice. *Of* Luxury *and* Sumptuary Laws. *Private Intemperance the Cause and Fore-runner of* Slavery. *Private Intemperance, as well as* Publick, *ought to be Restrained by* Law. *Of the* Vertues *accompanying* Temperance. *Of* Moderation, *and* Temporizing. *Of* Modesty, *and the several Sorts of it. Of* Honesty, Continency, *and* Abstinence. *The Great Excellency of these* Vertues. *The Contrary* Vices, *how Foul and Odious. The Mischiefs of* Lust *and* Drunkenness. *Instances of the* Great Temperance *of the* Ancients.

IN tracing the ordinary and established Course of Nature, we may easily find, that there is a Perpetual War, and Contention between the Mind and the Body; and that in this Struggle and Tumult raised within us, we are often Obstructed and Diverted from our Necessary Attendance upon the Proper Duties of Life, and Offices of Vertue. The Desires and Appetites, Temptations and Blandishments of the Body, are at a Continual Enmity with the Mind, and ever labouring to get a Full and Entire Power and Dominion over it: Whilst, on the other hand, the Mind is, or ought always to be, upon its Guard; and Endeavour, with all its Forces, to Support and Maintain its own Dignity. This Vertue of the Soul, in the Strength of which, it manfully Resists and Repells the Rebellious Appetites, and keeps them

them under, and in due Subjection to its own Authority, is properly and strictly called, *Temperance:* By which, at the Command, and according to the Directions of our Reason, we are led into all Good, and preserved from Evil, and are instructed how to Chuse the One, and to Reject the Other. This Vertue chiefly shews itself in an Aversion to, and Contempt of Pleasures, especially of Those, which properly belong to the *Sensations* of *Touching* and *Tasting*. It is by no means an Enemy to all Pleasure whatsoever, but to such only, or to the Excesses of them, which are Inconsistent with True Vertue. There are some Honest and Lawful Pleasures, and some that are not so: In Both which, the Mind, as well as the Body, has its due Share and Proportion. The Proper Perception and Judgment of them, belongs to the Senses, which are as it were the Domestick Attendants upon all our Pleasures. The Perfection Mankind ought to aim at, extends itself to the Mind, as well as the Body; and without Vertue we can never Attain it. The Use and Exercise of Vertue, in the Regulation and Good Government of our Bodies, is the Sum of that Particular Accomplishment, called, *Temperance*; which keeps our Body in Subjection to our Reason, and renders our Life agreeable to the Dignity of our Nature. Our Pleasures are Born and Bred with us, and are Familiar to us from our very Cradles. So that we cannot long or easily Abstain from them, and especially from Those, which are more Delectable to the Body, than the Mind; though these are the Foulest, the most Beastly and Dishonourable. We ought therefore to use our Best Endeavours, in bringing our Bodies under, and in keeping them always Dependent upon, and Subject to the Superior Jurisdiction of the Mind; that they may never be separated in their Inclinations and Enjoyments. For in this Subjection and Dependence, consists the Whole Dignity and Perfection of our Nature. Nothing conduces more to the Ease and Happiness of Life, than *Temperance*; because it keeps

us

us within the Bounds of Justice and Honesty, sets us above all Low and Vulgar Temptations; and by moderating our Appetites, and preventing any Undue Digressions, makes us Firm and Steady, both in Word and Deed, and Establishes our Constancy and Resolution. All the Vertues, in their several Degrees, are so many Blessings to a State, and are the Sure Means of making a Commonwealth Safe and Happy: But *Temperance* is the Keeper and Preserver of this Publick Happiness; and effectually Prevents Luxury and Intemperance, the usual Fore-runners and Fatal Causes of a Nation's Overthrow. For these Reasons, every Wise Government, that is Well-provided with Good and Wholsome Laws, and with a Body of People well-informed in the Principles, and inured to the Practice of their Duty, will take Care at the same Time, to Guard and Defend its Subjects from Luxury and Profuseness; which never fail to introduce Avarice, the Parent of all Vice, and the Root of all Evil. Among the *Romans*, there were many *Sumptuary* and *Vestuary* Laws and Edicts, by which the People were confined to a Plain, Honest, and Frugal Way of Living. The *Lacedæmonians* always dined in Publick, on purpose to let the World see, that they were not given to Gluttony and Luxury. The *Old Belgians* would never suffer any Delicacies to be Imported into their Country; lest the People should be thereby tainted with Softness and Effeminacy. And at this very Day, a too Sumptuous and Extravagant Way of Living is, in some Cities of *Italy*, publickly forbidden by the Laws. *Intemperance* is a Devouring and Insatiable Vice; and unless it be Restrained by Law, will never cease, till it has Poisoned the whole Mass of the People, and made a Government ripe for Destruction. Of this we have a Notorious Instance, in that Infamous Gang of Conspirators, who were the Followers of *Cataline*. When they had made a Sacrifice of their own Substance to their Lusts, Luxury, and Intemperance, they were for reimbursing themselves

out

out of the Spoils and Ravage of their Native Country; and therefore began a Civil War, on purpose to fling all Things into Confusion. Every Commonwealth, therefore, should be Careful of Training all its Subjects to Temperance, and of Preventing their being Sunk and Lost in Ease and Luxury. Such a Timely Care will preserve the Publick Happiness and Tranquillity, the Health, Strength, and Fortunes of the People; whereby they will be always Prepared and in Readiness to undergo any Difficulties, Dangers, or Fatigues of War, for the Sake of their Country; and on these Honourable Occasions, will Submitt to any Wants, or Hardships, or Forego any Pleasures; the Dread of Want, and the Love of Pleasure, being the Two most Prevailing Arguments, that usually tempt Men to give up their Freedom, and to become Voluntary Slaves. It is also for the Publick Interest, that all Intemperance should be Prohibited, as well in Private, as in Publick Life; and that the Subject should be Restrained from wasting his own Patrimony or Inheritance, by Luxury and Debauchery. The Temperate and Sober Life of Private Subjects, is a Part and a Shining Proof of the Publick Happiness. All Extravagances ought therefore to be laid under a Penalty, as being the Rise and Occasion of many Great and Dangerous Evils; and the *Good Senator* ought to be Watchful over the Lives of Others, as well as his own. The *Censorian Severity*, which kept Temperance and Modesty so long Resident in *Rome*, may be of like Use to some other States. It is certain, that no Care ought to be omitted in Suppressing Intemperance, either by Private Admonition, or Publick Chastisement: And so Dangerous and Pernicious a Vice, very well deserves a Strict and Rigorous Prosecution.

Temperance is a very Easy and Natural Introduction to many other Eminent and Useful Vertues, such as *Moderation, Modesty, Honesty,* and *Continency:* By which the Happiness of our Lives is Increased, and Adorned at the same Time. *Moderation* is a Vertue, as the *Stoicks* describe it, *that consists in a Right Knowledge and Choice of the Proper Times and Occasions, on which to say or do any thing, in such a Manner, as that it may effectually Answer some Good End and Purpose.* For in every thing we Say or Do, there is a *Mean* or *Medium*, and a Measure of Decency to be observed; lest by our Words or Actions we give an Unnecessary Offence, and thereby Defeat our own Present Prospect and Designs. *Not to Overdo any Thing,* is a Rule of Action, laid down by *Solon*, of great Use and Benefit in Life. And on some Occasions, it may be our Duty to *Temporize* and comply with the Times, and to adapt our Affairs to their Proper Seasons. For by the Missing of an Occasion, or by the Abuse of an Opportunity, the Noblest Projects may Miscarry, and the Best Designs prove Abortive. The *Senator* therefore, whenever he Speaks or Enters upon Action, must observe an Exact Decorum, even in his Look and Countenance, his Gestures, Motions and Deportment, and temper all his Outward Behaviour, with such a Graceful *Moderation*, that it may thereby adorn his Vertue and Honesty, bespeak the Favour and Countenance of the World, and establish a Clear, Durable, and Shining Credit and Reputation among Men.

Modesty is also a very Becoming Vertue, and the Great Defender and Preserver of an Honest Life; by which our Actions are kept clear of all Foul Stains and Marks of Infamy. As *Justice* obliges us not to offer any violence to others, so does *Modesty* restrain us from giving them any real Scandal or Cause of Offence. A Good Man will look upon it not only as his Duty and Choice, not to offend others; but as the Grace and Ornament of a *Modest* and Inoffensive Behaviour. He will be Ashamed, as well as Afraid, of doing any the least Act of Injustice. The *Modesty* which ought to appear in a *Senator*, is not of that Bashful Sort, which is often seen in Raw and Unexperienced Youth; nor that Consciousness,

ousness, which sometimes shews itself in Wicked Men, and is really the Effect of their Guilt: All such Commotions and Pains of the Mind, are rather a Disgrace, than an Ornament, to the Good Character of a Truly Grave and *Temperate Man*. But Genuine *Modesty* is an Exact Resemblance and Imitation of Vertue, and is an Habit of the Mind, confirming us in our Enmity and Aversion to Vice. If through Ignorance we are betrayed into a Crime, our Modesty will be seen in our Shame; and to be thus affected, is Decent and Laudable. When *Cæsar* fought with the Junior *Pompey* at *Corduba*, and saw his Men betake themselves to Flight, he advanced boldly in the Front of the Battle, and for a while stood the Shock of his Enemies, with Incredible Intrepidity: At which Sight the *Fugitives* could by no means contain themselves; but Rallied and Renewed the Fight, as well in regard to their *General's* Example, as to their own *Shame*, and for the Saving of their Modesty.

There is in the Mind and Disposition of every Man, a Secret Impulse and Instinct of *Honesty*, by which he is led on to do what is Just and Honourable, and to abstain from what is Mean, Base, and Ignominious. In tracing all the Ways of *Honesty* from its Rise and First Setting out, Vertue is our Best and Surest Guide. All the Splendor and Dignity of *Honesty* are wholly borrowed from Vertue; and are often seen in the Glory and Lustre of a Good Name, and attested by a General Prevailing Opinion, and the Evidence of Popular Fame and Applause. When by diligent Search and Enquiry we are able fully to discern what Rule and Measure of Behaviour we are to Conform ourselves to, what Course and Order we are to observe, and what Dignity in Life we are capable of Attaining: And when in all our Words and Actions, we behave agreeably to the Beauty, Decency, and Order, so set out and limited, as the End and Perfection of our Conduct: Whilst, at the same time, we take Care to avoid all Effeminacy, Lust

Lust, and Indecency; we shall by these means be fully and compleatly furnished with the Amiable Vertues of Modesty and Honesty. And so great is the Force and Efficacy of *Honesty* alone, that this Vertue is of itself sufficient and able to preserve us from all Vice and Infamy.

Continency and *Abstinence* are the Last-mentioned, but not the Meanest Vertues, that contribute to the Accomplishment of the *Senatorial* Character, in what relates to Good Manners and External Behaviour. By these we are instructed, how to guard against all the Temptations of Pleasure, and to restrain all our Inordinate Appetites and Desires, our Hands, our Eyes, our Mind, from wandering after any Forbidden Objects and Gratifications. To see a Man perfectly contented with what is his own, and an Entire Stranger to Inordinate Desires, is one of the most amiable Spectacles in Life. Remarkable is the Example of *Paulus Aemilius*, who out of all the Spoils and Treasure, which he brought home from *Spain* and *Macedonia*, reserved nothing for himself, but flung it all into the Publick Treasury; and chose rather to be called an Abstemious Poor Man, than a Publick Plunderer. For when all his Goods and Effects were upon his Death disposed of at a Publick Sale, there was hardly enough left to give his Widow a Dowry. *Scipio* is another admirable Instance of Continency: For at the Demolition of *New Carthage*, when he was only Twenty Years Old, and had among the Spoils of that City a very Beautiful Virgin for his Captive; he not only offered no Violence to her Chastity, but gave her in Marriage to the Person to whom she was engaged; and with her a Fortune, the whole Sum that her Friends had offered him for her Redemption. I pass by the Example of *Alexander the Great*, and of many others, whose Reputation and Renown, gained by their Continency, was as Great as was the Glory of their Arms, or the Lustre of their Triumphs. Let the *Good Senator* therefore distinguish himself, by a Strict Observation

servation of this Vertue, and always remember that excellent Saying of *Pericles*, who, when his Colleague *Sophocles* sate openly with him in the *Prætorian Office*, and occasionally commended the Beauty of a Person then present before them, did not scruple to charge him with Incontinency, and told him, *That a* Prætor *ought to keep his Eyes from Inordinate Wandering, as well as his Hands from Inordinate Gain.* The Wisdom of *Cato* is very justly applauded, for expelling (when he was *Censor*) *L. Quintius Flaminius* from the *Senate*, on Account of his Libidinous Character. For during his *Consulship*, and whilst he was in *Gaul*, he was prevailed upon, at a Publick Entertainment, by a Common Strumpet, to Behead a Criminal then in Prison, and under Sentence of Death. Even for so small a Fault as kissing his Wife in the Presence of his Daughter, *Manilius* was removed from the *Senate:* And *Salust* was entirely deprived of all *Senatorial Dignity*, on Account of his Many Debaucheries, and Notorious Adulteries. There is indeed no Vice whatsoever, that Strikes so Foul, so Deep, and so Lasting a Stain and Blemish, upon the Honour and Dignity of a *Senator*, as Lust and Lasciviousness. These Vices are enough Scandalous even in Private Life, but in a Publick Station and Character perfectly Intolerable. *Sardanapalus*, would often spend whole Days in the Womens Apartments, and omitted no Means or Opportunities of Indulging and Gratifying his Lusts. In his own Lifetime, he ordered his *Sepulchral Monument* to be Erected, and this *Epitaph* to be Engraven on it.

> *Since Thou art Mortal, Eat, and Drink, and Play*
> *For there's no Bliss beyond the Present Day.*
> *Enjoy what Nature gives, and Lust can crave:*
> *There's no Delight nor Pleasure in the Grave.*
> *I, who am now a Ghost, no Joy can find,*
> *From all the Pomp and Wealth I left behind.*

What I once had, is now my Only Bliss:
Hear this, and from the Dead learn to be Wise.

Aristotle, happening to pass by this *Monument*, stopped to read the *Inscription*, and when he had gone through the *First Part* of it, burst into a Loud Laughter, and said to himself; *Would not this* Epitaph *have fitted a* Bull, *as well as a* Monarch? But when he had gone through the *Whole*, he added this Remarkable Observation; *I wonder* (says he) *that this dead* Monarch *should say,* He has now any Enjoyment of what he once Possessed; *since he never Enjoyed what he did Possess; unless Swallowing and Devouring may be called Enjoyment.*

All Pleasures whatsoever, unless they are some way or other Serviceable to the Ends and Purposes of Honesty and Necessity, are in themselves Unlawful. And particularly the Two Sorts of Pleasure belonging to the *Sensations* of *Touching* and *Tasting*, by which we are generally betrayed into the Foulest and most Ignominious Vices. Among the Pleasures, belonging to the *Sensation* of *Touching*, may be reckoned all *Venereal* and *Libidinous* Enormities, the Lascivious and Immoderate Uses of *Bathing*, all Immodest and Wanton Habits and Gestures, and whatever contributes to the Gratification of our Inordinate and Beastly Lusts: And among the Pleasures belonging to the *Sensation* of *Tasting*, are to be reckoned, all Intemperancies of the *Palate* and *Belly*, which are really the Occasion of almost all the Vices and Iniquities that bring Infamy and Disgrace upon Human Nature. The *Good Senator* must use his best Endeavours, to rescue his Fellow-Citizens from these Foul and Odious Vices, and to preserve the Vertues of *Temperance* and *Chastity* in their Full Force and Vigour. All Impure and Dishonest Pleasures ought to be Restrained by Strict Laws and Severe Penalties: And whatever gives Occasion, or Administers to a Loose, Immodest, Vicious, and Intemperate Way of Living,

Living, ought to be Removed and Taken away. The *Lacedæmonians,* when any of their Servants were Drunk, would expose them and their Ridiculous Behaviour to their Children, on purpose to Deterr them from any such Vulgar, Filthy, and Brutish Folly. It is much to be wished, that we were as well prepared to imitate the Examples of the *Ancients*, as to Commemorate and Applaud them. Our Forefathers were Sparing and Moderate in their Diet, Frugal and Temperate in the Use of those Good Things, which are Necessary and Convenient for the Support of Life. They did Eat to Live, and not Live to Eat. Whilst in these our Times, Intemperance hath so far Prevailed among us, that more Men have been Lost by Lust and Luxury, than have fallen by the Edge of the Sword; and some Whole Nations may be easily found, who Live as if they were Persuaded, that Man's Life consisted of nothing else but Drinking. Surely the Temperance of *M. Curius*, a *Roman Senator*, is well worth our Best Commendations; whom the *Samnian Ambassadors*, in a Visit they made him, found Eating his Supper out of a Wooden Dish; and heard him Bravely refuse the Gold they then offered him, with this Memorable Saying, *That he had rather have Authority over Rich Men, than be Rich himself.* I pass by the *Fabricii,* the *Tubero's,* the *Fabii,* the *Cato's,* and *Scipio's,* who have gained Immortal Reputation by Sobriety and a Temperate Life. *Hortensius* underwent a very Severe Censure, because at an *Angural Supper,* he had among other Dishes entertained his Guests with a Boiled Peacock. *Cossius* was noted for Intemperance, because in a Publick Assembly, he had called for Water to Drink, and had thereby convinced the Spectators, how little able he was to endure Thirst only for a few Moments. And *Duronius* was deprived of his Seat in the *Senate-House*, because when he was *Tribune,* he had Abrogated the Law for restraining Expensive and Costly Entertainments. Happy was the *Roman State* in such *Senators!* And Happy the
Times,

Times, in which *Senators* not only made Good Laws, but set the People a Good Example, of Manners and Vertue. How Great the *Temperance* of the *Roman People* at that time was, we may learn from this Single Instance: When *Pyrrhus*, King of *Epirus*, was miserably Broken, and at last totally Defeated in the War he had for some time maintained with the *Romans*, and in order to make his Peace, and bespeak the Favour of the *People* of *Rome*, had sent an Immense Collection of many Rich and Valuable Presents, which were Publickly carried about the City, and offered to every one who would accept of them; not a *Roman* was found, who would open his Hand to receive any Part thereof; whereby *Pyrrhus* might have learned, that the *Romans* were as much Superior to him in Vertue, as they had been in War. But when Luxury from the *Conquered Provinces* of *Asia*, made its Way into *Italy*, and the People began to Indulge themselves in Peace and Plenty, and were melted down and dissolved in Ease and Wantonness; the Discipline of *Temperance*, Parsimony, and Sobriety, was entirely Forgotten, and Avarice prevailed, and Introduced a Train of Impure and Filthy Vices, which (in the Judgment of *Salust*) were the Sole Cause of the Decay, and Final Overthrow of that Empire. The *Good Senator* therefore Exerts himself, as much as possibly he can, to Prevent the Rise and Growth of Luxury; a Vice which never fails to interrupt the Publick Peace and Happiness, and to make a People Wanton, Delicate, and Effeminate; and in the End, Poor, and Miserable. As *Diogenes* was one day reading a *Proscription*, or *Advertisement* by which the House of a Certain Luxurious Person was exposed to Sale, *I knew* (says he) *that the Master of this House, who had Stocked it with so many Rich Wines, and other Delicacies, would one Day Swallow and Devour his own Habitation.* Overloading the Stomach, is a Practice particularly Fatal to *Senators* and Statesmen; because it Clogs the Reason, Damps the Mind, and renders it unfit for Counsel and Advice;

Advice; and at the same time Disables the Body, by Diseases and Infirmities, and Disqualifies the Whole Man for Action, or any Great Enterprize. *Solon* made a Severe but very Remarkable Law, that a *Nobleman* guilty of *Notorious Drunkenness, should be put to Death*. When *Philip of Macedon*, in one of his Drunken Fitts, had Condemned a Woman without hearing her Cause; the poor Criminal offered an *Appeal*, and being asked, *To whom she Appealed ? I Appeal* (says she) *from King* Philip *Overtaken by Wine, to King* Philip *when he is Sober*. Excess of Wine always perverts the Judgment, makes a Slave of a King, a Child of an Old Man, a Madman of one that is Sober, an Orator of an Infant, a Fool of a Philosopher, and turns Weakness into downright Stupidity. The *Senator* therefore should be very Temperate and Abstemious in the Use of Wine, and drink no more than will supply the Necessities of Nature, without answering the Demands of Intemperance. What *Anacharsis* observed, is well worth our Notice, That the *First Measure of Wine* was intended for *Necessity*, the *Second* for *Drunkenness*, and the *Third* for *Madness*. It is Scandalous for a *Senator* to appear in Publick, with an Inflamed Countenance, Eyes Swoln and Sparkling with Rage and Fury, and a Mouth full of Foul and Arrogant Language; and that these Stains and Blemishes, the Usual Marks and Symptoms of Drunkenness, should be exposed to the General View and Observation. In the midst of such foul Excesses, when the Body is Overcharged, there is a Necessity of taking a more than ordinary Measure of Sleep, in order to shake off and get rid of the Load; and even this Intemperance in Sleeping, takes up too much of the *Senator's* Time, and is inconsistent with that Care and Vigilance, which are at least a Graceful and Ornamental Part of his Character.

How far *Temperance*, and Moderation in Eating and Drinking, are of Use to us, even in Low and Ordinary Life, and how much they contribute to the Preservation of Health, and to the Fitting us for Action, and especially for any Great and Noble Undertaking, every one's Experience may easily convince him. By *Temperance*, all the Parts and Faculties, both of the Body and of the Mind, are kept Clear and Sound, and in their Full Strength and Vigour; so that we can Exert and Employ them with so much the more Readiness and Facility, in the Affairs of Life, and for the Uses and Purposes, for which they were given us. A continual and excessive Repletion of the Belly, is in effect the making a Grave of our Body, wherein to Bury our Mind. Parsimony and Frugality are the Great and Shining Ornaments, both of Private and Publick Life. But then on the other hand, we must beware of running into the Opposite Extreme. There is an Excess even in Parsimony, and we must have a Care of being Over-tenacious and Continent; lest we fall into the Abject and Sordid Vices of Covetousness and Misery. We must Live up to our Dignity and Station, and not Lessen our Honour, to Enlarge our Fortunes. By avoiding Private Luxury, we may be the better enabled to bear the Expences of Publick Magnificence. We may abstain from Profuse Banquetings, and yet keep a Good Table, and maintain the Character of Decency and Hospitality. Extravagant and Sumptuous Expences will soon bring a Burden upon us; but a Way of Life, that is Decent and Generous, will give us a Lustre and Reputation among Men. In adjusting these Differences, there is a Rational Estimate and Computation to be made, and we must consider Times and Places, Men and Things, as also our own Station and Circumstances; before we can settle the Account between what is due to ourselves in Private Life, and what is required of us, in regard to our Publick Dignity and Station, and to our Interest and Credit among Men. We must take our Turns of Labour and Refreshment, and must proportion our Diligence and Attendance accordingly. *Q. Tubero*, because at an Entertainment he made for his Friends, his Beds were covered

with

with *Kid-Skins*, was openly Censured for his Folly, and for Breach of the Laws of Decency and Frugality, and was thereupon deprived of the *Prætorship*. But let what we have hitherto said, suffice for the Explaining and Illustrating the Great Vertue of *Temperance*. It is now Time we should proceed to what, in the Order of this Discourse, we proposed to speak of; which was, to Set out and Explain the several Good Things, Gifts, and Endowments, belonging to the Body, which contribute to the *Senator's* Happiness, and Adorn his Character, without which, it cannot be made Perfect.

CHAP. VIII.

The CONTENTS.

Of Bodily Accomplishments *and* Perfections. *How far Useful and Advantageous to those of the* Mind. *Of the* Nurture *and* Care *of* Youth. *Of Regulating* Marriage. *Of* Health, *and the* Temperament *of the* Body. *Of* Beauty *and* Dress. *Of* Bodily Strength. *Of the* Senator's Age. *Of the* Goods *of* Fortune. *Of the* Senator's Wealth *and* Estate. *Of* Nobility, Honour, *and* Glory. Posterity *the Best Judge of* Merit. *Of* Reputation, *and* Renown. *Of* Clients, Friends, *and* Followers. *Of* Issue *or* Children. *Of* Riches *and* Money. *Of* Husbandry. *Of* the Privileges *and* Respect, *due to the* Accomplish'd Senator. *Of* his Last *and* Greatest Reward.

SINCE the Body is a Necessary Part of our Being, and Serves as a *Case* and *Tabernacle* to the Mind; it is a Duty incumbent upon us, by the Care we take of the One, as well as of the Other, to render our Lives as Perfect as we can, and complete the Fulness of our Nature. In a Weak and Infirm Body, Vertue can never Exert all its Strength and Activity, or be Exact in the Performance of all its Offices: Nor can the Body, when joined to a Weak Mind, execute the Functions of all its Parts and Members, with that Perfection, of which Nature made it capable. There is such a Close Union, Mixture, and Connection of the Soul and Body, put together, that as a Master cannot Give his Commands, without a Servant to Obey them, so neither can the Mind put its Designs in Execution, without the Concurrent Aid and Assistance of the Body. As there is a Natural, so

there

there is also a Political Conjunction of these Two Parts: And without the Proper Arts and Discipline belonging to Both, Man can never come to be of Use and Benefit to Publick Society. The *Political* Perfection of the Mind, is established by Good Laws and Civil Discipline, and is preserved by Justice and Judgment: And the Perfection of the Body, is owing to the Free Gifts and Endowments of *Nature*, is confirmed by *Exercise*, and preserved by *Physick*. Hence it was, that every Wise and Well-constituted Government, hath Regulated *Matrimony* by Particular Laws, and confined it to a certain Age and Season of Life, and hath Provided for the Discipline and Education of Youth, that Nature and Art might both Conspire in Perfecting the Bodies, as well as the Minds of its Subjects and Citizens. But since we have already spoken of the Endowments and Perfections of the Mind, we shall now speak of those Gifts and Perfections of the Body, which are Necessary for the *Good Senator* to be Possessed of, that he may be Perfect both in Body and Mind; a State, very well becoming his High Dignity and Character.

It is a Well-known Truth, and agreeable to the Sentiments of the *Academicks*, that Human Happiness cannot subsist altogether upon the Accomplishments and Acquisitions of the Mind; but requires the Additional Good Things and Endowments of the Body, before it can be completed. For though these Bodily Perfections add nothing to the Real Worth and Praise of a Man, yet since Vertue is wholly Employed in the Right Use of them, they are on this Account very Desirable Things, and worth the Pains we bestow in Acquiring them. Now of the Perfections belonging to the Body, some belong to it in the Whole, and others only in Part. Of the Former Sort are, *Health, Beauty, Strength*, and the *Integrity*, or the *Soundness*, of all the Limbs put together: And of the Latter Sort are, the *Perfections* of the *severaly Particular Members*, that contribute to the Offices of *Sensation*, and of

such

such others, as are Remarkable for some one Excellency more than the rest; as the Hand for Strength, and the Foot for Swiftness. There is a General Agreement and Intercourse between the Soul and the Body, which the *Greeks* call *Sympathy*; and so is there a Reciprocal Harmony between the Vertues and Perfections, belonging to both. *Health* resembles *Justice*, because by an Equitable Temperament of the Parts, it preserves the Whole. *Beauty* resembles *Temperance:* For One is the Parent of the Other, and Both in their Turns reciprocally serve for their own Ornaments. *Fortitude* comes nearest to *Strength:* For in all Dangers and Enterprizes, they are Mutual Supports to each other; and *Prudence* as nearly resembles the *Soundness* and *Integrity* of the *Parts* and *Members:* For as all Judgments and Opinions concurr in the Formation of Prudence, so do all the Parts and Members in the Formation of a Sound and Perfect Body.

Common Experience teaches us, how necessary Health is, to a Comfortable and Happy Life. A Good or Ill State of Health will accordingly have its Influence upon all the Successes, or Miscarriages of our Conduct. This Blessing well befits every Publick Minister or Officer, but especially the *Senator*; whereby he may be enabled to labour and bestir himself, in the Publick Interests and Affairs; may execute his own Proper Function with Diligence; and may make his own Life Easy and Happy, and free from all Care and Solicitude. Our *Maker* is the First Cause and Author of our Health, by giving to every one of us a Sound, Perfect, and Wholsome Body; and the Secondary Cause of it, is from ourselves, by the due Use of Study and Exercise. Negligence and Intemperance are the Decay and Ruin of it. Health (as *Cicero* well advises) is Preserved by making an Intimate Acquaintance with our own Constitution; by distinguishing between what is Good and Wholsome, and what is Pernicious and Hurtful for us; by regulating our Diet, and all Provisions necessary for the Support

Support and Maintenance of the Body; and by restraining from the Excesses of our Inordinate Lusts and Appetites. Whatever else is necessary for us to know, relating to this Subject, we must look for in *Galen* and *Hippocrates:* But by the way, *Diogenes* would Laugh heartily at those Men, who sacrificed to the *Gods*, and implored Health at their Hands, whilst at the same time they lived in all manner of Luxury and Debauchery. For he said, *They were Fools to Trouble the Gods for the Sake of Obtaining That Blessing, which it was in their own Power to bestow upon themselves, if they would but live up to the Laws and Rules of Temperance.*

A Good Temperament of Body, is also a Great Blessing to a *Senator.* And if, as the Physicians speak, he be of a Sanguine and Cholerick Humour, his Disposition to a Vertuous and an Active Life, will be so much the Stronger. For Men of this Temper are, generally speaking, Witty and Docible, and have a Good Genius and Memory. *Aristotle* ascribes Ingenuity to those who are of a Melancholy Disposition, and imagines, that when they are Rouzed to a Degree of Rage and Fury, they have something of a Divine Impulse upon them, and a Sure Foresight and Prospect of Futurity. Such Men, however, are unfit for the Service of the State and the *Senate*, and are Slow in the Undertaking and Performance of any Great Action. For the Black Choler that reigns in their Constitutions, always gets the Better of their Wisdom and Prudence. And because the Dry and Cold Humours prevail in their Constitution, therefore all their Thoughts are turned to Solitude, Envy, Ill-will, Sorrow, and Sadness. As *Cicero* was one Day perusing *Aristotle*'s Opinion, concerning Melancholy, (as I have already Quoted it) he is said to have Smiled to himself, and to have Thanked the Gods, *That Himself was made rather of a Dull and Heavy, than of a Melancholy Disposition.* As a Fat merry Fellow was one Day censured in the Hearing of *C. Cæsar*, for being too Free and Gay in his Conversation, the

Person

Person that Censured him, was Checked by the *Emperor*, who said, *That Men of Mirth and Corpulency were far less Dangerous, than Lean, Spare, and Meagre Persons;* and at the same time Pointed to *Brutus* and *Cassius*. Phlegm is also another Fault in the Constitution of a *Senator*, and not to be borne with, even in those of the *Pedarian* Order. For this Distemper always makes Men Slow and Heavy, both in Body and Mind.

There is a Beauty and Gracefulness in the Exterior Form, which is in some measure an Indication of the Mind, and Strikes an Additional Lustre upon the Vertues that Adorn it. Whence the *Poet* makes this Just Remark:

Vertue, to Beauty join'd, is doubly Graceful.

This agreeable Appearance of the Look and Shape, recommends Persons to the Publick View and Notice, but especially so very Publick a Person as the *Senator* is supposed to be. When I ascribe Beauty to him, I mean by it such a Noble and Manly Form, as is quite different from the Softer and more Delicate Allurements of the Other Sex; and which shews itself in the Stature, as well as in the Countenance. The Former ought to be neither Dwarfish nor Gigantick, but Middle-sized, and of a Just Proportion. Because Vertue consists in a *Medium*, *Aristotle* thinks it Misplaced, or Ill seated, in too Large or too Little a Body. The Gross and Corpulent are as Unfit for Action, as the Lean and Dry are for Toil and Fatigue: And they who are Lame, or have any Defect in their Limbs, or any Oblique Cast and Distortion in their Eyes, or are of a Mean and Dwarfish Stature, are generally noted for their Falshood and Treachery, and are as Disagreeable to us, as any other Monstrous and Uncouth Spectacles in Nature. Such Unhappy Men, do by no Means become a Publick Station, unless they

they are eminently Good, and by their Inward Vertues, take Care to make Amends for their Outward Deformities.

    A Good Countenance is also Recommended by its Colour and Complexion, which serves as a Portal or Inlet to the Mind. For the Natural Covering of the Body is very often an Indication of the Soul. *Philopæmen*, General of the *Achaians*, retired on Account of his Deformity, and employed himself in Hewing of Wood: At this Work being one Day surprized by his Friends, he told them by way of Excuse, *That he was making an Atonement for his Deformity*. A Grave and Serious Face, with a Mixture of Pleasantry, and a Look not Stern or Severe, but Composed and full of Sedate and Awful Sweetness, serve to recommend a Publick Officer, or Magistrate, to the Good Opinion and Esteem of the People. Not that the Outward Form is always to be depended upon, as an Infallible Mark of the Inward Frame and Disposition of the Mind. There are many Men of an Ill-made and Deformed Body, but of a Mind perfectly Beautiful and Handsome, and furnished with the Amiable Vertues of Justice, Prudence, and Temperance. No Deformity of the Body can Stain and Blemish the Mind, but the Beauty of the Mind always communicates its Lustre and Graces to the Body. Vertue is not necessarily confined either to a Handsome or Deformed Personage: It depends upon its own Internal Graces and Native Ornaments, and bestows a Share of them upon the Exterior Form. In our Judgment of Mankind, we must not depend upon our Eyes, but our Reason; and in Determining and Fixing the *Senatorial Character*, we must take a Full Survey of the Mind, and not proceed altogether upon the Evidence of the Shape and Features. For the Beauty of the Soul is always Preferable to that of the Body. This Latter Sort of Beauty is indeed enough Desirable, but by no means absolutely Necessary to the Perfection of our Nature.

The better to support the Dignity and Advantages of the Exterior Form, some Regard must be also had to *Dress* and *Habit*, which serve to recommend the United Beauties both of Body and Mind, and to bespeak the Regard and Notice of Mankind. The *Senator* ought to be Distinguished from other Men, by a Particular and Proper Habit. For such has the Practice been in all Wise and Well-constituted Commonwealths. The *Romans* had their Robe or Gown, which was the Distinguishing Ornament of their *Senators*, and they had also their Sandals cut and turned up in the Shape of a *Crescent*, which were a Part of the Habit peculiar to Noblemen, and those of the First Rank. This particular Ornament they borrowed from Foreigners, and in all Probability from the *Hebrew Nation*. For *Isaiah*, in his Prophecy, threatens the *Jewish* Women, that GOD would take from them the *Tinkling Ornaments of their Feet, and their Round Tires like the Moon*. By the way, *Plutarch* gives us Four Reasons, why this Sort of Sandals was in Use among the *Romans*; which, because there is some little Pleasantry in them, I shall therefore venture to mention. The *First* is, because they were persuaded, that their Heroes and Great Men, upon their Departure out of this Life, went immediately to Heaven, and had their Residence assigned them, near the Sphere and Orbit of the *Moon*. The *Second* Reason was, because the *Moon* had been a Sign of Great Antiquity, in much Repute among the *Arcadians*, who under the Leading of *Evander*, came and settled themselves in *Italy*, and boasted that they were a Nation much Older than the *Moon*. The *Third* Reason was, that considering the Uncertainty and Volubility of Human Affairs, they should never be too much Elated or Transported, by the Success and Prosperous Condition of their Affairs: For as the *Moon* has Two Parts, one Bright and Shining, and the other Dark and Obscure, so has the Life of Man, which has no Splendor or Dignity, but what is sometimes Overcast and Eclipsed by Adversity.

sity. The *Fourth* and *Last* Reason was, because the *Moon* gives us a Signal of Modesty and Obedience, as well as of Government and Authority, which we are directed to ask for at the Hands of our *Maker*, and from whom we borrow them, as the *Moon* does her Lustre and Glory from the *Sun*. Some Authors have been of Opinion, that in Fact the *Romans* did not make Use of the Sign of the *Moon* in their Sandals, but of the Letter *C*, out of Respect to the *Hundred Senators* or *Counsellors*, who were Elected and Brought together, by the immediate Direction and Order of *Romulus*. But this, however, is certain, That in every Well-constituted Government, the Order and Station of every Private Subject is as easily known by his Habit, as by any Description extant in the Laws of his Country; and that this Distinction of Habits tends to the Restraining and Confining of Men to their Proper Duty and Station, which produces Ease and Contentment, the Natural Consequences of an Established and Regular Way of Living. Hence it was, that *Purple* came to be a Colour commonly used among the *Romans*, by their *Senators*, *Priests*, *Magistrates*, and *Sons* of *Noblemen*. I pass by their *Rings*, *Chains*, and *Bracelets*, which were Honorary Ornaments and Marks of Distinction, commonly used among them. How these Ensigns of Honour are Confounded and Mingled together in these Modern Times, to which we belong, common Experience may easily convince us; and we plainly see a very great Difference and Alteration, not only in the Things themselves, but in the Manners and Customs of the World. There seems at present to be no Distinction of *Soldiers*, *Magistrates*, and *Senators*, from Merchants, Mechanicks, Servants, Boors, and Rusticks. No Man's Quality or Station is now Distinguished by any Particular Ensigns or Ornaments; nor are any of those Honours Ascertained and Appropriated, which were once looked upon as Incitements and Provocations to the Greatest and Noblest Enterprizes; and as Preservatives of the Honour and Reputation,

putation, which Men of Merit are possessed of. The *Sceptre*, the *Crown*, the *Bracelet*, the *Ring*, the *Gown*, the *Robe*, the *Chair*, and the *Throne*, had their Proper Use and Value among the *Ancients*. They were by no means Real Dignities in themselves, but the Marks of Dignity in those who wore them; whereby Others were Allured and Invited to exert themselves in the Execution of their Proper Duty and Offices, in adorning their Pre-eminence and Station among Men, and in making Additions to their own Glory and Reputation. *Livy* tells us, that when *Romulus* had drawn together a Body of Men, who for the Generality were Entire Strangers to him; the better to reconcile them to the Laws he was then about to Prescribe, and to his own Authority, which it was then necessary should be had in Reverence and Esteem among them, he appeared in a more Illustrious Habit than ordinary, and had his *Twelve Lictors* always attending him. The *Good Senator*, therefore, ought to Dress in such a Manner, as that he may be able to Attract the Reverence and Regard due to his Gravity, Dignity, and Vertue; and to be particularly Careful, not to betray the Levity and Inconstancy of his Mind, by the Variety and Frequent Changes of his Habit. There is, on this Occasion, a Proper Decency to be observed; a Solid and Manly, and not a Delicate and Effeminate Decency; an Elegant and Well-regulated Decency, without any Suspicion of Roughness and Rusticity. For in every Motion and Gesture, in every Step, and Air of Deportment, and in all the Postures of Sitting and Lying down, the *Senatorial* Gravity ought always to be Preserved, with the Utmost Strictness and Severity.

It is also much for the Advantage of the *Good Senator*, that he be provided with a sufficient Share of *Strength*, with a Sett of Clean and Able Nerves, and with all the Bodily Vigour and Activity, which are necessary to Qualify him for any Great and Laudable Undertaking. These Accomplishments, as they are entirely

owing

owing to the Good-will and Bounty of Nature, we ought to be more busy in Cultivating and Improving, than Active and Diligent in Acquiring and Obtaining them. All Strength whatsoever, in a Firm, Sound, and Well-grown Body, is capable of Increase or Decrease, according to the Different Periods and Stages of Life. Youth is Fiery and Vigorous, Manhood Strong and Robust, and Old Age Weak and Infirm. We do not therefore require so much Vigour and Strength in a *Senator*, as may possibly be required in a Wrestler or Gladiator, but only so much as Nature requires, in discharge of the Common Duties and Offices of Life. When *Milo* was grown Old, and (as it happened) was one Day looking upon the Sports and Exercises in which the Youth of his Age were engaged, it is said, that upon a Survey taken of his own Nerves and Sinews, he declared them to be Dead and Defunct, and thereupon Wept. Which Resentment of his, we can (in my Opinion) impute to nothing else, but the Conscious Guilt of having Forfeited or Impaired, by some Vices or Ill-habits, That Noble Vigour, which is the First of all Bodily Accomplishments.

What That Particular Age and Time of Life is, in which the Faculties both of Body and Mind appear to the greatest Advantage, and in which, the *Senatorial* Dignity is displayed with the Utmost Lustre, we are now at Leisure to Enquire. They who treat of the Stages, Periods, and Duration of Human Life, have differed in the Bounds or Limits, which they usually set to it. *Solon* confines it to the *Eightieth*, and *Plato* to the *Eighty First* Year; but the more General Computation is, That of Seventy Years; which Number is Subdivided, according to the several Great Changes and Alterations, to which our Bodies are liable. The *First Seven* Years are the Time of our *Infancy:* The *Second Seven* of our *Youth*; the *Third* of the *Fulness* of our *Stature*; the *Fourth*, of our *Corpulency*; the *Fifth*, of our *Strength*; the *Sixth*, of our *Desires;*

sires; the *Seventh*, of our *Wisdom*; the *Eighth* is the completion of our *Maturity*; the *Ninth* puts an End to our *Vigour*, and the *Tenth* to our Lives. There are Other *Authors*, who limit every Great Change in our Constitution to every *Ninth* Year of our Age: And there are some, who limit it to every *Odd Year*, computing till they come to *One and Twenty*. *Pythagoras* tells us, that our *Eightieth* is the most *Fatal Year*, and he divides the Time of our Life into *Four Twenties*; the *First*, the Time of our *Childhood*; the *Second* of our *Youth*, the *Third* of our *Manhood*, and the *Fourth* of our *Old Age*. These *Four Periods*, he compares to the *Four Seasons* of the Year; *Childhood* to the *Spring*, *Youth* to *Summer*, *Manhood* to *Autumn*, and *Old Age* to *Winter*. *Varro* sets out Life into *Five Stages*, and to every Stage assigns *Fifteen Years:* The *First Fifteen* are the Time of our *Childhood:* At *Thirty Years* we are *Full-grown*, and Perfect in our Bodily Parts and Stature: At *Forty Five* Years, we are in Full Strength, and Well-qualified to serve our country, in any Civil or Military Employment; and at *Sixty Years,* we are in Full Maturity, and entring upon the Decline and Decay of *Old Age*. This Computation and *Division of Life,* we readily give into: For the Other *Numerical Computations* fall more properly under the Cognizance of *Physicians*, and of Those who are Employed in the Care of our Bodies, and in the Cure of such Distempers, as are Incident to them. It is their Business to observe Times and Days, especially those which are called *Critical* by the *Greeks*, and *Indiciary* by the *Latins*. What is most proper for us to observe on this Occasion, is, that the *Forty Fifth Year* of Life is that Particular Period, in which the *Senator* may be supposed to be at the Height, and in the Utmost Perfection of his Character, with regard to the Accomplishments both of Body and Mind. Besides, it is the *Half-Way Stage*, and *Middle Period* of Life, at which time it may be expected, that our Strength and Reason are in their full Vigour and Maturity.
For

For at this Age, our Mind is supposed to have gotten the Better of our Appetites and Desires, and to have established its Dominion over the Lusts and Passions: And it is taken for granted, that we are entirely under the Direction of Good Counsel, Wisdom, and Experience. Whilst the *Roman* Commonwealth was in its most Flourishing State, this Time and Period of Life was looked upon as the Properest Age, at which to admitt Men into the *Senate-House:* Because the Mind was then best Turned for Counsel and Advice, and in its most Perfect State; whilst all the Heats and Fire of Youth were cooled, allayed, and qualified: For the Mind Decreases and Increases in Strength, just as the Body does; according to the Different Stages and Periods of Life. It is indeed True, that some Men are Old in Wisdom and Experience, even at the Age of *Thirty*; and because they grow Old soon, their Old Age is of so much the longer Continuance. The *Romans* frequently chose Men of this Age into their *Senate-House:* For it is not a Number of Years, but of Vertues, that makes a Man truly Old: And hence it was, that the *Ancients* called their *Sages* Wise or Good Men, and their Old Men by one and the same Name. This, however, all Good Governments and Commonwealths ought to be very Careful of, that the Administration of their Affairs should be always entrusted in the Hands of the Aged and Experienced: And accordingly *Plutarch* delcares That State to be Happy and Durable, in which the *Elders* are employed *in the Giving of Advice*, and the *Juniors* in the *Discipline and Exercise of the Spear:* And Remarkable is the Saying of *Euripedes*, as we find it extant in *Stobæus:*

'Tis a Well-known, and an Undoubted Truth;
Old Men *for* Counsel, *and for* Action, Youth.

The

The *Athenians* admitted to all Citizens whatsoever to their Publick Consultations, after the Age of *Fifty*. And it was a Custom among the *Romans*, that every Citizen, of the Age of *Sixty*, had a right to come into the *Senate-House*, whenever he pleased, though he had not been duly Elected into the *Senatorial Office*. After the Age of *Sixty*, all *Senators* were permitted to Retire, and were upon their Petition discharged from the Toil and Trouble of all Publick Employments whatsoever. The Particular Laws and Customs of every Commonwealth are, on this Occasion, chiefly to be regarded, and always strictly observed: And even Those of *Nestor*'s Age ought not to be Excluded the *Senate*, so long as they are Capable of Serving their Country, and are, on all Occasions, and at all Times, ready to assist their Fellow-Subjects, by their Counsel and Wisdom. Whilst it is in our Power, we must do Good to the Publick: And to Decline this Service, is a Just Cause of Reproach, to any Private citizen; but in a *Senator*, it is notoriously Wicked and Infamous. Though we have (as *Plato* speaks) *One Foot in the Grave, yet with the Other we ought to sit down in Counsel, so long as we are Capable of Serving our Country*. When we are too far Advanced in Years, and are come to Dotage, and our Senses and Intellects begin to Decay, it is then High Time for us to Quit the *Council-Board* and *Senate-House*. For such Superannuated *Sages* deal more in Surmise and Opinion, than in Solid Wisdom and Counsel; and we hear little else from them, but Perhaps and It May Be, or some such Conjectural and Indeterminate Expressions: And the Load of Experience is so Heavy upon them, that they are always afraid of every Danger and Evil, of which they have had the Least Feeling and Experience.

Since Human Felicity cannot be made Perfect, without the Additional Enjoyment of the External Blessings and Good Things of this Life, it is Necessary the *Good Senator* should be Possessed of these in a Competent Measure; not only for the Maintenance and support of his Proper Dignity, but as a Means of Reducing all his Vertues to Action and Exercise. Upon this Subject, the *Philosophers* are much divided in their Opinions. Some of them assert the Perfection of Human Happiness, without the Possession of these External *Good Things*; and others maintain, that without them, it is impossible for us to be truly Happy. Now if we look to the Final Issues and End of Life, as well as to our own Present Station and Circumstances, both these disagreeing Parties are certainly in the Right. They who confine all their Vertues to Private Life, may, with a very Low and Mean Fortune, make themselves Perfectly Happy: But they, whose Vertues are to Shine out in a Higher Sphere, who are Stationed in some Publick Office or Employment, and placed in the Open View of their Fellow-Subjects, and have the Care of Governing and Presiding over them, can never be able, without a Due Supply of Fortune's Goods, to exert their Generosity, Magnificence, or Liberality, or to Carry on and Finish any Great or Glorious Undertaking. A Competency of Wealth and Riches is necessary to the Good government of the Commonwealth, and to the Display and Exercise of our Vertues. Without these Advantages, we can never effectually Interpose, to the Saving and Relieving our Fellow-Subjects, or the Publick, when in any Calamity and Distress, or under the Apprehension of any Great or Imminent Danger. Without a Sufficient Stock or Treasure, a Commonwealth cannot long Subsist, or make any Pretension to Prosperity and Happiness. And therefore the Contending *Philosophers* would have found it more for their Purpose, if instead of Disputing about Riches themselves, they had Disputed altogether about the Use and Application of them. For Life itself, as well as the Happiness of it, cannot well be Supported, without the Affluence and Accession of these Goods of Fortune; a Proportion of which is required for

the

the Maintenance of every Man's particular Station and Character, in order to make Life Sweet and Comfortable. The Happiness of *Diogenes* was quite different from that of *Alexander the Great:* One was Poor, and the Other Rich: *Alexander's* Ambition was not satisfied with the Conquest of the Whole World: Whilst *Diogenes* lived contentedly in a Cottage, resembling a *Tub*. The Lives of these Two Men were quite Different, and so consequently were their Notions of Happiness. Both were *Philosophers*, the One Happy in Publick, and the Other in Private Life. The Former had a Just Title to all imaginable Praise, and the Latter was by no means Vile or Infamous. GOD, or Nature, or our own Choice, has assigned to every one of us, our Particular Study and Way of Life. To this we are confined, and this we are obliged to Follow and Retain, and to Adorn it in such a Manner, as GOD and Nature, or our own Reason and Vertue, shall direct. Some Men had rather Live in a Low and Mean, than in an Exalted State: Others had rather be Learned than Rich, or Soldiers rather than Priests; and a Third Sort preferr Privacy and Retirement to all Publick Honours and Offices whatsoever. Let every one Chuse the Way of Life which is most agreeable to him, and afterwards take care to Improve and Adorn it. But now, since the Life of the *Good Senator*, and his Happiness, are set in so Full and Fair a Light, and constantly exposed to the Publick View and Inspection; the Use of these External Blessings and Goods of Fortune is absolutely Necessary to the Support and Maintenance of his Character. These are Birth and Pedigree, Reputation, Honour, and Renown, a Number of Friends, the Good-Will of all about him, Children, Lands, and Money. Let him be the Issue either of the Nobility or Gentry, and descended of a Stock or Family, which can carry up their Pedigree from Father to Grandfather, to a Sett of Noble and Illustrious Ancestors. For Nobility and Descent are as Pledges deposited with our Country, by our Forefathers, obliging

ging us, in its Defence, to Sacrifice every Thing, even Life itself. Hence it was, that the *Romans* had a Law among them, that no *Senator* should marry the Daughter of a Man, who was not *Born*, but only *made Free*, or the Daughter of a *Plebeian*, or on one who had followed any Ludicrous Art or Employment. I would be far from Reflecting upon those Men, who look only to themselves for the Proofs and Instances of their Nobility, and ground all their Pretensions to it, in their own Personal Vertues. The same Vertues make *Upstarts* and *Hereditary Nobles*, both alike; and whoever depends upon Vertue, as his Best Title to Honour, is never Deceived or Disappointed. *Cato*, upon some little Difference that happened between him and *Scipio Africanus*, is said to have Expressed himself with a Sneer, in the following Manner; *That it would be well for the* Roman State, *if the* Nobility *would engross all the Vertues to themselves, in such a Manner, as that the* Plebeians *should have none left; or if the* Plebeians (*of which Number himself was One*) *would fairly Contend with the* Nobility, *which Order of the* Two *had most Vertues belonging to it*. This, however, in an Up-start or New-raised Family, is always to be considered; By what Steps and Pretensions to Merit, or by what Particular Vertues they acquired their Nobility. For a Person of Mean Birth, when Advanced to Honour, is by no means Inferior to Hereditary Noblemen, if the Vertues, to which he owes his Rise, are not either Fictitious and Imaginary, or of the Softer and Gentler Sort, but the Rough, Manly, and Laborious Vertues, among which are always to be reckoned the Military and Senatorial, as ever Preferable, not only to the Qualifications of Wealth and Fortune, but to all the Other Vertues whatsoever, which are only Fitted to a Life of Privacy and Retirement.

Honour and *Glory* are the Rewards commonly bestowed by a Wise Government, upon Great and Deserving Men; and these Acquisitions give them a Just Pretension to the Title of *Fortunate*.

Honour

Honour consists either in the Possession of some High and Considerable Posts, or Offices in the State, or in the Favourable Opinion, Applause, and Affection, bestowed by Wise and Good Men, upon those of Superior Accomplishments and Merit. True *Honour* (as *Tully* well observes) *is the Portion of Men of Worth and Renown, assigned to them, in Return for their High Deserts and Good Services already performed; and not barely as an Incitement to their Hopes, or to Encourage them in any future Undertakings or Exploits*. The truly *Honourable* will have very little Regard to *Pictures, Statues,* and *Images*; but will depend altogether on those Vertues, to which so much Greater and more Durable Rewards are deservedly annexed. When *Cato* saw such an Abundance of Publick *Statues* in *Rome*, he would not suffer his own to be put up, but said, *He had rather Men should guess at the Reason why it was not Erected, than be at a Loss to find one, why it was:* And doubtless the *Honours* due to a *First-rate Vertue*, are not made of any Brittle or Perishing Materials, but are Perpetual and Everlasting. Of the *Thirty Statues* erected to *Demetrius*, not one remained to try the Teeth of Time, or to wear the Marks of Antiquity; but they were all Demolished, even in the Life-time of the Original. *Glory*, or *Renown*, is the Desirable Blessing, which the *Senator* is allowed to Aim at, and is indeed the Highest Reward of Vertue. The Excesses of *Glory* ought always to be Proportioned to those of Vertue; and these Two should be Constant and Inseparable Companions; thus the Shadow is Proportioned to the Substance, upon which it constantly attends. *Theseus* had but *Three Things* to ask of the GODS; *Good Fortune*, and *Success*; a *Mind free from Care and Pain*; and *a Name adorned with True, Genuine, and Unspotted Glory*. They who make Glory the Great End and Aim of all their Vertues and Conduct, will never bear with any the Least Baseness or Ignominy, in their Own, or in the Character of Others; and will always measure the Share of Honour

and

and Reputation, which they have in the World, by the Approbation and Good Opinion of their Wise and Vertuous Fellow-Subjects. A Man of a Generous Birth, and Liberal Education, has no Greater Pleasure in Life, than to hear his Friends and Fellow-Citizens, and even Strangers and Foreigners speak well of him, and to be able to Transmitt the Glory, which the Present Age hath unanimously Conferred on him, to his Latest Posterity. The *Good Senator*, therefore, ought above all other Men, to be particularly Cautious of having the Least Stain or Blemish affixed to his Name or Character. For any thing of this Sort is seldom or ever worne out, or atoned for, either by our own After-Conduct, or by the Vertues and Reputation of those that come after us. The *Present Generation* will sometimes speak out; but *Posterity* is never Silent and Reserved, and will not forego its Liberty and right of Enquiring into, and Censuring the Behaviour and Actions of Other Men. The Good and Vertuous do not only, in their own Persons, reap the Fruits and Benefits of an Honourable Reputation, but Transmitt a Share of it to their Neighbours, Friends, and Children, and to a Succession of many Generations. For *Posterity* never fails to give Good Men their Just Due, to Admire their Lives, and Extoll their Vertues, and to bestow all imaginable Praises and Commendations upon the Times in which they Lived, the Laws which were of their Making, and the State and Government in which they Presided. Whilst we are upon Earth, we ought to take Care, that the Bravery, Fidelity, Piety, and other Vertues of our Ancestors, the Reputation and Glory of which they Bequeathed to us, and Entrusted in our Hands, may not be Lessened or Diminished. We ought to keep up to the Dignity of their Character, the Observation of their Precepts and Institutions, and the Example of their Vertues; and we ought to Transmitt all the Vertues, Discipline, Good Manners, Piety, and Fidelity, which we Learned and Received from them, to our Children's Children.

Fame

Fame is the Sure Foundation of a Lasting and Perpetual Glory, and this alone is sufficient to restrain us from all Appearances of Vice, lest in the pursuit thereof, we leave our Character and Reputation behind us; the Loss of which can never be Repaired, or made Good to us. The *Romans* had a Law, that no Man should be chosen a *Senator,* who was *Stained* and *Infamous in his Character:* And in this Number they always reckoned those Men, who were *Noted Gamesters,* or had given *False Evidence,* or had been *Convicted of Theft,* or had *Betrayed their Trust,* or their *Words, Pupils,* and *Clients,* or had *Prostituted their Eloquence* for a Bribe, or had *Changed their Religion,* or were *Disfranchized* and *Deprived* of the *Freedom of their own City,* or were *publickly Noted and Stigmatized,* for any *Scandalous Crime or Enormity,* that condemns a Man to *Infamy,* and brings a Lasting and Indelible Spot and Blemish upon his *Good Name* and *Reputation.* The *Athenians* erected a Court, or *Judicatory,* called the *Dokimacy,* in which the Life and Character of every Man were enquired into, who was Proposed as a *Candidate* for the *Senatorial Dignity:* For *Solon* had, by one of his Laws, prohibited the Introducing into the *Senate-House* any Person whatsoever, whose *Name* had been Stained with any *Publick Blemish,* or *Mark of Infamy.* To this we agree, and would have all such Men excluded from the *Senate.* For they, who are unfit for *Common Conversation,* are by no means Qualified to be *Members of any such Assembly.* Let, therefore, the *Good Senator*'s Life and Character be searched and sifted to the Bottom, that it may Stand the Test of Vertue and Honesty. For upon this Foundation, all the Glory, Fame, Reputation, Praise, Splendor, and Dignity of Human Life, are to be Raised and Erected.

A Number and Multitude of *Friends, Clients,* and *Followers,* and their Good Affections and Offers of Service, are a Considerable Addition to the *Senator*'s Dignity, and contribute very much to his Satisfaction and Happiness in Life. There is a Pleasure and Ease

Ease of Mind, in communcating our Affairs and Interests to our Friends, and in enjoying the Fruits of their Fidelity, Benevolence, and Good-will towards us; and a good deal of Satisfaction and Security, in Depending on their Aid and Assistance, in any Juncture, or on any Emergent Occasion, either of Publick or Private Life. When *Alexander the Great* was asked, *Where his Treasury was?* He readily answered, *With his Friends:* Thereby intimating, that the Good Will and Assistance of our Friends often stand us in more Stead, than our own Wealth, or the Contributions of Others.

Whoever regards the Good and Welfare of Posterity, will look upon a Number of Children, as a very Great Blessing, especially if they are Well-disposed, and Trained to Vertue. A *Senator* cannot well ask of Heaven any Greater Benefit, or which contributes more effectually to his own Private Happiness. For *Progeny* is a Sort of Interest and *Usury* added to the *Sum Total* of our *Years*, in the *Accounts* of Life, and our Name and Family are thereby made Lasting, and perhaps Perpetual. When *Bercilidas*, the *Spartan General*, took his Seat in Publick, none of his *Juniors* (as the Custom was) would Rise up to do him Honour, thereby Upbraiding him with Want of Children, and because he could leave none behind him to pay the same Compliment to their *Seniors*. Among the *Romans*, the Fathers of a Numerous Issue were always Excused in the *Censor*'s Books, and were afterwards dignified with the Title of *Proletarians*.

I come now to speak of Money and Riches, the Possession of which is absolutely Necessary to the Support of the *Senatorial Character*, and to the Carrying on of all Private and Publick Business; without which, all Great Undertakings are at a Stand, and all the Vertues dwindle to mere Speculations and Inactivity. *Majesty*, without this Support, is never Safe; and *Prudence* and *Wisdom* are often made Retainers and Slaves to Folly. The *First* Share
and

and Dividend of Wealth is, when a Man has really as much as he Wants; and the *Second* is, when a Man possesses as much as ought to Satisfy and Content him. *Plato* would have the Keepers or Governors of every City, neither too Rich, nor too Poor: For by too much Wealth, Men come to be Idle, Wanton, and Luxurious; and by too much Poverty, to be Weak, Sordid, and Contemptible. Whatever Wealth a *Senator* acquires, he ought to acquire only by Honest Means, and not to make a Fortune at the Expence of his Character. There are (according to *Aristotle*) *Two Ways* of Acquiring Wealth, the One *Honourable*, and according to Nature; and the Other *Dishonourable*, and consequently *Unnatural*. The *Natural Way*, is by Agriculture, Hunting, Fishing, Fowling, or some other such Method of Supplying our Necessities, without Interest of Money, Usury, or Exchange of Commodities. *There is no Trade or Profession,* (as *Cicero* very well observes) *more Honourable and Profitable than Husbandry, or more becoming a Liberal and Free-born Citizen*. *Cato* being asked, *By what means a Man might come to be Rich?* Answered, *By Feeding:* And being again asked, *How must he Feed, in order to grow Rich?* Answered, *He must Feed Well*; thereby hinting at the Care we ought to take of our Cattle, and of the Grounds and Pastures to which they belong, as the Proper Means of Enlarging our Fortune. *A Good Man*, and a *Good Husbandman*, were Equivalent Phrases and Terms of Commendation among the *Romans:* And their Great Men were frequently called from the *Plough*, to some Publick Office or Employment. This, among many Others, was the Case of *L. Quintius Cicinna*, when he was Advanced to the *Dictatorship:* And by the way it is to be noted, that the *Ancients* did not make Choice of this Rurual Way of Life out of Necessity, but merely for the Sake of Pleasure, and to Ease and Unbend their Minds, when Embarrassed and Overloaded with Publick Business. There is something Unnatural in Trade, Merchandize

dize, and Usury; because it is so very Difficult to keep within the Bounds of Honest Gain and Profit. *Cato* being asked, *What he thought of Usury?* demanded of the Querist, *What he thought of Murder?* All Unreasonable and Dishonest Gain, is what the *Good Senator* ought to have a Just Contempt of. For a Vulgar and Sordid Eagerness in acquiring Wealth, is a notorious Blemish to the Honour and Dignity of his Character. Hence it was, that among the *Romans*, all Usury or Unlawful Gain was strictly prohibited by the *Fathers*, among those of their own Order; and no *Senator* could be Owner of a Ship, above a certain Moderate Burthen. It is hardly possible for a Man to be governed altogether by a Principle of Honour and Honesty, in transacting the Affairs of the Publick, who has no Regard to any thing so much, as his own Profit, in his Private Employment and Commerce with Mankind. For which Reason, all Followers of Usury and Unlawful Gain, were Excluded the *Senate*. Money, Lands, Farms, *Villa's*, Mannors, Houshold Goods, Flocks, Herds, and a Competent Number of Servants, were heretofore reckoned as the Honest and Liberal Substance, of which a Subject might be lawfully Possessed, and well Employed in the Management of them. Of these Possessions, certain *Rates* or *Cense-Books* were commonly made in most Commonwealths, distinguishing the Names and Degrees of the several Owners thereof; and accordingly as they were Rated in these Books, Men were qualified for, and chosen into the *Senatorial Office*. *Solon* divided his People into *Four Classes*; the *Three First* differed according to the Proportions that are between *Five*, *Three*, and *Two*; and in the *Fourth Class*, were included Traders, Mechanicks, and all the Poorer Sort. They, who were in the *Second Class*, were commonly those of the *Equestrian Order:* They in the *Third*, were generally such as kept a *Single Horse*; and They in the *First*, were the Nobles, Magistrates, and Senators. Among the *Lacedæmonians*, no Man was admitted to any Office

in

in the Magistracy, or Government of the Commonwealth, who was not a Contributor to the Publick Feasts, commonly called the *Phidicia:* Which Entertainments were held once a Month, and every Contributor brought a certain Quantity of Bread, Wine, Cheese, Figs, and Money. *Plato,* in like manner, divided the Subjects of his Commonwealth into *Four Classes,* under which were ranged the several Orders of Citizens, according to what they were Worth in Money. The *Romans* had also their *Cense-Books;* but they differed, according to the several Changes and Alterations, which That Commonwealth underwent. Such a Practice is of great Use in all Governments whatsoever: For by this means the several Orders of Subjects are kept up and distinguished; the Publick Tributes, Tolls and Duties, are secured and ascertained; the Precedency of Families settled and adjusted; and a Way is opened, for Reforming the Manners of a People, for Suppressing Luxury, and for Provoking even the Meanest Subjects to be Active and Diligent in their Care and Concern for the Safety and Welfare of the Publick. The *Roman Censors* were the Masters and Overseers of the Order, Good Discipline, and Behaviour of their Fellow-Subjects, and were instituted in Imitation of the *Grecian Nomophylaces.* But after all, I venture to give my humble Opinion, in an entire Deference to better Judgments, that Wealth is by no means the Only Qualification, that ought to recommend a Man to the *Senatorial Dignity.* The Resigning of a Government into the Hands of the Wealthy, is like committing the Care of a Vessel, not to the most Skilful, but to the Richest Person aboard; which can end in nothing else, but the Danger or Loss both of Ship and Cargo. When *Pliny* censured the *Roman* State, the Vices of their Magistrates, and the Corruptions of their People; he imputed all their Degeneracy to the Partiality of their *Cense-Books: For when* (says he) *a* Senator *is chosen, or a* Magistrate, *or* Judge *appointed, only for the Sake of his Wealth;*

he

he will, in the Course of his Administration, and in all his Proceedings, have no Regard to the Lives, but only to the Properties and Fortunes of his Fellow-Subjects. Wealth, without Vertue, is of little Use; but when Both are in Conjunction, they complete the Happiness of Human Life. And therefore in the Choice of *Senators*, Vertue is always more to be regarded than Riches. Where a Person is both Good and Wealthy too, and yet chuses to decline the *Senatorial Office*, he ought to be compelled to accept of it, by a *Censorian Law*. For a Man cannot well be Guilty of a more Infamous Act of Ingratitude, than by refusing to serve That Country and Nation, to which he owes his Birth and Life, and all the Honours, Benefits, and Advantages, which serve to make Life Pleasant, Comfortable, and Glorious. This Caution however is, by the way, always to be observed, That Men, whose Folly is equal to their Wealth, ought never to be Advanced to any Publick Office. For Honour turns Fools into Madmen. It is Reasonable enough, that Rich Men should be Preferred in a State, because they have more Abilities and Opportunities of doing Good than other Men; especially if their Learning, Prudence, and Justice, are Proportioned to their Wealth: But to Exalt Men only for their Wealth's Sake, is perfectly Unjust: For Wealth, without Wisdom and Vertue, only enables Men to Oppress the Poor, and to attempt Changes and Innovations in a Well-established Government.

I come now, in the Last place, to speak of the Rewards justly due to a *Good Senator*; of the Fruits he ought to reap by his Labour and Diligence, and of the Debt of Honour and Profit, which his Country really owes him. We are all Incited and Spurred on to Action, to the Service of our Country, and to the Performance of Honest, Vertuous, Great, and Laudable Undertakings, by the Hopes and Prospect of a Sure and Sufficient Reward. Whatever we Undertake, whether it be of Little or of

very

very Great Consequence, we always look for some Advantage in the Accomplishment and Performance of it. *Solon* observed, *That Rewards and Punishments were the Preservation of every Government;* and unless these are Proportioned to every Man's Vertues and Vices, a State must necessarily be Unhappy and Miserable. Every *Good Senator* is therefore justly Entitled to a Proper Support of his Dignity, and to the Rewards due to his Vertues. *All Publick Rewards* (in the Opinion of *Cicero*) *are bestowed, either as Favours to distinguish a Man, or as Additions to his Income and Fortune, or as a Maintenance for his Superior Quality and Dignity.* For some of these Rewards, we must apply to Heaven; and for the rest to our own Country. But of all the Rewards, which a Grateful Commonwealth can possibly bestow upon a *Good Senator*, there is none more truly Valuable and Desirable, than that of *Glory* and *Renown*; which a Good and Vertuous Man will look upon as the Completion of his Hopes, and as the End and Crown of all his Labours. All his Honest Endeavours are enough recompenced, by the Approbation, Praises, and Encomiums of his Fellow-Subjects. For, as *Xenophon* speaks, *The Pleasure Men take in Honour and Glory, is the same that the Divine Being is most Delighted with.* The Benefits conferred upon us by the *Deity*, are so Many and so Great, that we can never, either by Word or Deed, be enough Grateful or Thankful for them; and yet all the Recompence and Compensation which He expects from us, is only the Return of *Praise* and *Thanksgiving.* Now though no Honour can be paid to the *Divine Being*, so Great and Ample, as to answer the Obligations we have to him; yet since the Honour we do Pay him, is the Utmost we are capable of Paying, and this he is pleased to accept; the *Good Senator* may make the *Deity* his Pattern in this, as in many other Things, and may accept the Honour, Glory, and Renown, which his Fellow-Subjects bestow upon him, as the Best Return

his

his Country can make him, and a Sufficient Reward for all his Vertues and Services.

  Every Good Man looks up to *Honour*, as the Reward of his Vertues; and both the *Soldier* and *General* have This always in View, as the Recompence of their Good Behaviour, and their many Victories. All the Glory a *Senator* is capable of, can be acquired by no other Means, than by Saving his Fellow-Citizens, by Defending his Country, and by Distinguishing himself in some Great and Glorious Enterprize. But still the Greatest and Highest Reward of Vertue, is the Attainment of the *Senatorial Dignity*; and as Honour is really a Disgrace, when it falls upon an Unworthy Person, so it is truly Valuable, when it is the Reward of Real and Undoubted Merit. For the Greatness of the Honour, is always proportioned to the Greatness of the Man who possesses it. To be Admired, Respected, and Esteemed, by all our Fellow-Subjects, to be Observed, Reverenced, and Extolled, by all about us; to have a Name Clear, Bright, and Shining, and always mentioned with the Additional Ornaments of Praise and Glory; to be called the *Parent*, the *Father*, the *Preserver*, or the *Deliverer* of one's *Country*; These are Great and Desirable Blessings, that approach very near to Divine Honours. And these Ensigns of Fame are not liable to Decay and Perishing, but bid fair for Eternity, and are always remaining upon the Tongues, and in the Ears of a Whole Nation, and in the Minds and Memories of Late Posterity. Such Glory, and such Honours, are of a Large and Wide Extent: For a Part of them is Communicated, or Descends to our Children, our Neighbours, our Friends, and to all who are any way Related or Attached to us; and Posterity, by our Example, is provoked to Copy our Actions, to Follow our Vertues, and to vye with us in Honour and Renown. By the Desire and Attainment of Glory, the *Good Senator* propagates his own Character, spreads his own Example through many Families, and lays the

Foundation

Foundation of many Seminaries and Nurseries of Vertue, whence the Publick reaps a Plentiful Harvest of many National Benefits and Blessings.

Honour and *Reverence* are a Tribute and Return of Gratitude, justly due from every *Good Subject*, to every *Good Senator*; and the Publick ought to take Care, that it may always by Fully and Regularly paid. Were it only on Account of his Age, he has a Natural Claim of Right to Respect and Veneration; but this is Common to many Others of the same Age; and a Double Portion of it belongs to him, when we consider his Particular Station, Dignity, and Character, and how Great his Prudence, Fidelity, and Diligence have been, in the Care and Government of the Commonwealth. All Insults, Injuries, and Offences, by which the *Senatorial Honour* is Lessened or Impaired, ought to be severely Punished by the Laws: And so very careful was the *Roman State*, in protecting the Honour of their Magistrates, that to Injure or Offend any one of That Order, was made a Capital Crime. They had one Law in particular, by which, if any Citizen Assaulted or Mal-treated the Person of a *Tribune, Aedile, Judge,* or any one of the *Decemviri*, his Life was Forfeited, and his Children and Family exposed to Sale, at the *Temple of Ceres. Servilius Isauricus,* of the *Consular Order*, walking one Day in the Streets, and meeting a Person on Horseback in a very Narrow Pass, who did not alight, and pay him the Respect due to his Character, but happened afterwards to appear in Judgment before him; upon a Relation made of the Fact, to the rest of the Judges upon the Bench, the Criminal was without Hearing immediately Condemned: For the Court was justly transported with Indignation, and readily believed, that the Man who was capable of Affronting a Superior of the Highest Quality, would not Scruple any other Enormous Crime or Iniquity whatsoever. The *Law of Treason*, made by *Honorius*, takes in all those, who offered any Injury to, or Conspired against, the Life and Honour of a *Prince* or *Senator:* Both which Characters and Dignity were put upon a Level, and held in the same Esteem and Reverence; and the Subject was expressly and severely prohibited from Reviling their Names, or Lessening their Credit, by any Verbal Reproaches, or Written *Satyrs* and *Libels*. *Cicero* recounts the several Rewards and Ornaments of the *Senatorial Character*, and mentions *Place* or *Precedence, Power* and *Authority*, a Splendid *Houshold, Equipage,* and *Attendance,* a *Name* and *Reputation* among Foreigners, the *Gown* or *Robe*, the *Currule Chair, Lictors, Fasces*, and other Ensigns of Outward Grandeur, *Military Offices* and *Commands*, and the *Government* of *Cities, Provinces*, and *Kingdoms*. I pass by the *Statues, Chariots,* and other Honorary Marks of Distinction, too Numerous to be easily Recounted: Of all which there is a very Curious and Exact Detail, now extant in a *Book*, written by our Countryman *John Samoski*, and by him Dedicated to *Peter Misovius, Vice-Chancellor* of *Poland*; a Work justly Valuable for a great deal of Elegant and Useful Learning, and for giving us an Uncommon Insight into the *Roman Antiquities*.

Every *Senator* therefore is justly entitled to a Due Share and Proportion of Honour, and either Sitting or Walking, ought to be Distinguished by his Proper Place and Precedence, and by other Marks and Instances of Dignity and Renown. As often as *Augustus* came into the *Senate-House*, he always Saluted every Particular *Senator* by Name; and at his Departure, took Leave in a Handsome Formal Manner, whilst the *Senators* kept their Places, and continued the Session in his Absence. The Emperor *Adrian*, observing one Day a servant of his own, and his Particular Favourite, crouding into the House, and taking his Place among the *Senators*, sent another Servant to him, with Orders to Smite him on the Face, and to Admonish him of his Duty; which was to Serve and Obey the *Senate*, instead of presuming to sit down

in

in so Illustrious an Assembly. When a *Senator*, by any of his Publick Actions or Exploits, had deserved well of the *Athenian State*, with the Concurrence of a Full and General Assembly, they commonly bestowed on him a *Crown*, or *Chaplet*, as a Mark of the Publick Gratitude, and at the same time presented him with a Purse of Money: Though, in our Opinion, a State ought to be very Cautious, how they part with their Money on these Occasions, unless to such Good Men as really want it. The Man of Real Merit will content himself with such External Marks of Approbation, Praise, Honour, and Renown, as his Country shall in Gratitude think fit to bestow upon him: Our Private and Personal Profit is the last Thing we ought to have an Eye to, in the Course of Publick Services and Employments; and a truly Just, Prudent, Magnanimous, and Noble Spirited Patriot, will despise it, in comparison with true Honour and Glory. It can never be well with a Government, when its *Senators* and *Magistrates* are invited into the Publick Service, upon no other Prospects, but their own Personal Interest, and the Advancement of their Fortunes: Such a Practice most commonly obtains in *Popular States*; where the Poor, as well as the Rich, have the same Pretensions to Power and Authority, and must consequently be Supported at the Publick Expence, in the Execution of their Offices: And it cannot well be otherwise in a Poor and Distressed Commonwealth, where the Magistrate's Private Fortune is by no means sufficient to Support his Publick Character. But all such Magistrates, during the Course of their Administration, ought to be more than commonly Careful of advancing the Publick, rather than their own Private Interest. And in general it is to be observed, that there is hardly any one Government, in which the *Senator* is not entitled to some Special Immunities, Prerogatives, and Privileges. Every Commonwealth must adhere Strictly to the Observation of its own Laws and Customs, and every *Good Senator*

CHAP. VIII.   *SENATOR*   329

nator must be more ready to expend his own Private Fortune in the Publick Service, than to add to and improve it: For this is most agreeable to the Generosity, Justice, Magnanimity, and all the other Vertues that establish and adorn the Senatorial Character and Dignity. Those Men certainly deserve the utmost Praise and Honour belonging to Mankind, who spare no Pains or Expences in a Publick Cause, who dedicate their Lives and Fortunes to the Service of their Country; and who, in all their Conduct and Management, aim at nothing more than the making of their own People Happy, Quiet, and Flourishing, at the Hazard of their Lives, and the Expence of their Private Fortunes: Freeing and Delivering them from the Malice and Animosity of Parties and Factions, and from all Tumultuous and Seditious Disorders whatsoever. If the Gratitude of his Country, the Monuments of Glory and Renown, and the Honour due to his Name and Memory, should fall short of the *Good Senator*'s Merit and just Expectations, he has this Comfort and Consolation left, that the Greater will his Reward and Happiness be hereafter. What his *Maker* has laid up for him, is far more Splendid, Ample, and Glorious, far more Lasting and Durable, than what a Mortal and Corruptible Body of Men can possibly bestow upon him. Posterity will be sure to do him Justice, and his Fellow-Citizens will remember his Name with Gratitude: Or if these should fail him, his *God* will give him a Place near Himself, in the Highest Heavens; will conferr upon him Everlasting Honour and Happiness, and a Crown Eternal and Incorruptible; than which nothing can be Thought of or Desired, more truly Glorious and Delectable. A *Senator*, thus Advanced, and who has failed in his Expectations of every Earthly Reward, may then apply to himself, what is said by a certain *African* Poet; and may say,

——Heav'n sometimes is by Yielding won:
And thus I make the Upper World my own.

All

All the Appetites and Desires of our Souls, and all our Endeavours to attain the Sum and Perfection of all Vertue whatsoever, ought to return back to the Fountain whence they issued, and were at first derived. The Great End and Aim of our Lives, and of all our Labours and Industry, is this; That (if possible) we may bring ourselves to Resemble our *Maker* in Vertue and Goodness, and rise by Degrees to an Imitation of the Divine Excellencies and Perfections. For as in This Life and State, they who Excell in Vertue, and come nearest to the Divine Original, are best entitled to the Praises and Applauses of Mankind; so in the Other Life and Future State, the more Vertuous and Excellent a Man is, the Greater will the Rewards of his Vertue and Honesty be. Whence we may conclude, that of all other Orders of Men, the *Good Senator*, as the most Useful and Beneficial to the World, is entitled, both in the Present and Future State, in This and the Next Life, to all the Honours, Pleasures, and Dignities, Perfect and Divine, which it is possible for us to Conceive or Imagine.

These Rules, Precepts, and Institutions, are such, as I thought proper to lay down and prescribe for the Better Direction of the *Good Senator*, in the Exercise of all the Vertues, in the Support and Maintenance of his Honour and Dignity, and in the Execution of his Office. And here, in the Conclusion, I Exhort all those of the *Senatorial Order*, to make the Preservation and Improvement of the Tranquillity and Happiness of their Country, the main Scope of all their Studies, and the chief End of all their Labours. I have some Reason to flatter myself, that what I have said upon this Subject, may give the *Reader* a Just, tho' not a *Perfect Idea* of a *Good Magistrate* and *Governor of his People:* And if Men will seriously attend to what I have advanced, their own Experience will (I believe) soon convince them, that all I have said is Just and True, and Useful to the Publick, in making the Governors of a State Wise, and the Subjects Happy.

A TABLE

A TABLE OF THE CONTENTS.

BOOK I. CHAP. I.

THE Excellency of Political *Knowledge. The Dignity of the* Senatorial *Character. It differs according to the Differences in the several* Forms *of Government. Which* Form *the most Perfect.* Man *the Governor of this Lower World. How nearly related to his* Maker. *How deputed by Him in the Government of the Earth.* God *the Author of all* Political *Wisdom. How we must Apply to him for it. Our* Reason *a Part of the* Divine Image. *When our* Reason *is in its best State.* Philosophy *the highest Improvement of* Reason. *The Praise and Excellency of* Philosophy. Philosophy *a sure Introduction to the* Art *of Government. Of the several Kinds of* Government. Pag. 1

CHAP. II.

The Peripatetick Philosophy *recommended. Wherein* Human *Happiness consists. Of communicating our Happiness to others. Of* Civil *and* Philosophical Life. *A* mix'd Life, *most truly* Divine. Plato's *Account of the* Formation of Mankind. *Of the* Monarchical *State. How* Kings *may be said to be* Gods. *Of the* Aristocratical Form. *How it differs from the* Democratical, *or* Popular *Form. The Preference due to* Monarchy

The CONTENTS.

Monarchy and Aristocracy. *How these Two* Forms *are to be Mixed or United. The Glory and Advantages of this* Union. *What we are to understand by the Word* People. *Of the* Good Things *belonging to a* Nation. *The several Orders of Subjects. Of Counsellors and Soldiers. The Dignity of the Priesthood.* P. 22

CHAP. III.

Instances of some particular Forms of Government. The Old Athenian *State. Of the* Lacedæmonian *and* Roman. *Of the* German, French, Spanish, Polish, English, *and* Venetian *Constitutions. What Things contribute to the Publick Happiness. Law is the Great and only Rule of Government. The General Qualifications of all Candidates, for any Publick Office. Of the Three Powers in every Monarchical State. The Original and Necessity of the Senatorial Order. Instances of its Rise among the* Romans *and* Spartans. *What a Senate is, and what is meant by the Word* Senator. *More Proofs of the Dignity of this Character. The General Qualifications for this Office. Every* Senator *ought to be a Native of that Country in which he is chosen, or advanced to any Place of* Trust. P. 47

CHAP. IV.

What a Citizen *or* Subject *is. The several Ranks and Orders of Citizens. How they stood among the* Romans. *The Differences between the* People *and the* Populace, *or* Mob. *Out of what Order of Citizens the* Senator *should be Chosen. What True* Nobility *is, and whence derived. The Qualifications for* Nobility. *Of Birth and Vertue. The several Sorts and Degrees of* Nobility. *Of Military and Pacifick Nobles. The Statesman Superior to the* Soldier. *Of Private and Publick* Vertue. *Of the Goods of the Body, Mind, and Fortune. Of the Strength of a Nation, and its Standing Forces. How they are to be Regulated. The Character of a Good* Soldier. P. 65

CHAP. V.

Three Things required to make our Nature Perfect. The Origin of all Human Imperfections. How They are to be Repaired. Of the Use and Benefits of Philosophy. *Objections commonly made to* Philosophy. *Some Philosophers unfit to be Statesmen. Of Speculative and Recluse* Philosophers. *Of the Middle Class or Order. What Sort of Philosophy most Proper for the* Senator. *His Genius and Natural Disposition. The Education of the* Senator. *Of Academical Discipline. The Advantages*

The CONTENTS.

vantages and Defects of it. Of Classical Learning. Of Philosophy in all its Parts and Branches. Of Natural and Mathematical Knowledge. Of Speculative and Practical Philosophy. Of History and Travel. The Dignity and Usefulness of Schoolmasters and Tutors. Which Sect of Philosophers the most Excellent. The Benefits of Eloquence. The Manner of Speaking in the Senate. Of the Study of the Law, and the Abuses of it. P. 80

CHAP. VI.

Of Civil Wisdom and Discipline. Of Bodily Improvements and Exercise. What are the most Manly Exercises. Of Good Generals, and Good Senators. The Romans remarkable for These Two Characters. Of Good Laws and Statutes. An Encomium on the Greek Commonwealths. The Length of Art, and shortness of Life. The End and Aim of every Man's Accomplishments. The Grounds and Foundation of the Polish Policy. The Perfection and Happiness of the Golden Age. The Fall of Man, and Rise of Philosophy. Which Sort of Philosophy deserves the Preference. P. 107

CHAP. VII.

Of the Manner of Electing the Senator. All Canvassing Unlawful. The Ways of attaining to Honours and Offices. Avarice fatal to a State. Honours ought not to be Sold. All Elections ought to be under one Established Rule. Magistrates should set the People a Good Example. Mal-Administration the Ordinary Cause of all State-Revolutions. Out of what Order of Subjects the Senator should be Elected. The Manner of Electing as different as the Forms of Government. Of Elections by Lot. How the Greeks Elected their Senators. How Candidates ought to be Qualified. Who ought to be the Electors. The Ill Practices of Ambitious Candidates. The Mob excluded from all Elections. Of the Interest of the Crown in Elections. How the Romans Elected their Senators. P. 122

The CONTENTS.

BOOK II. CHAP. I.

THE *Connection and Argument of the* Second Book. *The* Senator *ought to be* Well-acquainted *with the* Constitution *and* Laws *of his own* Country. *It is greater to* Preserve *than to* Found *a Commonwealth. Every* Polish Senator *is a* Mediator *between* King *and* People. *The* Senator *how* Posted *in a* State. *The* Common Artifices *of* Tyrants. *The* Office *and* Duty *of a* King. *How He ought to* Regard *his* Senate. *The* Humours *of the* Mix'd Multitude, *and* Rise *of all* Seditions. *The* Mixture *and* Harmony *of the* Three Estates *of a* Kingdom. *How* Tumults *and* Seditions *may be* appeased. *Every* Order *or* Estate *in a* Government *ought to be* Zealous *in maintaining the* Rights *of the* Other Two. *Of the* Doctrine *of* Equality. *The* Rights *of the* Subject. *Of* Demagogues, *and* Alterations *in* Religion. *Of the* Four Cardinal Vertues, *the Great and Necessary* Qualifications *for the* Senatorial Office.   P.145

CHAP. II.

Of Prudence; *its* Excellencies, *and how far* Preferable *to the* Other Vertues. Prudence *Defined and Described. The* Difference *between* Speculative Wisdom *and* Prudence. *Of* Civil *and* Domestick Prudence. *This* Vertue *limited by* Truth *and* Justice. Honesty *and* Profit *the* Scope *of all* Human Endeavours. *The* Two Great Errors *of the* Imprudent. *Of* Laws, Good Examples, *and* Wholsome Exercises. *A* Caution *to be observed in making of* Laws. *Of the* Vigilance *and* Extensive Knowledge *of the* Senator. *They who* Love *not their own* Country, *are worse than* Brutes. *Of the* Lesser Vertues, *Attendant upon, and the Companions of* Prudence. *Of* Ingenuity, Docibility, *and a* Good Memory. *Of* Intelligence, Sensation, *and* Reflection. *Of* Circumspection. *Of the* Use *of* Standing Forces. *Of the* Administration *of* Justice. *Of* Human Foresight. *Of* False Pretences *to* Foresight. *Whence the* Senatorial Foresight *is derived. Of the* Good Genius. *Of* Example, Experience, *and* History. *Of* Caution. *Some Rules to be Observed in Speaking in the* Senate. *Of* Sagacity. *Of* Cunning *and* Artifice.   P.169

CHAP. III.

Of Consultation *and* Deliberation. *Of the Subject Matter of all* Deliberations. *Of* Raising Money *by* Taxation. *Of* Exports *and* Imports.

Of

The CONTENTS.

Of making War *and* Peace. *Of the* Defence *and* Safeguard *of the* Realm. *Of* Trade *and* Commerce. *Of the Making of Good and Wholesome* Laws. Good Counsel *the Result of all Wise* Deliberations. *Of Things* Honest *and* Profitable, *and the Differences between them.* Fortune *ought never to be depended upon. Of* Subtle *and* Bold Undertakings. *Of* Rashness *and* Expedition. *Of* Preliminary Consultations. *Of Giving* Sentence *and* Opinion. *The Benefits of* Experience. *Of* True *and* False Oratory. *Of the Manner of* Voting *and* Giving Opinions. *Rules to be observed in* Speaking *and* Debating. *Of* Personal Attendance *in the* Senate. *The* Perfection *of the* Senatorial *Character. Of* False Patriots.   P.196

CHAP. IV.

Of Natural Justice. *Of Mutual* Benevolence *and* Good-will. *Of* Piety. *Of* Self-Preservation, *or the* Justice *due to ourselves. Of* Divine Justice, *or the* Justice *which is due to our* Maker. *Of* Natural Religion. *Of* Publick Worship. *Of the* Christian Institution *and* Priesthood. *The Danger of attempting to Alter the* Established Religion. *How such Innovations come to be Fatal to a* State. Religion, *how far advantageous to a* Government. *Examples of the ill Consequences of* Religious Innovations. *Of the Character of* Sanctity *as annexed to the* Senate. *Of the Method of* Opening *every* Senatorial Assembly. *Of* Human *or* Civil Justice. *All* Justice *is founded in fidelity. The Character of a* Faithful Man. *Of* Justice *in the Distribution of* Honours. *Of the* Ancient Method *of* Decreeing Honours. *How Those of a* Publick Character *are* Distinguished *by the* Moderns. *Of* Numerical *and* Judicial Equality. Duelling *condemned. Of* Executive Justice. *Of* Primitive Justice. *The End and Design of all* Good Laws. *Of* Idleness *and* Luxury. Industry *ought to be Encouraged. The* Old Laws *of a* State *ought rather to be* Amended *than* Repealed. *Every* Senator *ought to be Punctual in the Observation of the* Laws. *Of the* Judge's Duty. *Of* Severity *and* Moderation.   P.213

CHAP. V.

Of the Vertues *attending upon* Justice. *Of* Piety. *Of the Great Obstructions to* Piety, Heresy, *and* Superstition. *Of* Goodness. *Of* Innocence *and* Integrity. *Of* Affability, *and how it ought to be Tempered with* Gravity. *Of* Benignity *and its Concomitant Vertues,* Humanity, Condescension, Lenity, Clemency, *and* Moderation. *Of* Clemency, Mercy, *and* Pity. *The Doctrine of the* Stoicks *condemned. Of* Liberality, *and the Rise of This Vertue. How it ought to be Regulated, and the Extent*

of

The CONTENTS.

of it. Of Magnificence, *and how it differs from* Liberality. Luxury *ought to be Restrained by* Legal Penalties. *Of* Friendship *and* Amity, *and how these Affections ought to be Formed and Regulated. Of* Hospitality. *Of* Concord. P. 243

CHAP. VI.

Of the Third Cardinal *Vertue,* Fortitude. *Its Excellency and Usefulness. How far Superior to the other* Vertues. *Private and* Publick Fortitude. *Of Military* Fortitude. *Of the* Vertues *accompanying* Fortitude. *Of* Magnanimity. *Of* Ambition, *and the Acquiring of* Honours. *Of* Constancy, *and the Love of* Truth. *How we ought to Behave, towards* Superiors, Equals, Inferiors, *and* Enemies. *Of* Perseverance. State-Secrets *ought to be kept. Of* Patience, Civil *and* Military. *Of* Confidence, *and of the* Good *and* Evil Genius. *Of* Security. *Its Faults and Advantages. Of True* Heroism. Military Men *ought to be Encouraged. Of* Despair, Anger *and* Fortune. P. 264

CHAP. VII.

Of the Fourth Cardinal *Vertue,* Temperance. *Whence this* Vertue *has its Rise. Of the Two Sorts of* Pleasures. *Wherein* Temperance *consists. How far Beneficial to a* State. *The Mischiefs of* Avarice. *Of* Luxury *and* Sumptuary Laws. Private Intemperance *the Cause and Forerunner of* Slavery. Private Intemperance, *as well as* Publick, *ought to be Restrained by* Law. *Of the* Vertues *accompanying* Temperance. *Of* Moderation, *and* Temporizing. *Of* Modesty, *and the several Sorts of it. Of* Honesty, Continency, *and* Abstinence. *The Great Excellency of these* Vertues. *The Contrary* Vices, *how Foul and Odious. The Mischiefs of* Lust *and* Drunkenness. *Instances of the* Great Temperance *of the* Ancients. P. 286

CHAP. VIII.

Of Bodily Accomplishments *and* Perfections. *How far Useful and Advantageous to those of the* Mind. *Of the* Nurture *and* Care *of* Youth. *Of Regulating* Marriage. *Of* Health, *and the* Temperament *of the* Body. *Of* Beauty *and* Dress. *Of* Bodily Strength. *Of the* Senator's Age. *Of the* Goods *of* Fortune. *Of the* Senator's Wealth *and* Estate. *Of* Nobility, Honour, *and* Glory. Posterity *the Best Judge of* Merit. *Of* Reputation, *and* Renown. *Of* Clients, Friends, *and* Followers. *Of* Issue *or* Children. *Of* Riches *and* Money. *Of* Husbandry. *Of the* Privileges *and* Respect, *due to the* Accomplish'd Senator. *Of his* Last *and* Greatest Reward. P. 300

F I N I S.